Britain in Egypt

Britain in Egypt

Egyptian Nationalism and Imperial Strategy 1919–1931

Jayne Gifford

I.B.TAURIS
LONDON · NEW YORK · OXFORD · NEW DELHI · SYDNEY

I.B. TAURIS
Bloomsbury Publishing Plc
50 Bedford Square, London, WC1B 3DP, UK
1385 Broadway, New York, NY 10018, USA
29 Earlsfort Terrace, Dublin 2, Ireland

BLOOMSBURY, I.B. TAURIS and the I.B. Tauris logo
are trademarks of Bloomsbury Publishing Plc

First published in Great Britain 2020
Paperback edition first published 2021

Copyright © Jayne Gifford, 2020

Jayne Gifford has asserted her right under the Copyright,
Designs and Patents Act, 1988, to be identified as Author of this work.

For legal purposes the Acknowledgements on p. vi constitute
an extension of this copyright page.

Cover design by Charlotte James
Cover image: 'Egypt Asks for More' by Raven-Hill, Leonard. Punch,
11 Apr. 1928. (© Punch Historical Archive, 1841–1992/TopFoto)

All rights reserved. No part of this publication may be reproduced or
transmitted in any form or by any means, electronic or mechanical,
including photocopying, recording, or any information storage or retrieval
system, without prior permission in writing from the publishers.

Bloomsbury Publishing Plc does not have any control over, or responsibility for,
any third-party websites referred to or in this book. All internet addresses given
in this book were correct at the time of going to press. The author and publisher
regret any inconvenience caused if addresses have changed or sites have
ceased to exist, but can accept no responsibility for any such changes.

A catalogue record for this book is available from the British Library.

A catalogue record for this book is available from the Library of Congress.

ISBN: HB: 978-1-7845-3804-0
PB: 978-0-7556-3668-6
ePDF: 978-1-8386-0494-3
eBook: 978-1-8386-0495-0

Typeset by Integra Software Services Pvt. Ltd.

To find out more about our authors and books visit
www.bloomsbury.com and sign up for our newsletters.

Contents

Acknowledgments		vi
Introduction		1
1	Between Two Worlds: Britain and Egypt in Africa and the Middle East	7
2	Riots and Resistance: Britain and Egypt, 1918–1922	31
3	Negotiating at Home and Abroad: The CID, Labour and the Egyptian Nationalists, 1924	71
4	The 'Colonized Colonizer': The Anglo-Egyptian Sudan	87
5	The Assassination of Sir Lee Stack: The British Lion's Final Roar?	117
6	'I Wish Austen Were Less of an Old Woman and Less Occupied with His Tea Parties in Geneva': The Conservative Government and the Anglo-Egyptian Treaty Negotiations	133
7	'The Two Ends Just Didn't Meet': The Labour Government and Anglo-Egyptian Treaty Negotiations	149
Conclusion		179
Notes		186
Bibliography		239
Index		258

Acknowledgments

Academic research can often be a lonely and isolating pursuit. The culmination of this hard work, however, is the product of much professional and emotional support from colleagues, friends and family alike.

This project is the result of a fascination and respect I have held for Egypt since my first primary school project all those years ago. My interest in diplomatic relations and the impact individuals have on policy formulation (something which is not lost in today's world) was fostered and encouraged during my undergraduate and postgraduate years at the University of the West of England, where I was fortunate to be taught by some of the leading lights in this area: Thomas Otte, Martin Thomas, Glyn Stone, Geoff Swain, Phil Ollerenshaw, Moira Martin, John Fisher and Joe Dunthorn. I am also grateful to Joe for his perseverance and good humour in educating me in both the English and French language all the while regaling his tales of adventure from his travels abroad, instilling the importance of every single word either spoken or written. Joe innately knows how to make even the driest of subjects fun and memorable.

I am indebted to Kent Fedorowich who, as my doctoral supervisor, provided invaluable guidance, support, and has continued to offer generous help in uncovering the story of the British World through the archives as well as the associated wine regions! Gudrun, your insights, advice and hospitality have been priceless.

During my time at the University of East Anglia I have been incredibly fortunate to meet some of the most inspiring, hard-working, supportive, kind and generous people who are not only my colleagues but of whom I am privileged to call my friends. Stephen Church, Thomas Otte, Becky Taylor, Malcolm Gaskill and Anthony Howe, thank you for finding the time to discuss my research and in helping me push through some of the more problematic aspects of the writing process. Emma Griffin, thank you for being my mentor, champion of women in academia as well as early career researchers, and for reading a full draft of the manuscript. Richard Deswarte, Jan Vermeiren, Matthew D'Auria, thank you for the companionship, chocolate and coffee! Rob Liddiard, Tom Williamson, Camilla Schofield and Geoff Hicks, you never fail to make me smile even during the busiest of semesters. Ben Jones, Amanda Dillon, Cathie Carmichael, Richard Mills, Chris Jones, Sarah Spooner and Jon Gregory, thank you for always being prepared to lend a sympathetic ear. Without the support, kindness and humanity of Jessica Sharkey and Matthias Neumann, I would not be where I am today. Jennifer Davey, Emily Cockayne, Joel Halcomb and Helena Carr, words cannot do justice to the debt of gratitude I owe: wise counsel, thoughtful words, and good humour – thank you.

I wish to thank the staff of the following archives and libraries for their helpful and friendly assistance with my research: the Bodleian Library, Oxford, particularly Colin Harris whose knowledge of the collections is unsurpassed; The National Archives of

Scotland; the Asia, Pacific and Africa Collections, London; the British Library, London; the University of Durham Library, Sudan Archive; Cambridge University Library; the Churchill Archive Centre, Cambridge; the Liddell Hart Centre for Military Archives, King's College London; the Middle East Centre Archive, Oxford; the House of Lords Record Office, London; the Special Collections, University of Birmingham; Rhodes House Library, University of Oxford; and The National Archives, Kew. I also wish to thank the Master and Fellows of Churchill College, Cambridge for permission to quote from papers held in their collections.

I am extremely grateful to I. B. Tauris for their patience in walking me through the publication process, especially Tomasz Hoskins, Nayiri Kencir, Giles Herman and, from Integra, Viswasirasini Govindarajan. I would also like to thank the peer-reviewers for their valuable suggestions and comments, and the copy-editors and Sally Osborn for their meticulous observations and keen eye. Any remaining mistakes and errors of interpretation are, of course, my own. I am grateful to the University of Toronto Press for allowing me to reuse material from an earlier journal article 'Extracting the Best Deal for Britain: The Assassination of Sir Lee Stack in November 1924 and the Revision of Britain's Nile Valley Policy', *Canadian Journal of History/Annales canadiennes d'histoire* XLVIII, Spring/summer (2013), pp. 87-114.

To those outside of academia it can appear a bizarre and baffling world. Nev, your patient understanding and assistance with the logistics of archival research has been amazing. To the Cornwall crew who have been some of the most welcoming people I have met and who have been instrumental in educating me in the importance of approaching life in a 'dreckly' manner, thank you.

Academic life is a roller-coaster of emotions and I consider myself extremely lucky to have such a generous partner, Ryan, and a family whose love and support is unconditional. It is to mum and dad that this book is dedicated.

Introduction

If the Suez Canal is our back door to the East, it is the front door to the Europe of Australia, New Zealand and India. If you like to mix your metaphors it is, in fact, the swing door of the British Empire, which has got to keep continually revolving if our communications are to be what they should.
 Speech by Anthony Eden to the House of Commons, 23 December 1929.[1]

The US-led invasion of Iraq in 2003 and the Arab Spring at the end of 2010 have once more brought the Middle Eastern region to the fore of international relations. This, in fact, represents a continuity in policy that owes its genesis to the nineteenth century when Western European diplomacy, in particular, that of Britain, was focussed upon maintaining the territorial integrity of the 'sick man of Europe' – the Ottoman Empire. During the twentieth century, Western diplomacy continued to focus upon the former Ottoman provinces by attempting to incorporate them into their colonial empires or spheres of influence. It is the immediate post–First World War period and the evolving Anglo-Egyptian relationship throughout the 1920s that deserve examination since they formed the backbone of Britain's imperial defence network.

At the heart of British policy within Egypt was the importance of maintaining control of the Suez Canal to safeguard imperial communication, trade and power across Britain's far-flung Empire. The First World War only served to underline this importance when Britain was faced with a global threat to its dominance. The 1920s also witnessed a technological revolution with the explosion in air, telegraph and land railway routes that now linked Africa, India and the Far East, thereby making Egypt the 'Clapham Junction' of imperial communications.[2] If Egypt was such an integral piece of the imperial puzzle, why was it not permanently incorporated into the formal British Empire? J Darwin has reminded us that, in its most basic form, the British Empire consisted of 'two parallel sub-systems divergent in style but common in purpose'.[3] Informal empire was exercised where British policymakers could be sure that commercial or strategic objectives were secure without the added expense and embroilment of annexation or direct rule through a 'compliant or obliging' local elite.[4] Whilst there was no outward symbol of British preponderance, Britain's tentacles of power undoubtedly reached deep into local matters and thereby constricted the freedom of action of nominally sovereign governments, especially in external relations. Where British influence or interests were challenged, whether by the indigenous elite or by foreign powers, Britain would revert to the formal alternative and impose direct

British rule.⁵ These were not mutually exclusive. There existed a great deal of freedom of movement within each of these systems. Egypt is a perfect example of this flexibility in British policymaking – moving from the declaration of a Protectorate in December 1914, shortly after the outbreak of war, to nominal independence in 1922 and a full-fledged alliance partner in 1936.

As a result, the British tenure of Egypt cannot be viewed in a monolithic sense. This is exemplified by the differing ways in which the pro-Consuls, later known as High Commissioners between 1914 and 1936 upon the declaration of a Protectorate and as Ambassadors following the conclusion of the Anglo-Egyptian alliance, exercised their powers. Sir Evelyn Baring (September 1883–May 1907), later made Lord Cromer in 1892, was nicknamed 'The Lord' for his characteristic tutelage of Egypt. This was in direct contrast to Sir Eldon Gorst (1907–11), whose term resembled that of complete independence. Gorst's replacement by Lord Kitchener (1911–15) represented a return to what became labelled 'Cromerism'. However, the terms of Sir Henry McMahon (January 1915–December 1916), Sir Reginald Wingate (December 1916–January 1919), Field-Marshal Edmund Allenby (March 1919–June 1925) and George Lloyd (October 1925–July 1929) all earned the ire of Whitehall.⁶

This study seeks to address several key themes with in the Anglo-Egyptian relationship. Firstly, the nature of British rule within the Nile Valley. How does British rule respond to threats of an internal nature, such as Egyptian nationalism? Why was Egyptian nationalism, after its wholesale destruction in 1882 of the fledgling movement under Colonel Ahmed Arabi, able to challenge British hegemony so violently in 1919? Furthermore, how did British rule manage the extraneous pressures it faced at home – the financial retrenchment needed in order to pay its Atlantic debtor, the United States, which required the scaling back of its military services at a time when its colonial reach marked its zenith? That Tsarist Russia, so long a preoccupation of imperial administrators and the threat it posed to Britain's empire, was convulsed by revolution simply meant that Russian imperialism was replaced by a new and deadly threat – Bolshevism. As M Thomas reminds us [in *Empires of Intelligence. Security Services and Colonial Disorder after 1914*] Bolshevism possessed the 'capacity to mobilise mass support'. It rejected a 'capitalist international system predicated on the supremacy of white-ruled empires'.⁷ What concerned the British was that Bolshevism could transcend imperial borders and 'appeal to colonial subjects to unite [...] in opposition to European control'.⁸

Was this Bolshevik menace real or imagined? It was certainly closely monitored by the British in Egypt during the 1920s and formed a consistent body of comment in situation and intelligence reports to the Foreign Office. However, any idea of a Bolshevik-inspired uprising against the British was largely smoke and mirrors and care must be exercised when these threat perceptions, based upon local intelligence gathering, are examined. Stung by criticism that the 1919 Egyptian nationalist revolts were missed by the British authorities in Cairo 'the security services in Cairo and Khartoum also conjured up Communist demons where none existed'.⁹ These tended to be used by those on the spot to force a definitive line of policy from London, particularly in the immediate post-war era when only the most pressing problems were consistently addressed. As Mohammed Nuri El-Amin has argued, [in 'International

Communism, the Egyptian Wafd Party and the Sudan'] 'Zaghlul completely turned his back on any leftist or revolutionary approach to Egyptian politics, and opted instead for a gradualist political struggle for independence'.[10] Zaghlul, in the words of the editor of *The Communist Review,* 'made use of the utmost demagogy to deceive the Egyptian people in order to place himself in power – this being his only single object'.[11] He was therefore not about to supplant the British yoke of imperialism for that of Bolshevik string pulling instead.

Britain approached her governance of Egypt in a two-fold manner – the military stick and the diplomatic carrot. Diplomacy was used as a means of limiting Britain's liabilities, reducing her military commitments – a treaty was much preferable to the indefinite and costly retention of large military garrisons. But, nevertheless, and despite Sir Henry Wilson's lament that 'in no single theatre are we strong enough', the military stick could still be deployed when Britain's vital strategic interests were threatened. The rise of Japanese power in the East and the non-renewal of the Anglo-Japanese alliance made navigation of the Suez Canal by the Royal Navy vital. It was preferable to London, both financially and under the international gaze of the League of Nations, if this mobility of the fleet could be secured by diplomatic means but, in the final analysis, Britain would not hesitate to enforce her strategic interests by military force if necessary.

Understanding the vicissitudes of British rule naturally fits into the second theme of this study – who exercised the greatest influence in shaping British policy towards Egypt. To ensure Britain's continued dominance of the Nile Valley, effective communication and co-ordination were required not only between members of the Cabinet, Service Ministries and officials at the Foreign Office, under whose remit Egypt fell, but also between those men-on-the-spot whose appreciations and assessments formed the basis of policy formulation. This triangle of communication between Khartoum, Cairo and London was vital in ensuring a clear line of policy. The breakdown of this linkage can be seen following the assassination of Sir Lee Stack, *Sirdar* and Governor-General of the Sudan, in November 1924 and the Foreign Office's overriding of Lord Lloyd's concerns regarding treaty negotiations with the Egyptians in 1927. It is therefore this ever-changing and -evolving nature of the Anglo-Egyptian relationship which forms the subject of this book. By formulating an understanding of the lines of influence and communication with the microcosm of the Nile Valley, it provides a lens through which to view the genesis and application of policy to the problems of empire in the post-war era.

As already mentioned, Egypt was never formally incorporated into the British Empire, despite the existence of significant pressures for this to become a reality, particularly towards the end of the First World War. Egypt therefore remained under the governance of the Foreign Office. But this has often meant that when examining the Anglo-Egyptian relationship, it becomes slightly more complex since Egypt occupied a unique position between the mandated Middle East and the closely administered African possessions. Although Egypt was a product of the Scramble for Africa, it was also perceived as an essential piece of the strategic nexus of the Middle East for the maintenance of Britain's wider imperial communications. The 1920s are also traditionally viewed as a period of retrenchment but Egypt remained crucial by continuing to provide the financial keystone for all three military services who were under constant threat from a parsimonious Treasury. Therefore, budgetary cuts were staved off by military strategists on grounds of imperial strategy, the maintenance of internal order and the security of the bases of the new aerial forms of communications, as well as the provision of ideal training conditions for the fledgling Royal Air Force.

Although Egypt was largely tranquil during the First World War, she certainly did not escape the ravages of this cataclysm. During the course of the war, British Middle Eastern thinking had to be revised as a result of wartime exigencies concerning Arab independence. This, coupled with the heavy-handedness of British policies in fighting the war and President Woodrow Wilson's pronouncements of self-determination, contributed to uniting the country in demanding an end to martial law and the granting of complete independence. The immediate post-war period witnessed the emergence of the nationalist Delegation, or Wafd Party, under Saad Zaghlul. Chapter 2 examines the causes of the March 1919 disorders and the co-ordination of the British response in the form of a swift military repression followed by a more political approach with the despatch of a mission under Lord Alfred Milner. The Foreign Office, preoccupied as it was with the Paris Peace Conference, believed that Wingate had mishandled the emergence of the nationalist cause within Egypt which, in their view, had led directly to the outbreak of violence in March 1919. As a consequence, it resulted in his supersession by General Sir Edmund Allenby in the same month. The origins of these riots brought into sharp relief not only how out-of-touch Whitehall had become with Egyptian affairs but also the difference of opinion between the Residency and the Foreign Office in the search for a diplomatic solution.

The despatch of the Milner Mission to Egypt in December 1919 at least demonstrated a willingness to resolve Anglo-Egyptian relations and decide upon a definitive course for British policy in the post-war world. However, the recommendations of the Mission highlighted the sharp divergence of opinion and interests between the departments involved in the formulation of Egyptian policy. Of course, Britain's Egyptian experience cannot be viewed in isolation and must be placed within the wider context of Britain's post-war Empire. It was not only departmental rivalries that influenced policy formulation but the trials and tribulations of Empire elsewhere. The Irish War of Independence between 1919 and 1920, Afghanistan's war against the British Empire in May 1919, the Amritsar massacre of April 1919, the Kurdish and Shi'ite tribesmen's insurrection against the British Army of occupation in Mesopotamia between 1919 and 1920 and Mohandas (Mahatma) Gandhi's non-cooperation movement between 1919 and 1922 played a role in influencing the nature and extent of British rule across both her formal and informal areas of Empire.[12] As a result, it is possible to discern during 1920–21 a gradual realization that by becoming embroiled in Egyptian internal affairs, Britain provided a rallying call for the Egyptian nationalists to oust their colonial master and thereby weaken Britain's imperial strength and prestige. In 1922 the Cabinet, and heavily pressured by Allenby, finally accepted that Britain's interests were best served by lessening the imperial burden with the Declaration of Independence, with the caveat that Britain's vital strategic interests were protected.

An important aspect of the Anglo-Egyptian relationship centred around the Sudan. Egypt perceived the Sudan to be part of the Nile Valley – a view largely justified following the Anglo-Egyptian conquest of the Sudan from Mahdist forces and the establishment of the Anglo-Egyptian Condominium over the area in 1899. From the British perspective, large-scale investment in irrigation schemes accorded the Sudan a growing prominence within the Empire. More importantly, British concerns centred around the dissemination of Egyptian propaganda into the Sudan encouraging some form of politically unified Nile valley. These fears only increased with the inception of the League of the White Flag in July 1920, believed to have direct links with Egyptian nationalists. The failed Sudanese mutiny in August 1924 whilst a popularly elected nationalist Wafd government was in power in Cairo seemed only to confirm British fears of Egyptian meddling. The development of Sudanese nationalism and how the British attempted to manipulate it for their own ends are the focus of Chapter 4. The perceived threat posed by encroaching Egyptian nationalism was taken seriously by both the men-on-the-spot and those within the Foreign Office to the extent that Britain was prepared to act with vigour in protecting her interests there and finally ejecting the Egyptians from the Sudan once and for all.

That the Sudan formed an important role within the Anglo-Egyptian relationship was exemplified by the assassination of Sir Lee Stack in November 1924. Chapter 5 examines the role played by political violence at the turn of the twentieth century and British attempts to combat the challenge to their presence through the Public Security Department and the police commands. From the British perspective, the assassination of Stack was the culmination of an intensive nationalist Egyptian propaganda campaign which Zaghlul had failed to discourage. With a new Conservative administration installed at Westminster in October 1924, it would be expected that British demands for recompense would be severe. However, in the aftermath of Stack's assassination a schism opened up between the new foreign secretary, Austen Chamberlain, and Allenby in Cairo. Allenby's ultimatum to Zaghlul, which included the evacuation of all Egyptian troops from the Sudan, without London's prior approval, bears all the hallmarks of a High Commissioner acting with scant regard for his superiors. However, upon closer investigation, Allenby's actions can be viewed as a continuity in policy enacted by the Labour administration under Ramsay MacDonald, particularly in light of the collapse of the 1924 treaty negotiations as discussed in Chapter 3. Despite earning Chamberlain's ire over the demands presented to the nationalist Wafd, Britain achieved her aims within the Nile Valley. Zaghlul resigned and his successor Ahmed Ziwar accepted all of Allenby's demands on 30 November. This ensured Britain's dominance within the Sudan and checked Egyptian nationalism since the Residency and palace authority once again dominated Egyptian political life.

Indeed, although Egypt had obtained nominal independence in 1922, Britain preserved its vital interests and upheld the *status quo* by utilizing Egypt's political landscape to its advantage. A number of attempts to negotiate a treaty were undertaken between 1924 and 1931 in order to resolve the four reserved points[13] and place Britain's presence within Egypt upon a firm legal footing. For Britain, the central problem revolved around the issue of attaining a method that would square the circle of traditional British foreign policy – the principle of self-determination and non-intervention in the internal affairs of another country, and the protection of vital imperial communications. How this was to be achieved divided the Chiefs of Staff (COS), the Foreign Office and the Cabinet. Chapters 6 and 7 explore this division between the government departments, particularly the relationship between the High Commissioner and the Foreign Office. It is interesting to note that both the Conservative and Labour administrations were prepared to overrule COS concerns in order to normalize Anglo-Egyptian relations. The Foreign Office recognized that no matter how vital British imperial communications were they could never be secure in the face of a hostile indigenous population. Moreover, the cost of maintaining an imperial force sufficient to deal with any internal uprising was impossible during the economically straitened post-war years. A diplomatic negotiated solution was the best method of both securing and preserving Britain's imperial requirements.

Since the main aim of this study is to assess the development of British policy towards Egypt and the Sudan within Whitehall and the Residency and the communication linkages between London, Cairo and Khartoum, a heavy reliance upon British archives at The National Archives, Kew, was therefore necessary. The systematic investigation of the Cabinet Office, Foreign Office, Service Ministries, Colonial Office and Treasury files has been complemented by the private papers of key British politicians, civil servants, police and armed forces personnel who were at the sharp end of policymaking and its implementation in Egypt and the Sudan. These private papers are housed across the UK and include: Sir Austen Chamberlain held at the University of Birmingham Special Collections; Sir Maurice Hankey, Leo Amery and Lord and Lady Lloyd held at the Churchill Archives Centre, University of Cambridge; the papers of Stanley Baldwin and Charles Hardinge held at Cambridge University Library; the papers and diaries of Sir Walford Selby, Viscount Milner, Violet Milner and Sir John Simon held at the Bodleian Library, University of Oxford; Thomas Russell Pasha held at the Middle East Centre Archive at St Antony's College, Oxford; Lord Curzon and Viscount Chelmsford held at the British Library; Sir Reginald Wingate and a number of officials working in the Sudan at the Sudan Archive, University of Durham; the papers of Lord Edmund Allenby at the Liddell Hart Centre for Military Archives, Kings College London; the House of Lords Record Office which contains those of prime ministers David Lloyd George and Andrew Bonar Law; and the papers of Philip Kerr, later Lord Lothian, and Arthur Balfour held at the Scottish National Archives.

It is the shaping of attitudes in the aftermath of the upheaval and structural changes wrought by the First World War upon the British Empire and how Britain attempted to respond to these challenges and underwrite its position in the post-war years that form the main thrust of this study.

1

Between Two Worlds: Britain and Egypt in Africa and the Middle East

The nature of British rule

British involvement in Egypt was long-standing. August 1882, and the arrival of British troops in Egypt, signalled the inception of British domination of the country. Britain was to enjoy this supremacy in a number of guises until after the Second World War. The various political and military organizations that were established as a result of the British occupation ensured that throughout Britain's 'moment in the Middle East', no other foreign power could exert the same degree of influence over Egyptian affairs as Britain. An examination of Egypt's position within the British imperial system presents an almost schizophrenic picture – Egypt, at once a product of the Scramble for Africa, was also a vital piece of the strategic puzzle in the Middle East helping Britain to maintain a wider imperial reach.

The construction of the Suez Canal, begun in the 1850s under Ferdinand de Lesseps, a former French consul in Egypt–turned–engineer, marked the first considerable penetration of Egypt by foreign capital. The Suez Canal Company was formed in Paris, largely with French money, and floated its 800,000 shares in 1858. Khedive Sa'id Pasha (1854–63 as Khedive) purchased 353,204 shares while French shareholders procured 400,000 and other European interests bought 46,796 shares.[1] During this period, Egypt also became an important market for goods produced by British industrialization and as a supplier of raw materials, such as cotton and grain, vital since the American Civil War had disrupted cotton supplies. This provided further incentive for investment in the infrastructure of Egypt, such as the construction of railway lines between Cairo and Alexandria, and Cairo to Suez, in order to facilitate the transportation of goods.[2] In attempting to model Egypt on Western lines, Khedive Ismail Pasha (1863–79 as Khedive) embarked upon a number of other ambitious construction projects. These included heavy expenditure not only on his court and surroundings but also on 8,400 miles of irrigation canals, 5,000 miles of telegraph communications, the construction of 430 bridges, the Alexandria harbour and the docks at Suez, the completion of 15 lighthouses and 64 sugar mills, and the area of arable land was increased from 4 million to nearly five and a half million acres. To finance these schemes, often suggested and undertaken by British capitalists, Egypt borrowed heavily and by 1874 Egypt's foreign debts amounted to

£19,917,160. Servicing the interest on the debts, approximately £6 million, took the majority of Egypt's revenue which amounted to less than £10 million a year.[3]

It was unsurprising then that Egypt's finances soon reached a state of insolvency. Moreover, it is still less surprising that British and French experts were willing to offer their services when the details of the loans are examined. For example, the contractors for the three loans of 1862, 1864 and 1866 were the firm of Frühling & Goschen, of which Charles Hermann Goschen, a director of the Bank of England, was senior partner, and George Joachim Goschen, later Chancellor of the Exchequer, was a member.[4] The first example of direct British interference in Egyptian affairs came in 1875 when British creditors forced the Khedive to sell his shares in the Suez Canal for £4 million.[5] British and French financial missions furthered Anglo-French interference with the establishment of the Caisse of Public Debt in May 1876 and dual control was extended over Egypt through the appointment of two executive Controllers-General: Mr Romaine, a former Judge Advocate of the Indian Army, for revenue, and Baron de Malavet for expenditure. Captain Evelyn Baring, formerly Secretary to the Viceroy of India, was appointed to the post of Commissioner on the Caisse.

This financial quagmire provided the backdrop to the political opposition that erupted in the form of the National Revolution in 1881–82 under the leadership of Colonel Ahmed Arabi.[6] Stirrings of unrest among Egyptians over foreign financial control had already manifested itself in 1876 with Sadik Pasha's, Ismail's Minister of Finance, opposition to dual control. As conditions worsened a further outbreak of protest occurred in 1879 when a group of Egyptian officers seized the Egyptian Prime Minister, Nubar Pasha, and the British Finance Minister, Sir Rivers Wilson, and detained them in the Finance Ministry. Although the officials were immediately released on the orders of the Khedive, this event had several significant consequences: it demonstrated that the Khedive still possessed a certain amount of authority; it signalled the beginning of a widespread revolt against foreign control among the upper- and middle-class sections of Egyptian society; and, most importantly, it prompted Ismail to form an Egyptian ministry, headed by Sherif Pasha, to displace the European ministry. The new Cabinet was to be responsible to an elected assembly and the Cairo correspondent of *The Times* described how 'foreign assistance which came to regenerate the country has only given birth to a national party distinctly opposed to all rule from outside and avowedly working from the standpoint of Egypt for the Egyptians'.[7]

Egyptian failure to meet the required debt repayments in full and the deposition of Khedive Ismail in favour of his eldest son, Prince Muhammad Tawfiq (Khedive 1879–92), by the Ottoman Sultan and at the behest of the European powers, allowed the Controllers a role within the Egyptian Cabinet. The army, the only indigenous institution remaining within the state apparatus, now became the centre of discontent at foreign controls. Under Arabi, a protest movement began over the non-payment of salaries and the unfair system of promotion within the army itself and grew into a nationalist programme that included the dismissal of the whole ministry, the granting of a constitution and an increase in the strength of the army to the full 18,000 permitted.[8] Arabi's agitation was successful in attracting different sections of the population from landlords who objected to the foreign exploitation of Egypt's new resources to *fellahin* soldiers who were increasingly burdened by taxation in order to satisfy Egypt's foreign debtors. S Huffaker points out that 'as the ambitions and aims of Arabi and his supporters increasingly came into conflict with British business and government interests [...] the Victorian periodical and newspaper press came to portray him in increasingly negative terms'.[9] Arabi became the 'ultimate representative of Egypt and Egyptians' as the Anglo-Egyptian crisis grew.[10]

The struggle for dominance between the Khedive, Arabi and the European powers against the ambivalent influence of the Ottoman Sultan reached fatal consequences on 11 June 1882 when riots erupted in Alexandria. The exact cause remains unknown, but it resulted in several hundred people being killed or injured, including fifty Europeans. Charles Cookson, Acting British Consul, was badly wounded and a petty officer from HMS *Superb* was killed.[11] This was against the backdrop of a deteriorating situation in Ireland and M E Chamberlain has argued that since Arabi was either unable or unwilling to control the situation the security of the Suez Canal was at risk and this therefore justified the occupation of Egypt. Huffaker maintains that the representation of Arabi in the Victorian press was 'interwoven with a hegemonic world-view, which supported Britain's imperial role and increasingly masked other motivations for the invasion'.[12] The riots in Alexandria were critical in influencing the British occupation of Egypt. Predisposed by the deteriorating situation in Ireland, the massacre 'convinced the waverers, including Gladstone himself, that law and order had broken down, that the Egyptian army led by Arabi was either unable or unwilling to control the situation, that European lives were in danger and that, in a longer view, the safety of the Suez Canal could not be guaranteed'.[13]

In view of the events in Alexandria, the French called for a joint conference of the six powers with interests in Egypt – Britain, France, Italy, Germany, Austria and Russia. The conference convened at Constantinople on 23 June 1882, and a self-denying protocol was agreed. This was an undertaking 'not to seek any territorial advantage, nor any concession of any exclusive privilege, nor any commercial advantage for their subjects other than those which any other nation can equally obtain'.[14] It was also agreed that none of the Powers should undertake isolated action in Egypt, except in case of special emergency and that an appeal should be sent to the Sultan to dispatch troops to restore the *status quo* in Egypt. However, despite these agreements, sixteen days later, the British fleet bombarded Alexandria. The pretext for the attack was Arabi's refusal to halt the construction of batteries and the placement of guns at Alexandria which could be used against the British fleet. This bombardment was followed by a landing of British troops, with the support of the Khedive, to restore order. As the British occupation progressed, pressure was exerted on the Ottomans to issue a decree declaring that Arabi had led a mutiny against the Khedive. Once this was achieved, the support of the Islamic and Arab world for Arabi rapidly declined as his main defence was that he was protecting the Sultan's rights.[15] Arabi and his followers were defeated at Tel-el-Kebir and Cairo was occupied by the British two days later. On 17 September the Khedive disbanded the army and established a new force under the auspices of the British.[16] The British occupation of Egypt was now an economic, political and military fact.[17]

Egypt and the scramble for Africa

The British occupation was an important development since Egypt now took on a whole new strategic dimension. The opening of the Suez Canal in November 1869 had overnight supplanted the Cape of Good Hope's advantage in freight carried between Europe and the Far East. The Canal, at just over a hundred miles in length, shortened the distances from the Port of London to Bombay by 4,543 miles, to Calcutta by 3,667 miles and to Melbourne by 645 miles. The Canal therefore acquired increasing importance for British trade. Before 1914, India accounted for over half of the Canal's traffic; trade with the Far East increased tenfold, and high volume exports from Australia became possible. By 1928, exports to Britain from India and Burma formed 35.1 per cent of south-north traffic whilst British flagged ships constituted the largest users of the Canal.[18]

Despite Britain's obvious economic interests in the Canal and the fact that it formed the shortest route to the 'jewel in the imperial crown' – India – the Canal did not make the British occupation of Egypt a foregone conclusion. William Gladstone, writing in 1877 and whose government occupied Egypt five years later, opposed Edward Dicey's view that Britain should occupy a bankrupt Egypt.[19] Gladstone believed that it would draw Britain into creating a vast British Empire in Africa:

> Our first site in Egypt, be it by larceny or be it by exemption, will be the almost certain egg of a North African Empire, that will grow and grow until another Victoria and another Albert, title of the Lake – sources of the White Nile, come within our borders: and till we finally join hands across the Equator with Natal and Cape Town, to say nothing of the Transvaal and the Orange River on the South, or of Abyssinia or Zanzibar, to be swallowed by way of viaticum on our journey.[20]

Gladstone argued that such an Empire would drag Britain into:

> Consequent embroilments with France and the other Powers. There would be no limit to the responsibilities Britain would have to undertake, dealing with all oppression, and undertaking the entire taxation. It would end forever the realisation of that lofty aim, the founding not of a terrestrial but moral empire – the enthronement of this idea of public right as the governing idea of European policy.[21]

Indeed, M Thomas and R Toye have recently argued that we should examine the dynamics of British party politics of the time and the role that attitudes towards France played in influencing the British government's approach to Egypt.[22] Domestically, Gladstone's rhetoric during the 'Midlothian Campaign' of 1879–80 was centred upon the 'allegedly sinister and autocratic system of government' with which Disraelian 'Imperialism' was 'intimately entwined'.[23] For Gladstone it was the 'governing style' that was at the centre of the debate as opposed to territorial expansion.[24] Indeed, 'it was the relationship between morality and national self-interest that marked the fault-line between Gladstonian and Conservative imperial views'.[25] As Thomas and Toye outline 'for high-minded Liberals, improvements in native welfare, to be worked for as part of a sacred trust that had been bequeathed them, were the only justification for an empire which Britain, in the last analysis, did not actually need for her survival'.[26] The Conservatives, on the other hand, possessed 'their own concept of imperial "duty" – albeit a duty to develop British character much more than one to improve native welfare'.[27]

From the beginning, there existed a moral opposition to the British occupation of Egypt. It was argued that 'expansion provided careers, or profits, for privileged groups at British taxpayers' cost'.[28] One such example was Seymour Keay's *Spoiling the Egyptians: A Tale of Shame* (1882), which depicted the Cabinet simply as pawns to bondholders and financiers.[29] This was countered by explorers or pro-consular figures who emphasized the 'need to forestall competitors or lose trade, and to "civilise" Africans'.[30] A Milner's *England in Egypt* (1892) perceived Britain's task in Egypt following Arabi's defeat at Tel el-Kebir as 'one of the most thankless roles thrust upon an unwilling actor'.[31] To Milner and his imperial compatriots, British control of Egypt was necessary for two reasons. Firstly, Britain's substantial and increasing commercial interests within Egypt were an important consideration and were vulnerable to indigenous Egyptian mismanagement. More significantly, Milner argued that Egypt's strategic position within the British Empire warranted attention to her internal political makeup. He believed that Britain had nothing to gain by annexing Egypt, but a great deal to fear if it fell into the possession of another power. To avoid this possibility, Milner advocated providing Egypt with a 'decent native government [… these] efforts are not philanthropy, they are business. But they are business of a perfectly straightforward and honourable kind, and possessing the characteristic of all good business – namely, that both parties concerned are benefited'.[32]

However, not everyone agreed with this 'constructive' imperialist ideal. J A Hobson, a Radical publicist, published *Imperialism: A Study* in 1902. His imperial faith, destroyed by the Jameson Raid (1895–96) and the Second Anglo-Boer War (1899–1902), argued that the 'sectional interest of finance capitalism, bankers, Egyptian bondholders, and Transvaal gold companies had usurped control of the state to create secure markets for their investments'.[33] Hobson was quick to note the difficulties in defining imperialism but perceived that it was closely related to its other kindred terms – nationalism, internationalism and colonialism.[34]

Seeing a direct linkage between nationalism, colonialism and imperialism, Hobson believed that it was the 'debasement of this genuine nationalism, by attempts to overflow its national banks and absorb the near or distant territory of reluctant and unassimilable peoples, that marks the passage from nationalism to a spurious colonialism on the one hand, imperialism on the other'. It was this imperialism, also compelled by an 'ever keener "fight for markets"', that Hobson believed to be a retrograde step for civilization. The doctrines of national destiny and imperial missions of civilization were seen by Hobson as mere propaganda for popular consumption in order to justify a 'calculating, greedy type of Machiavellianism'. Hobson was unapologetic in his belief that imperialism, as witnessed in the Scramble for Africa, was 'a depraved choice of national life, imposed by self-seeking interests which appeal to the lists of quantitative acquisitiveness and a forceful domination'.[35]

The carnage of the First World War and the publication of V I Lenin's *Imperialism: the Highest Stage of Capitalism* (1916) which argued that 'imperialism', the latest stage of monopolistic industrial capitalism, was the cause of the war, gave weight to writers of the Left who continued to question the idea of a fair and just British Empire with its civilizing mission.[36] For example, Elinor Burns in *Imperialism in Egypt* perceived the British occupation as pure exploitation of the peasants and workers by British capital.[37] Even the abolition of the *corvée* (forced labour) by the British authorities, advertised as one of their greatest achievements, was criticized by Burns as it was merely replaced by a system of wage labour at the lowest rates possible. Burns concluded that Britain would be unable to reconcile its interests within Egypt with those of the nationalist movement.[38]

Ronald Robinson and John Gallagher's seminal *Africa and the Victorians* (1961) sought to eschew the traditional explanations for the Scramble for Africa that took a Eurocentric focus – from the new imperial spirit in Europe, to structural changes in European industrial capitalism, or on the intensifying rivalries within the European balance of power to events in Africa itself. For Robinson and Gallagher the Empire should not be viewed as a homogenous imperial state. Any study of the Scramble for Africa needed to include the informal empire of trade and influence into its considerations since formal empire often had deep historical roots in informal empire that preceded it. Indeed, the circumstances from within the empire, as opposed to a centrally directed policy, were the primary factors in governing the timing and forms of imperial intervention.[39]

Indeed, the idea that an expanding Victorian economy was the *raison d'être* for the Scramble failed to convince Robinson and Gallagher. Instead, it was a more subtle and complex relationship – political action aiding the growth of commercial supremacy, this supremacy in turn strengthening political influence. By incorporating a number of areas into their study – the policies of imperial expansion within the metropole; the concept of informal empire in relation to the empire of rule; the idea that the chances of local co-operation and crises of local resistance played as large a role as agents of expansion in determining the different forms of imperialism in differing regions; the notion that there was no unified imperial state, but many different kinds of empire with as many different connections with Britain as there were countries under her sway – the Scramble for Africa was one of 'central continuity and regional discontinuity'.[40]

In their analysis they discovered that the Victorians had 'given much less weight to economic interests and much more to strategic factors in Africa'.[41] But, at the same time, empire for empire's sake was not the policymakers' motive either. Instead, it was the cold, hard system of ensuring national safety that prompted the ruling elite to search for greater security in the Mediterranean and the East – a continuity in policy formulation that had been handed down from Pitt, Palmerston and Disraeli. The territorial and commercial gains that Britain acquired were therefore 'little more than by-products'.[42]

So, British advances were prompted by different interests and circumstances in different regions. In the case of Egypt, Robinson and Gallagher argued that Egypt was occupied as a direct result of the collapse of the Khedival regime. In the centre a variety of different interests – religious and humanitarian, commercial or financial and imperial – all lobbied the government for territorial acquisitions. Ministers listened to these pleas only when it suited their purpose – it was one consideration and one consideration alone which entered into all the major decisions north of the three Rhodesian protectorates and that was the safety of routes to the East – the safe communication between India, the Far East and the British Isles. This determined the order of priorities in the Middle East, Asia and Africa and, ultimately, Britain's position within the world. It was only when the traditional forms of security by influence began to break down as a result of internal nationalist crises within Egypt, coupled with rivalries in Europe, that ministers were to intervene in order to 'regain by territorial claims and occupation that security which could no longer be had by influence alone'.[43]

Critics of Robinson and Gallagher, such as D C M Platt, question whether they had distorted the African case at the expense of other regions across the globe. In *Finance, Trade and Politics in British Foreign Policy 1815–1914* (1968), Platt examined how far commerce influenced the formulation of foreign policy during the nineteenth century throughout the world. He argued that by stressing factors, such as the security of the routes to the East, the part played in British policy by the need to protect the position of British trade in world markets had been consigned to one of insignificance. Since the protection of commerce was a major factor in determining policy in China and Latin America, could it really be of such little consequence in the partition of Africa? Platt believes that it was actually the fear of being excluded from prospective as well as existing markets that underlay British policy in West and Central Africa since nobody at the time could accurately estimate what these markets might be worth in the future.[44]

Indeed, many critics believe that Robinson and Gallagher over argue their case with regard to Egypt. Jean Stengers points out that political and commercial rivalry existed in the Congo independently of the Egyptian question. Historians of West Africa also take issue with Robinson and Gallagher, believing that it was France between 1879 and 1882, and not Britain, that initiated the Scramble for Africa.

Furthermore, P J Cain and A G Hopkins' examination of British imperialism in *British Imperialism: Innovation and Expansion, 1688–1914* (1993) and *British Imperialism: Crisis and Destruction, 1914–1990* (1993) sought to put the metropolitan economy back at the centre of the analysis. Criticizing Marxist historians for often misjudging both the development of the British economy and its links with overseas expansion, Cain and Hopkins advocated a reconsideration of capitalism both as a concept and in its historical application. By examining British imperialism through the lens of several interacting forms of capitalist enterprise – agriculture, commerce, finance and industry – and a reappraisal of the social agents of capitalist enterprise, such as the English gentleman, Cain and Hopkins hoped to 'reunite the history of the centre and of its diverse peripheries'.[45]

As regards Egypt, Cain and Hopkins disagreed with Robinson and Gallagher's view that the British occupation was a result of a crisis on the periphery sparked by a proto-nationalist revolt and Britain's need to restore law and order to protect its strategic asset in the Suez Canal as the route to India. Cain and Hopkins instead suggest that 1882 can be seen as a 'moment of conjuncture arising out of the long term interaction between the expansion of British interests and the aspirations of Egypt's rulers'.[46] Anglo-Egyptian commercial ties had grown rapidly after 1815 based around the exchange of cotton goods for raw cotton. The purchase of the Egyptian Government's shares in the Suez Canal in 1875 and the consolidation of the public debt in 1880 meant that Britain was the principal creditor when Egypt slid into bankruptcy in 1876. Cain and Hopkins view the forward policy followed by Benjamin Disraeli's Conservative Government (1874–80) and largely continued by Gladstone's Liberal administration after 1880 as assertive because of the need to defend Britain's substantial economic interests in Egypt. Moreover, Disraeli and Gladstone believed that these interests could be secured quickly and inexpensively and that this would also produce political benefits at home.[47]

Cain and Hopkins continued this line of argument in relation to Britain's relationship with the Sudan. They argued that it was actually Egypt's indebtedness and not the need to protect the Suez route to India that prompted Britain's involvement in the Sudan, particularly since Britain could not allow disorder to persist in the Sudan if it endangered the settlement that had just been imposed upon Egypt.[48] This again demonstrates the linkage between the metropole and periphery and the impact that the economy, in terms of finance and the service sector, had on shaping both national policy and Britain's informal presence abroad.

Indeed, Cain takes this argument one stage further and links Egypt's indebtedness to the rhetoric of character that British governing elites used to justify their presence in Egypt as well as the financial policies they adopted. British imperial representatives believed that this character was both the product of centuries of external experience and the response to a complex set of internal crises, such as the Protestant reformation and the Civil War, perceived alongside the development of constitutional and religious structures after 1688 that were observed as progressive.[49] These events had laid the basis for the 'agrarian, commercial and industrial transformations' that catapulted Britain to the leading global and imperial power of the nineteenth and early twentieth centuries. This, coupled with Britain's technological and military superiority over Africa and Asia, permitted the development of both a moral and material superiority over indigenous populations that was underwritten by technological advancements and military firepower. This economic context permitted the idea of a 'good character' to be linked with attributes such as 'industry, energy, self-help and self-discipline, thrift, honesty, integrity, devotion to duty',[50] and masculinity. Gladstone perceived that an 'enforcement of financial disciplines was [...] vital to the survival of both public and private morality and, ultimately, to national prosperity and social order'.[51] Viewed in this light and considering Britain's economic and strategic interests in the region, the British occupation is unsurprising whilst disguised behind the thinly veiled rhetoric of character or 'good government' when Egyptians 'deserved liberty just as much'.[52]

Britain and Egypt in the Middle East: The development of nationalism

Egypt's declaration of independence on 28 February 1922 has been regarded by traditionalist scholars, such as historian Arnold Toynbee and former British diplomat Alec Kirkbride as an abdication of British rule in the Middle East and symptomatic of its decline as a world power. In Toynbee's *Survey of International Affairs. The*

World after the Peace Conference (1925), he suggests that militant Middle Eastern nationalism, assisted by the policy of national self-determination, gradually subverted the agreements made by the victorious powers at the Paris Peace Conference[53]; for example, the Egyptian rising against the British regime in March 1919, Afghanistan's war against the British Empire in May 1919, and the Kurdish and Shi'ite tribal insurrection against the British Army of occupation in Mesopotamia between 1919 and 1920. According to Toynbee, these armed rebellions, however reckless, were justified by the political results they achieved because they demonstrated a latent weakness or lack of will on the part of the British. For instance, Egypt gained nominal independence even after a sharp repression. The Iraqi rebellion collapsed after six months, but the British still abandoned direct administration and established a National Government under British guidance. And, even though defeated by Britain, Afghanistan secured release from British dominance. In Toynbee's view the forces of nationalism had promoted the cause of national sovereignty and independence across the Middle East.[54]

This image of Britain as a weary Titan was continued, to a certain degree, by Elizabeth Monroe's *Britain's Moment in the Middle East, 1914–1971* (1981). Written in response to the rise of the neo-colonial school, Monroe argued that the various measures Britain was forced to exercise in the Middle East in order to maintain its position had long-term repercussions that reduced both British repute and power. Monroe's argument can be divided into two parts: the internal complications of British dominance in the region and the external strategic consequences.

According to Monroe, Britain's 'moment' in the Middle East extended from the British capture of Baghdad and Jerusalem in 1917 until the Suez Crisis of 1956. Although this paled in comparison to the recorded history of the region extending over four millennia, those officials participating in this moment perceived it as long enough for the accomplishment of services beneficial to both Britain and the Arab peoples, Britain's civilizing mission.[55] However, Monroe was quick to emphasize the underlying strategic factor behind Britain's effort: to 'keep the route to India orderly and secure'.[56] In fact, Monroe emphasized the enormous role played by India in the British Empire. It was accorded its own Secretary of State, was an Empire in its own right and possessed an Indian Army numbering nearly a quarter of a million men. It provided valuable training conditions and was to be utilized as a pivot for operations as far east as China and as far west as Egypt. After the collapse of Tsarist Russia in 1917–18, Britain began to extend her commitments in the Middle East in order to fill the vacuum left by the Ottoman Empire and to maintain the tranquillity that Britain long thought vital to her strategic interests.[57]

Internally, British dominance over the indigenous peoples of Egypt and the Middle East was assured by the 'despondency, uncertainty and division of opinion into which the Arab nationalists were plunged by the fruitlessness of their effort between 1916 and 1918'.[58] Rather than forging an independent nation, they merely changed their master, from Ottoman Turk to British. The presence of foreign troops coupled with America ignoring nationalist pleas for self-determination allowed Britain to take advantage of the Arab inability to combine as a single force.[59]

So was Britain's position in Egypt and the Middle East purely a result of luck rather than calculated judgement? The introduction of the thirty-year rule for access to government archives in 1967 allowed a more far-reaching and sympathetic approach to the latent problems surrounding the inter-war period and historians engaged in pluralist analyses. Elie Kedourie's revisionist *The Chatham House Version and Other Middle Eastern Studies* constituted a stinging polemical attack upon this traditionalist interpretation. By examining events from a largely Arab perspective, Kedourie warned against simply imposing the post–Second World War state of mind, more particularly after 1956, on the inter-war period.[60]

It is true that military expenditure was scaled down in the immediate post-war years. However, this was because ministers believed that there was little prospect of a major European conflagration in the near future. There is no evidence to suggest that ministers were guided by the belief that the empire was entering its twilight years, or that nationalism was a sufficiently powerful force to render British control of India and the Middle East obsolete. Of course, there were some armed uprisings in India, Egypt, Iraq and Palestine during 1919 and 1920, but these were quelled with relative ease. It was only after these short-lived disturbances were quashed that policymakers decided that British imperial interests could be preserved more economically and with less trouble if local leaders were installed in power, their co-operation secured through treaties, and this co-operation ultimately guaranteed by British military and naval preponderance in the region.[61] Whilst traditionalist interpretations perceived the British abdication of power in the Middle East as inevitable, Kedourie argues that British policies were adopted as a matter of choice and not under compulsion.[62]

John Darwin continued Kedourie's revisionist stance by investigating Middle Eastern affairs from a largely British perspective. In *Britain, Egypt and the Middle East. Imperial Policy in the Aftermath of War* (1981), Darwin refuted the belief that the outbreak of the First World War was a decisive watershed in Britain's imperial experience. Traditionally, the First World War has been viewed as 'separating the era of strength and success from the era of decline and dissolution'.[63] Darwin contends that, on the surface, this is a completely plausible argument to accept. Indeed, following the conclusion of hostilities, several factors made the capability of the British to control their vast Empire appear uncertain. Firstly, the white Dominions' rejection of any subjugation to the mother country combined with progress towards full national sovereignty appeared more assured and absolute. Secondly, nationalist movements in Ireland, India and Egypt exerted a significant strain upon British imperial policy as they gained a wider support base whilst also devising more effective tactics to confront British authority. Thirdly, following the stresses of the Great War, coupled with the significant growth in the industrial and naval power of the United States and Japan, Britain's position as the great economic powerhouse of the world appeared less certain. Finally, the advent of mass democracy in Britain after the war and the existence of ineradicable social and economic problems diminished the ability of the British Government to effectively 'divert resources into the protection and defence of Britain's imperial system [...] and the preoccupation of politicians with issues of domestic rather than international significance was correspondingly greater'.[64] Thus, the policymaker's willingness to either concede formal independence or accelerate progress towards self-rule seemed only to confirm the accepted interpretation.

By examining Egypt and the Middle East from the perspective of Downing Street, Whitehall and occasionally Westminster, Darwin argues that British policy continued to adapt in order to deal with the altered international situation. For instance, the Egyptian Declaration of Independence of 1922, rather than being symptomatic of an irreversible loosening of Britain's hold over Egypt, actually exemplified a stalemate in the struggle for Egyptian independence. What ministers actually sanctioned was an adjustment in Anglo-Egyptian relations: 'the shrugging off of commitments that had become over-extended during the war and which […] were undermining the real purpose of the British presence'.[65]

Darwin argues against an innate pessimism permeating the corridors of power post-1918 and a tendency to view pre-1914 as a golden age, free from anxiety. What troubled the policymakers was not whether the imperial system could survive. The more pressing problem was how to contain the side effects of war on the internal and international security of the imperial system. The idea of abandoning the empire was never considered, but a general recognition that 'old objects must be served by new methods'[66] came to exist.

This situation would endure so long as Britain remained powerful enough to prohibit its imperial rivals from a direct voice in Egyptian affairs and while the evolution of a single focus of power eluded Egyptian politicians. Darwin maintains that in 1922 'the disappearance of either of these fundamental conditions of British power and control seemed so remote as to be almost inconceivable'.[67] Indeed, Britain's imperial security lay not in her capacity to defeat nationalist forces, but in her 'ability to divide or defeat those powers whose military and economic strength matched her own, and to prevent them from rupturing the thin skein of naval power and political influence which held the imperial system and its outworks together'.[68]

The awakening of proto-nationalisms, as outlined by Robinson and Gallagher, has provided historians with another lens through which to assess Britain's moment within the region. In *Redefining the Egyptian Nation, 1930–45* (1995), James Jankowski and Israel Gershoni focus upon the creation and dissemination of new Egyptian national images and frameworks of identity. They contend that, in part, 'the history of Egyptian nationalism involves the contest for political authority and the competition among rival political forces; but it also involves the larger historical process of Egyptian collective self-definition'.[69] Overarching these individual nationalist variants was the common feature of a *supra-Egyptian* character. During the 1920s, nationalism can be viewed as developing within a territorially defined area. The 1930s, by contrast, demonstrated a desire to extend Egyptian national identity to peoples and regions beyond the Nile Valley. The concept of supra-Egyptianism encompassed several new definitions of Egyptian national identity – Easternism, Islamicism, Arabism and an integral Egyptian nationalism. According to Jankowski and Gershoni, 'the first three linked Egyptian national identity to the external referent of the Islamic community, the Arab nation and the "East"; the last expressed the conviction that Egypt had a role of leadership extending to the same peoples and regions'.[70]

Jankowski and Gershoni therefore perceive Egyptian nationalism as constituting two distinct phases. The first, which gained primacy immediately after the First World War, was founded upon the territorial and Western-influenced image of

Egypt. This was based upon Egypt's geographical setting and its ancient history. The only external association this territorial nationalist ideology acknowledged was the culture and values of Mediterranean civilization and the modern West. In political terms it assumed a necessary identity between the state and nation and drew sharp lines between the nation-state and the surrounding world. Socially, the creation of Egypt's Westernized elite strove to reconstruct Egyptian society on a Western model.[71]

The 1930s and 1940s, however, witnessed the evolution of alternative ideas of conceptualizing Egypt. These were based upon cultural, religious and linguistic sources instead of concepts originating from Egypt's geographical setting and its ancient history. Supra-Egyptian nationalism was not from the Islamic-Arab heritage that Egypt shared with peoples beyond the Nile valley. The West was now perceived as alien and aggressive and Egypt's real external association rested with the peoples of the Arab, Muslim and Eastern worlds.[72]

The origin of this shift lies in several factors. The internal crises experienced throughout the 1930s resulted in significant consequences for Egyptian nationalism: the economic depression of the 1930s accompanied by its social upheavals; the continuation of British dominance resulting in the perception that the 1919 uprising had failed to produce any tangible results; the repressive Ismail Sidqi regime; Palace manipulation of political life; and the general corrupt nature of the political establishment, which led to a loss of faith in the parliamentary and Western-orientated system conceived in the 1920s.

As a consequence, Jankowski and Gershoni contend that 'all this served to undermine Egyptian territorial nationalism and led Egyptians to search for other, presumably more effective, nationalist alternatives'.[73] Externally, the crisis of democracy across Europe also contributed to a movement towards greater Arab co-operation as the Egyptians became disillusioned with the European model, while marvelling at the new regional prospects that a re-evaluation of their relationship with their neighbours could supply. At the same time, however, a cultural crisis of contradictions within Egyptian nationalism bubbled beneath the surface. Egyptian nationalism had simultaneously to fight European imperialism whilst borrowing appropriate models and methods for modern community from the West and, at the same time, creating its own cultural and psychological distinctiveness from the West.[74]

A further factor that marked the shift from territorial to supra-Egyptian nationalism was the creation of the new *effendiyya* class. Technological change, industrialization, education and the spread of literacy produced a 'broad stratum of urban, literate, modern occupational groups'.[75] These groups became the most significant producers and consumers of nationalist imaginings, disseminating the new concepts of nation both upward and downward in the social strata. In conclusion, therefore, Jankowski and Gershoni put forward that:

> The more Egyptian nationalism moved from being the exclusive property of elitist intellectuals and spread among the wider strata of society, the more it became less Pharonic-Western and more Islamic-Arab. Egyptian nationalism was disseminated and popularised only through its Islamification and Arabisation.[76]

In broadening their analysis, Jankowski and Gershoni's, *Rethinking Nationalism in the Arab Middle East* (1997) evaluates the role of nationalism in shaping the wider Fertile Crescent. Traditional accounts of Arab nationalism, such as John Marlowe's *Arab Nationalism and British Imperialism* (1961), have recounted the development of nationalist movements against the background of the struggle against European imperialism, or have defined nationalist ideology as that as expressed by the educated elite and party spokesmen. Arab nationalism has often been explained as a result of three factors. Firstly, as a response to European imperialism and the demise of Ottoman/Islamic order. Secondly, as imitative, as Arab intellectuals became fascinated by European culture. Thirdly, as diffusionist, as nationalist concepts gradually disseminated from their European homeland to the Middle East. Other features such as the social and psychological bases of nationalism, the spread of new identities within society and the non-elite dimensions of nationalism have largely been ignored by Western historians.[77]

Jankowski and Gershoni contend that the story of nationalism in the Arab Middle East is dynamic, a clash of rival national identities and agendas. As a result, writing the history of Arab nationalism consists of explaining 'the interplay among alternative nationalist visions and programs [sic]'.[78] The collection of essays within *Rethinking Nationalism in the Arab Middle East* therefore attempts to cultivate a multi-faceted viewpoint on nationalism. As the diverse histories of different forms of nationalism in Arab societies are being uncovered, the notion of a homogenous and hegemonic Arab nationalism so often projected by ideologues is being broadened. Instead, the genesis and evolution of nationalism is increasingly being viewed as a multi-dimensional process whose roots lie in the socio-economic processes of the modern era and whose meaning extends beyond elites to broader sections of societies.[79]

Indeed, much of the examination of the development of Egyptian nationalism has been top-down. Z Fahmy in *Ordinary Egyptians: Creating the Modern Nation through Popular Culture* (2011) attempts to rectify this imbalance through the examination of colloquial Egyptian mass culture from newspapers to the recording industry as a lens through which to understand the development of nationalism as a growing number of inhabitants of the Nile Valley began to identify as being Egyptian. Fahmy points out that many of these individuals were illiterate and simply did not read, nor were they exposed to the intellectual writings of Taha Husayn, Lutfi al-Sayyid or the nationalistic fictional novels of Najib Mahfuz. For those who could read, these works were simply not in a 'language' or format with which they could engage.[80] So how was this idea of Egyptian collective identity communicated? Fahmy argues that it was the mode of transmission that holds the key. It was 'newspapers, especially the satirical press, recorded and performed colloquial Egyptian songs and the vernacular theatre that were the principal and most effective mediators and broadcasters of cultural ideologies',[81] as opposed to the more formalized, literary Fusha variety of Arabic. This development in mass media, aided by the development of technologies and communication networks, facilitated a mediation between the 'written Fusha discourses of the "bourgeois nationalists" and the colloquial expressions of the Egyptian urban masses',[82] in the development of a collective Egyptian national identity and usefully moves this discussion out of the realms of elite politics.

The British conceptualization of Egypt produces an interesting dichotomy. The construction and opening of the Suez Canal, the forefront of technological development, were perceived as a confirmation of European modernity, the progress of European civilization. However, as E A Haddad has shown in 'Digging to India: Modernity, Imperialism and the Suez Canal', *Victorian Studies* (2005), this was juxtaposed against Victorian accounts of a certain nostalgia for the Egyptian pharaonic and medieval past, so readily visible on journeys through Egypt. Against the backdrop of rapid industrialization at home, Victorian Britons looked to 'medieval British feudalism or to their more recent agricultural heritage, the objects of their nostalgia were rural and [...] often explicitly anti-urban'.[83] This perhaps, in part, explains policymakers innate conviction that their primary role in the administration of Egypt was that of protecting the Egyptian *fellahin* against the inefficiencies of the Egyptian landowning elite. Indeed, D M Reid in 'Cromer and the Classics: Imperialism, Nationalism and the Greco-Roman Past in Modern Egypt', *Middle Eastern Studies* (1996), tackles this idea of perception by focussing upon the uses Europeans and Egyptians made of classical Greek and Roman discourse. He notes that Alfred Milner, imperial administrator and politician, used the classics as a lens through which to play with the Egyptian enigma: 'Egypt is still, like the Egypt of Herodotus, the chosen home of what is strange and unexampled and paradoxical. Imagine a people that most docile and good-tempered in the world in the grip of a religion the most intolerant and fanatical'.[84] As Reid points out, Egyptian nationalists detected this Western fascination with ancient Egypt, but the *ulema* and the masses identified with the more recent Islamic past.[85] This thereby represents a discombobulated layering between class and their identification with the Egyptian past. The nationalists could use the classics to their advantage and appeal to enlightened European elites. For example, Ahmad Lutfi al-Sayyid translated Aristotle's *Nichomachaean Ethics* into Arabic in 1924. Al-Sayyid declared that Aristotle could establish Egypt's nationalist awakening 'on the same rational foundation as the European Renaissance'.[86] In essence, it is impossible to study Egypt in the late nineteenth and early twentieth centuries without taking into account the 'classical mind-set which so many Westerners used to make sense of Egypt and the Middle East' and which is, in turn, reflected in the rhetoric of politicians and colonial administrators. Reid concludes that 'whatever the virtues of a classical education and of values expressed in classical idiom, such a way of viewing Egypt at best warped perception of contemporary realities and at worst conjured up a full-blown mirage'.[87]

J Whidden's 'Expatriates in Cosmopolitan Egypt: 1864–1956' continues this theme that class as opposed to race was integral to the foundations of British power within Egypt. Whidden emphasizes the social as opposed to the purely political/imperial aspect of Anglo-Egyptian relations and describes them as 'a richly layered social and cultural milieu',[88] particularly during the inter-war years. As more Egyptian men and women were educated in foreign schools during this period 'British and middle- or upper-class Egyptians often shared a common set of values, forged at the schools, clubs and other cultural institutions that actively encouraged cultural exchange'.[89] It was, in fact, these interdependent Anglo-Egyptian social relations as opposed to pure imperial power that underwrote the British presence in Egypt.

Britain and Egypt: The Sudan

These studies examine the complex relationship between British imperialism and Arab nationalism, but an equally interesting story was unfolding south of the Egyptian border in the Sudan. Accounts by former officials, such as Sir Harold MacMichael, *The Anglo-Egyptian Sudan* (1934), maintain that Britain's reconquest of the former Egyptian territory (lost during the Mahdist uprising of 1881) was necessary to secure Egypt from any Sudanese threat and to prevent any other European powers from annexing the Sudan during the Scramble for Africa and thereby exercise a stranglehold over the flow of the Nile waters into Egypt. The Condominium Agreement of 1899 ensured Britain's virtual trusteeship of the Sudan through British control of the administrative machinery and the final approval of the appointment of consuls. The sovereign rights of Egypt in the Sudan no longer existed after 1884 save in so far as they were recreated in conjunction with the sovereign rights accruing to Britain by right of conquest in 1899. MacMicheal was convinced that 'Britain has undertaken a trusteeship for the welfare of the Sudanese [...] She cannot abandon that trust, nor hand it over to any party who is not fitted by natural genius of character combined with practical experience to carry it out'.[90] The extent to which this belief permeated official circles was demonstrated by Prime Minister Ramsay MacDonald in a broadcast speech reported in *The Times* of 26 May 1930:

> We have undertaken the care of people who could not take care of themselves. They were doomed to civil war or systems of government, which cut them off from the benefits of civilisation. We have duties regarding them. We must see so far as we are able that weakness in our part or a too ready withdrawal from the guardianship we have assumed does not abandon them so that they relapse into the conditions from which our intervention rescued them [...] We dare not lay down our burdens. We dare not leave our task unfinished.[91]

It is possible to see a healthy dose of Liberal Victorian rhetoric in MacDonald's speech but this time extended to the Sudan as opposed to Egypt.

Heather J Sharkey in *Living with Colonialism, Nationalism and Culture in the Anglo-Egyptian Sudan* (2003) focuses on the importance of the lives and careers of the local functionaries to the operation of the colonial state, the mediation of cultural change and the elaboration of communal identities. In line with the Robinson and Gallagher thesis, Sharkey argues that the idea a lone British ruler could bring the continent to heel through intelligence, civilization and character was a myth. In fact, the British Empire worked on the ground because it relied upon a vast army of local clerks, technicians, teachers and doctors who administered the day-to-day tasks of colonialism. 'As petty employees these individuals produced domination in its most prosaic forms, but as early nationalists they dreamed of displacing imperial power. These were colonialism's intimate enemies, making colonial rule a reality while hoping to see it undone.'[92] The enemy from within.

With this as the foundation, Sharkey examines three areas: how colonialism worked on a day-to-day basis; how nationalism grew out of the banal activities and myriad exchanges that occurred on the ground and in print; and, lastly, how the colonial state took shape and evolved into a nation-state with its lasting social consequences.[93] The colonial system depended upon a wide participatory base and 'the great British achievement was in managing these staffs and deploying limited financial, educational and military resources to the maximum advantage of the colonial state'.[94] The indigenous employees who occupied minor administrative roles were very often highly educated and literate men and were as much part of the colonial system as the Britons who ruled it. By utilizing the power of the written word as well as that of visual images they have left a vivid record of their lives and careers. Indeed, it is the use of this writing and imagery that made these minor colonial employees early nationalists by cultivating their own cultural image.[95]

For the British, the use of local recruits for the administration of the colony was a double-edged sword. Whilst on the one hand the heavy use of civilian support staff provided a low-cost solution to the personnel problem, conveying an impression of solidity and thereby neutralizing opposition among the newly educated classes, this in itself sowed the seed of dissatisfaction. It was the actual conditions of colonial employment that were conducive to the advent and growth of nationalism. The fact that they attended British-style schools, developed a familiarity with the medium of print and film, possessed a connection with the ruling class and periodically moved postings within the colonial territory's borders aided the imagining of a nation-state. As a result, the indigenous recruits became increasingly frustrated as they found their ascent within the bureaucratic system blocked by Britons who cast them as social inferiors, and this led to the development and perpetuation of nationalist ideologies based on evident anticolonial foundations. 'In this way, the nationalist challenge to colonialism arose from within the colonial system and swelled to fill the borders that empire had imposed.'[96]

Moreover, the very conditions that allowed the consolidation of the British Empire, such as developing technologies in transport and communication,[97] aided the development and growth of nationalism. Sharkey argues that the daily life of the colonized began to adapt to the new order in the way people travelled, dressed, conducted business, ate and treated illnesses. Social groups also began to redefine themselves and their relations to others as contacts with Britons and other expatriates intensified, and as rates of migration rose, especially towards towns and cities. In addition to communal identities based upon religion, sect, language or clan, Sharkey perceives a new identity emerging. One which was 'an ideological manifestation of compound social changes that colonialism set in motion. It responded not only to the idea of foreign domination, but also, and perhaps more importantly, to political and cultural change'.[98]

Furthermore, as in Egypt, the printed word was essential to the development and proliferation of ideas associated with nationalism. Cheap printing allowed educated groups not only to read the ideas of others but also to publish journals, newspapers and books of their own. However, although encouraging early nationalism, the print culture also confirmed its elitism within African and Asian societies. In this way, Sharkey extends our understanding of the connected histories of colonialism and nationalism in Africa during the twentieth century.

Other studies have provided a deeper analysis of the complex triangular colonialism of the Anglo-Egyptian relationship within the Sudan. Eve M Troutt Powell's *A Difference Shade of Colonialism. Egypt, Great Britain and the Mastery of the Sudan* (2003) demonstrates how central the issue of the Sudan was to Egyptian identity and Egyptian nationalism and highlights the deep ambivalence in Egyptian attitudes towards the British Empire and the resulting ambiguities and paradoxes that were essential components of the nationalist movement. Troutt Powell dismisses the Manichean binary relationship between colonizer and the colonized and advances the idea that actually a greater fluidity existed between the nations involved within the Nile Valley where the colonizers came from more than one continent. 'The colonized could aspire to be a colonizer not only by adopting the tools of the British, or the traditions of the Ottomans, but also by assimilating the Sudan to be a part of what defined Egypt as truly Egyptian.'[99]

Martin Daly's *Empire on the Nile. The Anglo-Egyptian Sudan, 1898–1934* (1986) pioneered the view that colonial rule in the Sudan existed on two levels. The most important was that of the maintenance of order. 'Administration was a profession, the proper work of "political" officers, while the business of education, health, social welfare, economic development, and so forth was secondary, incidental, to be left to others'. Daly states that while the Sudanese Government presented an 'imposing edifice, rock-solid, permanent', this was merely a façade and instead relied upon personality, not policy to maintain British superiority in the region.[100] Personalities such as Lord Kitchener, Lord Cromer, Reginald Wingate, C A Willis (Head of Intelligence), Sir Lee Stack (1919–1924), Sir Geoffrey Archer (1924–1926), Sir John Maffey (1926–1934) (Sudan's Governor-Generals), Colonel Hubert Huddleston (Adjutant-General of the British military authorities in the Sudan), Lord Allenby, Saad Zaghlul and Jack Murray at the Foreign Office determined the course of the Condominium. That British rule rested on a fragile house of cards could be seen at every level.

Indeed, A Kirk-Greene's study of these imperial administrators reinforces this point. The District Commissioner was the centre of the imperial machine. For these imperial administrators their top priority was the 'maintenance of law and order', the 'application of justice' and the 'imperative of paternalism' and that this rested upon 'a generous measure of White Man's Bluff'. That the District Commissioner administered with the aid of a 'mystique of authority created by and built on his own self-confidence […] it was a fundamental sense of one kind or another of superiority (cultural, moral, intellectual, socio-racial, technological or organisational know-how), at once unquestioned and unquestioning, which enabled the expatriate colonial administrator – be he an experienced Commissioner or greenhorn cadet – to advise, to act, to accomplish, and indeed to be'.[101]

Britain and Egypt: The strategic dimension

The concept of imperial defence 'as an intellectual exercise, was, despite a lack of consistency in image or manifestation, a reality'.[102] Egypt formed the cornerstone of Britain's imperial security during the inter-war period for all three services. For the

Royal Navy the Suez Canal provided the 'jugular vein' to the Far Eastern Empire and antipodean dominions and facilitated the existence of a highly mobile fleet in a post-Washington Naval Conference era.[103] For the newly formed Royal Air Force (RAF), Egypt provided ideal training conditions and a significant base in the Middle East. For the British Army the defence of the Suez Canal, the guarding against any internal disturbances caused by a 'sudden rising of the population, [or] political intrigue on Bolshevik lines',[104] coupled with its mandate commitments in Palestine also meant that Egypt occupied an area of strategic significance.

The 1920s are largely associated with factors such as the 'ten-year' rule and the overarching power of the Treasury. John Ferris's *The Evolution of British Strategic Policy, 1919–26* (1989) examines these perceptions by arguing that the Treasury and the ten-year rule only shaped service policies between 1925 and 1928, once the government had altered the basis of strategic policy, and it came to dominate them only between 1929 and 1931.[105] Indeed, historians examining the military position of Britain in the inter-war years need to make a distinction between the 1920s and 1930s when assessing the influence of the Treasury over the armed services.[106]

Rather than viewing the inter-war period along traditional lines, the 1920s as a time of arms limitation and the 1930s as one of rearmament, Ferris argues that 1921–27 should instead be viewed as a 'peak of British military preparations in peacetime, not as a trough.'[107] Indeed, Ferris contends that Britain did possess a strategic policy between 1919 and 1926 – one which attempted to co-ordinate the diplomatic, financial and military elements of British strength with a view to supporting its aims as a great power. He maintains that it was only after 1926, when the world appeared to be stable, that service spending was subordinated to social, financial and diplomatic considerations. Since it was believed that there would be a warning period of several years in the course of which Britain's position could be strengthened, programmes for Britain's security were deferred until threats became imminent. Nonetheless, Britain enjoyed a powerful strategic position, and Ferris states that by 1929 the services were more effective than in 1925.[108]

Moreover, even though the government deferred a modest part of the approved service programmes of 1925, over fears of provoking an arms race which prevented the navy from maintaining its lead in naval aviation, Ferries believes that 'these actions were anything but fatal.'[109] Instead, it was the actions of the governments between 1929 and 1936 that created the dangerous situation of the later 1930s – cuts in defence spending to protect Britain's fragile economy, the decision at the London Naval Conference in 1930[110] not to allow the Royal Navy to match the size of the Imperial Japanese Navy and any other European power, and the cancellation of the Singapore Naval base, which restricted Britain's naval strategy – all had far-reaching consequences for Britain's imperial security.

For the Royal Navy at the end of the First World War, its dominance appeared secure. Indeed, Greg Kennedy argues that in terms of most areas of important technological innovation and modern ship numbers, combat experience, manpower management, naval bases and store installations, supported by communication networks, intelligence systems gleaning information from human, cable and radio sources, and doctrinal and training methods 'while not always recognised as such, were the most advanced in the world'.[111] Kennedy acknowledges the pressures that faced the Royal Navy throughout the 1920s, such as world financial crises, a growth in pacifism, calls for collective security measures and the challenge of air power to the Royal Navy's traditional role as the primary securer of imperial defence. Nonetheless, he recognizes that the Admiralty continued to pursue a determined naval policy. This was supported by British politicians who 'acknowledged the need for a strong, viable naval service in order to give authority to imperial policies in the Middle and Far East', in order to demonstrate the 'will' of the British Empire.[112]

The enduring importance of the Royal Navy throughout the 1920s is demonstrated in Britain's imperial defence strategy, which rested upon the mobility of the fleets between East and West, whereupon the Suez Canal became a key strategic node. The post–First World War period presented a new naval situation. Prior to the war, the principal foreign naval power was concentrated in Europe, therefore necessitating a smaller concentration of British naval forces across the British Empire. After the war however, the strategic position had altered with Britain's two most serious naval rivals – Japan and the United States – situated in widely separate areas of the globe. It was deemed impracticable and certainly too expensive to maintain the fleet at a sufficient strength to effect the double concentration in Home waters and in the East to meet the situation satisfactorily. As a result, the Admiralty believed that to make up for its lack of preponderance across all oceans, its ability to effect a quick passage to any threatened portion of the Empire was its greatest asset. In this question of mobility the Suez Canal played a vital role. The alternative route to the East, via the Cape, was far longer. Hence, time would play an important role since the security or loss of an outpost of Empire, like Hong Kong, would be decided by the accessibility of the Canal route:

> The Suez Canal and its approaches are the most delicate link in the chain of Naval communications with the East, since the narrow and shallow nature of these waterways renders them more easily open to attack from land or sea than any other portion of the route.[113]

A mobile fleet was central to imperial defence strategy and remained a pivotal feature of military appreciations throughout the 1920s. The Naval Staff in 1923 commented:

> The Canal has always been an important link in our Imperial communications; the rise of a strong power in the East and the shifting of the strategic centres to distant waters had made it a link of such vital importance that it is difficult to envisage the possibility of our embarking on a war in the East unless we were quite certain that it could not be severed.[114]

Moreover, by signing Article XIX of the Washington Treaty for the Limitation of Naval Armaments, the United States had voluntarily renounced her power of intervention with armed forces in the Western Pacific. This left Britain the task of countering with the requisite naval forces any aggressive tendencies on the part of Japan. Thus, the Naval Staff warned that:

under present conditions [...] it would appear that the pressure of British seapower could at a critical moment be neutralised, and preparations, such as the establishment of oil fuel reserves and Naval bases in the East, rendered abortive by a simple act on the part of Japan requiring little preparation or foresight. The time factor would be all-important, and the delay imposed on our Fleet by the blocking of the Canal might admit of the Japanese scoring such striking initial triumphs, such as the seizure or destruction of Singapore and Hong Kong, as to render it difficult, if not impossible for us to wage war with any prospect of success.[115]

Indeed, the Admiralty was concerned that not only would the safety of Britain's Eastern bases – Singapore, Hong Kong – and with them the means of maintaining the Fleet in an efficient and mobile state (i.e. oil reserves at Trincomali, Colombo and Aden) be seriously imperilled, but British imperial trade, communications and territories in the East would be exposed to heavy attack, and denied protection over an indefinite period.[116]

Of course, being such an important nodal point in imperial communications meant that the Suez Canal also needed to be defended on the ground. Not only was the British army charged with defending the Suez Canal but also British air communications to the Near and Middle East. This included the protection of aerodromes and other necessary air force establishments used by the RAF for the defence of Palestine, Iraq and India. This commitment for the British Army was typical in the inter-war period – where the defence of Empire was paramount, and where the greatest emphasis during the first half of the 1920s was 'placed on the need to prepare for wars outside Europe'.[117] Indeed, David French argues that Britain 'did not maintain a single army to defend their empire, they maintained several'.[118] These comprised, for example, the British army, recruited exclusively in the UK, the British-Indian army and other, smaller forces, such as the Royal West African Frontier Force (RWAFF) and the King's African rifles. The roles that these forces performed also varied. They acted as an imperial reserve to counteract resistance to British rule and maintain law and order; they projected British power by showing the flag; garrisoned naval bases and coaling stations which formed the mainstay of the Royal Navy's global influence; acted as an imperial policeman along the North-West Frontier of India; and, occasionally, took part in global wars.[119]

Within Egypt itself, British policy was primarily based upon the Declaration to Egypt of 28 February 1922 in which, whilst recognizing Egypt as an independent sovereign state, Britain reserved to her absolute discretion four points pending the conclusion of an agreement with Egypt. These were:

a) the security of the communications of the British Empire in Egypt;
b) the defence of Egypt against all foreign aggression or interference, direct or indirect;
c) the protection of foreign interests in Egypt; and
d) the Sudan.

As a consequence, the British army was committed to Egypt in two ways. Firstly, to the defence of Egyptian territory. It was deemed that as long as Britain held the command of the Mediterranean and the mandate for Palestine, the defence of Egypt against foreign aggression was secure. Secondly, Britain was committed to the defence of British communication in Egypt and the protection of foreign interests. By extension, so long as British troops remained in Egypt – and without their presence, the defence of British communications could not be ensured – Britain was committed to the maintenance of internal order. To fulfil these obligations, the High Commissioner needed to rely on a British force strong enough to look after itself and to lend the requisite weight to the recommendations which the High Commissioner might have to make or to enforce the advice which he might give.[120]

For this Britain largely relied on projecting an image of strength in order to disguise what French describes as 'its slender reality'.[121] Using cavalcades for officials, parades, colourful uniforms, flag flying and military ceremonies helped to hide the 'enormous discrepancy between the population of the colony and its British garrison [...] The British Empire was administered on a shoestring and the military was no exception'.[122] Consequently, much of British imperial administration relied upon the co-operation and/or the collaboration and acquiescence of the indigenous population with British administrators – Egypt was no exception. Of course, if this balance did break down, as it did in Egypt in 1919, troops were swiftly summoned to assist the civil power to regain law and order. This was not without its own intractable problems as the 1919 uprising coincided with the 'Irish ulcer' which had also reached a critical point.[123]

Indeed, as Brian Bond suggests, an examination of the annual budgets and strategic priorities of the army between the wars would point to a 'story of political neglect':

> The line would plunge steeply from the Armistice, where there were over 3.5 million troops on the British establishment, to the end of 1920 when there were only 370,000. Another sharp drop was effected in 1922 when the Geddes Axe drastically reduced both numbers and expenditure, and thereafter the army's annual budget fell steadily every year from just over £43.5 million in 1923 to just under £36 million in 1932.[124]

Unsurprisingly, in comparison with the traditional priority accorded to the Royal Navy and the growing competition for expenditure with the RAF, the Army perceived itself as the 'Cinderella Service'. It was 'criticised in the press, always short of men despite continuing high unemployment, and increasingly dependent on obsolete weapons and equipment'.[125] Although its post-war role of imperial policeman in India, Egypt, Iraq and Ireland certainly placed a strain upon the resources of the Army, the War Office saw it as a fulfilling and necessary role.[126] Not only 'against the RAF's claims to perform this function more effectively and more cheaply', but, more particularly, since Egypt did offer the advantage of being a training ground, facilities for which were 'peculiarly lacking in Gibraltar and Malta'.[127]

The Army's commitment to the garrisoning of Egypt, despite its overstretch, was shown by its determination to remain in important Egyptian cities, such as Cairo and Alexandria, rather than withdraw to the Suez Canal zone. In order to facilitate a political agreement between Britain and Egypt, the withdrawal of British forces to the Canal Zone formed a major part of the Committee of Imperial Defence (CID) discussions between the armed services and the Foreign Office throughout the 1920s. However, the British General Staff were reluctant to see any British withdrawal from the major cities since the garrisons were a strong deterrent to internal disturbances. The retention of a garrison in Cairo was also deemed to be a strategic necessity in order to protect the freshwater canal that provided drinking water to the forces stationed in the Canal Zone. Moreover, the successful suppression of an uprising could be accomplished only by the retention of troops at the disorder's source, deemed to be Cairo 'where the brains and centre of disturbance will be'.[128] The General Staff placed such importance on this that they advocated making every effort to overcome political opposition in Egypt and elsewhere, and to make the Egyptian Government realize that the presence of a strong British garrison in Egypt and the location of British troops in Cairo would accrue political, commercial and military advantages to both countries. Egypt was not considered in isolation but was an important link in Britain's chain of imperial communications. As with the Royal Navy, the Army was keenly aware of the shift in the centre of gravity further East. The strategic reasons for this were fourfold:

a) Britain's post-war position *vis-à-vis* Turkey and the obligations imposed upon Britain by the Palestinian mandate;
b) the enhanced importance of the Suez Canal for the passage of the fleet to Eastern waters;
c) the need for safeguarding the Canal against the additional dangers inherent in the change on the status of Egypt;
d) the liability to support Iraq so long as Britain remained responsible for that country as a mandatory power.[129]

These concerns were closely reflected in the priorities of the Royal Navy and demonstrate that, even in an era of post-war retrenchment, the Army viewed Egypt as a crucial part of the Mediterranean and Middle Eastern region and as an integral link to the Empire in the East in a global context.

Britain's position in the Middle East also took on a new importance because of the air route to India. Robin Higham's *Britain's Imperial Air Routes, 1918–1939* (1960) lambasts the slow progress made by British overseas air transport in the inter-war years, blaming the 'failure of the Governments of the day to reach a far-sighted and statesmanlike view of the role to be played by air transport in Imperial affairs'.[130] In Higham's view, although much was done in laying down a useful network of routes and services, progress was restricted due to an:

> alternation of political leadership at the Air Ministry (including occasional lack of Cabinet rank), politics, RAF rearmament, failure to develop civil prototypes (a responsibility of both the Ministry and Industry) and, until 1930, economically unsuitable airliners, paucity of suitable personnel, and a scarcity of risk capital in the pre-dividend days.[131]

Despite advice from the Civil Aerial Transport Committee in 1918 on the need to maintain civil aviation in order to support the RAF, government policy, as expounded by Winston Churchill, dictated that 'civil aviation must fly by itself'.[132] As a consequence, the RAF was reduced to its bare bones everywhere, except the Middle East where it vied for the role of military policeman with the army.

But even this, as James Corum argues, was not assured. Despite the acknowledgement of the key role that airpower played in the First World War, its survival was not guaranteed:

> Both the army and the navy staffs, with strong agreement in the Cabinet, wanted to see the RAF disestablished as an independent service, and its squadrons revert to the army and navy, who would, to be sure, maintain strong air arms – but firmly under the control of the army and navy staffs.[133]

Despite this pressure from the older, more established services the application of air power as a tool of colonial control continued to be demonstrated in Afghanistan, India and Iraq and, once again, proved the worth of the RAF. Sir Hugh Trenchard (Chief of the Air Staff) argued that the RAF could police several of Britain's new responsibilities through air control, i.e., air strikes, as opposed to the more costly punitive expeditions by ground forces. During the 1919 uprising in Egypt, for instance, British aircraft 'patrolled communications, scattered propaganda, delivered mail, relieved garrisons and even attacked groups of Bedouin and demonstrators'.[134] Corum argues that, in the final analysis, the RAF's programme of colonial control could be considered as 'fairly effective, with it also delivering Trenchard's promise of reducing the costs of policing the Empire'.[135] This echoed earlier assessments of the RAF's contribution to Empire.[136] David Omissi's *Air Power and Colonial Control. The Royal Air Force, 1919–1939* (1990) also emphasizes the two-way relationship between the RAF and the areas it policed. Although the deserts, swamps and mountains of the margins of Empire (along with its inhabitants) were exploited as an ideal training ground for British bombers, Empire experiences also partly formulated Air Staff doctrine whilst the particular need of policing shaped the design of some British military aircraft.[137]

There is no doubt that Egypt became the cornerstone of the RAF scheme:

> Its ideal flying climate gave on average forty per cent more flying hours than in England, enabling faster training; Egypt formed a semi mobile squadron reserve for the Near East and Middle East [...] In short, Egypt was the most important junction in the world from an imperial air route point of view.[138]

This was reflected in Foreign Office discussions concerning the development of commercial routes through Egypt. Concerning the RAF it is important to remember that the size of the squadrons maintained in Egypt was not governed purely by the requirements for the defence of the Suez Canal. The Air Staff believed that for air operations in the Middle and Far East it was essential to have a base nearer than England for reinforcements and supplies. Both strategically and economically, the RAF saw Egypt as by far the most suitable place for such a base, where a significant amount of money had already been spent in establishing British air forces. For the defence of the Canal, in co-operation with the Army, it was estimated that only two squadrons would be required. The Air Staff warned that any British withdrawal from Iraq or any threatening developments in that country, Palestine or the Far East would necessitate an immediate increase in the number of squadrons stationed in Egypt for the purposes of reserve or reinforcement or, in other words, for imperial defence. Indeed, the Air Staff argued that 'Egypt must be for the Air Force what Singapore is to be for the Navy – an advanced post on the route to the East'.[139]

The study of this region is vital since the Nile Valley is where competing imperial rivalries, the development of nationalism and a burgeoning imperial defence strategy converge.

2

Riots and Resistance: Britain and Egypt, 1918–1922

The signing of the Armistice of Mudros by the Entente Powers and Turkey on 30 October 1918 officially ended hostilities in the Middle East. The situation, however, remained fluid. Clause 7 of the Armistice 'enabled the Allies to occupy any strategic points should events in the Middle East threaten their security'.[1] Elsewhere the Allies secured further gains with Batum and Baku in the Caucasus, and Turkish evacuation of North-West Persia and possibly the remainder of Trans-Caucasia.[2] Between 1915 and 1918 military strategy and events on the battlefield determined the course of international relations. By 1919, however, the emphasis was upon diplomatic manoeuvring within the council chambers at Versailles. It is important to remember that 'only two months separated these two phases as the nations and their leaders, weary from the protracted war effort, turned without respite to the challenges of peace'.[3]

The period 1918–22 shows Egypt's importance in terms of imperial strategy with the despatch of the Milner Mission to deal with the growing threat posed by Egyptian nationalism. Moreover, this period illustrates the indecision over whether Egypt should be considered within the wider Near/Middle Eastern question, particularly with its religious ties to Turkey and the Caliphate, or, given the strategic significance of the Suez Canal, as part of the British Empire.

Egypt and the wider Middle East

During the course of the war, British Middle Eastern thinking on Arab independence was revised. In the controversial McMahon-Husayn correspondence of 1915, McMahon, with certain exceptions, accepted the territorial demands put forward by Husayn.[4] The Sykes-Picot agreement of May 1916 appeared, however, to mark a stark divergence. In this agreement, Britain and France proposed to divide the Arab lands of the Ottoman Empire into distinct spheres of influence.[5] But, almost immediately, this agreement came under fire from some of Britain's eastern experts such as David George Hogarth of the Arab Bureau and Colonel Gilbert Clayton, head of the Arab Bureau and later Edmund Allenby's Chief Political Officer, as well as Lord Curzon, who believed it had given too much to France and the remainder of the war and its immediate aftermath were spent retreating from its provisions.[6] Thereafter, British

Middle Eastern policy appeared to be one of freeing Arabs from their Turkish yoke.[7] This change in direction culminated on 7 November 1918 when a joint Anglo-French declaration stated that the 'Allied war aim in the East was to establish national governments and administrations deriving their authority from the initiative and free choice of the indigenous populations'.[8]

Since 1917 British policy on the Middle East had been formulated by a series of committees. Each of these was chaired by Lord Curzon and was composed of representatives from various departments with a stake in the future development of the region. The Inter-departmental Persia and Mesopotamian Administration Committees (1917) were followed by the Middle East Committee (1917–18), and then the Eastern Committee (April 1918 to January 1919)[9] only to be succeeded by an interdepartmental conference on Middle Eastern Affairs (IDCE) in 1919–20.[10] According to Timothy Paris, and in contrast to Erik Goldstein, none of these committees were particularly effective in directing Middle Eastern policy formulation. Attempts to create a Middle East office, or to bring Middle Eastern Affairs under the umbrella of an existing department, all foundered until the end of 1920.[11] This was largely due to 'Curzon's resolute insistence on the committee approach'.[12] Egyptian affairs continued to be handled by the Foreign Office and in 1917 an Egyptian Department within the Foreign Office was created.

Whilst British policy accepted, or feigned acceptance of, the existence of national aspirations in some areas of the Middle East, British attitudes regarding Egypt's future had changed little. British policy towards Egypt was based upon the assumption that constitutional progress would be slow, and would take place under the Protectorate proclaimed in 1914. Indeed, Hogarth and Clayton were 'utterly contemptuous of the notion of Egyptians aspiring to the same goals that they were deftly dangling before the Sharif [Husayn ibn Ali, King of the Hejaz]'.[13] Following Clayton's active encouragement of declaring a Protectorate at the outset of the First World War, and later annexation in 1917, he wrote:

> All this claptrap about Sultans and self-government is rot. They are not really ready for it and if you have a Palace, every ounce of power and self-government which you think you are giving to the people will go straight to the Sultan [...] and be used against you. Beautiful theories are all very nice, but hard facts remain.[14]

Hogarth expressed a similar derision towards Egyptian nationalism:

> Of course Egyptians are not Arabs at all but sons of Ham, with a sprinkling of prophet progeny: and all this talk of Arab nationality is fudge. Really they have no interest in anything but the cotton crop [...] and [...] family feuds. What can you do with such but rule them, whether they like it or not.[15]

Wingate receives the Nationalist Delegation

Nonetheless, the heavy-handedness of British policies to meet the exigencies of the prolonged war contributed to a growing sense of dissatisfaction with British control. On 14 November 1918 Wingate reported privately to Charles Hardinge, Permanent-under-Secretary at the Foreign Office (1916–20) and a former Viceroy of India (1910–16), that he had received a deputation from three prominent Egyptians – Saad Pasha Zaghlul, formerly Minister of Education and currently Vice-President of the Legislative Assembly; Abd al-Aziz Fahmi, a well-known Nationalist lawyer; and Ali Pasha Sharawi, a wealthy landowner and prominent member of the Legislative Assembly. Wingate reported that their aim appeared to be representation at the Paris Peace Conference in order to state their own case for either 'a much larger share in the Government of this country [Egypt] than they now have, or even complete autonomy'.[16] The deputation argued that since Egypt had shown a great spirit of loyalty during the war and had provided men and money in its prosecution, they now expected their reward. Furthermore, as Wingate had already warned the Foreign Office in a private telegram on 8 November 1918, Woodrow Wilson's professions of self-determination and, more particularly, the Anglo-French declaration of self-determination for the Arabs led them to claim the same rights, especially since they considered themselves far more capable of conducting a well-ordered government.[17] The deputation were prepared to accept a measure of financial supervision in regard to the Public Debt and to guarantee special facilities for British ships using the Suez Canal, but the future Anglo-Egyptian relationship would be governed by an alliance of perpetual peace and friendship.[18] Wingate considered that these Egyptian demands were the logical result of British rule over the past forty years that Britain was 'about to reap the results of our patient labours […] in seeing a complete Egyptian regeneration on political lines dear to the British democracy'.[19]

Zaghlul, Fahmy and Sharawi had also visited Rushdy Pasha, the Prime Minister, who now advocated that these three Nationalists should accompany him and Adli Yakan, Minister of Education, to London to take part in the Peace discussions. Rushdy urged that 'there could not be a more favourable time than the present to settle once and for all the future of Egypt'.[20] To this Wingate agreed:

> If these burning questions are not settled now, we are likely to have considerable difficulty in the future. The general spirit of self-determination to which the war has given birth, has taken a firm hold in Egypt and I think it only just that the Sultan, his Ministers and the Egyptians generally should be told how they stand, but presumably such conversations as are now suggested would be conducted entirely through His Majesty's Government and Egypt (being a British Protectorate) would in no sense come within the scope of the International Peace Conference, though the fact that India, the Dominions etc. are to be consulted, has naturally given our Egyptian friends hopes of similar consideration.[21]

The Foreign Office, however, did not share Wingate's view and he received short shrift:

> It cannot be concealed that the fact of any responsible leaders of Egyptian opinion having advanced such extravagant demands has created an unfortunate impression here. I trust that they received no encouragement from the Sultan or his Ministers […]

> His Majesty's Government desire to act on the principle which they have always followed of giving the Egyptians an ever increasing share in the government of the country, and the rate of Egyptian progress towards self-government must depend on Egyptians themselves. As you are well aware, the stage has not been reached at which self-government is possible.[22]

Hardinge followed this up in a private letter to Wingate encouraging him to 'do all you can to snub these gentlemen who are going in for self-determination and home rule in Egypt. A little firmness now will save us from a peck of trouble later on'.[23] The nationalist leaders' request to visit London was rejected and although a visit from Rushdy and Adli Pasha would be welcome, at the present time it was seen as inopportune due to the pressures of the Peace Conference. The Foreign Office, critical of Wingate's reception of the Nationalists at the Residency, ordered Wingate to manage the resulting agitation by means of the suppression of public meetings, public demonstrations and the distribution of circulars.[24]

Signs of a growing Nationalist movement continued to be reported by Wingate throughout the latter half of November 1918. 'There are indications of an organised campaign directed against the Protectorate [...] circulars have been issued, [...] attempts have been made to interfere with pupils in the schools, and that a wave of political feeling is being artificially engendered'.[25] What Wingate was attempting to convey to London was that whilst there did not appear to be, as yet, any signs of a 'militant spirit nor of attempts to excite religious fanaticism or anti-European feeling',[26] the distinguishing feature was that calls for complete autonomy for Egypt were permeating the substratum of Egyptian society and were not merely confined to the political elite.

As a result of London's refusal to receive the Egyptian ministers, Rushdy and Adli tendered their resignations. But as Britain was in no rush to form a new Egyptian ministry, a split began to emerge between the Egyptian ministers and the Nationalists as each interest group vied for position to represent Egypt's aspirations.[27] Moreover, Wingate believed that if the ministers were permitted to travel to London, the Sultan would dissociate himself from the extremists and thereby further separate the extremist faction from the more moderate party. Wingate felt that these demands for greater liberty represented 'something more than a fresh outcrop of Egyptian Nationalist sentiment'.[28] In fact, Egypt's detachment from Turkey as a result of the Protectorate had stimulated the idea of an Egyptian as opposed to a Turkish nationality as well as the idea of Egypt taking the leading place among Muslim countries. 'It is quite possible', Wingate postulated, that the

> cry for independence or autonomy is not only concerned with political liberties, but also based on apprehension that, if too openly subjected to Christian protection, Egypt can never hope to regain supremacy she once held in [the] Islamic world. Sultan Fuad is intensely jealous of position now attained by ruler of Hedjaz [sic], and views our dealings with him with expressed disapprobation.[29]

As a result of Wingate's despatches, Balfour allowed Rushdy and Adli Pasha to proceed to London for discussions about Egyptian reforms in March. However, concern was expressed at the propensity to connect the question of Egyptian reforms with the Peace negotiations and, for that reason, the Egyptian ministers were not permitted to go to Paris during the Peace Conference.[30]

With Balfour now in Paris for the peace negotiations, the day-to-day running of the Foreign Office was entrusted to Curzon. The division of the Foreign Office between London and Paris was seldom clear and therefore hardly conducive to a coherent policymaking strategy at such a critical period in the post-war settlement. Indeed, David Gilmour, Curzon's biographer,[31] notes that a clear delineation of responsibilities was lacking. 'Lloyd George dealing with matters that interested him and Curzon administering most of the others' whilst Balfour himself behaved 'more like a deputy Prime Minister than a Foreign Secretary'.[32]

Despite Rushdy and Adli's invitation to London, the situation within Egypt had already developed beyond the Foreign Office's remit. The ministers claimed that even if they went to London, they would have to resign later, unless they could obtain some measure of popular support. They insisted that the Nationalist leaders would always be able to outbid them, unless they too were allowed to go to England and be discredited by their failure to gain a hearing from the British Government. It was essential for Zaghlul and his associates to 'leave Egypt and return empty-handed'.[33] Wingate believed the sincerity of the two Ministers and he recommended the relaxation of restrictions placed upon the movements of the nationalist leaders. Wingate was sure that the refusal to accept the resignation of the Ministers had had 'a good effect' in demonstrating that the task of governing would continue despite the lack of an Egyptian Cabinet. However, Wingate warned that whilst 'ordinary administration continues without inconvenience, reconstructive work [such as the Capitulations Commission] will be seriously interrupted if present situation is prolonged'.[34] Indeed, Wingate admitted that 'real co-operation with leading Egyptians has, in fact, become an essential part of our machinery, and I trust that you will consider very carefully method of conciliation, which I have now advanced after prolonged discussion, and in agreement with my principal advisers'.[35] It was clear that London was being forced to react to circumstances rather than dictate the pace of policy and, although Wingate's despatches had contained warnings to the Foreign Office, from as early as December 1917, that a demonstration of nationalist aspirations at war's end was highly likely, it was not always easy to gauge the extent and seriousness of the nationalist movement. As a result, Wingate was summoned to London in order to discuss Egyptian affairs.

The view of the Foreign Office differed significantly from that of Wingate. It perceived the Nationalist leaders as having placed themselves at the head of a disloyal movement whose aim was to expel the British from Egypt. The Foreign Office believed that they had no right to be received in London and that to accede to the Ministers' demands would only be interpreted as a sign of weakness in Egypt. 'The idea that the Nationalists should be brought here in order to be snubbed and turned down scarcely seems to savour fair play, and would be likely to increase the bitterness of their feeling against us.'[36] Furthermore, the fact that the Egyptian Ministers should be able to dictate the terms of their visit to the British Government was also viewed as an undesirable development. Balfour largely agreed with the telegram drafted by Curzon which renewed the British Government's invitation to Rushdy and Adli Pasha only, thereby excluding the Nationalists and continuing to adhere to the same attitude already expressed by the British Government.[37] The memorandum also hinted at the fact that Wingate's view was not shared by everyone. Indeed, Ronald Graham, acting permanent under-secretary at the Foreign Office whilst Hardinge was in Paris and also a former Counsellor at the British Residency in Cairo, had received a private verbal message from Milne Cheetham, now acting High Commissioner in Wingate's absence, that trouble had been brewing in Egypt all summer. According to Cheetham, the Nationalists had been actively discussing with the Sultan and Ministers what form their activities should take and that this had been known to Wingate. Instead of dealing with this through the Residency staff and the Anglo-Egyptian officials at the Ministry of the Interior, Wingate chose to manage the situation through Colonel George Stewart Symes, Wingate's Political Intelligence Officer, with whom a number of conversations took place and whereby the Nationalists were encouraged rather than otherwise. Thus, when the 'storm burst' it came as no surprise to Wingate and he must have known that by meeting the nationalists he had given the Nationalist movement tacit recognition.[38] This does seem a rather harsh indictment of Wingate's actions, especially since he had warned the Foreign Office of Nationalist agitation in December 1917. One thing that was clear, however, as the Foreign Office attempted to assert control over policymaking in Egypt, Wingate would not be returning to his position of High Commissioner of Egypt and the Sudan and instead would be fashioned into a scapegoat for the British difficulties. Indeed, in writing to Hardinge in October 1919, Wingate referred to the 'relations which existed between yourself [Hardinge] and Graham on the one hand and a high authority [Curzon] on the other – there is little doubt in my own mind, that these unfortunate relations, as well as the conflict of views between Paris and London, have had much to say to the many mistakes which have been made'.[39]

During February Cheetham announced a distinct improvement in the political atmosphere. Rushdy Pasha, Adli Pasha and Zaghlul's popularity had slumped as manifest divisions were appearing in the nationalist camp.[40] The agitation was dying out, which Cheetham assessed to have been 'entirely pacific in character' from the beginning.[41] While Cheetham believed that 'we still no doubt have to reckon with discontent amongst upper classes, the landed proprietors and professional element', he did not believe that the situation differed materially from that of 1914. He perceived that 'there seems no reason why it should affect the decisions of His Majesty's Government on constitutional questions and proper form to be given to the Protectorate'.[42] Cheetham's reports served only to reinforce the Foreign Office's belief that their policy was the correct one and their corresponding lack of faith in Wingate.[43]

As a result of the Foreign Office's rebuff, the Egyptian ministers, whose resignations had remained suspended, were duly accepted by the Sultan. On 6 March Cheetham reported that Zaghlul, severely irritated by Britain's refusal to allow him to proceed to Europe, was doing all he could to prevent the formation of a new government by threatening those politicians willing to accept office with their lives. Cheetham added that Zaghlul had intimidated the Sultan, and discouraged his co-operation with British authorities in re-establishing the Council of Ministers. Being refused admission into Abdin Palace, Zaghlul left the Sultan a signed petition repudiating the Protectorate, warning His Highness against accepting the advice of the Residency and issuing thinly veiled threats against him should he continue to assist in creating a Ministry. The Sultan was shaken by the terms of the petition and 'earnestly appealed [to Cheetham] for protection against further insults'.⁴⁴ Cheetham voiced concern that if Zaghlul and his activities were left unchecked, the British could expect intrigues, the encouragement of dissent within the Egyptian service and difficulty in finding a competent and popular minister. He did not believe that a warning to Zaghlul and his followers by the General Officer Commanding-in-Chief Egypt, General Bulfin, would be sufficient and therefore recommended, in consultation with his personal advisers, the immediate arrest and deportation of Zaghlul 'whose insidious propaganda made him more dangerous than any of the agitators interned at Malta since the beginning of the war'.⁴⁵ Cheetham claimed that the more moderate and more sensible Egyptians were 'wondering why we have permitted it to go so long unchecked'.⁴⁶ The assent of the Foreign Office was received the following day and on 8 March Zaghlul, along with those most closely associated with him in his campaign of deliberate intimidation, such as Ismail Pasha Sidqi, Mohammed Pasha Mahmoud and Hamed Pasha El Basal, was arrested and deported to Malta.⁴⁷

Outbreak of Unrest

Reaction to Zaghlul's deportation began with an outbreak of protest in Cairo on 10 March 1919 among the students of the higher colleges.⁴⁸ Since Zaghlul had been a popular Minister of Education, a reaction on the part of the students was, to some degree, expected. R Wellesley, an Inspector returning from Lower Egypt, wrote to London and assured Graham that there 'is no sympathy with the present agitation among the better class of native notables or among the *fellahin*'.⁴⁹ However, Cheetham's daily reports marked a deteriorating situation: continued rioting in Cairo; strikes of clerks in the Ministries of Public Works and Education; and outbreaks with loss of life at Tanta, Damietta and Mansura in the Nile Delta. Contact with Upper Egypt was interrupted and required many more troops to maintain communications.⁵⁰ On 15 March, Cheetham reported that the Nationalist resistance was stronger than expected. On 17 March General Bulfin reported that it was impossible to safeguard railway communications between Cairo, Alexandria and Port Said in addition to restoring communications with Upper Egypt.⁵¹ By 19 March, the disturbances had spread to Lower Egypt. A train from Beni Suez arrived with the bodies of six murdered British officers.⁵²

There is no doubt that the rapidity with which the disorders spread caught both the Residency and London by surprise.⁵³ Balfour, devoid of any Egyptian experts in Paris, referred all decision-making to Curzon.⁵⁴ Because of the extent of the disorders, General Bulfin returned from Palestine and the War Office approved the despatch of reinforcements to Egypt, which would increase the total number of troops to 10,000.⁵⁵ Curzon also appointed General Sir Edmund Allenby as Special High Commissioner for Egypt and the Sudan and conferred upon him supreme authority in all matters military and civil in order to restore law and order. Victorious in Palestine during the First World War as commander of the Egyptian Expeditionary Force, Allenby was well respected.⁵⁶ Although nicknamed 'The Bull', according to Major-General George de Symons Barrow, Commander of the 4th Division in the BEF in 1918, Allenby was 'always glad to listen to other opinions and advice, provided this was backed by knowledge and common sense. What angered him was stupidity, negligence and, most of all, disregard of orders'.⁵⁷ In writing to inform his mother of his new appointment, Allenby remarked 'I think my return as Special High Commissioner, will have a calming effect, but the unrest has got a deep root, and will be hard work to do'.⁵⁸

Wingate, still in London, became increasingly frustrated at his own exile. He perceived the Egyptian movement to be 'little short of a revolution and [it] must be suppressed with a strong hand at once'.⁵⁹ With his 'personal and intimate knowledge' of Egypt and the Sudan and his long experience in these countries, Wingate believed that his return would have a tranquilizing effect and therefore expressed his desire to return to Egypt.⁶⁰ Curzon, however, disagreed and felt that Wingate's presence in Britain was 'for the moment essential'. Wingate now believed that the propitious time for allowing the Egyptian nationalists to come to London had passed and repeated an earlier suggestion, of 9 March, for despatching a mission to enquire into the whole situation in order to rally Anglophile Egyptians to the British side and to temper some of the strong anti-British language. This had also been repeated to Curzon as a suggestion of General Bulfin on 17 March, although Cheetham doubted its efficacy in the present excited state of public feeling.⁶¹

Throughout the remainder of March and April, order was gradually restored as the actions of the military authorities began to take effect. With the immediate emergency over, it allowed the authorities within the Foreign Office and the Residency a period of reflection. What had shaken the British the most was the depth and extent of the violent movement. Whilst dissatisfaction was expected among the educated and professional classes, whose political ideas had been excited by the cry for national self-determination and who had suffered greatly with the rise in prices during the war without any corresponding gain, it was the violent upheaval amongst the agricultural classes, the *fellahin*, that posed both an unwelcome and unexpected development in the Protectorate. The British had perceived, inaccurately, the *fellahin* to be the bedrock of Britain's occupation of Egypt, they took little interest in politics and the war had brought them great prosperity.

The nature and violence of this unrest also led the British authorities to conclude that it was a well-planned, co-ordinated attack by external forces. Four explanations were offered by the British authorities for this united solidarity. Firstly, German propaganda prior to and during the war encouraged discontent. Secondly, pro-Turkish elements were perceived as ready and willing to be the tools of pro-Turkish agents. Thirdly, Bolshevist propaganda, which was 'spread by a body of low class foreigners, chiefly anarchists or Levantines, who were in touch with Continental Bolshevism, and could easily gain a hearing amongst the ignorant and violently inclined mobs of the larger towns'.⁶² And, fourthly, the pupils of Al-Azhar University who had had their feelings roused and their popular influence increased by the collapse of Turkey. In addition, the student class was being encouraged by the maxim of liberalism.⁶³ Cheetham himself admitted in hindsight that some upheaval was sooner or later inevitable. This led the Foreign Office to ask how the Anglo-Egyptian authorities were so greatly out of touch with indigenous sentiment. 'They have indeed shown a complete lack of foreknowledge for which it is almost impossible to account'.[64] This assessment was perhaps a little unfair since Wingate had repeatedly warned the Foreign Office of Egyptian opinion.

> Nationalism has been in the air for the last twenty-five years in Egypt – but its dormant embers were fanned into a bright flame by the Great War and the self-determinating ideas which were so widely propagated during the many months prior to the signing of the Armistice.
>
> To anyone conversant with Egyptian politics and mentality and to myself in particular, the effect of all this public talk and the situation in India, South Africa and in territories liberated from Turkey, the attitude of the Egyptian Nationalist did not come as a complete surprise and in my various letters to the Foreign Office since I have been High Commissioner I emphasised this fact.[65]

Nevertheless, the Foreign Office largely blamed the Residency for the course of events, defending their decision not to allow the Nationalist leaders to be received in London so as to avoid giving 'official sanction to the movement for independence, and to have recognised their mandate as true representatives of the Egyptian nation'.[66]

Zaghlul and the Wafd: The development of Egyptian nationalism

On 31 March 1919 Allenby reported that he had received a long memorandum from the extremists. It stated that the agitation was due to the feeling that Egyptian views had been refused expression, and requested that travel restrictions be removed, which would restore tranquillity and guarantee the formation of a Ministry.[67] Allenby continued to press his point that although he had outwardly suppressed the movement by force of arms, the causes of unrest and ill feeling remained as strong as ever. Allenby warned that:

> the nationalist movement which was at first purely political is now taking a religious turn. Centre of religious disturbance is Azhar Mosque, where seditious and inflammatory speeches are made all day and night. Owing to sacred character of Azhar Mosque, which is revered throughout the Moslem world, its frequenters cannot be entirely restrained by force.
>
> There is evidence that movement is influencing Palestine and Syria, besides Egypt, and danger is a very real one.[68]

The Foreign Office, supported by Wingate, was reluctant to lift the existing travel restrictions. Graham, in the hope of influencing those in Paris, wrote to Hardinge:

> I am in despair about Allenby's attitude on the question of the Nationalists. It means immediate calm and the eventual loss of Egypt – this is not putting it too strongly. Whatever the rights or wrongs of the previous decisions may have been and I believe we were perfectly right; to surrender now would be entirely fatal and

we should not have a friend left in Egypt. I do not believe that Allenby, splendid soldier and administrator as he is, knows anything of Egyptian politics and he has let himself be swayed by the plausible Egyptian politicians who are all out for their own hand. A firm attitude at present is absolutely vital and I trust you will do all you can to support this view.[69]

Instead, the Foreign Office suggested the despatch of a mission to Egypt, with Lord Milner at its head.[70] The purpose of the mission was to investigate existing conditions in Egypt, enquire into the causes which had led to the present outbreak and to determine the future form of the British Protectorate and the extent and nature of the constitutional reform and administrative changes that might be necessary.[71] In advocating the idea of a Commission, the Foreign Office felt that it would be able to transfer the focus of political unrest away from the Peace Conference in Paris back to Cairo, and therefore make it easier to satisfy Egyptian demands without appearing to yield to violence.[72] However, since Allenby had sent his telegram to Balfour in Paris advocating the removal of travel restrictions, a third cog had been added to the decision-making process. Both Balfour and Lloyd George supported Allenby because, since he was appointed Special High Commissioner to deal with the situation there, his advice could not very well be disregarded.

While we agree with you [Curzon] that it is desirable he [Allenby] should be aware of your suggestion for a Commission we think that it would be better that this should be put forward tentatively in a separate telegram and as a measure of help towards a final settlement of political difficulty. We consider that it should be treated as entirely distinct from passport question [...] It is important to avoid any appearance of mistrusting his [Allenby's] present policy. Ultimately, it may prove desirable to adopt both plans [...] we must remember that whilst he has full knowledge of our views we are not fully seized of present local conditions.[73]

Despite Curzon's forwarding of Wingate's reservations and Foreign Office concern that Allenby's advice over travel restrictions had been offered in ignorance of the mission policy, the view of the Prime Minister and Balfour overrode Curzon's concerns. The stance in Paris was to give Allenby their fullest support and accept his recommendations.[74] As a result, Allenby announced the lifting of travel restrictions and the release of Zaghlul and the three other ringleaders from internment in Malta. The subsequent relaxation in tension allowed the formation of a new Ministry on 9 April and the announcement that a delegation of eighteen Nationalist leaders, including Zaghlul and his three comrades, would be shortly arriving in Britain.

The fact that the nationalist leaders, including those deported to Malta, were to be received in London was perceived as a climbdown by the Foreign Office and a blow to British prestige at a critical time. The Foreign Office seemed dumbfounded that even with full discretionary powers at their disposal, the British authorities had 'shown themselves unable, or unwilling' to stand up to nationalist fervour. 'The principle at issue has been surrendered [...] Thus a fortnight of violence has achieved what four months of persuasion failed to accomplish. The object lesson will not be lost in

Egypt and throughout the East'.[75] Indeed, the disdain of the Foreign Office after being overruled by Paris was shown in Curzon's reply to Wingate of 13 April:

> I am personally entirely opposed to receiving the Nationalist Deputation from Egypt. I regard them as responsible for the troubles occurring the past three weeks and would have no truck with them.
> What Mr Balfour may wish to do, I have no idea. He, and not I, is responsible for bringing them over, and if he desires to see them the responsibility will be his.[76]

Wingate himself continued to receive letters from George Stewart Symes, Wingate's private secretary, updating him on the situation in Egypt. Allenby had explained to Symes that the release of the detainees from Malta was taken with a view to 'cleaning the slate', and Symes had commented 'no one but a victorious General could afford to risk the effect of the impression of weakness involved', Symes continued:

> I think perhaps in taking this action he [Allenby] over-estimated the influence of his personal prestige upon the native's mind. The transport of reckless joy into which the natives fell after learning of his decision [...] had the aspect of a religious frenzy but was inspired, almost entirely by political enthusiasm.[77]

Symes believed that this admission of weakness would reverberate across the whole of the Middle East and India.[78]

Causes of the unrest

With the immediate emergency over, the Foreign Office could reflect upon the causes of the disturbances. It was believed that their immediate cause lay in the general wave of dissatisfaction and vague political aspirations passing across the globe as a result of the four years of war. In the large towns the British position had always been exposed to hostile outbreaks of this kind – the rich pashas were seen as pro-Turkish 'the harems have hotbeds of Young Turk intrigue and propaganda',[79] whilst the students and professional classes, doctors, lawyers and a good number of the younger government officials were described as being nationalist in sympathies and followers of Zaghlul. Much blame was placed at the door of the Wilsonian idea of 'self-determination':

> Thinking Egyptians had realised that Egypt was defenceless, and must rely on the Protection of some strong Power, and on the whole, they preferred British tutelage as being less onerous than that of any other great Power. But they now see in the League of Nations a fairy godmother, remote and unobtrusive in their internal affairs, but always ready to step in and save them the trouble and anxiety of defending themselves from aggrieved or aggressive neighbours.

Moreover, Egyptian *amour-propre* had been wounded by the absence of Egyptian representation at the Peace Conference when India, and still worse, the 'disliked and despised Bedouin of the Hejaz',[80] had been represented. To this was added the Anglo-French declaration to the Arabs which had raised hopes and jealousies. Thus, the Foreign Office could easily rationalize why a certain amount of dissatisfaction existed among the educated and professional classes. Not only had their political ideas been excited but they had also suffered from the rise in prices during the war without any corresponding gain.

It was more difficult for the Foreign Office, however, to account for the violent upheaval among the agricultural classes who were perceived to take little interest in politics and to whom the war had brought great prosperity. However, although the war had brought a spike of prosperity, the continued expansion of Egypt's resources by foreign enterprise and capital served only to mask underlying problems associated with Egypt's rapid economic development which had taken place without the necessary support from its political and social institutions. More importantly, Egypt's path of development had not allowed the growth of an indigenous bourgeoisie. As a consequence, foreign involvement, of course to foreigners' own interests, led to a number of problems. Firstly, the greater share of Egypt's increased prosperity was accrued by foreigners. Secondly, it was easier to develop Egypt's cotton industry, in which Egypt enjoyed an advantage, by extending the irrigated area rather than diversifying the economy. Thus, after the First World War, when the supply of readily available land was exhausted and the relative price of cotton began to fall, the agricultural classes felt it the most. Thirdly, educational and technological development failed to keep pace with Egypt's economic development. Finally, the existence of a foreign bourgeoisie pursuing Egypt's development inhibited the growth of an indigenous entrepreneurial bourgeoisie.[81]

These pressures were exacerbated by the war. The requisitioning of the *fellahin's* fodder for the army at below its market value and, even more so, the forced requisitioning of their services for the Labour and Camel transport Corps in the Egyptian Expeditionary Force created much ill-feeling. Although 10,000 to 20,000 Egyptians did volunteer initially, as the military demands increased it was left to the indigenous authorities, under the supervision of a very small body of British inspectors, for each district, to produce its quota of men. Inevitably, forms of compulsion had to be employed which allowed corruption and favouritism to seep in. A 'rankling sense of injustice and resentment had been left among them which has, no doubt, found expression and relief in a violent campaign of destruction'.[82]

As British control was extended because of the exigencies of war, traditional customs, privileges and immunities were shown little consideration. The declaration of martial law, which limited free movement, and the collection of fewer than 100,000 firearms from the *fellahin* by the Ministry of the Interior during 1915–16 were resented and felt as exemplifying increased British political authority.[83] 'Real and imaginary grievances have shaken the peasants' old belief in British honesty, the belief on which our control is ultimately based, and he [the peasants] has joined in the almost general demand that the English should clear out of Egypt'.[84]

The emergence of the Wafd at the close of the First World War marked a new departure in Egyptian politics. The Wafd now formed a specifically Egyptian nationalist movement dedicated exclusively to the cause of Egyptian independence.[85] Its leaders subscribed neither to the Pan-Islamic pro-Ottoman sentimentalism of Shaykh Ali

Yusuf and his collaborators at the turn of the century, nor to the romanticism of Mustafa Kamil's National Party.[86] The leadership of the Wafd was largely composed of aristocrats or urban bourgeois who were tired of deferring to their British overlords in final decisions and disagreed with the policy of 'preventing able Egyptians from rising to meaningful policy-making positions'.[87] As Janice Terry points out, even the monarchy was complicit in encouraging the early nationalist demands. Sultan Fuad saw that a British withdrawal would free him from the shackles of the High Commissioner and 'advisers' who were his superiors. 'In an independent Egypt, Fuad would have the opportunity to rule as a real King, not as a puppet performing in front of the façade of Egyptian self-government'.[88] Thus, in the early days of nationalist demands, the aims of the Palace and Wafd coincided and this triangular contest between the Wafd, Palace and the Residency became a feature of the Egyptian political landscape throughout the interwar years as each vied for hegemony. What made the Wafd such a powerful force was its ability to unite all facets of Egyptian society in support of its calls for independence:

> The aristocracy and the bourgeoisie were the first movers of the Wafd, but students, workers, peasants, women (for a lively feminist movement emerged in post-war Egypt) and religious minorities [such as the Copts who provided considerable financial support] quickly rallied behind the Wafdist demands.[89]

Zaghlul quickly emerged as the leader of the Wafd and dominated the party until his death in 1927.[90]

> A man with a grievance against the British. But a man, too, whose Nationalist professions and activities were kept within bounds by consideration of self-interest and the lack of opportunity. Circumstances changed, however; openings for profitability exploiting an extreme nationalism presented themselves; ambition, self-interest and opportunity alike urged him to the course he now hastens to follow.[91]

The March 1919 uprising resulted in a number of short- and long-term effects upon Britain's Egyptian policy. In the short term, it brought into focus not only how out of touch Whitehall was with Egyptian affairs but the conflict of opinion between the Residency and the Foreign Office in how to handle the situation. This difference was also evident between Curzon and his Foreign Office officials, principally Graham, in London and Balfour and Lloyd George in Paris. In the longer term it was the decision to despatch the Milner Mission to Egypt that signalled a resolve to examine and decide upon a definite course for British policy in Egypt, something which had been rumbling on since the declaration of the Protectorate at the outset of war.

The Milner Mission: Background

Since mid-November 1918 and Balfour's description of a visit by Egyptian ministers to London as inopportune, British policy had undergone a complete revision. In the space of five months, Foreign Office policy had moved from berating Wingate for even entertaining the complaints of the Egyptian ministers to implicitly recognizing the nationalist leaders as representatives of the Egyptian people by acquiescing in Allenby's recommendations. Two significant factors contributed to this change in policy. Firstly, the scale of the agitation throughout March shocked and embarrassed many British officials who were busy securing international recognition of the Protectorate. Secondly, Allenby's appointment provided the Residency with greater authority in London than previously enjoyed. The confidence that Lloyd George, Balfour and Andrew Bonar Law, Lord Privy Seal and leader of the Conservative Party and House of Commons, accorded to Allenby allowed a certain amount of freedom for the Residency from Whitehall interference.

Zaghlul and his fellow Nationalists were permitted to proceed to the Paris Peace Conference. They held high hopes that the agitation would cause the interruption of the Peace Conference and that finally the Egyptian Question would be internationalized. The Foreign Office was concerned to remind Balfour in Paris of the peril of giving too much encouragement to Zaghlul's views and even advocated a sharp and public rebuff of Zaghlul's opinions; even better if this could be administered by the Allied and especially American delegations. Zaghlul's arrival in Paris had the effect that the Wafd were increasingly regarded as representative of Egyptian opinion. As a consequence, ministers in Cairo 'feeling ground [sic] crumbling under their feet and hope of native support disappearing, are inclined to throw up the sponge', thereby making the task of creating a Ministry affable to British policy even more difficult. The Foreign Office continued:

> General Allenby draws a distinction between Zaghloul [sic] and his party and the Extreme nationalists. I would however remind you that avowed programme of Zaghloul in November last was 'complete autonomy for Egypt which would leave to Great Britain only a right of supervision in the matter of public debt and facilities for our ships traversing the Suez Canal' [...] No useful purpose can be served by negotiations with Egyptians holding such opinions [...]
>
> We seem likely to arrive at a position in Egypt in which we shall only be able to obtain Ministers from ranks of Zaghloul's party and this would render satisfactory Government of the country almost impossible.[92]

It was clear that the Foreign Office was at odds with the line of policy advocated by Cairo and Paris.

Nonetheless, Egyptian hopes were dashed when America recognized the British Protectorate, contrary to President Wilson's Fourteen Points that advocated self-determination for all nationalities. In fact, Zaghlul kept a copy of Wilson's Fourteen Points in his pocket with the inspirational self-determination point underscored in red. With Britain refusing to sanction the claim that Zaghlul and his followers represented Egyptian opinion, the nationalists received nothing more than a calculated snub in Paris. Britain's maximum publicity of American recognition of the Protectorate[93] served only to alienate further the Egyptian-educated elite who believed that Britain had once again proved her entrenched hostility and hypocrisy towards Egypt.

Despite the nationalists' rebuff at Paris, the Egyptian issue was far from resolved. A civil service strike which had begun on 2 April continued to hamper the administration of the various departments and as attempts to form a new ministry dragged on, Curzon telegraphed Allenby on 18 April informing him that the British Government had decided to despatch an important commission under Lord Milner to Egypt at an early date. This commission would not only investigate the existing conditions in Egypt, but also examine the causes of the present disturbances and determine the future form of the British Protectorate.[94]

The Residency and Foreign Office were once again at odds with one another. Allenby had assumed that the mission would be working with him to investigate the disturbances and Britain's future policy there. Curzon, however, perceived it very differently. In fact, the mission was to be entirely independent of the Residency and was to be represented as a necessary stage in the constitutional evolution of the country, rather than as a step that had been directly forced upon Britain by the recent rising. Originally, Allenby had suggested that the mission proceed to Egypt in mid-May but its delay in departure, some eight months after its original announcement, was due to a number of factors. Milner was not available until the end of the year and it was no easy task to find suitable members at such short notice. Moreover, to undertake such a task during the hot season would not be conducive to the mission's work.[95] Milner also wanted to exercise complete control over the approach and methods of the mission. In response to Allenby's telegram, which suggested an immediate announcement and possible terms of reference, Milner entirely dissented and was 'not *prepared* to accept the Mission under these conditions'.[96] Unfortunately, and much to Milner's chagrin, the Foreign Office had already sent a telegram to Allenby on the same day as Milner's letter to Curzon, which authorized the announcement of the mission.[97] Nonetheless, Milner's persuasive influence can be seen in the drafting of the terms of reference as Curzon readily submitted to Milner's suggestions. Indeed, it appears from Milner's letter to Curzon on 25 April that it was Milner, initially at least, who wished to delay the announcement and departure of the mission:

> The more I think of it, the clearer it is to me, that it would be a mistake to make this, or any fresh move, now. It would be a repetition on a much milder form, of the great blunder made by Allenby, when, [...] he made the concession about passports and the release of Zaghlul and Co. [...] The moment is a bad one to announce a new move on our part. It looks as if we were flustered, afraid of the situation created by the non-existence of an Egyptian Ministry and the naked assertion of British authority, and felt that something must be done at once to get us out of a hole.[98]

Milner felt strongly that the restoration of order was the preserve of Allenby whilst it was the business of the mission to lay the foundations of a new system of government. Otherwise the mission would be regarded as:

> a fresh expedient for inducing the Egyptians to keep quiet, an emergency measure, a sop to Cerberus. It will revive hopes and intrigues and in fact keep the pot of

agitation boiling. So strongly do I feel this that I really am not prepared to be fired out to Egypt merely to meet the immediate difficulty of meeting Parliament with a declaration of Policy. The whole thing is doomed to failure if we are going to let ourselves be hustled over it.[99]

Moreover, the formation of a new ministry under Mohammed Said Pasha on 22 May 1919 removed the urgency from the despatch of the mission and also eased some of the pressure on the Residency.[100] The critical moment for the time being having passed, Allenby found no need to press the Foreign Office for an earlier departure than the recommended time of September.[101] Whatever the underlying reason for delay, the official line taken by Curzon in a speech to the House of Lords on 25 November 1919 was that it had been:

> Intended to despatch the Mission at as early a date as its composition could be completed. But difficulties were experienced in more ways than one. It was not found easy to find available members with the requisite authority and experience; the Summer is not exactly the best time in which to conduct investigations in the interior of the country with the Egyptian climate; it was felt desirable to give the newly-formed Egyptian Administration an opportunity of firmly establishing itself; and, it was thought that the Peace Conference at Paris might address itself before the Autumn to the solution of the Eastern problem. Lord Allenby, upon whose judgement HM Government placed great reliance, informed us that the Sultan of Egypt and the Prime Minister both favoured a postponement till the Autumn, and that he agreed with their views. It was in these circumstances that the date of the departure of the Mission was deferred.[102]

The prevailing idea within the Foreign Office and the Residency was that time would settle many of the present troubles within Egypt, but this was perhaps Britain's greatest enemy. The delay in the mission's departure allowed the newly formed Central Committee of the Wafd[103] time to decide how best to combat this new British strategy.

The idea of boycotting the mission originated over the course of the summer between Zaghlul and Abd al-Rahman Fahmi, General Secretary of the Wafd's Central Committee. Whilst Allenby was on leave, Acting High Commissioner Cheetham reported in early October that Zaghlul, in a letter to the President of the Cairo Committee of the Extremist Party, had advocated the boycott of the Milner Mission. This new development was further confirmed by Lord Derby, British Ambassador to France, also in October, who reported that in an interview for the *Journal*, Zaghlul had said that 'the Milner Commission is useless; it has been appointed merely to tranquilise opposition in Parliament'.[104] Cheetham reported that articles in the press and pamphlets emphasized that to recognize the mission would imply Egypt's acquiescence in the British Protectorate.[105]

The extent of Wafd influence over the press was a worrying development. The tentacles of Wafd control were such that any pro-British support on the part of any particular journal 'resulted in such a diminution of sales as to threaten bankruptcy'.[106] Clayton warned that 'until public opinion ceases to be dominated by the extremist party who have a powerful weapon in the Press, it is hopeless to expect the formation into a solid block of that large body of "moderates" who are now intimidated into silence'.[107] This opposition to the mission which had now become the war cry of the nationalists came to the attention of British authorities as early as July 1919. Admiralty intelligence consistently linked the disturbances and industrial unrest with the imminent arrival of the Milner Mission. According to these reports the unrest was being stirred and supported by the nationalists whose idea was to 'paralyse transport and business in order to create a crisis that will pave the way for another revolution [for independence]'.[108]

These reports also conveyed an underlying concern over the development of three other movements that challenged Britain's hegemony within Egypt. Firstly, Italian dissatisfaction with the Paris Peace terms was openly demonstrated by the establishment of friendly relations with the Nationalist Party and Italian encouragement of the independence movement in every possible way.[109] The Italian newspaper, *Roma*, encouraged hostility towards America, Britain and the French Government, making capital out of Indian, Korean, Maltese and Egyptian national aspirations for this purpose. It even went so far as to associate itself with Pan-Islamic and pro-Turkish propaganda.[110] Furthermore, Italian socialists, such as Giuseppe Pizzuto, a print worker, actively worked to form trade unions among Egyptians and foreign workers, the immediate consequence being the spread of the strike movement among all classes of workers and employees.[111] There were also fears that the Socialist unions in Italy were sending demobilized soldiers to secretly direct the trade union movement in Egypt.[112]

The rise of Bolshevism in Egypt was also closely watched as there was a concern that trade unionism bred Bolshevism.[113] However, officials comforted themselves with the fact that whilst the Bolshevist cause would enjoy a certain amount of success if the Bolsheviks confined themselves to Egyptian Nationalist ideals, it would be difficult to assess how far they would succeed in 'Bolshevising' the Egyptians. 'As of the four great sects in Islam, Egypt is officially Hanafi, and their tenets and those of Bolshevism would appear to be diametrically opposed to one another, and the Mufti, as head of the sect, has recently issued his Fatwa against Bolshevism'.[114]

As the discussion over peace terms with Turkey dragged on, there was considerable concern over a revival of the Pan-Islamic movement within Egypt. Reports from British officials stationed in Berne suggested a League between Egyptians and Turks in Switzerland had formed that also encompassed Tunisians, Arabs, Indians and Central Asian Muslims, which would operate branches in all Muslim countries, their aim being to free such countries from foreign rule.[115] Concern was expressed that the longer the settlement of the Turkish question was delayed, the greater the danger posed by this upheaval of Islam. Abdel Aziz Shawish, leader of the Egyptians in Switzerland, had received news from Egypt that the revolutionary movement had made great progress and was ready to break out again soon.[116]

The men-on-the-spot therefore clearly perceived the British position to be under threat from a number of angles. It is clear that on the surface a nervous calm existed, but underneath bubbled a volatile nationalist movement ready to make itself heard upon Milner's arrival.

Composition of the Milner Mission

The events since Allenby's assumption to the position of Special High Commissioner of Egypt and the Sudan had given Curzon pause for thought over Allenby's inexperience, especially when dealing with the intrigues of the Pasha class. The mission's underlying aims therefore were twofold: to bring Egyptian administration under more experienced direction, and to circumvent an open confrontation with a general who enjoyed great influence and respect in both London and Cairo. Curzon was sure that, with Milner in charge of the mission, its findings would validate his own view of the necessity for political discipline and imperial control.

The Milner Mission was composed of six members, three of whom possessed first-hand experience of Egypt. Lord Milner, as head of the Mission, had received his formal education at Balliol College, Oxford, the same college as two of its other members, Sir James Rennell Rodd and John Alfred Spender. Curzon, who had appointed the delegates to the Mission, was also a product of Balliol.[117] Milner's early views on imperialism and Empire were largely developed while studying at Balliol and were heavily influenced by George Parkin, a Canadian schoolmaster and imperial patriot. In a speech at the Oxford Union, Parkin urged the cause of a United Empire and 'such Imperial federation will secure the representation of the more important Colonies in the Imperial Councils'.[118] Parkin, like so many other imperialists of this age, believed in the idea of race. He was certain that a united British Empire, bound by some kind of federal government, was possible because 'a special capacity for political organisation may, without race vanity, be fairly claimed for Anglo-Saxon people'.[119] It is possible to see how Milner absorbed these ideas when writing in 1894 about Britain's role in Egypt, where he spent three years as Director General of Accounts and then Under-Secretary for Finance between 1889 and 1892.[120] He believed that Britain had no desire to annex Egypt to the Empire, but had every reason to prevent any rival power from controlling Egypt. Britain would be able to achieve this by building up a system of government stable enough to resist any future foreign intervention. According to Milner, Britain was best equipped to do this with 'the number of her sons who have special aptitude and special experience in the work of governing or directing more backward nations'.[121] An advocate of enlightened imperial rule, Milner believed that Britain's reforming zeal should take prominence above any Egyptian incorporation into the Empire.

Of the others who shared first-hand experience of Egypt was Rennell Rodd, a career diplomat who had served at the Cairo Residency between 1894 and 1901. A long-standing friend of Curzon, Rodd had also served as British Ambassador to Italy from 1908 until 1919. General Sir John Maxwell boasted a long association with Egypt that began as an *aide-de-camp* to one of the generals on Sir Garnet Wolseley's staff during the battle of Tel-el-Kebir. Maxwell subsequently served under Cromer and upon the outbreak of the First World War assumed the post of General-Officer-Commanding troops in Egypt from September 1914 until January 1916. Maxwell also served as a Governor of Pretoria. Described as popular amongst Egyptians because of his geniality, he was 'reputed to be deeply interested in the welfare of Egypt'.[122] Sir Cecil Hurst, Principal Legal Adviser to the Foreign Office, and Brigadier-General Sir Owen Thomas, an expert on African agriculture and a Labour MP, were also appointed to the Mission. Finally, J A Spender, former editor of the *Westminster Gazette* and prominent liberal, completed the six members of the Mission. A T Loyd, formerly of the Egyptian Civil Service, and Edward Ingram, from the Foreign Office, accompanied the Mission as secretary and assistant secretary, respectively. Ingram also acted as Milner's private secretary.[123]

The fact that it took three months to decide the composition of the mission demonstrates the sheer volume of work that preoccupied the Foreign Office in the immediate post-war era. More importantly, the weight of experience and expertise the Mission embodied allowed the Mission to forge its own path without reference to London or the Residency. Milner's own high standing and influence allowed him to enjoy a freedom impossible for any other politician heading the mission. Even before Milner's arrival in Egypt he held broad views which established the guiding principles and approach of the Mission.

Prior to Milner's arrival, Zaghlul sent a telegram to Curzon stating 'the British Authorities have made the great mistake of underrating the Egyptian movement for independence, just as their forefathers did in America in 1775. The present movement is deep, spontaneous, and universal'. Zaghlul continued that Egypt no longer required the protection of Britain against external threats since the League of Nations now represented a sufficient guarantor of Egyptian independence.[124] It is clear that the mission faced an uphill struggle not only within Egypt itself but at home as well, between the expectations of Curzon and the Foreign Office and of the British public.

The Milner Mission

When the mission arrived in Egypt on 7 December 1919, it was to a country where strikes, disturbances and attacks on individuals continued. In spite of martial law, Zaghlul and his followers progressively strengthened their grip on the country, as their demand for a boycott of the Milner Mission was 'very thorough'.[125] Writing to the Prime Minister after three weeks in Cairo Milner described Egypt as being:

> in a much worse state than I imagined when I started. Partly from mismanagement, but partly also from a good deal of sheer bad luck, we have lost ground terribly since I was last here some 8 years ago. Indeed, I think we have been going back ever since Cromer, though not so rapidly as in quite recent days.[126]

This view seemed to be confirmed in an interview between Milner and Osmond Walrond on 8 December. Walrond, a confidential advisor to Wingate and a Secret Intelligence Service officer, painted the situation 'pretty black – believing that the moderates were thoroughly frightened by, and under the thumb of the extremists, and that no Egyptian, however friendly, would venture to have much to do with the Mission [...] the present Ministry were men of straw, who carried no weight what so ever in the country'.[127] However, at this early stage of the mission, whilst Milner saw men such as Walrond as useful for providing him with a point of view that would have otherwise remained unknown to him since Walrond resided amongst Egyptians, Milner nonetheless discounted 'all this pretty heavily'.[128]

Milner's investigations appeared to confirm his preconceptions. In an interview with Maxwell, who had been seeing ministers and ex-ministers, he concluded that:

> it becomes more and more apparent that the grievance of the more moderate Egyptian malcontents is that they are "priest-ridden", i.e. kept too much in leading strings by an ever-increasing number of British officials. On the other hand, the British officials themselves, finding that, for all their conscientious discharge of duty, they get nothing but unpopularity and abuse, are disheartened and on the defensive [...] Question. Are we trying to do too much for these people, and getting ourselves disliked without materially benefiting them?[129]

In a memorandum circulated to the Mission soon after their arrival in Cairo, Milner set out its objectives. Milner did not want to spend a great deal of time on the causes of the March disorders or the sputtering unrest which had continued since. In his view, the general causes were pretty clear and would obviously be recorded in any report submitted by the Mission. Instead, Milner wished to concentrate upon a scheme for the better government of Egypt. 'The "veiled Protectorate" has definitely come to an end. It was perhaps the best system possible, but it was necessarily temporary [...] Something has to be substituted for it, having a more definite and open character'.[130]

In order to achieve this, two key areas needed to be examined. Firstly, how much authority should Britain try and exercise in Egypt; and, secondly, whether an agreement could be reached by which the Egyptians themselves would recognize Britain's right to exercise such authority. In answering the first question, Milner suggested a systematic review of all the main branches of Egyptian administration: Finance, Interior, Public Works, Justice, Education, Agriculture and Defence, they should assess whether it was possible to take the indirect method of Britons doing the work or through direct orders. In regard to the second point this was more problematical since the continuing boycott prevented meaningful discussion with influential Egyptians. Moreover, Milner was acutely aware of the negative connotations surrounding the term 'Protectorate', and whilst, at this point, he did not advocate abandoning the term, he recognized that 'something else, not inconsistent with it'[131] needed to be found that would take its place in the mind of Egyptians.

As a result, Milner floated the idea of an understanding being reached between Britain and the moderate Egyptian elements by which Britain would undertake to guarantee an agreed constitution for Egypt against foreign interference and internal disorder. In return for that guarantee, Egypt would acknowledge Britain's right to maintain an army of occupation and to retain certain posts in the administration, as well as control of the Sudan.[132] Almost immediately the Mission's aim now became not one of enquiry but of negotiation. Instead of analysing the situation, it was attempting to construct an informal agreement with the leading politicians as to the allocation powers under a revised system of British control.

Milner was certain that the boycott of the Mission would eventually crumble.[133] In a meeting with Sarwat Pasha on 13 December, he emphasized:

the absurdity of the attempted 'boycott of the Commission, which meant that the native party, anxious to obtain a greater measure of independence for Egypt would lose the opportunity now presented to them of putting their case and that we should be obliged to arrive at decisions without regard for them. The present childish proceedings, if persisted in, would afford the strongest evidence of the political incapacity of the Egyptians and of their unfitness for self-government. If sensible native opinion, which condemned these proceedings, was unable to keep a lot of school-boys and hooligans in order, how could we expect the better elements to take over the whole government of the country?'[134]

Nonetheless, the boycott of the Mission was so effective that within three weeks Milner recognized that Egypt was united behind Zaghlul in opposing the Mission. According to Milner, Egyptian opposition stemmed from a belief that the chief object of the Mission was to 'effect the confirmation of the Protectorate'.[135] As a result Milner believed that in order to make progress it was necessary to jettison the label 'Protectorate'. Allenby expressed some doubts over this course of action 'anxious lest he should seem in any way to budge from "the Protectorate", which is his anchor, and the thing he is specially sent here to defend'.[136] Once Milner assured him that the declaration in no way abandoned the essential character of the Protectorate but simply threw open the door to discussion, Allenby was satisfied. On 29 December the mission issued a declaration stating that its object was to 'reconcile the aspirations of the Egyptians with the special interests of Great Britain and the rights of all foreigners in Egypt. And that we were ready to hear the views of all men of good will, such discussion being "without prejudice" on both sides'.[137] Milner's object in this declaration was to parry the favourite argument of the extremists that it was dangerous even to approach the Mission, because anybody who did so *ipso facto* abandoned the cause of Egypt. In response, Zaghlul stated in a letter to Ibrahim Pasha that it 'did not warrant suspension of the boycott nor the return of Zaghlul to Egypt to undertake negotiations'.[138]

The publication of this declaration demonstrated that Milner was forced to abandon the hope of an agreement between Britain and the moderates, thereby isolating the so-called extremists. The solidarity of indigenous opinion across all classes, the reluctance of those whom the British believed were powerful and influential to engage with the Mission and the eagerness of the moderates to include Zaghlul in any negotiations forced the Mission to realize that it had been unsuccessful in reaching the real sources of power within Egyptian society.

Despite Allenby's misgivings, all attempts to cajole Zaghlul into a discussion over constitutional reform, such as the release of a number of notables of Zaghlulist persuasion, failed.[139] Milner grew more despondent over the Mission's objective of direct consultation with the leaders of indigenous opinion and wrote on 6 January 1920 'the amount worth recording grows less and less as time passes. There is such a fearful amount of repetition. In a country where backbone and sincerity are at such a discount, the kaleidoscope of opinion, once the various colours are known, hardly seems worth following'.[140] As a result the mission almost discarded its search for a negotiated settlement and reverted to a detailed investigation into the governmental machinery and administration of the country. The mission left Egypt in early March 1920.

The mission had been a comprehensive failure. Milner wrote to Curzon on 12 January advising him of what he could expect from it:

> What you have therefore to look forward to, *unless the situation undergoes a complete change in the next few weeks*, is a Report, which will, I hope, be a thorough piece of work, but the recommendations of which cannot by any possibility be represented as having been made with Egyptian public opinion. For the information of the Government, or, in so far as it is publishable, for that of the British public, such a Report may be of use. But it will not solve the Egyptian Question. For even supposing that our recommendations were fully approved at home, we should still be faced with the problem, how to set up an Egyptian Constitution without the help and in the face of the vehement protests of all that is vocal in Egypt. It will be something like the Irish situation all over again.[141]

These observations were repeated to Lloyd George at the end of February. Milner noted that however much the moderate party wished to come to terms with Britain, they were unable to pluck up the courage to do so. They wanted Zaghlul to lead them and, Milner believed that, Zaghlul wished to do so but 'he was afraid of the Frankenstein he had himself created'. This resulted in the Extremists having free reign and the 'monstrous refrain of "complete independence" goes up incessantly from the Press, the mosques, and is repeated endlessly in resolutions, letters, telegrams and from colleges, schools, local Councils and so on'.[142] Milner believed that the majority of the peasantry and small landholders – 'the non-vocal class in fact are quite out of sympathy with the racket [...] But the agitators, who have heaps of money, continue to make untold efforts to stir them up again'. Indeed, the recent rise in price of common articles of food – wheat, maize and rice – coupled with rumours that British irrigation schemes in the Sudan would deprive Egypt of water added new and disquieting features to the current situation. Milner's sense of despondency was also conveyed in a letter to Lady Edward Cecil:

> The more I see of Egypt the more convinced I am that, quite apart from our muddles, there are very troublesome times ahead. It would take a great deal more than this mission to get to the bottom of the problem, much more to solve it. I think we have done some good, we may do some more. But new difficulties are springing up on every side, and unless we can find a real statesman to give the best years of his life to the job – and where is he? Allenby is a good man, and a fine soldier, but he is not equal to the job – I am afraid we shall go on floundering. Cromer's task here was difficult enough, but I think the task before the High Commissioner now is even more difficult. It is certainly more complex. A weak Sultan, a weak Ministry [...] an *enormously wealthy* Pasha class, with [...] nothing to do with their money except to spend it on gambling and intrigue, a rapidly growing poor population, too numerous for so small an area of cultivated land, and an unsettled world all around – Islamic fanaticism, Zionism, Bolshevism (the last quite a new factor). What a kettle of fish![143]

What made the achievement of any settlement in Milner's mind even more difficult was the 'failure to wind up the Turkish business'. The wider implications for Britain's position in Egypt were not lost on Milner. 'What we do here, much depends to a large extent on what we are doing in Palestine and Mesopotamia. The whole Near East is One Question'.[144]

Milner's convictions remained essentially the same. His proposals advocated the abandonment of all wartime administrative changes, which had led to tighter British control, and the replacement of the Protectorate by a negotiated treaty conceding to Egypt a significant degree of internal autonomy. 'It should be the aim of British policy to give scope to the spirit of independence and the increased capacity and desire of Egyptians to govern themselves. We should seek to give to the future status of Egypt the greatest appearance of independence compatible with the maintenance of the absolutely indispensable minimum of British control'.[145] The new order of Anglo-Egyptian relations was to be the recognition of Egypt's independence in return for her acquiescence in remaining Britain's satellite in diplomatic and strategic matters. This policy is understandable once it is recognized that Milner did not believe in a monolithic relationship between the mother country and all of her dependencies. He certainly did not believe that the incorporation of Egypt into the British Empire on the model of India or tropical Africa was the solution.

The Milner-Zaghlul discussions

In May 1920 Milner issued a personal invitation to Zaghlul to proceed to London in order to begin discussions with the mission over a negotiated settlement of the Egyptian problem. This differed from earlier attempts at a negotiated settlement as the delegation that would proceed to London was to be unofficial thereby allowing the parties to 'feel their way and discover whether there really was a possibility of agreement', without either the Egyptian or British Government being committed to a formal negotiation 'the failure of which would be disastrous'.[146] From Milner's actions it is possible to discern that, in his own mind, although the mission had returned from Egypt, it did not signal the end of its working contribution in the shaping of British policy. Indeed, the Foreign Office's lack of supervision of the original Milner Mission and the referral of information received in the Foreign Office from Egypt to Milner for comment contributed to this belief.

The Milner-Zaghlul conversations began on 9 June. However, the watchful gaze of the Watanists – extremists, reactionary in character with pro-Turkish and pan-Islamic ideals – and extreme Zaghlulists, ready to criticize all advances towards a compromise, undoubtedly exercised a certain amount of influence over Zaghlul's actions.[147] Even Milner did not feel much optimism over the outcome of the talks, in particular in winning over Zaghlul's followers in Egypt if a settlement was reached.[148] This sentiment was echoed by Allenby.[149]

The basis upon which agreement was being attempted was a treaty of alliance between Britain and Egypt whereby Britain would guarantee the integrity and independence of Egypt. In return, Egypt would recognize the right of Britain to maintain a military force in the country, and to nominate Englishmen to certain posts within the Egyptian service to ensure the fulfilment of Egypt's international obligations, such as the payment of the Debt, maintenance of the Mixed Courts, an efficient police and the protection of the lives and property of foreigners. At the end of June, Curzon telegraphed Allenby to say that the conversations were proceeding slowly but amicably. According to Curzon, Zaghlul and his associates were anxious to come to terms. They would be willing to accept and support an arrangement, not inconsistent with the maintenance of essentials of British control over Egypt, if in form it did not conflict too violently with what they had claimed and had led Egyptians to expect. Within Egypt, political writings in all sections of the Arabic language press had been tuned to the 'accommodationist' note, in spite of the chief differences of opinion over the custody of the Suez Canal, the status of the Sudan and the representation of Egypt abroad.[150]

However, a number of difficulties remained. Firstly, Zaghlul and his associates felt unable to accept the necessary reservations, which constituted substantial limitations on complete independence. Secondly, even if Zaghlul and his party accepted, they would be unable to carry the bulk of their followers with them. The latter would break away and join the Watanists, in which case it would be impossible to obtain the crucial endorsement of the Egyptian National Assembly. Such endorsement was essential to British policy. Thirdly, the proposed Treaty of Alliance would be between the British monarch and the Sultan. The latter must, therefore, be brought into the negotiations. This was a delicate point, as the Sultan had naturally been suspicious of the whole proceeding. The time was fast approaching when, if the conversations continued to progress well in London, it would be necessary to pass from this preliminary stage to a conference with regularly appointed representatives of the Egyptian Government. These representatives could be appointed only by the Sultan, who would thus take the lead and desire to include representatives sharing his views and not those of the present delegation.[151]

During July 1920 the negotiations reached an impasse. With Zaghlul and the delegation ready to leave England, Adli persuaded Milner to make one final attempt to reach an Anglo-Egyptian understanding. Milner noted to Spender that 'the Egyptian kaleidoscope has had another shake'. Adli gave Milner the impression that Zaghlul and his associates were now in a 'very chastened frame of mind', and that there was a 'chance of creating a strong Moderate party among Egyptian Nationalists which, if allowed to pass, might never recur'.[152] Milner did not hold out much hope but 'after all the months we have spent trying to bring the thing off, I am unwilling not to give Adli – who has certainly helped us very loyally throughout – a last chance of converting the Wafd to his point of view, especially as he seems very sanguine of being able to do so'.[153]

With the talks on the verge of collapse Milner presented the Egyptian delegation with a memorandum on 18 August. The memorandum proposed that Britain and Egypt should enter into a treaty on the following terms: Britain would recognize the independence of Egypt as a constitutional monarchy with representative institutions, whilst Egypt would confer upon Britain such rights as necessary to safeguard her special interests and enable Britain to furnish the guarantees that must be given to foreign Powers to secure the relinquishment of their capitulatory rights. Under the same treaty, an alliance would be concluded in which Britain would undertake to support Egypt and defend the integrity of her territory whilst Egypt would agree, in case of war, and even when the integrity of Egypt was not affected, to render Britain all the assistance in her power within her borders, including the use of harbours, aerodromes and means of communication for military purposes. The proposed treaty would also incorporate a number of stipulations. Egypt would enjoy the right to representation abroad so long as she did not adopt an attitude or enter into any agreements prejudicial to British interests. Britain would maintain a military force in Egypt for the protection of her imperial communications but the stationing of these forces would be fixed by the treaty. The appointment, with Britain's concurrence, of an Egyptian adviser to the Ministries of Finance and Justice would be sanctioned. Britain would also exercise a degree of protection over religious minorities.[154] This memorandum, a result of the Milner-Zaghlul discussions, was meant to serve as the basis for formal negotiations between the properly accredited representatives of the British and Egyptian governments. It essentially encompassed the body of the mission's 'General Conclusions'.

The Milner Mission and subsequent discussions represented a significant milestone in Anglo-Egyptian relations. It may be perceived as an important attempt to impose a constitutional framework that separated local administration, which often led to damaging confrontations between British officials and local politicians, from the wider strategic imperatives of Britain's political, military and commercial interests within the eastern Mediterranean and wider Middle East. Milner hoped to achieve this goal by collaborating with those who represented popular opinion – Zaghlul and his followers – thereby circumscribing the Sultan's power. Milner truly believed that by harnessing the populist elements of the Egyptian political scene to the British imperial wagon, he was strengthening Britain's imperial position, not weakening it.

In Egypt, the news of the proposed understanding with Britain was at first acclaimed by the Zaghlulist Party with enthusiasm at finding that so much had been achieved. However, Zaghlul's non-committal attitude towards the agreement encouraged the extremists to reject the memorandum.[155] His issue of a lukewarm manifesto upon the return to Egypt of the four delegates charged with resolving the disagreements modified the enthusiasm that had initially greeted the proposed settlement. Although the activities of the delegation were criticized by the Foreign Office in a later report as calculated not to advance matters quickly and satisfactorily,[156] the authorities on the spot held a different opinion commenting that:

> the quiet and unrhetorical manner in which the delegates laid their proposals before the nation has proved a successful innovation in Egyptian politics. It has not prevented public opinion from moving rapidly in their favour, while it is largely responsible for the tone of moderation and sincerity with which the question has been discussed.[157]

According to the British authorities this led to an overwhelming degree of support for the Milner-Zaghlul proposal, whilst the weakness of the opposition grew steadily more manifest. More importantly, for the British it was judged that political excitement was confined to the educated classes whilst the poor and *fellahin* seemed to be hardly aware at all that the delegates had returned.[158]

The London Arena

Milner's deliberate lack of communication to his Cabinet colleagues over the objectives and procedure of his mission served only to complicate the situation. As a result, some members of the Cabinet learned of the Zaghlul-Milner Agreement through *The Times* newspaper.[159] Winston Churchill, Secretary of State for War, noted that 'this is another of those turning points', and pleaded with Lloyd George that 'you shd join with us in asking that no irrecoverable step shd be taken about Egypt until we come back [from the summer recess]'.[160] In the meantime, Churchill led the opposition against the agreement on four counts. Firstly, the mission was castigated for concluding an agreement without prior approval from the Government:

> While the British will be held committed to approving the proposals of this character, the Egyptian Nationalists will be free to take them merely as a starting point for further demands; thus, even from this point of view of bargaining, the disclosures which have taken place seem to be regrettable. The cession of territory, which has been definitely incorporated in the British Dominions, is, however, a matter, which requires the assent not only of the Cabinet, but also of Crown and Parliament.[161]

Secondly, it was questioned whether Milner's reforms to allow Egyptian independence were real or a manoeuvre. If, as Churchill expected, they were a mirage, would the nationalists be satisfied with this state of affairs? Thirdly, the mission was criticized for its failure to consult the government's military experts. Finally, Churchill alarmed his colleagues by warning that concessions to extremists only generated further demands. Moreover, he emphasized the dangerous repercussions of these proposals on Irish and Indian nationalism:

> If we leave out the word 'Egypt' […] and substitute the word 'Ireland' it would, with very small omissions, make perfectly good sense, and world constitute a complete acceptance of Mr. De Valera's demands […] The ideal which Mr Montagu has been endeavouring to hold up before Indian eyes of India as a great self-governing Dominion within the orbit of the British Empire and under the supreme authority of the British monarchy will be discarded in favour of an independent Indian Empire.[162]

Although Churchill's arguments represented genuine concerns about Britain's imperial security, they also signified an attempt to assert his influence in policymaking within the Middle East.[163] British policy in the Middle East was divided between four departments of state – the War Office, the India Office, the Colonial Office and the Foreign Office. This system contributed to a paralysis of policymaking in the region since rivalries and conflicting interests were played out between the department heads – Churchill, Edwin Montagu, Lord Milner and Lord Curzon, respectively.[164] Churchill's criticisms forced Milner to suspend discussions with Zaghlul in November 1920.

Churchill's negative assessment of the proposals had the full support of the three fighting services. The Chief of the Imperial General Staff, Sir Henry Wilson, highlighted that this draft agreement would have 'a far-reaching effect on the military situation of the British Empire, since [...] Egypt is the "Clapham Junction" of imperial communication'.[165] Wilson also raised the question of the Sudan's status if and when Egypt achieved independence. The General Staff clearly desired that the Sudan be entirely separated from Egypt and be directly administered by the Imperial Government, dependent, of course, on the financial consideration involved. The General Staff actually advocated a policy that gradually eliminated the Egyptian element from the army in the Sudan, and which reconstituted it on a Sudanese and Arab basis whilst also extending the police force.[166]

The Admiralty also had special interests in Egypt, or more precisely the Suez Canal's status. The Suez Canal provided one of the main arteries of sea communications between Britain, India, Australia and the Far East. Any threat to this route would prove disastrous to imperial strategy since Britain's two serious naval rivals – Japan and the United States – were at opposite ends of the globe. It was impracticable and financially impossible during the inter-war years of retrenchment to maintain the fleet at sufficient strength to effect the double concentration at home and in the East to meet any situation satisfactorily. The fleet therefore had to make up for its lack of preponderance in all oceans by its mobility. By facilitating quick passage to any threatened portion of the Empire, the Suez Canal played a pivotal role. The alternative route to the East, via the Cape, was far longer. In a situation where time would be a deciding factor, the security or loss of an outpost of Empire such as Hong Kong would be decided by the availability of the canal route.[167]

Thus, the Admiralty showed concern over how the proposals would affect the Canal. It believed that the Suez Canal and Egypt could not be separated and voiced unease over the possibility that the Egyptians might claim that the Canal was specially regulated by the Suez Canal Convention of 29 October 1888. 'Egypt has a very valuable asset in the Canal and she might in her negotiation for the renewal of the lease, use it as a lever to secure alterations in the present proposed Political Agreement and Convention'.[168]

The Admiralty's concerns were, however, given short shrift by Curzon at the Foreign office. Although alive to the importance of protecting the Suez Canal, Curzon did not 'consider it necessary to make any special reference to the protection of the Canal'.[169] He believed that the Egyptians had no desire to question the paramount interests of Britain. 'It has indeed been the policy of Egypt to put forward the Suez Canal as constituting the main, if not sole reason for the retention of British troops on Egyptian soil and it has even been suggested that in future, British armed forces in Egypt should be relegated to the zone of the Canal'.[170]

The Air Ministry, fighting for its existence as an autonomous service in the 1920s, outlined their concerns in a more forceful manner. The importance of Egypt to the RAF was reflected by the fact that Hugh Trenchard, Chief of the Air Staff, took the proposals to heart. 'The changed status of Egypt, if *The Times* reports are true, is causing me considerable anxiety [...] the Air Force has a particular interest in Egypt'.[171] According to the Air Ministry, Milner's proposals affected the RAF's policy in the 'gravest possible manner'.[172] For the RAF, Egypt was the keystone of their survival.

It is, on account of its climate, an admirable training ground for airmen; it is the headquarters of the Air Force throughout the Near and Middle East; in the country are stationed squadrons which form a semi-mobile reserve for these areas; large expenses have been incurred in the provision of workshops and depots, and a proposal is in hand to form in the country a large rigid airship base, and finally, it is possibly the most important junction in the world for an Imperial air route point of view.[173]

The forcefulness with which these concerns were voiced no doubt reflected the stake which each of the armed services held in Egypt.

The Secretary of State for India, Edwin Montagu, supported Churchill in his criticisms of Milner. Montagu feared that negotiation and concession with, what he termed, the extremist elements of Egyptian nationalism would increase agitation in other troubled hotspots, such as India and Ireland.[174] Montagu's criticism was also influenced by more personal considerations. It is possible that his denigration of Milner's proposals was a defence of his and the Viceroy of India, Frederic Thesiger Chelmsford's own reforms in India, which were coming under increasing fire from British officials in the Indian territories.[175] Indeed, Hardinge regarded Milner's scheme as 'most dangerous, while what has been and is being done in Egypt will make the situation in India far more difficult [...] I feel very gloomy about it all, and it is a great misfortune that it is the views of idealists rather than practical men that are listened to now in higher circles'.[176] The struggle for supremacy over the control of Middle Eastern affairs between the India and Foreign Office was a further factor in Montagu's censure.

In response to these concerns, Milner acknowledged that the proposals appeared to look like a step backward 'but to a more secure position than that which we now occupy'.[177] The Mission had allowed Milner to use the Egyptian situation as a lens through which to view both Britain's position in the wider Middle East and the means with which to tackle post-war dislocation. It provided the opportunity for Britain to recast her relationship with the hotspots of nationalist aspirations and place Britain's position on a much firmer footing. In that vein, Milner countered Churchill's claim over the status of Egypt within the British Empire:

> The proclamation of a Protectorate over a foreign country may mean much or little, but it is certainly not equivalent to annexation [...] We went out of our way to represent our action as intended to defend Egypt against the dangers threatening her independence! And we at the same time raised the status of the rule of Egypt from that of 'Khedive', the vassal of Turkey, to that of "Sultan", the title of his former 'overlord'! Whatever may have been the effect of these curious and somewhat contradictory acts and declarations, which may have been very differently interpreted by us and the Egyptians, it is certainly difficult to contend that they constituted an incorporation of Egypt in the British Empire.[178]

Milner argued that the proposals would define Egypt's political status whilst also conferring an unquestionable legal basis to Britain's rights through a treaty confirmed by a National Assembly. Milner believed this would satisfy the moderates and saner elements of the nationalist movement. Indeed, he viewed the proposed concessions to Egyptian nationalism as 'just and polite, and as calculated to strengthen and not to weaken our Imperial position'.[179] Milner argued that unless Egypt's political status was clearly defined, the nationalist movement would continue to grow and the agitation against Britain would be carried on all over Europe and America by Nationalist emissaries. 'The middle and lower ranks of the bureaucracy and the Egyptian officers of the army are permeated with the spirit of repugnance to British control [...] with the whole native civil service permanently disaffected, the amount of grit in the administrative machine is bound to make it work very badly.'[180] Although holding some reservations over the attitude of the Capitulatory Powers to these proposals, Milner clearly believed that the 'blessed word "independence" will get us round many awkward corners just as the unfortunate word "Protectorate" would make even paradise unattractive to the Egyptians'.[181]

Milner's strength of feeling over the subject was indisputable. In explaining his continued absence to his wife, Violet, Milner complained that:

> Our affairs here are in a really indescribable condition of confusion and crisis. I wish most heartily I had nothing to do with them, and every day strengthens my conviction that I am in the wrong box and my anxiety to get out of it. But, being where I unfortunately am, I should feel it was a really shabby thing to absent myself, when matters of the most serious kind are under discussion almost every hour, matters about which I have rather a strong line [...] and in which my presence may just stop the 'rot', which has set in and is making such alarming progress.[182]

This says much about the critically important matters that continued to face ministers in the post-war period. Confronted with a plethora of difficulties within Britain's Empire, ministers had to make decisions on ever-changing situations that would have far-reaching consequences:

> Ireland, Mesopotamia, Persia [...] I am committed up to the hilt about the latter two, and even the former, though it is not in the same sense my 'pigeon', it is not a thing about which I could not consent, being still in the Government, to make a surrender. It is one thing to stick to your guns, and, if you are beaten, to go, but it would be a hopeless position to be deliberately absent, when a vital decision was taken, and then resign, because one did not agree with it, not having been at pains to be present when it was known to be imminent and fought against it to the last.[183]

In regard to his, Milner's, proposals and Egypt, it was a close call:

> We have been at it hammer and tongs [...] So far two or three of us have held the pass, and kept L.G from toppling over on the wrong side [...] Some things have been said and done which I greatly resent, but *no decision* has been taken against my views on vital points, and while they hang in the balance, I can't desert the ship.[184]

Nevertheless, any Cabinet decision rested with Lloyd George and Bonar Law, as leader of the Conservatives within the coalition government. Both painfully aware of the delicate nature of their coalition, they generally tended to err on the side of caution and stuck with tried-and-tested means of imperial control. Their unenthusiastic reaction to the proposals was therefore somewhat unsurprising. Bonar Law wrote to Curzon stating that 'the whole of these Egyptian proposals came to me as a great shock and I think that will be the effect on public opinion here when they are known'.[185]

Milner's proposals were not discussed until 1 November 1920 in a specially convened ministerial conference.[186] Milner was at pains to emphasize that Britain would attain much greater efficiency in Egypt if 'we gave up direct control and relied more on influence'.[187] Cabinet debate over the issue centred upon external and internal strategic concerns, particularly around the level of influence British officials would possess in the Egyptian administration under Milner's scheme.[188] Although Allenby offered a measure of encouragement for Milner's scheme, wider support was lacking. Milner emphasized that the Egyptians were better disposed to Britain than anyone else; that with British sea power 'we could do practically what we liked strategically'.[189] As regards foreign intrigue under the proposed scheme, Egypt would be in 'Alliance with us, and with us only'.[190] The Cabinet remained unconvinced. Bonar Law thought that with good will on the part of the Egyptians, the proposed scheme 'might work', but if not, it appeared 'to be hopeless'. Furthermore, it was doubtful that the fourteen foreign powers that possessed Capitulatory rights[191] would be willing to agree to the proposals. Serious doubts remained over how, under Milner's scheme, it would be possible to prevent the French or any other Power from intriguing within Egypt and gradually gaining a foothold. Egyptian press reports stating that the Milner Commission recommended measures amounting to independent government had also found their way to William Hughes, Prime Minister of Australia. Hughes complained that 'in absence of any direct information [the] Commonwealth Government is completely in darkness as to what facts are but is much perturbed at such a policy as recommended by Lord Milner's Commission'.[192] Primarily concerned over the impact any Anglo-Egyptian agreement would have over the control of the Suez Canal 'one of the main arteries [of the] imperial body', Hughes raised the comparison of India and requested that no alteration of policy be made until the Imperial Conference of June 1921. 'The Government has given India a measure of self-government: has it satisfied or pacified India? It certainly would not appear so.'[193] It was clear that Milner would have an uphill battle – the Cabinet wanted to turn back the clock to the power and influence of Lord Cromer's rule. Lord Milner was at pains to point out that this was simply impossible, that in the post-war era a new relationship with Egypt needed to be forged rather than one based upon a Colony or Protectorate.

Cabinet discussion resumed on 4 November 1920. Again, concern was raised that Milner's scheme gave great opportunity for anti-British intrigue, by allowing Egypt to enjoy the right to representation in foreign countries, for instance. It was pointed out that British control over Egyptian foreign relations would be safeguarded in a large measure by the provision that Egypt would not be able to enter into an agreement with a foreign Power that was prejudicial to British interests. Finally, Cabinet opinion was coming round to the idea that an alternative needed to be found for Britain's position in Egypt if only to enable troop reductions to be made and therefore savings. The question centred upon whether Milner's proposal was the best possible. Allenby, who was due to return to Egypt on the following day, was not opposed to Milner's proposals but only to their constituting a basis for consultation with a representative Egyptian delegation to be nominated by the Sultan. Allenby made it clear that 'he did not like the manner in which negotiations had been carried out with Zaghlul, who is our enemy, instead of the Egyptian Government'.[194] He also felt that Britain was now committed, to a considerable extent, to a scheme. Allenby advocated that future policy should concentrate on supporting Britain's friends – at present the Egyptian ministry and Sultan – rather than 'trying vainly to conciliate our enemies'.[195] As a result of the Cabinet discussion, the Prime Minister, with the agreement of his fellow colleagues, instructed Allenby to make it clear to Egypt that the British government was not totally committed to the scheme. The next step would be for an Egyptian delegation to proceed to London either to discuss the details of the scheme already accepted in principle, or merely to reopen the whole question. Again, these awkward questions of policy were left for later consideration.

Nevertheless, Milner could console himself in the knowledge that his warnings had made some impact in getting the Cabinet to recognize the necessity for change in Egypt's status. In the meantime the members of the mission continued to work on the final report. Spender noted in December, whilst working on the final revisions, that 'M[ilner] prepares some snorting passages and then very good-naturedly submits while I comb them out'.[196] Spender himself believed in the work of the mission commenting that whilst it would be possible to quell dissatisfaction and improve public order by employing a sufficient British military force and a strong and consistent administration 'no reduction of the British forces in Egypt or relief to the British taxpayer could be expected from this method, and little or no advance in the general civilisation of the country'.[197] The delay in the publication of the final report meant that a decision over the Egyptian question was delayed until the New Year. Milner, although originally hoping that a Government decision on policy would have been reached in December 1920, was not unduly concerned. 'The Egyptian prospect is not quite as bad as it looks. I don't mean to say that it is good. Delay is dangerous, and we are in for delay, but perhaps for not very long. The Cabinet was pretty equally divided, and, in the last week of the year, tired out and listless'. However, Milner believed that with pressure from both Allenby and Egypt the Cabinet would consider the Egyptian question 'very shortly'.[198] Milner also informed Spender that once the Missions' report was published he would be standing down from the Colonial Office.

> This had fortunately been decided some time ago (I was only hanging on till the Report was finished). If I had not been, I should almost necessarily have had to go over this business. As it is, though my position remains very difficult, I think as far as Egyptian policy is concerned, I may be of more use now, if I am outside without having had an open breach with my colleagues. I can speak up for the policy of the Report with more freedom when I am not hampered by my Ministerial position.[199]

A concern over the postponement of discussing the Egyptian question was something that Milner and Spender shared. Spender complained to his wife that:

> The Report, as I conjectured, is the object of opinions, Cabinet dissensions and instead of [the Report] being sent to Egypt is held out here to be fought over. So, as in Ireland, the propitious moment may pass and the whole month be wasted. But M[ilner], I am glad to say, is for action and [...] declares that he is going to fight. He says that, if he hadn't resigned before, he would have had to resign over this.[200]

Spender noted that 'I am determined to do all I can to help them [the moderate nationalists], but I feel up against a brick wall with this government'. He wondered, wryly, over the propensity of the Government to 'hold back reports of Committees and Committees appointed by themselves, as in Ireland, and Egypt, because they don't happen to agree with their conclusions'.[201]

However, it was only after Curzon's memorandum to the Cabinet, accompanied by the support of Allenby in the form of a suggested declaration to the Sultan,[202] that Egypt once again pre-occupied the Cabinet in February 1921.[203] During the Cabinet meeting Milner warned that:

> The basis of our relations must be that it was bi-lateral and not unilateral. He [Milner] was in agreement that Egypt should be effectively within the ring-fence of the British Empire, but their status must not be that of a British Dominion [...] in his view the present moment was a favourable one for stating our attitude. If we did not take advantage of it the present relatively favourable situation might deteriorate, and six months hence, if nothing were done, might become thoroughly bad.[204]

Whilst still harbouring misgivings over some important details of the mission's report, Curzon 'warmly supported the two essential features of Allenby's formula. That: the status of a Protectorate over Egypt was no longer satisfactory; and, that the Protectorate should be substituted by a Treaty of Alliance which would still retain Egypt within the bounds of the British imperial system'. Indeed, in a letter to Lloyd George prior to the Cabinet meeting where Curzon's memorandum would be considered, Curzon warned that 'if we do not take some such action I am afraid we shall never get an Egyptian solution at all and that we shall miss the tide'.[205] These points were, of course, the essence of Milner's recommendations.[206] After a lengthy discussion, Allenby's formula was finally adopted, but even then it was later subject to alteration.[207] Whilst this did not go as far as Milner advocated, the Cabinet had come a long way in recognizing the need for negotiating a fresh relationship with Egypt.[208] This was received in Cairo with appreciation.

The Negotiations

In March 1921, Adli formed a new Ministry. Its composition was welcomed by Jack Murray of the Foreign Office as 'probably the best possible combination in the present circumstances'.[209] Whilst it did not contain any Zaghlulists, Adli hoped to induce Zaghlul and possibly two of his followers to serve on the official delegation to London. It was Zaghlul's move and London perceived him to be 'on the horns of a dilemma. Either he must join the delegation with one or two of his adherents who will restrain him from extreme courses; or he will refuse, and then his adherents who do not yet dare to disavow him, will do so, and he will be in a position of both open and real discredit'.[210] The Foreign Office was concerned to impress upon Allenby the importance of the Egyptian delegation's not only including one or more members with the power to sign any arrangement that might be reached, but also that its composition was so authoritative as to make it reasonably certain that his recommendations would be ratified by the representative assembly.

In response to Adli's request for Zaghlul's co-operation, Zaghlul made his participation conditional upon the abolition of the Protectorate and the acceptance of further demands made by the Wafd, which Milner had rejected in November 1920, before serious discussions could even begin. Furthermore, if these conditions were accepted, Zaghlul demanded that he should not only head the delegation but that the majority of its members be Wafdist.[211] Adli, who refused to participate in a delegation under the presidency of Zaghlul, now turned to Allenby. In the Foreign Office the message was clear: 'we cannot go an inch further than we have gone in the Cabinet's declaration of February 22. This is axiomatic.'[212]

Both Murray and Ronald Lindsay, Under-Secretary of Finance in the Egyptian government, expressed disappointment at Adli's 'unduly timorous' attitude. They believed that Zaghlul's actions had left him:

> virtually isolated. His influential adherents had fallen away from him in everything but appearance. And yet from Paris, where he has only two supporters, he dictates an ultimatum to the Ministry in almost insolent terms, reaffirming all his most extreme demands of the old days. In any other country he would be left high and dry by the receding flood: but the disquieting feature is that Adli [...] is not at all convinced that Zaghlul will ruin himself politically by the attitude he has taken up.[213]

The Foreign Office's other concern was that the Sultan, hating Adli and his programme of constitutionalism, would seize the opportunity to intrigue against him. Again, the Residency had to try and act as the fulcrum of Egyptian politics and balance the political agents – the Palace on the one hand and the Nationalists on the other. For the Foreign Office their position was clear: Zaghlul's ultimatum had to be met with a 'blunt refusal'.[214] The Cabinet's decision had been secured with the utmost difficulty and represented the limit of concession to which the British Government was prepared to go as a basis for negotiation. This had also been secured in the belief that it was satisfactory to all reasonable and moderate elements within Egypt. Curzon made it clear that 'if these now allow a situation to arise as a result of which the outstretched hand is refused the responsibility for possible consequences will not rest with His Majesty's Government, and I shall take care to make this plain'.[215]

Zaghlul returned to Egypt on 4 April and was 'greeted with delirious enthusiasm both in Cairo and Alexandria, and demonstrations and banquets in his honour were the order of the day for about a week'.[216] In a speech given on the day of his return to Egypt, he described the Milner recommendations as a 'veiled Protectorate – not independence'. Furthermore, in an interview with the *Egyptian Gazette*, Zaghlul demanded: the control of the Cabinet by the Zaghlulist delegation, rejection of the Milner Report, repeal of martial law, relinquishment of the Capitulations, no Judicial Adviser, curtailment of the powers of the Financial Adviser, no British troops except east of the Canal and the Sudan to become Egyptian territory.[217] Demonstrations in favour of Zaghlul continued, and he was elevated to the status of a national hero. Allenby reported that Egyptian Army officers were attaching themselves to Zaghlul and in Zaghlul's exalted and dictatorial state of mind, Allenby believed that it would not be beyond Zaghlul to attempt a *coup* similar to that of Arabi Pasha.

Nonetheless, and perhaps as a result of London's refusal to budge on the matter, Adli entered into discussions with Zaghlul over his support and inclusion in the delegation to London. By 15 April Allenby informed the Foreign Office that Adli's negotiations with Zaghlul were making good progress. Zaghlul had agreed to support the delegation on the terms offered by the British Government but he continued to insist upon being President of the delegation. The Foreign Office saw this as a major achievement, and although Zaghlul would 'no doubt be a nuisance on the delegation'[218] it thought it better that he was in London than left in Egypt.

However, these hopes proved to be over-optimistic. By the end of April an Egyptian delegation that included Wafd members looked unlikely. Allenby reported that negotiations between Adli and Zaghlul had reached deadlock over the presidency of the delegation and a breach between them now appeared likely. Adli maintained, with Britain's tacit approval, that it would not be in accordance with the political traditions of any country that the head of the government should take part in negotiations in a subordinate capacity.[219] In light of this development the Foreign Office had three alternatives: to leave matters entirely in Adli's hands, allowing him to send his delegation with or without the collaboration of the Wafd; to inform Adli that Britain could only negotiate with a representative delegation that would ensure the ratification of any agreement signed and so to hold off forming a delegation until the co-operation of the moderate nationalist elements was assured; or to suggest to Adli that he should force Zaghlul's hand by resigning and advising the Sultan to invite Zaghlul to form a Ministry with the negotiation of a political settlement with Britain as its first objective.

The first option obviously represented the line of least resistance, but in the longer term it would just store up larger problems. Any settlement negotiated under these auspices would never be ratified whilst, at the same time, it would represent a minimum from which all future demands would start. The second course would shift the burden onto Adli. The delay might create disturbances entailing the intervention of British troops, but Adli might achieve success in persuading moderates, such as Mohammed Mahmoud, Abd al-Aziz Fahmi and others to join him. The final option would largely be a bluff for it would be unthinkable that Zaghlul would accept it save on 'some absurd basis such as the withdrawal of martial law and the Protectorate as conditions precedent to taking office'.[220] If Zaghlul refused office, the Sultan could fall back on Adli whose position might be strengthened by Zaghlul's intransigence. However, none of these options were attractive to the Foreign Office as none really fulfilled Britain's wishes 'namely the formation of a sensible delegation enjoying such support in Egypt as will provide reasonable hope that a settlement which they accept will be ratified by an elected assembly'.²²¹ Indeed, as Milner noted in a letter to Spender 'certainly our role is to help them as much as we can by not sticking out over unessentials. I am sure the new plane of friendliness is what we must go for'.²²² But here was the intractable problem: what the Cabinet was prepared to accept did not meet the nationalists' demands, whilst any further outbreaks of violence would place further burdens on an already overstretched British military force. Furthermore, Lloyd George's unwillingness to weigh in on the Egyptian question provided a roadblock to a final resolution. 'I am sure that if L.G. would apply his mind to the subject […] in ½ an hour he would see the point at once. But the trouble is that he never will, as you know, attend to anything until it has got into a trough and he is called upon to save the situation.'²²³

By the beginning of May 1921 it was clear that Zaghlul and Adli could not reach an agreement. As a result, Adli advocated the formation of a delegation without Zaghlul as he believed nothing further would be gained by delay. Allenby agreed and did not believe there was any alternative to Adli's proposal. Even so, he remained sceptical over its chances of success. 'I cannot disguise my opinion that to arrive at an agreement with such a delegation and to secure ratification of such an agreement by an Egyptian Assembly will both be matters of the greatest difficulty.'²²⁴ Allenby continued that 'Adli's own attitude in negotiations will be greatly influenced by developments in Egypt which it is impossible to forecast. He will prove tractable or intractable according as Egyptian opinion shows signs of rallying to his standard and deserting Zaghlul, or vice versa'.²²⁵ A sense of despondency permeated the Foreign Office prior to the negotiations. Even at home the Foreign Office had to fend off the criticism of Cabinet ministers, notably Churchill. Curzon wrote to both Lloyd George and Churchill complaining of the latter's incursions into the arena of foreign affairs. 'Experience shows that incursions into Foreign Affairs by Ministers other than those directly responsible […] are seldom attended with much advantage, and not infrequently with some peril.'²²⁶ The Foreign Office was therefore left to navigate an almost impossible path between the limits demanded by the Cabinet²²⁷ coupled with the clauses in any agreement that the military were prepared to accept, and the desiderata of the Egyptian delegation.²²⁸

The Egyptian delegation arrived in London in July 1921 with the first meeting taking place on 13 July. In all, six conferences took place between the British and Egyptian negotiators throughout July and August.²²⁹ However, no community of interest could be found on Egypt's diplomatic status and the position of Britain's military occupation once independence was granted.²³⁰ But both parties were mindful of breaking off negotiations. For Curzon, this stalemate was preferable to having to return to his Cabinet colleagues confessing failure. He hoped that the lingering discussions would wear down the resolution of the Egyptian delegation. Adli was also loath to return to Egypt empty-handed where Zaghlulists would claim that the breakdown in discussion was a result of their campaign against the official delegation. Curzon attempted to break the deadlock by circulating a paper illustrating further concessions that might be offered. This was to be done in conjunction with the establishment of a Cabinet sub-committee to investigate the military requirements of imperial security should the negotiations breakdown.[231] Following a meeting of this Sub-Committee H A L Fisher, President of the Board of Education, wrote to Lloyd George, with whom he had enjoyed a friendship for some years. Fisher expressed his hope that Adli would be able to return to Egypt with an 'instrument which he was prepared to accept and with a programme which he was prepared to carry out'. Fisher rightly pointed out that whilst the immediate withdrawal of troops from Cairo and Alexandria would 'appear to be a confession of weakness and a concession to Zaghloul which we ought not to make', it would be a shame to see negotiations breakdown over this question when, perhaps in five years' time, the troops were removed anyway.[232] Fisher continued that he failed to see how it made 'any very material difference to our substantial hold upon Egypt whether the troops are within Cairo and Alexandria or within a striking distance of 24 hours from those two centres. We have to remember that whatever agreement we make we shall control the Sudan, the Canal and the Sea'.[233] The Irish spectre was once again raised: 'All I am concerned with is to send Redmond back with a good offer for fear that we may have to deal with a Michael Collins'.[234]

Curzon proposed several new concessions. Firstly, the withdrawal of British troops from Cairo and Alexandria to Abassia and Mustapha respectively following one year of tranquillity. British advisers in Egypt endorsed this option as safe; Allenby disliked it. Secondly, greater Egyptian involvement, but not a veto, in the negotiations over the abolition of the Capitulations and an alteration in the High Commissioner's title to Ambassador, both of which Allenby agreed with. Finally, the omission of the clause dealing with the extension of the Suez Canal concession.[235] Curzon emphasized his reluctance to suggest further concessions but stated that his hands were tied by the publication of the Milner Report in February 1921. Although he believed that these concessions would be refused, he wanted to 'show to the world that we [the British Government] had made the Egyptian Delegates a generous offer'.[236] Curzon again warned of the consequences of refusing any kind of concession:

> If they fail to obtain it [independence] their disappointment will be bitter and the country will unite against us. We can no doubt provide a sufficient force to prevent a general rising but there would no doubt be violence and assassination and a complete breakdown of the administration caused by a universal strike and the withdrawal of Government officials from their offices.[237]

However, Curzon met with strong opposition. Lloyd George believed that any further negotiation was impossible whilst Zaghlul was parading around Egypt denouncing the British government. Zaghlul's activities had made British public opinion hostile to any concessions and had also created a very bad atmosphere in the House of Commons where he was regarded as the representative of Egyptian nationalism. Lloyd George doubted whether any settlement except on the lines of the status quo could be carried through Parliament whilst Zaghlul continued his present activities.[238]

At a Cabinet meeting on 4 November 1921, and against the advice of Curzon and Allenby who advocated more liberal terms, the Cabinet decided that they would continue with the original terms of reference as agreed on 11 July 1921.[239] These terms were rejected by Adli who returned to Egypt. His nationalist credentials remained intact.[240]

To the Cairo Arena

Adli resigned upon his return to Egypt. The formation of a new ministry now became a matter of public interest and shifted the initiative from London back to the Residency in Cairo. Once it became clear that Zaghlul would not be called upon to form a ministry, the Residency was forced to deal with various and serious disturbances created by Zaghlul's campaign against the formation of any ministry. This agitation consisted of nightly demonstrations, attacks on the police, the shooting of two British soldiers and strikes by the Egyptian Bar, government officials and private schools. In response, Allenby ordered the arrest and deportation of Zaghlul and four of his associates on 23 December.[241]

On 8 January Sarwat Pasha agreed to form a ministry provided that the British government unilaterally declared the abolition of the Protectorate, that Egyptian independence was recognized and her control in foreign relations re-established. The Wafd extremists perceived Sarwat's conditions to be a treacherous bargain between the British, the Sultan and Sarwat himself. This fear was only increased by the deportation of Zaghlul.[242] With the prospect of further disorder and supported by his Cairo advisers, who advocated co-operation and partnership rather than forceful British leadership, Allenby approached London. Curzon, with the support of the Egyptian experts at the Foreign Office, endorsed Allenby's unilateral British declaration of Egyptian independence despite the threat of defeat at Churchill's hands which would result in an even greater loss of influence for Curzon and the Foreign Office. This time Curzon was mindful of Allenby's determination and accepted the argument that 'so long as Britain remained supreme in the eastern Mediterranean, and also the Canal, she had little to fear from an Egypt which, even if the Milner scheme were implemented to the full, would be no more independent than in the days of Cromer, Kitchener and Gorst'.[243] Moreover, the internment of Zaghlul and his followers ensured that the beneficiaries of any British concessions would be Zaghlul's adversaries.

Curzon put forward his proposal to the Cabinet on 18 January 1922. Churchill unsurprisingly opposed it. 'The suggestion that we should abolish the Protectorate before a treaty was made was in effect to concede to Egypt what we declined to grant to Sinn Fein.'[244] Lloyd George remained on the fence. In the absence of Austen Chamberlain, who was regarded as an accurate reader of Unionist backbench opinion, the Prime Minister refused to commit himself either way. This was largely a result of the nervousness over the Conservative reaction to the introduction of Lloyd George's Irish Treaty. Any further concession to Egyptian nationalism might have been interpreted as an indication of weakness and would have destroyed the fragile balance of the coalition. Instead, the Cabinet decided to summon to London Clayton and another official in order to gauge the accuracy of Allenby and Curzon's interpretation of events in Egypt.

Allenby had had enough and threatened to resign on 23 January. In response, senior Residency officials were authorized to offer a parliamentary resolution that would formally grant independence on the understanding that Egyptian ministers agreed to recognize Britain's reserved powers.[245] For Allenby this was not enough and he threatened to continue with his resignation. This action would be followed by the resignation of four principal advisers, including Amos and Clayton, from the Egyptian government 'virtually decapitating the imperial presence in Egypt at a critical moment'.[246] This latest development was met with a dim view by some in the Cabinet. 'The Cabinet should not be turned from its carefully considered policy by the pressure of our agents in Egypt. The whole British position was at stake; and it would be impossible to defend in Parliament the abandonment of the Protectorate yielding to the *force majeure*'.[247] Indeed, in a telegram that Curzon was instructed by the Cabinet to send to Allenby, Allenby's abilities to read and interpret the Egyptian atmosphere were called into question. 'If it be true that no Egyptian dare at present sign his name to anything short of complete independence, there must have been a change in Egyptian sentiment [...] We have as yet received no adequate explanation of this violent metamorphosis'.[248] From Paris, Hardinge, now British ambassador to France, observed:

> I have been watching with great interest the Egyptian negotiations and I would like to say how entirely I approve and sympathise with your attitude towards Allenby's proposals. With his big bluff external appearance, he really is the weakest man I have ever known, and since he has been there, he has given away the whole of our position in Egypt with the exception of the few vestiges that remain, which he would now like to surrender but for which I am glad to see you are fighting.[249]

It was even suggested that a replacement be found for Allenby.

Allenby was summoned to London for discussions. He met with Curzon for an hour and a half on 10 February. Curzon complained that 'he [Allenby] is unable to see any inconsistency over his own conduct or advice'. Curzon's real anxiety lay not in the 'loss of this particular agent (whose limitations we know) but from the feeling that his loss will involve us in a struggle in Egypt'.[250] Curzon urged Lloyd George to see Allenby with the least possible delay for the Prime Minister 'may succeed where I [Curzon] failed' in dissuading Allenby from resigning. Lloyd George duly met Allenby on 15 February and was greeted by Allenby's ultimatum. 'I have told you what I think is necessary; you won't accept it and I cannot make you. I have waited weeks for a decision and I cannot wait any longer so I shall ask Lady Allenby to come home'.[251] Lloyd George replied: 'You have waited five weeks for a decision, wait five minutes more'.[252]

Allenby achieved his goal. He could announce the unilateral declaration of the independence of Egypt so long as the reservations were referred to as explicitly as the concessions. Although a victory for Allenby, it was again suggested that he had not made clear to his advisers in Egypt the magnitude of the concessions involved in the offer of the British government and that he had failed to interpret the Cabinet's policy to the Egyptians just as he had failed to keep the Cabinet informed of the situation in Egypt.[253] Thus, with a distinct lack of supporters within the Cabinet, Allenby's apparent failure to communicate the seriousness of the situation was held responsible for the shortcomings of the British government in dealing swiftly and effectively with the Egyptian situation.

Nonetheless, Lloyd George's announcement to the Cabinet of the declaration passed unchallenged, indicative of his personal authority and of ministers' relief over the storm's passing which had threatened potential dangers at home and in Egypt. The contradictions and suspicions that underlay Britain's Egyptian policy since the agitation of March 1919 served only to emasculate Cabinet resistance when it faced Allenby's ultimatum. The conclusion of the Milner report and Allenby's intransigence made the Cabinet's will to resist more problematic. It was clear that, under the watchful gaze of the press and parliament, it would not be as easy to oust the respected Field Marshal as it had been with Wingate.[254]

The Allenby declaration

The Allenby declaration was announced on 28 February 1922. The recognition of Egypt as an independent state was conceded unilaterally in these terms:

1. The British Protectorate over Egypt is terminated, and Egypt is declared to be an independent sovereign state.
2. So soon as the Government of His Highness shall pass an Act of Indemnity with application to all inhabitants of Egypt, Martial Law as proclaimed on the 2 November 1914 shall be withdrawn.
3. The following matters are absolutely reserved to the discretion of His Majesty's Government until such time as it may be possible by free discussion and friendly accommodation on both sides to conclude agreements in regard thereto between His Majesty's Government and the Government of Egypt:
    a) The security of the communications of the British Empire in Egypt.
    b) The defence of Egypt against all foreign aggression or interference direct or indirect.
    c) The protection of foreign interests in Egypt and the protection of minorities.
    d) The Sudan.[255]

Conclusion

The 1922 Declaration has often been viewed as marking a watershed in Anglo-Egyptian relations: a tacit acceptance that after the massive struggle of the First World War Britain no longer possessed the strength and will to exercise her imperial prerogative. However, in reality, the declaration represented only the abandonment of imperial control, which had been imposed as a result of war against Egypt's suzerain power, and thus no different to the preceding period of Cromer, Gorst and Kitchener, that ministers regarded as the least important. A further complicating factor was the coalition government, the nature of its politics and personalities. Problems over imperial control within Egypt became inextricably linked with other domestic and imperial concerns, such as nationalism in India and Ireland, retrenchment and the importance of public opinion in maintaining the existence of the coalition. Furthermore, the vying for influence or attempts to claw back power lost during the ravages of prosecuting total war among the various personalities and departments, such as Curzon at the Foreign Office, Churchill as Secretary of State for War and later as head of the Colonial Office and Montagu as Secretary of State for India, all contributed to the confused vacillations evident in Whitehall.

The handling of Egyptian affairs was influenced by the difficulties of Empire elsewhere, ministerial rivalry and the domestic realities which faced ministers following the gargantuan effort exacted by the war. Throughout 1920 and 1921 it is possible to distinguish a gradual understanding that loosening the imperial bonds back to that of pre-1914 would not signal the end of Britain's dominance in the region. In fact, as a result of the war, Britain's dominance reached its zenith and by becoming bogged down in Egypt's internal affairs, Britain only increased its enemies and exhausted its imperial strength. In 1922 the Cabinet tentatively decided that Britain's interests were best served by lessening imperial control of Egypt's internal affairs as far as was compatible with safeguarding Britain's imperial interests, a return to informal Empire.

3

Negotiating at Home and Abroad: The CID, Labour and the Egyptian Nationalists, 1924

Following Britain's unilateral declaration of Egypt's independence in 1922, a number of attempts to negotiate a treaty were undertaken to resolve the reserved points and thereby place Britain's position within Egypt upon a firm legal footing. The negotiations tell us much about the divergent views and perceived needs of the political and military establishments in relation to the treaty's terms, the aims of the Egyptian politicians and the significance of the role of the High Commissioner in these negotiations. The negotiations across the whole of this period provide an insight into who was in charge of policymaking – Whitehall, the Chiefs of Staff (COS) or the Residency? How did the High Commissioner's relationship with the Foreign Office develop or change throughout the 1920s?[1] Importantly, the negotiations allow an assessment of both Labour and Conservative foreign policy approaches to the Egyptian Question prior to the formation of a National Government in 1931.

Egypt obtained nominal independence in 1922 but Britain had preserved its vital imperial interest and upheld the *status quo* by utilizing Egypt's political landscape to its advantage. For Britain, the Egyptian question centred on the problem of how to square the circle of traditional British foreign policy – the principle of non-intervention in the internal affairs of another country, and the vital necessity of protecting imperial communications.

1924 a Labour Government in Britain and the Nationalist Wafd in Egypt

The Wafd's electoral landslide in January 1924 under the new Constitution of 1923 and the formation of a Wafd ministry under Saad Zaghlul were based upon the programme of Egypt's right to real independence and the independence of the Sudan. As Zaghlul was assuming the office of Premier, Ramsay MacDonald was also taking office as Prime Minister and Foreign Secretary of the first Labour Government. Labour's frequent and outspoken expressions of sympathy with Egyptian nationalist aspiration could not but encourage Zaghlul to hope that he would receive more favourable treatment from the new Government, and that British policy would undergo a marked change. At the inaugural session of the Egyptian Parliament on 15 March 1924, a cordial telegram from Ramsay MacDonald was read out which offered negotiations in order to reach a settlement over the reserved points. The Egyptian response whilst welcoming was robust. Zaghlul defined the Egyptian position as one of entering negotiations in order to realize the complete independence of Egypt and the Sudan, declaring that Egypt was not bound by the 1922 Declaration.[2]

The gulf between the British and Egyptian positions soon became apparent. MacDonald instructed Allenby to undertake negotiations with Zaghlul in Cairo and to proceed to London only to sign any agreement reached. MacDonald hoped that low-key conversations would not attract the glare and criticism of the press and public that a fully publicized trip to London would. The failed Adli-Curzon negotiations were clearly at the forefront of MacDonald's mind: 'a breakdown would be fraught with even more unfortunate consequences'.[3] However, after observing Zaghlul and his style of conducting public affairs, Allenby believed it would be impossible to hold unostentatious negotiations in Cairo. 'We should find ourselves negotiating not with him but with the Egyptian public and press and in [an atmosphere of intense popular excitement].'[4] If negotiations were conducted in Cairo, Allenby feared that Zaghlul would be driven from a policy of compromise to one of extremism and emphasized Zaghlul's belief that MacDonald's accession to office enhanced his prospects of gaining a favourable settlement. 'He [Zaghlul] sees in personal contact with yourself more advantages than indirect communication through channels associated with your predecessors, and I think in the case of negotiations, arguments coming from you would have an effect on him very different from any communication to him by myself on your behalf.'[5] Allenby advocated that negotiations should begin as early as June in order to take full advantage of Zaghlul's strong position at the time and warned that any postponement of a visit to London would be compared to that of 1918 when Britain refused to allow a delegation to leave Egypt.

> He [Zaghlul] is on the crest of a wave. His position could not well be stronger, and I think that we should not only endeavour to take full advantage of it, but avoid any action that might prejudice it since it would be in virtue of his position only that he could [...] induce Egyptians to acquiesce in [a] solution that falls short of their maximum demands.[6]

MacDonald reluctantly agreed to Allenby's suggestion but requested that he should ascertain the general lines along which Zaghlul was prepared to negotiate. MacDonald added that 'until I have some indication that his aspirations do not conflict too hopelessly with our irreducible requirements regarding the Soudan [sic] and the defence of the Canal in particular, I would be unwilling to ask him to undertake negotiations in London.'[7] Although Allenby perceived current relations with Zaghlul to be favourable, they remained delicate.

> Whether or not negotiations be successful, our main occupation should be, I think, to make our position before the world secure against the least suggestion of bad faith. By appearing to put obstacles in the way of Zaghlul going to London, we should expose ourselves to the charge that our proposal was not honest, and that we were trying to evade the last step on the policy of [the] February declaration.[8]

Allenby's concerns seemed to be borne out by the reaction of the independent *al-Ahram* and the Zaghlulist *al-Balagh*. *Al-Ahram* perceived any negotiations that were held in Cairo as a sign that Britain considered they should avoid direct contact in London with an Egyptian delegation representative of the nation. *Al-Balagh* hoped that negotiations in London would result in a goodwill and confidence between the Wafd and the new Labour Government, something that was seen as impossible with their Conservative predecessors.[9]

In the face of such pressure and coupled with a warning from the Financial and Director-General of the European Department that a state of danger existed in the minds of the masses,[10] MacDonald relented and invited Zaghlul to London for negotiations at the end of June.[11] Zaghlul assured Allenby that although the opposition had become 'very Red', he had the Egyptian Parliament well in hand and could guarantee that it would approve any settlement that he himself accepted. However, he was in agreement with the opposition over the complete withdrawal of British troops from Egyptian territory and over the Sudan's independence. Of course this was in stark contrast to even the minimum requirements acceptable by the Committee of Imperial Defence (CID).[12]

The Committee of Imperial Defence

The CID had already begun examining the reserved points in 1923 when the Egyptian Constitution was settled. Concerns raised by the War Office over the poor accommodation and welfare of existing troops in Egypt meant that a decision over their location had to be reached, and quickly. In writing to the Chancellor of the Exchequer, Stanley Baldwin, in order to secure funds, Edward Stanley, the seventeenth Earl of Derby and Secretary of State for War, outlined that all of the men and most of the families at Moascar were under canvas. 'The ground there is sand subject to heavy drifting in storms and the temperature reaches at time [*sic*] as much as 112 Fahrenheit inside the double fly tent [...] If sickness were to break out amongst the troops and married families so situated I should find it extremely difficult to defend our inaction.'[13] By linking the health and welfare of the existing troops in terms of the construction of at least temporary accommodation to the question of their future location under any agreement reached with Egypt, Derby was attempting to assert the War Office's strategic necessities over the Foreign Office's political imperatives. Derby continued:

> I am convinced that there can be no question of reducing the Egyptian Garrison at present and I am sure that the military authorities would not agree to withdraw British troops and concentrate them at Alexandria, as suggested by Lord Curzon.[14]

In a War Office memorandum Derby argued that the 'protection of our interests in Egypt cannot be ensured by local defence of the Canal area'.[15] What concerned the General-Officer-Commanding British troops in Egypt, and which Allenby and the General Staff endorsed, was that internal disturbances caused by a sudden uprising of the population, political intrigue along Bolshevik lines or the defection of the Egyptian

Army could only be suppressed by retaining British troops in Cairo.[16] A British garrison in Cairo would not only be a deterrent to disturbances, but if the capital needed to be evacuated in the event of a serious uprising, and then re-occupied, this would be 'an operation of considerable difficulty', entailing 'serious loss of life and damage to property'.[17] The General Staff therefore recommended that British troops should be located in Cairo and its immediate vicinity, Alexandria and Moascar.

Inevitably the Foreign Office took a decidedly different view. From its political perspective, it pointed out that Britain's current position in Egypt could not be reconciled with the recent statement on the Franco-Belgium occupation of the Ruhr in the House of Commons.[18] Any popularly elected Egyptian Parliament would be no more accommodating over the question of British troops than Adli Pasha had been in 1921. The Foreign Office therefore believed that the most that could be hoped for was a temporary arrangement liable to revision after a relatively short period. The 'apparent willingness of the War Office to relinquish Kasr-el-Nil barracks [situated in Cairo] might facilitate the negotiations, and would, at any rate, furnish evidence to Egyptian opinion of the intention of HM Government to honour their undertakings [in the 1922 Declaration]'.[19]

The Foreign Office was also concerned that if negotiations failed, Egypt might bring the question before the League of Nations, there being no ground for British opposition to her candidature for League membership. The Foreign Office argued that rigid insistence on the permanent occupation of the interior of Egypt would give rise, at some point, to acute political difficulties. In the view of the Foreign Office, the undoubted physical advantages of Egypt as a base for a British Expeditionary Force was discounted by the political drawbacks and that any defence scheme for the Suez Canal had to take into account political as well as purely military considerations. Indeed, the Foreign Office recommended that effective British control of the Sudan and Palestine and over the Sinai Peninsula would secure the Suez Canal and, as a consequence, Egypt.[20]

Concerns over the military aspects of the Egyptian question were not only confined to the War Office. To the Navy, the Suez Canal was a vital link in Britain's imperial communications:

> The rise of a strong power in the East and the shifting of the strategic centre to distant waters has made it a link of such vital importance that it is difficult to envisage the possibility of our embarking on a war in the East unless we were quite certain that it could not be severed.[21]

Indeed, in an era of retrenchment the idea and costs associated with a review of naval plans from an entirely different standpoint – such as new fuelling bases and their 'high scale' defence protection – 'could hardly be contemplated'.[22] With alternative sea communications ruled out for reasons of financial expedience, it was left to the War Office to prepare for the defence of the Suez Canal.

The Colonial Office also expressed significant concerns pointing out that the Palestinian mandate only permitted British troops for the defence of Palestine and not as a base for British military requirements in Egypt and the Middle East generally.[23] As a result of these conflicting departmental concerns it was clear that two distinct and yet interlinked questions emerged: the defence of the Suez Canal and military policy within Egypt. These questions were examined by the Chiefs of Staff sub-committee on 28 September 1923. The Chiefs of Staff agreed that the most important consideration was the security of the Suez Canal, which could not be guaranteed without the presence of British forces in Egypt. To ensure the safety of the Canal and to maintain internal order, British forces needed to be stationed within the immediate vicinity of the main centres of population – Cairo and Alexandria. In the case of Cairo, this meant the stationing of troops at Abbassia,[24] a revision of the War Office stance expressed in July. It was stressed that if Britain failed to protect the lives and property of European residents, it would not be improbable that other countries would seek to establish a system of legation guards to safeguard the interests of their own nationals. There was also the wider issue protecting the status and position of the Army during this period of retrenchment across the military forces. If the War Office admitted that the Egyptian garrison could be reduced, or even withdrawn, 'everyone will say that the garrison is superfluous and the British Army can be reduced proportionately'.[25] Indeed, Derby agreed with Kenneth Lyon's, Derby's private secretary, assessment. 'We must stick to it that Egypt is the place, and the only place, for us to keep our troops. I am certain if once we relax our military hold over Egypt that we should not only put British interests in that country in grave danger but we might imperil the safety of the Sudan. The size of the Garrison for the defence of Egypt is for us to decide.'[26]

The importance of the RAF establishment at Aboukir was also emphasized. This base was vital to operations not only within Egypt but across the Middle East. Aboukir relied upon the British garrison at Alexandria for its protection, the withdrawal of which would necessitate a move to a site nearer to the cantonments selected for the troops and a loss of £500,000 already spent on the base.[27]

During the subsequent meeting of the CID to discuss the military policy within Egypt, Lord Derby acknowledged that:

> There would appear to be a divergence of opinion between the Departments as to the future location of the [British] troops. The Foreign Office [...] had suggested the Sinai Peninsula. In the opinion of the General Staff, Egypt was the only suitable place for the location of the troops with the object of protecting the Canal from outside aggression and also from internal disorder. The City of Cairo was the key to the position.[28]

While Derby was prepared to give up the Kasr-el-Nil barracks he wished the occupation of the Cairo Citadel to remain and also stipulated that it was essential to retain troops at Abbassia to protect the fresh water canal and Cairo. This was a view largely endorsed by Lord Cavan, Chief of the Imperial General Staff, who believed it was necessary to maintain sufficient troops in the immediate vicinity of Cairo.[29] Indeed, Lord Derby reported to the King that he hoped the future garrison of Egypt would be 'satisfactorily settled' within the next few days.[30] Leo Amery, First Lord of the Admiralty, supported the 'strong line taken by Derby [...] over the need for keeping troops in Egypt not merely on the Canal but within reach of Cairo and Alexandria',[31] but also recognized the Foreign Office point of view of avoiding unnecessary irritation to the sensibilities of the Egyptian people, by retaining troops in the Citadel for example. As regards the Canal, he suggested that as opportunity arose, the British Government should endeavour to obtain a further block of shares in the Suez Canal Company and appoint more British pilots to the Canal Service as vacancies arose.³² Sir Samuel Hoare, Secretary of State for Air, agreed. What concerned him was that Aboukir was the central depot for the air service across the whole of the Middle East, upon which large sums of money had already been spent as on the base at Heliopolis. Any withdrawal of British troops would entail the relocation of units then stationed in Egypt.³³

On the other side, Lord Curzon, Secretary of State for Foreign Affairs, emphasized that the question had to be examined from the strategic and political point of view. 'He was not prepared to dispute the strategical arguments [...] but] he was of the opinion, however, that the War Office were inclined somewhat to exaggerate their case.'³⁴ In consultation with Allenby, Curzon 'considered it to be wise and also to be safe', to withdraw the troops from the two capitals, Cairo and Alexandria. In his opinion, the Kasr-el-Nil barracks had to be evacuated and he further argued that the Citadel should also be cleared of troops. 'It would be most offensive to the *amour-propre* of the Egyptians if the British flag were to continue to fly from the highest point in the centre of the city.'³⁵ Curzon also suggested that those troops stationed in Alexandria should be withdrawn to the Mustapha barracks, two miles outside of the city.

Curzon underlined that in any forthcoming negotiations, he would argue that it was essential for Britain to maintain a considerable garrison within Egypt. However, he also encouraged the War Office to consider a reduction in the strength of the existing garrison in order to strengthen Britain's bargaining position. Lord Derby, however, was not prepared to agree to any reduction in the existing garrison until negotiations on the reserved subjects had been satisfactorily completed. Curzon refused to give way and pointed out that during the negotiations it might be necessary to fix a term of years within which the garrison would be reduced to a minimum. Curzon's steadfastness prevailed and it was agreed that they would be located outside Cairo and Alexandria at the Abbassia and Mustapha barracks, respectively.³⁶

Discussions over the military disposition were reconvened following the general election of December 1923 that brought a minority Labour Government into power for the first time. Although the divergence between the political and the military point of view persisted at a CID meeting on 4 February 1924, the Foreign Office position was undoubtedly strengthened by the recent Labour victory at the polls. Sir Eyre Crowe, Permanent Under-Secretary of State, was supported by Philip Snowden, Chancellor of the Exchequer, in emphasizing the importance of maintaining the British garrison in the Canal Zone. Snowden asked: 'Might not a contented Egypt [...] provide a better security than a strong garrison?'³⁷ Sir Sydney Oliver, Secretary of State for India, even commented on the notion of retaining a garrison in Egypt 'when we had only recently declared it to be an independent and sovereign state'.³⁸ Lord Cavan, Chief of the Imperial General Staff, stated that whilst the War Office might accept the stationing of troops at Abbassia on the outskirts of Cairo, an attack on the Canal would most likely come from a north-easterly direction. It was therefore necessary to maintain the bulk of the garrison close to Cairo so that it would not find itself with an actual enemy on one side and a hostile Egypt behind it. 'Internal order could only be assured by maintaining effective control over Cairo itself'.³⁹ A garrison in the vicinity of Cairo was also necessary to ensure the stability of the Sudan. Although the War Office had compromised slightly by agreeing to the stationing of troops at Abbassia if the Egyptian Government objected to the continued occupation of the Citadel and Kasr-el-Nil, it remained a military victory over the political point of view:

> In order to secure the safety of our vital communications through the Suez Canal, the best solution would be if the Egyptian Government could be induced to allow British troops to remain in Cairo and existing air stations at Heliopolis and Helouan. If this solution should prove impossible, the next best plan from a military point of view would be to negotiate for the retention of such a position as would enable a British garrison of moderate size, including air stations at Heliopolis and Helouan, to provide for the defence of Egypt from the north-east without being exposed to the danger of attack from the reverse side. The Air Force establishment at Aboukir should also be retained together with existing air stations on the Canal.[40]

The suggestion was even considered of offering the Egyptian Government rent for the continued use of the barracks within Cairo. This option, proposed by Stephen Walsh, the new Secretary of State for War, was cheaper than constructing new barracks at Abbassia at an estimated cost of £1,250,000.[41]

MacDonald found he had little room for manoeuvre between Zaghlul's demands for complete independence for Egypt and the Sudan and the CID's minimum requirements. Indeed, William Tyrrell, Assistant Under-Secretary of State at the Foreign Office, commented:

> As regards the Sudan and the British garrison in Egypt, we can make no substantial concessions to present Egyptian aspirations. The most we can hope for is that Zaghlul, if he finds himself confronted by a determination on our part to maintain our position with regard to these questions, may be inclined to ask for some face saving concessions.
>
> If, however, our Cairo reports faithfully represent the state of affairs in Egypt, I think we should only be deluding ourselves if we expected anything under the latter head: in other words we are faced with the prospect of having to settle our relations with Egypt in such a way as to leave no room for doubt that we mean to maintain our Imperial position in that country and retain unimpaired substantive control of the Sudan.[42]

This opinion was echoed in the 'gloomy views' expressed from Cairo by both Reginald Patterson, Financial Adviser, and Alexander Keown-Boyd, Oriental Secretary, 'both of whom ought to have their fingers on the pulse'. Similarly, Allenby's telegrams demonstrated 'how wide a gulf separates Egyptian aspirations from British requirements'.[43] In light of this, MacDonald added that 'unless there is reasonable chance of Zaghlul and myself agreeing, negotiations had better not begin'.[44] Zaghlul was also facing the prospect of difficulties at home. The re-organization of the opposition radical Nationalist Watanist Party had been undertaken in light of the impending discussions with Britain.[45]

Preparations for the negotiations

Under these difficult circumstances, MacDonald outlined his views on the negotiations to his Cabinet colleagues. 'Any Anglo-Egyptian agreement would have to be ratified by Parliament and therefore it would be impossible for Britain to evacuate the Sudan and to disinterest herself in that region.'[46] Perhaps in light of the Chiefs of Staff determined stance coupled with his minority in the House of Commons, it is notable that MacDonald's attitude towards the Anglo-Egyptian negotiations hardened. His statement in the House of Commons on 8 May 1924 referring to the February declaration was perceived in Egypt as an attempt to restrict the basis of negotiations to the reserved points.[47] The 1922 declaration and its reserved points were crucial to the Wafd, as the declaration had never been recognized by them or Zaghlul. Zaghlul made a counter-declaration informing the Egyptian Parliament that if Britain's invitation was qualified by any restrictions he would refuse and resign.[48] According to Allenby, Zaghlul desired to negotiate and in this he was supported by the majority of his ministers, influential partisans, the presidents of both houses and King Ahmed Fuad. However, opposition existed from his political opponents and certain elements within the Wafd 'who fear he is playing into our hands [and, therefore] he hesitates to take the plunge'.[49]

The principal area of contention for Zaghlul was that entering into negotiations on the basis of the reserved points would mean, even in their failure, an acceptance of the 1922 declaration and thus its bi-lateral character. Zaghlul's view, in Allenby's opinion, was that the declaration claimed for Britain 'rights which he [Zaghlul] does not admit, and [...] which he holds did not possess any legal basis'.[50] The Foreign Office was careful not to underestimate Zaghlul and was slightly more cautious than the Residency in pushing for negotiations. Murray noted that:

> Zaghloul [sic] Pasha is a political tactician of a very high order [...] Bearing in mind how successfully he outmanoeuvred Lord Milner in 1920 we must be careful to avoid being drawn into any admission which he could exploit to our disadvantage [...] The department may err on the side of caution, but Zaghloul Pasha as a negotiator is such a formidable opponent that it is only prudent to treat him with the utmost respect.[51]

This Foreign Office assessment of Zaghlul differed markedly from Allenby's which stressed that Zaghlul's manoeuvrings were a result of 'diplomatic inexperience, a natural shrinking from the precise, and apprehension of entanglement'.[52] Allenby attempted to smooth the path to the negotiations by re-affirming Zaghlul's good intentions and suggested that MacDonald should send a private letter to Zaghlul assuring him that it was not Britain's desire to tie his hands and that negotiations would probably take the form of a free and friendly exchange of views about Egypt.[53]

MacDonald, however, remained unmoved. Under pressure as a minority government to defend Britain's interests, MacDonald asserted that 'the position of Great Britain in Egypt, whatever the Egyptians may try to make out is juridical and internationally perfectly legal. Egypt was *de jure* and *de facto* a British protectorate'.[54]

It was apparent that MacDonald's chief reason for negotiating with Zaghlul was 'the probability that an agreement accepted by him would be endorsed by Egypt'.⁵⁵

In this seeming impasse, Zaghlul tendered his resignation to the Egyptian King on 29 June. However, this was later withdrawn in response to protestations from the King, parliamentary support for Zaghlul and public manifestations of unity. Allenby believed that the real object of Zaghlul's resignation might have been to free himself from ministerial responsibility while retaining power as head of the Wafd during any Anglo-Egyptian discussions, or to resume office after a demonstration of solidarity for him by the King, parliament and people behind him. Either way, it strengthened Zaghlul's position.

The prospects for successful negotiations continued to look slim following MacDonald's statement to the House of Commons over the Sudan. 'I should make clear to all concerned that I do not believe that this House would accept any arrangement which would break our pledges given to the Sudan or jeopardise the present administration and development of that country.'⁵⁶ This, coupled with some difficult debates in the Egyptian parliament over the Egyptian contribution to the upkeep of the British army in Egypt and the compensation of foreign officials leaving the service of the Egyptian government, prompted much local Arab language press comment. *Al-Balagh* opined that 'all the trouble comes from British commercial greed. The Sudan is to be a British cotton farm which will supply their looms and fill their pockets [...] and who propose to obtain their ends by brute force. Egypt should remain calm in the face of such provocation, and should concentrate on developing her propaganda in the Sudan'.⁵⁷ The more pro-British *Al-Mokattam* blamed the paralysis of Labour foreign policy on it having 'to bow before the joint Conservative and Liberal majority [...] for fear of being turned out of office'.⁵⁸ Whilst the Nationalist *Al-Liwa* drew attention to the success of Ghandi in India. 'Egypt could learn a lesson from the efforts of her Indian fellow sufferers'.⁵⁹ London complained that 'every action taken by HMG is consistently misrepresented by the Egyptian press'.⁶⁰ John Murray at the Foreign Office largely agreed and added that:

> I am afraid that Zaghlul is losing his grip on the situation. That he has done so is largely his own fault for he has allowed the wild men on his own side and in opposition, to push him along a road which, left to himself, he would have avoided.
>
> Politicians in Egypt are as irresponsible as the press whilst the public is ignorant, credulous and excitable: and to make matter matters more difficult, one and all suffer from that conceit which is the bane of most oriental nations.⁶¹

Nevertheless, and even after surviving a Watanist assassination attempt on his life, Zaghlul departed for Britain via France on 25 July.

The Sudan issue

There can be no doubt that in the run-up to the Anglo-Egyptian negotiations, the issue of the Sudan occupied a pivotal role. In Allenby's opinion, the Egyptians had six major concerns. These were: continued economic development in the Sudan, which could mean a shortage of water for Egypt; the fear of British interference with the flow of the Nile for political ends; an increase in the production of Sudanese cotton detrimental to the marketing of Egyptian cotton; a desire to share in the profits of the development of the Sudan; the security of Egypt's southern frontier; and a desire to use the Sudan as an outlet for Egyptian emigration.

Indeed, Sir Lee Stack, Governor-General of the Sudan and *Sirdar* of the Egyptian Army, reported in early May a considerable increase in Egyptian propaganda on behalf of their claims to the Sudan. Confined to the more populous northern towns, this propaganda was directed to 'the younger and more impressionable Soudanese, more particularly those in government employment', with promises of greater governmental control, political careers in the Egyptian parliament, improved prospects for promotion and the abolition of taxes.[62] Stack's fears were realized when rioting erupted in mid-June in Omdurman as a result of a political demonstration organized by Egyptian agitators. Egypt's reiterated claim to the Sudan and an increase in Egyptian propaganda lent encouragement, according to British sources, to 'minor Egyptian officials and discontented Sudanese ex-officers, and others who appear to furnish the element most susceptible to Egyptian propaganda'.[63] It was believed that this propaganda contributed to the disturbances at Atbara and Port Sudan and, of a far more serious nature, a demonstration by the military cadets at Khartoum School. Refusing to go on parade, the cadets instead marched through Khartoum with rifles and equipment proclaiming their loyalty and support for King Fuad, Saad Zaghlul and Ali Abd-el-Latif, leader of the White Flag League.[64]

From the British perspective, this demonstration called into question the future officering of the Arab and Sudanese units of the army.[65] The involvement of the railway battalion in the disturbances at Atbara gave further weight to Stack's suggestion of creating a Sudanese Defence Force and dividing his dual role of *Sirdar* of the Egyptian army and Governor-General of the Sudan. Although paid by the Sudan Government, the railway battalion was made up of 2,400 Egyptian conscripts. Stack clearly feared that increasing Egyptian propaganda would influence the attitude and discipline of the Egyptian army in the Sudan. 'There is not only the immediate fear of intrigues by Egyptian officers, but the further risk of the army itself becoming a menace to public security through its inevitable demoralisation, or as the result of its use as a political instrument'.[66] He continued: 'Practically all the younger Sudanese and Arab officers of the army are now more or less disaffected, and it is only a matter of time for the contagion to spread from the officers to the rank and file. Once this occurs a mutiny is inevitable.'[67] Moreover, with the coming to power of the nationalist Zaghlulist party, the dual office of *Sirdar* and Governor-General was increasingly untenable. The post of *Sirdar* was under the authority of the Egyptian Minister of War and under a compliant ministry this did not present any difficulties. However, the Zaghlulist government publicly announced that a British *Sirdar* was not 'in keeping with the dignity of Egypt as an independent country'.[68] The creation of a Sudan Defence Force was supported by Allenby who even went one stage further and advocated a policy of de-Egyptianisation within the Sudanese government 'even at the cost of administrative efficiency'.[69]

Much Egyptian propaganda in the Sudan was described as, on the one hand, demonstrating to the Sudanese the advantages of Egyptian rule for their co-religionists; while, on the other, it presented British policy in the Sudan generally, and the Gezira irrigation scheme in particular, as one of purely selfish exploitation. The Sudanese nationalist organization, League of the White Flag, formed in July 1920, was believed by C A Willis, head of Intelligence in the Sudan, to have close affiliations with Egyptian nationalists. Indeed, a memorandum on the League concluded that:

> It appears that the system is Egyptian, the advisers are Egyptian, the expenses have no other obvious sources and are attributed to Egyptians, the appeal is invariably to Egypt and the nature of the propaganda is Egyptian.[70]

Al-Mokattam compared the relationship between Egypt, the Sudan and Britain to that between France, Syria and Palestine. It accused France of placing artificial barriers between the Syrian and Palestinian people, just like those placed between Egypt and the Sudan by Britain. These barriers were maintained by force alone but that 'sooner or later the two peoples would affect political union'.[71] The Residency largely interpreted the Sudan disturbances as of an artificial rather than a spontaneous nature. Indeed, the Sudanese movement for closer Egyptian ties was perceived as an 'unhealthy growth [...] based upon no sincere national feeling of long standing'.[72] Nonetheless, the impact that this propaganda had upon the minds of the 'inexperienced and half educated, who play a considerable part in the politics of this country', was not to be underestimated. Clearly, Britain's and Egypt's future plans for the Sudan were greatly at variance but Allenby hoped that agreement could be reached on the basis of a continuance of the 1899 agreement.[73] Allenby confessed: 'I do not take a very sanguine view of the chances of arriving at an agreement with Egypt as to the future of the Sudan, but the advantages of an agreement would be so great that even [...] a slight chance should not be neglected.'[74] MacDonald concurred and in a debate over the Anglo-Egyptian position vis-à-vis the Sudan in the House of Commons, he stated:

> The position I have always taken up is, let us negotiate as quickly as possible. I know the great difficulties that Zaghloul [sic] Pasha has to meet. He has a new Parliament. It is a raw Parliament; it has not found its feet yet; it is a "heady" Parliament – in other words, it is a Parliament wherein human nature is represented. The more objective we are in these matters, the more good-humoured we shall be ourselves, and the more successful when we come to handle the questions that we have to find agreement. But I have felt that this cannot be allowed to drift, and drift, and drift. There must be plenty of time, but not too much of it. We must not be too slack about it. We must be reasonable, but not unreasonable.
>
> Therefore, I have quietly pushed to get this thing settled, to get the negotiations begun. But I have said this: While the negotiations are pending, neither Egypt nor ourselves ought to destroy the status quo. That must be honourably understood.[75]

Meanwhile, Stack's appreciation of the situation and his recommendations were wholly supported by the Foreign Office:

> They are [Stack's proposals] conceived in a practical and reasonable spirit but their acceptance by Zaghlul Pasha, who is not a free agent and who has committed

himself to the most extravagant claims in respect of the Sudan, can hardly be counted on with any confidence.

Sir Lee Stack has rightly emphasised that compromise or half measures in the case of the Sudan are out of the question. We must, therefore, be prepared to contemplate the situation which will arise if the negotiations with Zaghloul do not result in an agreement. It will be necessary for HMG to take some kind of unilateral action in respect of the army, financial control, and, in the fairly near future, the distribution of water.[76]

Murray and his colleagues did not hold out much hope that the British and Egyptian positions on the Sudan could be reconciled at this point. In fact, the Foreign Office was suspicious that Zaghlul was coming to England 'partly with the idea of gaining time so that the anti-British influences in the Sudan may continue their work, and partly with the hope, not so much of effecting an amicable settlement of outstanding Anglo-Egyptian difficulties, as of deriving some personal and political advantage from his visit'.[77] When examining the Sudan issue, the Foreign Office had to wrestle with two considerations. The first of these was British prestige if the Sudan question was brought before the League of Nations, all the time watched closely by the French, Italian and Belgian powers whose territories abutted the Sudan. Secondly, concern was expressed over Egyptian reaction to any strong measures taken by the British in the Sudan. The Sudan issue certainly coloured the approaching talks; MacDonald warned Zaghlul 'of how recent events are influencing me and how I regard them as making every prospect of friendly negotiation a mere figment of misplaced goodwill'.[78]

Allenby and Foreign Office recommendations

With Zaghlul's impending arrival, Allenby and the Foreign Office put forward their recommendations. In the Sudan, Allenby pushed for the continuation of the Anglo-Egyptian Condominium Agreement that incorporated Stack's proposals over the army, finance, personnel and legislative control, which substantially strengthened Britain's position. Allenby acknowledged that although this would 'certainly seem to constitute an obstacle to any extension or novel affirmation [of Egyptian] rights and interests in the Sudan',[79] the establishment of a Nile Water Board with a neutral chairman would be a substantial concession to Egyptian sensibilities. Allenby even argued that the proposal for the Governor-General to cease being the *Sirdar* of the Egyptian Army could also be regarded as a British concession. With this the Foreign Office concurred and asked for a clear definition of Zaghlul's position regarding both the 1899 Condominium Agreement and the recent disturbances in the Sudan.

Turning to Egypt and the protection of imperial communications, Allenby informed the Foreign Secretary that the Egyptian government would 'quite certainly not agree to the occupation of Cairo [by British troops] and it is almost equally certain that they would not agree to a concentration in Alexandria'.[80] The maintenance of a garrison in the Canal Zone was, however, 'not improbable'. The Foreign Office agreed with Allenby's assessment and in an unconcealed attack upon the position of the Chiefs of

Staff, War Office and the Air Ministry, declared that 'the maintenance of our troops in their present stations does not fit in with any logical line of policy except the eventual assumption of complete responsibility for the administration of Egypt; in other words, Crown Colony government'.[81] Instead, Allenby argued that by retaining the claim to protect foreigners, this actually provided Britain with the right of military re-entry or intervention in order to protect foreign interests, as opposed to purely British interests, as well as the right to protest against the military intervention of another Power to protect the interests of its own nationals. This would thereby allow the reduction of imperial troops that, in turn, would have a greater impact upon Egyptian sensibilities.[82]

It is clear that Allenby and the Foreign Office were largely of one mind in the run-up to negotiations, with Allenby infusing the discussions surrounding policy with a sense of realism that the CID assessments tended to lack. It is also interesting to note the conflicting assessments of Zaghlul by Allenby in Egypt and Stack in the Sudan. Allenby took a more genial attitude towards Zaghlul, believing that although:

> a bad starter and difficult to keep on course, I believe [Zaghlul] is really anxious to come to an agreement, that his first demands may seem to belie this intention but will probably prove to be a mere façade, and that not too much importance should be given to the apparently deep commitments of his parliamentary and public speeches.[83]

Stack, on the other hand, interpreted the recent statements and events as 'an attempt to defer a definite issue with the British Government and in the meanwhile to take all possible steps to undermine the British position in the Sudan. To allow him to pursue such a course would be fatal'.[84]

Thus, the men-on-the-spot strongly influenced preparations for negotiations and gave a sense of realism to the likelihood of their success. Indeed, the Foreign Office had learnt from its previous experience, with Lord Milner in 1920 and Lord Curzon in 1921. On both occasions it felt that Britain had been manoeuvred into a position of placing proposals before the Egyptian negotiators, which were then rejected. The Egyptians, therefore, had managed to secure concessions without conceding anything in return. The Foreign Office was not going to fall into this trap again and instead advised that Zaghlul should be asked: to define his attitude in regard to the Sudan; to formulate his suggestions for the protection of British imperial communications in Egypt; and to warn Zaghlul of the serious consequences for Egypt of default in the service of the Ottoman Loans of 1885, 1891 and 1894.[85] Again, the Foreign Office emphasized the importance of Zaghlul first producing adequate proposals and until that time 'we should confine ourselves to the role of critic'.[86]

The MacDonald-Zaghlul meetings

The first conversation between MacDonald and Zaghlul took place on 25 September 1924. It was also attended by Dr Hamid Mahmoud and Kamil Bey Selim on the Egyptian side and Walford Selby and John Murray from the Foreign Office. The conversations, after expressions of goodwill, immediately turned to the Sudan. After protracted wrangling over British and Egyptian actions in the Sudan, MacDonald attempted to tackle the heart of the matter – the organization and working of the Sudan Government. On paper there was a shared responsibility between Britain and Egypt, but in reality this was heavily weighted in Britain's favour. The Khedive could appoint and dismiss the Governor-General but only with the concurrence of Britain. Economic development and the maintenance of law and order in the Sudan were also dominated by Britain. What MacDonald wanted to know from Zaghlul was whether it was possible for the British government to fulfil what it believed to be Britain's moral obligations to the Sudanese, and, at the same time, satisfy the Egyptian government. MacDonald added, however, that 'it was absolutely impossible for them to agree to anything which would interfere with the fulfilment of those obligations'.[87] After this statement of position from the Prime Minister, Zaghlul was evasive for the remainder of the meeting, focussing instead upon the series of misconceptions between the two governments. A further conference was scheduled for 29 September.

At the second conference it was clear that the pressing issue for MacDonald remained the Sudan. His reluctance to begin talks over Britain's position in Egypt, even at Zaghlul's insistence, demonstrated that it was MacDonald's belief that the Sudan would be the real sticking point on which any agreement would fail and giving any ground over Britain's position in Egypt would be fruitless unless common ground could be found over the Sudan.[88] Furthermore, the amount of debate that the Sudan generated in the Houses of Parliament, particularly over the extension of credit to the Sudan Government for the development of cotton farming, was undoubtedly at the forefront of MacDonald's mind presiding, as he was, over a minority Labour Government.

Despite this, and only after much-dogged insistence by Zaghlul, MacDonald relented and the discussion turned to Egypt. Zaghlul emphasized that 'Egypt was his house and the house was his'.[89] The Egyptian proposals comprised: the removal of the British army from Egypt; the withdrawal of the Financial and Judicial Advisers; the British High Commissioner should become a minister like other diplomatic agents; Britain should drop its claim to protect foreigners and minorities in Egypt; and Britain should also relinquish the claim to protect the Suez Canal.[90] For his part, Zaghlul offered to make a 'special alliance' with Britain. MacDonald hinted that he 'might be able to get Parliament to agree to a good deal if he could assure them that Egypt and Great Britain were united by a treaty of such a nature that the two countries were in quite special relations of good friendship'.[91] With the principle of a treaty agreed, MacDonald suggested that Dr Mahmoud and Murray draw up a proposal, to which Zaghlul finally acquiesced.

At their third conference on 3 October, the discussion focussed on the details of an agreement. MacDonald demanded that British troops be stationed in positions to defend the Suez Canal. Zaghlul rejected this on the basis that it went against the very idea of an alliance. Zaghlul added that since the defeat of the Central Powers in the First World War, Britain now dominated the region, even barring the route to the Canal by her occupation of Palestine. MacDonald replied that this was inconsequential and that it would be impossible to protect the Canal from Palestine. He added that: 'The Canal was an essential British interest. No House of Commons could consent to give up its security in exchange for some paper assurance'.[92] Zaghlul offered that under the terms of an alliance both parties would share in the protection of the Canal whereby Egyptian soldiers would garrison the Canal and turn to Britain when help was required. For MacDonald this was, unsurprisingly, out of the question as the House of Commons would not accept anything less than a co-operative part for Britain in securing the security of the Canal. Equally, this was unacceptable to Zaghlul. 'It was quite impossible for the Egyptian nation and the Egyptian parliament to accept the existence of British military posts on the Canal or on any other part of Egyptian territory'.[93] With this, negotiations stalled. Excuses of inclement weather and a troublesome parliament in Cairo meant that the Egyptian delegation returned to Egypt without any agreement on the Sudan or on the protection of the Suez Canal.

Conclusion

In Egypt, throughout the conversations, press comment was restrained. The failure to reach any agreement was attributed to MacDonald's precarious political position. The opposition of the Liberal party to the Anglo-Soviet treaty, supported by the British press, coupled with the strength and influence of the CID and their insistence upon the strategic aspect of the Egyptian question were seen as forcing the hand of the Labour Party.[94]

Fundamentally it did not matter whether it was a Conservative or Labour Government in power in Britain or a nationalist Wafd Egyptian ministry; what mattered was that since the Egyptian Constitution of 1923 allowed a semblance of parliamentary democracy then any Anglo-Egyptian agreement would always be subject to the vicissitudes and criticisms of Egypt's opposition parties. This is where Egypt really does fall between two stools. Britain's policy of ruling through moderates applied in other areas of the empire, formal or not, simply could not be applied to Egypt due to its fledgling democracy.

4

The 'Colonized Colonizer': The Anglo-Egyptian Sudan

The Anglo-Egyptian re-conquest of the Sudan from Mahdist forces and the establishment of the Anglo-Egyptian Condominium in 1899 over the Sudan ensured that the area held a place of great significance in the Anglo-Egyptian relationship. Egyptian nationalists perceived the Sudan to be part of Egypt and the Nile Valley and so when Egypt's relationship with the Sudan is assessed, a dualism emerges. The nationalists themselves spoke from the perspective of the 'Colonized Colonizer'; they wished to bestow on the next generation of Egyptians 'an Egypt whose past greatness and regional power could be grasped once again in the Sudan, free of political and economic control of the British government'.[1] From the British perspective, large-scale investment in irrigation schemes accorded the Sudan a growing prominence within the Empire. More importantly, British concerns centred around the dissemination of Egyptian propaganda into the Sudan encouraging some form of politically unified Nile valley. These fears only increased with the inception of the League of the White Flag in July 1920, believed to have direct links with Egyptian nationalists. The failed Sudanese mutiny in August 1924 while a popularly elected nationalist Wafd Government was in power in Cairo seemed only to confirm British fears of Egyptian meddling.

This chapter will examine the development of Sudanese nationalism and its links to its Egyptian counterpart. How did the men-on-the-spot and their superiors in Whitehall perceive and interpret this nationalist threat? What was Khartoum's link with Cairo? What impact did the 1924 mutiny have on the Condominium relationship?

The 1899 Condominium agreement

The Anglo-Egyptian re-conquest of the Sudan under Major-General Kitchener was a military success, but the political problem remained. In British eyes it was impossible to conceive of the idea that the re-conquered lands be returned to Egypt, a country which had ruined the Sudan eighty years earlier and whose presence had been ejected by Mahdist forces. Similarly, British public opinion would not have acquiesced so easily in such a scheme. Moreover, Britain could not permit any foreign power to obtain supremacy in the Sudan and thereby threaten Egypt's fresh water supply and, by extension, British interests. Whilst these points suggested a British annexation of the Sudan, a number of other factors had to be carefully weighed up. The Scramble for Africa meant that the reaction of other, rival European Powers, especially France, was of 'paramount importance'.[2] Egyptian sensibilities had also to be taken into consideration. After all, the re-conquest had been undertaken in the Khedive's name and Egypt had contributed two-thirds of the campaign's cost. Moreover, there was concern that the Sudan would prove to be a white elephant. Lord Cromer asked, 'What was the point […] of acquiring on behalf of ourselves or the Egyptians large tracts of useless territory which it would be difficult and costly to administer properly?'[3]

Some form of hybrid government was necessary and as the Egyptian advance continued from Dongola to Khartoum, Cromer and the Foreign Office began to develop the idea of an Anglo-Egyptian condominium. This was enshrined in the 1899 Anglo-Egyptian Condominium Agreement whereby the Khedive of Egypt and the Queen of England would jointly rule the Sudan. Britain's claim to share in the governing and future development of the Sudan was based upon the right of conquest. According to the agreement, the Sudan was defined as the territories south of the 22nd parallel which had either never been evacuated by Egyptian troops or had been previously administered by Egypt and now re-conquered by the Anglo-Egyptian force, or those which might be re-conquered by the two governments in the future. Both the British and Egyptian flags were to fly together throughout the Sudan. Supreme civil and military command was vested in a Governor-General appointed by Khedival Decree on the recommendation of the British government and given full legislative powers. Any sort of internationalism was to be kept out of the Sudan, either through Egyptian legislation applying to the Sudan, Mixed Tribunals or consular agents.[4] The Sudan fell under Foreign Office jurisdiction rather than that of the Colonial Office and a separate Civil Service (the Sudan Political Service) distinguished the territory even further from other Colonial Office regions and therefore maintained the 'fiction of the Anglo-Egyptian partnership'.[5] Signed on 19 January 1899 by Lord Cromer and Butros Pasha Ghali, the Egyptian Minister for Foreign Affairs, this agreement was to be of a temporary nature but, in fact, it endured until Sudanese independence in 1956. Even though the Condominium Agreement remained in place M Daly points out that 'the salient point was that Britain had gained control of the Sudan, and while her policies and plans there would often have to take account of Egypt, that control was maintained by force, not by the Condominium Agreement'.[6]

The Sudan and the First World War

At the outbreak of the First World War the Sudan was nearly a million miles in extent, with a scattered population of approximately 4 million and governed by 110 British officers and officials distributed across fourteen provinces. The country could largely be divided into two: the north, mostly inhabited by Arab tribes, riverain and nomads; and the south, largely populated by black African tribes who were less closely administered and largely Christian.[7] Initially, the outbreak of hostilities with Turkey in 1914 created little excitement within the Sudan. Reginald Wingate, Governor-General of the Sudan and *Sirdar* of the Egyptian Army, believed that the exclusion of the word

Sudan from Britain's declaration of a Protectorate over Egypt largely contributed to this.[8] But even though the Sudan government received expressions of loyalty 'from all over the country,'[9] and the general Sudanese attitude was perceived as 'satisfactory', Wingate believed that:

> very careful watching is required – they are a bit nervous and excitable in temperament – [… and] I dare not go down to Egypt – all sorts of rumours and shaves would be the result and, with them, the personal equation of the G[overnor] G[eneral] and his British Officers and Officials bulks largely.[10]

Wingate continued that, on the whole, the senior Sudanese officers of the Egyptian Army approved of Britain's declaration of a Protectorate, but that the junior officers who had been brought up in the Egyptian nationalist schools felt that it had narrowed their career prospects. Nonetheless, he believed that there was 'nothing to worry about in this feeling, but they [would] require a little manipulation'.[11] This awareness of the link between Egyptian nationalism and its impact upon the Sudanese remained with Wingate when he assumed the position of High Commissioner for Egypt and the Sudan in January 1917.

Indeed, the First World War was to have a significant impact upon relations between the Sudanese government and the Cairo residency. Communication between Cairo and Khartoum was complicated by a duality of military and civil authority in Egypt and by the internal politics of the Residency.

> There appears to be two separate shows now. The GOC who of course comes into the administration a good deal under martial law and who corresponds with Lord K[itchener] directly on various matters without apparently bothering much about the [Sudan] Agency.
> Then there is the Triumverate (Cheetham, Graham and Cecil) who do the political side with the F[oreign] O[ffice] and whose deliberations are shrouded in mystery and secrecy.[12]

In terms of personnel, the war saw a number of significant changes. Lee Stack moved from his post of Sudan Agent in 1914 to that of Civil Secretary,[13] and was succeeded in Cairo by Gilbert Clayton, until then Wingate's Private Secretary.[14] When Wingate was appointed High Commissioner for Egypt in 1917, Clayton, a personal friend of Stack, remained as Sudan Agent. G S Symes, who had succeeded Clayton as Private Secretary in April 1914, and A W Keown-Boyd, Assistant Private Secretary, were both seconded to Egypt upon Wingate's transfer. This provided Wingate with 'a degree of continuity in his private office', but denuded Stack's from a wealth of experience.[15] As to their replacements, M J Wheatley and A B Howell became Private Secretary and Assistant Private Secretary respectively on 1 January 1917. R M Fielden replaced Stack as Civil Secretary while Wasey Sterry, a civil judge, replaced the retired Edgar Bonham Carter as Legal Secretary. R H Dun, formerly Advocate General, took over from Sterry as Chief Justice. Education did not escape unscathed either. James Currie, director since 1901, retired on the outbreak of the war and was replaced by J W Crowfoot, formerly Assistant Director.[16]

However, the most significant personnel change, and a direct result of the outbreak of war, was the resignation of the Inspector-General of the Intelligence Department, Slatin Pasha. An Austrian national, he was en route to the Sudan from leave in Austria when war was declared making his return impossible.[17] The replacement of Slatin Pasha was no simple task. As Inspector-General he had concentrated a great deal of knowledge solely in his hands. For example, secret agents were known to him alone and appointments were made on the basis of personal knowledge not personnel files. Moreover, although responsible for directing the Khartoum intelligence department, Slatin Pasha had 'neglected it, delegating work but not responsibility'. This meant that as the Sudan Government (and the Egyptian Army) entered the war they lacked any real system of intelligence gathering and assessment.[18] Finally, in 1915 'temporary assistance' was lent to the department which included a civilian inspector, C A Willis, who was later appointed Assistant Director at Khartoum in March 1916 and by May 1916 had 'effectively taken over the intelligence department'.[19] Slatin's departure left a massive void and it was one that remained vacant right up to the Sudanese mutiny in 1924.

Throughout the war, the Sudan Government was very much left to its own devices, to the evident frustration of Wingate who often felt as though he was excluded from discussions on policy over the status of Egypt.[20] In fact, Wingate largely relied upon Clayton and official communications to keep abreast of the situation in Cairo. Indeed, Wingate felt that the attitude of the Cairo administration had changed towards him personally under Sir Henry McMahon as Egyptian High Commissioner.[21] He felt personally affronted by the lack of importance accorded to the Sudan and the perceived rejection of his readiness to place himself and his experience at Cairo's disposal. This did much to sour relations between Khartoum and Cairo.[22]

Indeed, Wingate perceived the outbreak of war as an opportunity to advocate for the termination of the Condominium Agreement and establish direct British rule over the Sudan.[23] Wingate wrote in December 1914 that 'the present status of Egypt makes the Sudan more British than ever, and I am inclined to think that the time is not far distant when it may be possible to have a Sudan Army'.[24] With his many other preoccupations in Cairo, McMahon did little to discourage these ideas, simply leaving Sudan affairs to those more suitably qualified.

To ensure that the Sudan was not forgotten, Wingate used Herbert Kitchener, a former Egyptian Consul General and current Secretary of State for War, to 'promote the interests of the Sudan'.[25] For example, during 1915–16 and culminating in the conquest of Darfur, Wingate bypassed the Residency and consulted directly with Kitchener. This muddle of communication was lessened somewhat upon Wingate's replacement of McMahon as High Commissioner in Egypt in October 1917. Sir Edward Grey's offer of the High Commissionership came as a surprise to Wingate and although his life and work had been, and continued to be, the Sudan, the High Commissionership held great promise. It would mean that control of the Arab revolt and the operations in the Hejaz would be centred in one single authority, Wingate, as opposed to the current plethora of individuals – the Governor-General of the Sudan, the Arab Bureau, the High Commissioner in Cairo and the Commander-in-Chief of the Egyptian Expeditionary Force.[26]

In a social sense, the post of High Commissioner was also extremely onerous, requiring someone with ample private means. Wingate had none.[27] Nevertheless, he accepted Grey's offer the very next day but stipulated that he should 'continue to exercise supervision over Sudan affairs from Cairo'.[28] This was clearly in contradiction with the independence he had been attempting to cultivate in the Sudan for himself. Perhaps mindful of the economic and political problems that would face the Sudan once the war was over or to avoid the embarrassment of leaving the Sudan during the war for fear that the maintenance of order would crumble without his personal presence, his successor was to be appointed on an 'acting' basis only.[29] As to his replacement, Wingate nominated Colonel Lee Stack.[30] The expertise that Stack lost from both Symes's and Keown-Boyd's transfer to Cairo alongside Wingate ensured that Stack would rely upon Wingate and thereby allow Wingate a measure of control across the whole of the Nile Valley.[31] Unsurprisingly, once in Cairo, Wingate was overwhelmed by Egyptian and military affairs for the remainder of the war. In the same manner that Wingate had criticized McMahon, Stack also complained of 'how little time Wingate devoted to Sudan's affairs [… it was a case of] out of sight out of mind as far as the poor old Sudan was concerned'.[32]

All in all, the Sudan emerged from the First World War without having experienced any serious anti-government incidents. This was largely attributed to the circumstances within the Sudan rather than to any specific governmental policy to ensure Sudanese loyalty.[33]

In terms of military effort, the Sudan Government was involved in the war in a very limited way. The garrison consisted of about 14,000 men of the Egyptian army, composed of Egyptian, black and Arab regular units scattered in detachments over the country, with headquarters in Khartoum, where there was also a small British force consisting of one battalion of infantry and a detachment of garrison artillery.[34] With the outbreak of the Arab Revolt in 1916, a small force of Egyptian troops was sent in June to co-operate with the forces of the King of the Hejaz. The troops were first used in operations against Taif, provided garrisons at Yembo and Rabegh, and later transferred to Wejh and Akaba as the Sherifan army advanced. Mobile columns were also organized which carried out frequent raids on the Hejaz railway and telegraph lines, causing considerable damage to those services. In addition to these troops, the Egyptian army also provided officers and non-commissioned officer instructors to assist in training the Sherifan forces and provided large quantities of supplies, guns, rifles, ammunition and other war material. Throughout this campaign the Sudanese were 'interested and sympathetic, but did not seem especially concerned, looking at the Holy Places of the Hedjaz [sic] as being religious rather than political centres'.[35] The only other direct point at which the First World War touched the Sudan was in the south where a garrison was provided in 1916 for the northern districts of Uganda, all available troops in Uganda having been drawn off to the south to meet a possible menace from German East Africa.

The administration of the Sudan was handicapped by the difficulty of obtaining staff during the war. This was largely felt in the first two years of the war as 'vacancies occurred which could not be filled, and the strain on the experienced officials who remained was considerable'.[36] However, from late 1916 onwards it was possible to obtain a regular supply of officers, mainly invalided from the various theatres of war, for service with the Egyptian army. Many of these were then lent to the Sudan government for administrative work and thereby eased the shortage. As in Egypt, the British forces made exceptional demands on the Sudan for foodstuffs and animals. The burden of organizing the purchase and delivery of these supplies fell largely on the provincial officials, adding greatly to their normal workload. It was widely held that the success of British operations was, in large part, due to the 'efforts of the officials and loyal co-operation of the Sheikhs and Chiefs of tribes',[37] largely in the closely administered northern and central provinces. In the southern provinces, where administration was much looser, the main problems for the British were the maintenance of public security and the extension of government control over the remoter tribes.[38] Indeed, many of the disturbances experienced in the Sudan during the war tended to be of a tribal and local nature.

The official line, advanced by Sir Lee Stack in his annual report on the Sudan, was that the First World War had been a positive experience for the Sudan economically and politically:

> The war has on the whole been a period of marked economic prosperity for the Soudan. The possibilities and advantages of trade have been brought home to a larger number of the population than before, and there has been an advance in energy and initiative, particularly among those who make their living by cultivation.[39]

Politically Stack pointed to the support shown by the 'more intelligent and educated men' to the British cause. Their 'loyal messages and speeches' of support, coupled with their 'active assistance' to the British cause, were communicated to the mass of the people. In Stack's opinion this goodwill and loyalty manifested itself by the 'readiness with which they responded to the demand of camels, cattle, and grain for the Expeditionary force in Egypt'.[40] Stack's opinion does seem somewhat at odds with the conclusions of the Milner Mission to Egypt (written one month later) which blamed the 1919 uprising on the disaffection of the Egyptian upper and educated classes and the massive strains placed upon the *fellahin* by the labour corps and the requisitioning of food and animals. Nevertheless, Stack believed that this spirit of co-operation had drawn the people closer to the government, and induced a greater sense of unity among them which would have a high value in their future development.[41]

The post-war Nile valley

Ever since Britain's declaration of a Protectorate over Egypt at the outset of the First World War, Wingate and his colleagues had advocated the termination of the Anglo-Egyptian Condominium Agreement and the establishment of direct British rule in the Sudan.[42] In fact, the growing Egyptian nationalist movement at the end of the war made this option appear even more desirable. Moreover, both Wingate as High Commissioner in Cairo and Sir Lee Stack in Khartoum were at one in advocating some positive action from officials in Whitehall. With Egyptian nationalist propaganda beginning to permeate the northern reaches of the Sudan in late 1918, Wingate and Stack felt the status of the Sudan a real and pressing issue. Wingate was concerned over keeping the Egyptians out of the Sudan, pointing to Lord Cromer's pledge to the Sudanese that they need never fear again being ruled by the Egyptians from Cairo. To Wingate this meant that should the situation in Egypt alter in such a way as to give Egyptians self-government, their authority would not be allowed to extend to the Sudan. Wingate's reasoning:

> In the Sudanese, we have a people exceptionally loyal to the British, and who are quite content with the system of government which has been established – a system which makes the Sudan a British possession in practically everything but in name. As long as we hold the Sudan, we hold the key to Egypt, because we control the source of its water supply.[43]

Wingate clearly perceived the Sudan to be the lynchpin of Britain's position in the Nile valley.

> The Sudan is of the greatest importance to us strategically – besides being a future asset to the Empire of no mean value. But as an *appendage* of Egypt (under a form of independence or even quasi-independence), it would be a positive danger to us – for it would at once become a hotbed of Egyptian and foreign intrigue, and would draw into its sphere of disturbance the adjoining possessions of Central Africa, Abyssinia, Eritrea &c. I cannot too strongly emphasise this danger, nor can I too emphatically urge on His Majesty's Government the importance of maintaining the *status quo* of the Sudan.[44]

Indeed, Wingate advocated that the Sudan's divorce from Egypt could be rendered still more final by obtaining the assent of the Powers at the Peace Conference to its absorption into the British Empire. Furthermore, he suggested that the Sudan's incorporation into the British Empire might be compensation for allowing Egyptian nationalists a greater share in the government of Egypt.[45] For Wingate then, the Sudan continued to occupy a position of great importance.

Unsurprisingly, the Foreign Office adopted a more neutral attitude to both Wingate's and Stack's urgings. Whilst any attachment of the Sudan to Egypt was seen as 'dangerous', and likely to 'lead to trouble', it was also pointed out that the Egyptian Government had made large monetary advances to the Sudanese Government and therefore had 'a perfect right to be interested in the Sudan'.[46] Wingate's suggestion of raising the status of the Sudan at the Paris Peace Conference was also rejected. Ronald Graham, a former Counsellor at the Cairo Residency and Assistant Under-Secretary at the Foreign Office, minuted that 'there should be no danger of pressure being brought to bear upon us as regards concessions to native demands in Egypt'.[47] In fact, the single point of agreement between the Foreign Office and those on the spot was that Stack should be confirmed as Governor-General of the Sudan and *Sirdar* of the Egyptian Army, thereby dispelling 'any doubt there may be in the native mind as to the intentions of His Majesty's Govt in regard to the future of the Sudan'.[48]

This initial Foreign Office rejection did not deter Wingate. In London during the Egyptian disturbances he reflected upon the growth of Sudanese national aspirations. Wingate believed that Britain was now facing the early beginnings of a Sudanese nation and it was up to Britain to decide how to proceed.[49] Wingate was entirely in agreement with Stack's assessment of the Sudan situation and both advocated the 'loosening of the tie which now binds the two countries together'.[50] In practice, this would mean the elimination 'as soon as possible from the Government [of] the Egyptian element, both administrative and clerical'.[51] This policy had two main aspects – separation from Egyptian control and the promotion of a national idea among the Sudanese. As regards the first there existed several practical obstacles. Firstly, there were not enough educated Sudanese to replace existing Egyptians within the administration. Stack commented 'the Egyptians are too useful to be dispensed with hastily, even though they are not altogether liked by the people they have to govern'.[52] Secondly, the military needs of the Sudan would have to be supplied without the use of Egyptian troops as the use of military service amongst the Sudanese had not been undertaken on any large scale as yet. Thirdly, the question of finance was the most difficult of all. Although Sudan revenues could support the civil needs of the country, it could not yet support a sufficient military force without help from outside. Increased taxation to plug this gap was deemed to be unwise. Presumably this was why irrigation schemes, such as that at Gezira, were favoured because they increased the Sudan's cotton growing potential. It was believed that the establishment of the Gordon College at Khartoum, the military school and the school of medicine would eventually provide enough trained administrators to take over from their Egyptian counterparts and thereby allow the Sudanese to govern themselves.[53] Stack was also careful to take into consideration the significant Egyptian interests in the Sudan, such as the Nile upon which Egypt depended for its irrigation. Since the reconquest of the Sudan was originally undertaken to safeguard the frontier of Egypt, its ultimate development could not be determined in a way that would involve a breach of Britain's promise to Egypt.[54]

Therein lay the difficulty. Wingate and Stack wished to detach the Sudan from Egypt and tie it more closely to the British Empire using as a pretext the reported desire of Sudanese notables and the growth of Egyptian nationalism as a rationale for their policies. However, Egyptian-Sudanese relations were intricately linked, and if the Foreign Office refused to sanction a definite break between the two nations at the Paris Peace Conference then a number of policies would need to be instituted in order to encourage a de-Egyptianization of the Sudan.

Stack advocated using the education of a national idea amongst the Sudanese, to mould and nurture it in order to meet British ends.[55] Not only did Stack and Wingate emphasize the differences between Egypt and the Sudan as reasons for its detachment, but they continued to highlight the dangers posed by Egyptian political activity upon a tranquil Sudan.[56] Using Britain's heavy economic investment in cotton growing within the Sudan, Wingate advocated the acceleration of this de-Egyptianization policy and perhaps even to:

> find [...] a suitable moment to definitely take over the Sudan, thus eliminating the intensely unpopular Egyptian element and inflicting on the Egyptian Nationalists who have sought to gain their ends by lawlessness, pillage and murder, the

well-deserved punishment of losing a country which their misgovernment had forfeited many years ago and which could never have been regained without British aid, which has made the Sudan what it is today – a land with a great future and strategically and materially a most valuable asset to the British Empire.[57]

No doubt angry over the Egyptian disturbances and his enforced stay in London, Wingate believed that any failure to remove the Sudan from the Egyptian orbit would render the position of the Governor-General and his subordinates 'most difficult', and would also prepare the way for either 'Pan-Islamism and fraternisation with the Egyptians as the only alternative left open'.[58] As to the reaction amongst the Sudanese, Stack and Wingate pointed to the support they received from religious leaders who presented Stack with two signed letters in which they claimed to speak for the people of the Sudan and wished to disassociate themselves entirely from the Egyptian nationalists. They also made it clear that any claim on the part of Egyptians to speak for the Sudanese in demanding the withdrawal of the British was 'quite unfounded'.[59]

Stack's continuing communications with Wingate over policy even after his supersession by Allenby in 1919 demonstrated how close the former High Commissioner and Governor-General were on questions of policy. Allenby, preoccupied by Egyptian events and whose knowledge of the Sudan was less than Stack's, would unhesitatingly agree with Stack's assessments. In defence of the Foreign Office, the heady days that followed the end of the First World War were not conducive to establishing a definitive Sudanese policy, even more so since the Foreign Office was split between George Curzon in London and Arthur Balfour in Paris during the Peace Conference. However, perhaps it was Stack who inadvertently was the cause of the British government's paralysis over the Sudan. Since his despatches continued to stress the loyalty of the Sudanese to Britain and their antipathy to Egyptian rule, the Foreign Office felt that any action could be postponed because there were other more pressing matters to be dealt with.[60]

Stack's and Wingate's views were not just the preserve of a former chief and his deputy. On a visit to the Sudan in February 1920, Sir Milne Cheetham also reported the enthusiasm for Britain shown by 'all the classes of native population, and their openly-expressed desire for British as opposed to Egyptian administration'.[61] Cheetham also warned that a safe and proper outlet needed to be found for this excitement, especially since the older tribal chiefs who could remember Egyptian maladministration were a passing generation. Cheetham believed that failure to settle the status and future of the Sudan in relation to the British Empire could only lead to future trouble.[62]

The Milner Mission and the Sudan

Despite the Sudan's status not being within the original the remit of the Milner Mission,[63] Lord Milner delegated Alexander Keown-Boyd, formerly of the Sudan Political Service, to examine the Anglo-Egyptian relationship with the Sudan. Unsurprisingly, Keown-Boyd adopted the stance advocated by Stack and Wingate and suggested that the 'ideal solution would be an immediate clean cut from Egypt'.[64] This inclusion of the Sudan ensured that, upon publication of the Milner report, Stack's and Wingate's beliefs reached a much wider audience than hitherto possible. Indeed, the Milner report viewed the political bonds that had, in the past, united Egypt and the Sudan as fragile and that the Sudan had 'never been really subdued by, or in any sense amalgamated with, Egypt'.[65] The Sudan was perceived as being virtually in British hands under the Condominium Agreement under which the Sudan had flourished, materially and morally. In addition, Wingate's Governor-Generalship was rated by Milner as 'one of the brightest pages in the history of British rule over backward races'.[66] Britain's position in the Sudan was seen as popular, which led to peaceful and progressive conditions throughout the country, a theme endorsed by Stack and Wingate. The report was definitive in that the Sudan should not be subjugated to Egypt:

> While the contiguity of Egypt and the Soudan [sic] and their common interest in the Nile make it desirable that some political nexus between the two countries should always be maintained, it is out of the question that this connection should take the form of the subjection of the Soudan to Egypt [... The Soudan] is capable of and entitled to independent development in accordance with its own character and requirements.[67]

However, the report would not go so far as to say that the Sudan should come under the control of the British Empire, for the 1899 Convention had already defined the political connection between Egypt and the Sudan and did not envisage hampering the independent development of the latter country.[68] The Milner Mission believed that the Sudan should continue its development of a more decentralized administration under British supervision. A central bureaucracy similar to the Egyptian model was seen as unsuitable for the Sudan and indigenous 'agencies for simple administrative needs' should be used as far as possible in order to avoid retaining a large number of Egyptian officials in the civil service of the Sudan. This decentralization and de-Egyptianization represented an attempt by the British to ensure that anti-British nationalism, as demonstrated in Egypt in 1919, would not have the opportunity to develop in large urban centres or through Egyptian officials.

For Britain, maintaining the pretence of the 1899 Convention ensured that Egypt had to continue its annual subvention to the Sudanese Government until the revenues from cotton cultivation were firmly established. The report recognized that Egypt's primary interest in the Sudan was the flow of the Nile and that any development of the Sudan would present a conflict of interest. Britain was to be charged as the arbiter in any such contest as not only did it command the sources of the White Nile and possess an interest in the welfare and development of both Egypt and the Sudan, but it also had a 'special interest of its own in the increase of the cultivation of cotton' – a nod to the Lancashire mills.[69] It was believed that with a large number of engineering works for storing water and raising the river levels in the Sudan, and possibly Uganda, an efficient irrigation system would provide sufficient water for all. The Milner report therefore recommended the establishment of a permanent commission composed of technical experts and representatives of all the countries concerned – Egypt, the Sudan and Uganda – to settle all questions relating to the regulation of the Nile and to ensure the fair distribution of its waters.[70]

With regard to education, the report warned against educating the Sudanese in a system which fitted pupils for little else than employment in clerical and minor administrative posts. An overgrown body of aspirants to government employment, whose hopes would be disappointed, would create a body of malcontents susceptible to anti-British propaganda. According to the Milner Report there was 'no room in the Soudan for a host of petty officials'. Rather, education should be aimed towards agriculture, industry, commerce and engineering.[71]

Turning to the military aspect of Anglo-Sudanese relations, the military forces in the Sudan were part of the Egyptian army and were paid for by Egypt despite more than half the force comprising regiments that were recruited in the Sudan. The post of Governor-General and *Sirdar* of the Egyptian Army had been combined and the mission recommended that at the first convenient opportunity a civil Governor-General should be appointed, and the *Sirdar*, with his headquarters staff, should be re-transferred to Egypt. The report also alluded to the creation of a purely Sudanese Army under British command, although the main obstacle to this was finance since the revenue of the Sudan only just covered the cost of the civil administration. This financial dependence of the Sudan on Egypt was undesirable and provided an additional argument for reducing Sudanese military expenditure and thereby its financial reliance upon Egypt. Milner was adamant that 'the sooner the finances of the two countries can be entirely separated the better'.[72] It was believed that savings could also be found by rationalizing the Financial Department and relaxing its control over other departments. Accordingly, the appointment of an independent Auditor-General was recommended to oversee this streamlining. In relation to any negotiated Anglo-Egyptian settlement, the report emphasized that the 1899 Condominium Agreement had to be recognized in order to secure the independent development of the Sudan whilst safeguarding the vital interest of Egypt in the waters of the Nile. The report thereby dismissed any Egyptian nationalist claims to the Sudan as an exclusively Egyptian possession.

Thus, it is possible to see within the Milner Report reflections of the position advocated by Stack and Wingate. By actively encouraging the political, financial and military separation of the Sudan from Egypt, the Milner Report suggested the Sudan would look to Britain for support and guidance rather than the Egyptians north of the border. More importantly, this informal control of the Sudan would be significantly cheaper than any formal annexation to the British Empire in terms of financial and military costs and also possibly avoid any serious political repercussions in Cairo.

The peaceful and acquiescent nature of the Sudan was confirmed by Allenby's visit between January and February 1921. Allenby reported contentment amongst the religious leaders, merchants and notables over the existing government and loyalty to British rule.[73] Any Egyptian propaganda directed towards obtaining the support of the Sudan for a programme of Egyptian and Sudanese independence by Egyptian officials of the Sudan government was met, for the most part with 'contempt or ridicule'.[74] Thus, Allenby concurred with Stack's assessments of the Sudan in believing that 'we have little to fear from such [propaganda] attempts in the Soudan, so long as His Majesty's Government make it quite clear that they intend to continue to govern the Soudan, and that they will not consider any suggestion that the Egyptians should be given a larger share in the control of the Soudanese'.[75]

The loyalty of the Sudanese Arab and non-Muslim black troops runs throughout this period. From the time of the Egyptian disturbances of 1919 they were perceived as being unaffected by events in Egypt and could therefore be relied upon.[76] In British eyes it was the junior Egyptian officers who posed the greatest threat, either through disseminating anti-British propaganda or through more direct means of demonstrations or open revolt.[77] This was a view shared by Stack for two reasons. Firstly, although the Sudan was home to a large number of Egyptians, who had been strongly affected by the nationalist movement in Egypt, they were handicapped by the relative remoteness of the Sudan. Therefore, any active movement by Egyptian nationalists would have a very real chance of failing and possibly backfiring. Importantly, the composition of the Egyptians was a significant factor. Since they were all government servants without any independent element among them, such as lawyers, press-men or landowners, they had much more to lose than their counterparts in Egypt if they pitted themselves against the Sudanese government and failed.[78] Secondly, the Sudanese were perceived as having no sympathy with the movement. Stack commented:

> They are not in themselves politically ready for self-Government – they are not sufficiently organised or coherent for such an idea to occur to them, I think, for some time yet – and they much prefer us as rulers to the Egyptians.[79]

Even discussion by the Sudan's religious leaders of developing the Sudan as an independent nation and not as a 'mere appendage to Egypt' was interpreted in a more anti-Egyptian rather than anti-British manner. 'They [the Sudanese] know their interests to be bound up with the British, and that they look forward to a closer identification with the British Empire rather than the Egyptian Sultanate.'[80]

1924 Disturbances and the Anglo-Egyptian negotiations

The impending Anglo-Egyptian negotiations of 1924 concerning the reserved points of 1922, which included the Sudan question, once again permitted a reconsideration of Britain's position within the country and the future status of the Sudan. In a memorandum examining this issue, Stack advocated a set of proposals which were to 'define the continuance of British predominance in the Sudan in a more emphatic manner'.[81] Stack declared that at the heart of his analysis were the wishes and welfare of the Sudanese people themselves who he believed wished to remain under British administration. The declaration of Egypt's independence meant that three essential conditions needed to be met: the establishment of the best possible form of government for the Sudanese, the preservation for Egypt of the benefits for which she joined Britain in the reconquest of the Sudan – namely security from any disturbance or danger from invasion on Egypt's southern frontier, and the right of access to the Nile waters for existing and any future irrigation of land under cultivation. Any suggestions that these conditions could be met by a totally Egyptian administration were promptly dismissed. Stack believed that past Egyptian misrule coupled with its desire to restrict the development of the Sudan's irrigation schemes quite beyond what was necessary for the protection of Egypt's own interests would stunt the Sudan's development.

Of course, the Sudan itself was deemed as being unfit for 'self-government' with the greater part of its population composed of 'backward races'. Although the policy of Sudanization and the use of indigenous institutions for local administration was progressing,[82] it was thought that the overwhelming majority of the Sudanese people would be unfit to take any share in a joint Egyptian-Sudanese representative government. As a consequence, any subordination of the Sudan to Egypt would mean the domination of the Sudanese by the Egyptians.[83] Stack warned that Britain's position was under attack from a barrage of Egyptian propaganda in the form of seditious circulars, an intensive campaign in the Egyptian press and efforts by Egyptian officers and officials stationed in the Sudan to prejudice the indigenous inhabitants against British administration and enlist their sympathies with Egyptian aspirations.[84] As a result, Stack reminded the Foreign Office that 'the people are still easily worked upon by any movement of the moment which may attract their sympathy, while the potentialities for religious fanaticism lie at very little depth below the surface'.[85]

The vast area of the Sudan was governed by only 110 British officials, which meant that much relied upon their individual personalities. Stack warned that 'if that confidence [in the British Government] is [...] destroyed the whole foundation of the existing security would disappear'.[86] British prestige had been eroded in the last five years through British support of an independent kingdom of the Hejaz, the proposed withdrawal from Mesopotamia, the concessions to Egypt and the consequent discharge of British officials. This had produced in the indigenous mind an 'impression of uncertainty as to British policy, and put his [Sudanese] confidence in the British Government to a severe test'.[87] Stack was confident of the loyalty of the Sudanese as long as they were assured that Britain intended to remain. He therefore urged British policymakers that during the forthcoming Anglo-Egyptian negotiations it should be made clear 'beyond all doubt that a policy has been decided on, which means both in form and in fact the complete predominance of British control [over] the Sudan and the complete exclusion of any increase in Egyptian influence'.[88] Stack continued:

> This administration must be single, and not divided. Any concessions by the British to the Egyptians would be construed by the Sudanese as confirming their apprehensions of an ultimate British withdrawal, while, apart from this, it would be impossible to maintain their confidence and respect if the sequence of all the accusations and abuse of the last five years were seen to be, not the reaffirmation of British predominance, but the admission of the Egyptians into a still greater share in the administration.[89]

Although realizing that this would be unacceptable to the Egyptians, Stack argued that with the present state of public opinion in Egypt any arrangements which provided for the retention of any form of British control would be equally unsatisfactory to them. 'This factor is in itself a strong argument against half measures'.[90] Therefore, Stack urged that since the 'Egyptians will most probably be dissatisfied with and intrigue against any settlement which the British Government could possibly accept, it is not only useless, but dangerous, to propose any compromise which would open to the Egyptians effective opportunities for such intrigue'.[91]

It was not only political factors that had to be taken into consideration but economic ones too. Britain had invested heavily in irrigation schemes. For example, the British government had guaranteed interest up to 3 ½ per cent on loans of up to £3,000,000 for the Gezira scheme in 1914. In 1919 this was increased to £6,000,000 and rose further under the Trade Facilities Acts of 1922 and 1924 to £14,920,000.[92] Consequently, the Egyptian government could control and hamper the Sudan's financial policy, whilst the British government, which had an equally important stake, would have practically no machinery of control to counterbalance that of Egypt.[93] The Sudan's economic potential was highlighted by the growing Lancashire demands for cotton. Tom Shaw, the Labour Member of Parliament for Preston, stated that 'the organised employers and workmen of Lancashire were one in this matter: they wanted all the development possible'.[94] Indeed, William Henry Himbury, Managing Director of the British Cotton Growers Association, had toured the Sudan in 1923 and met Allenby as he travelled through Egypt. Himbury concluded that Gezira was 'one of the finest cotton propositions in the Empire'. However, the amount of water available, due to Egyptian sensibilities, limited this potential. 'The Sudan has truly the making of a great cotton country; that it will finally develop into one I am convinced because we shall get our water and solve our insect and disease troubles, therefore whatever happens the Sudan must remain British, and it is to Lancashire's interests more than any to see to it'.[95] Murray of the Foreign Office read Himbury's report with the 'greatest interest' and was 'gratified to find that you [Himbury] take such a favourable view of the position in the Sudan, a view which I feel will be justified by events'.[96] The Foreign Office stance, therefore, was unsurprising:

> Weakening of our position or, what comes to the same thing, strengthening of the Egyptian position in the Sudan will not mean that the country will merely be slightly less efficiently administered: it will mean an inevitable upheaval not, perhaps immediately but within a very few years. Africa is a powder magazine and such an upheaval might easily have an effect far beyond the confines of the Sudan.[97]

However, the Foreign Office's hands were largely tied by the Condominium Agreement. If Egypt refused to compromise, the British government could do little more than offer a general assurance that Britain would not 'agree to anything which would impair their power to fulfil [their moral] obligations' to the Sudanese.[98] The implication here was that the political and economic position would be secure.

In framing any Anglo-Egyptian settlement over the Sudan, three factors needed to be considered. These were the 1899 financial regulations, the Egyptian army and Egypt's water rights. The original 1899 Convention had tied Khartoum and Cairo together as the Sudan required Egyptian financial aid in its early years. This took the form of assistance to meet budget deficits; credits for capital expenditure on railways, housing, telegraphs and general development; and provision for military defence. Since 1912 Egyptian assistance to meet budget deficits and aid with capital expenditure was no longer necessary and therefore Stack advocated a rethinking of the current terms. In his view, the existence of the Sudanese debt to Egypt had to be recognized and the amount and terms for interest payments settled and incorporated into any Anglo-Egyptian agreement. Moreover, whilst the Cairo-Khartoum financial linkage was acceptable under a British Financial Adviser within the Egyptian government, any alteration of this under an Anglo-Egyptian agreement could prove detrimental to British involvement within the Sudan and provide such 'opportunities for vexatious interference as to seriously hamper the conduct of the normal financial business of the Government'.[99]

As a consequence, Stack proposed that any financial agreement would be overseen by a Joint Anglo-Egyptian Commission, sitting in London, and as long as the Sudan government met its obligations in regard to any settlement, the Joint Commission would have the right of access to the accounts and full information, but no right of interference in the conduct of normal financial policy. Even though this Joint Commission would have very little power, Stack believed it would go some way to satisfying Egyptian sensibilities, with London being its seat rather than Cairo in order to avoid questions of Sudanese finance being raised for debate in the Egyptian Parliament.[100]

The Egyptian army was by far the most important and difficult question of all. Apart from one British infantry battalion and a detachment of garrison artillery, the Egyptian army provided the bulk of the Sudan's military garrison. No part of the cost of maintaining this force was met by the Sudan and, in fact, through the traffic which it brought to the Sudan Railways, it actually provided a source of revenue to the Sudan government.[101] More importantly, the Governor-General's role as *Sirdar* of the whole of the Egyptian Army meant that he fell under the authority of the Egyptian Minister of War. This was acceptable so long as Egyptian policy was under British control. However, the Declaration of Independence of 1922 and the advent of a Zaghlulist ministry in February 1924 meant that a much more active interest was taken in military affairs by the Egyptian Government. For example, the *Sirdar's* discretionary power to replace British officers as vacancies occurred was made subject to the approval of the Egyptian Council of Ministers. Under Saad Zaghlul's regime this was extended and the Minister of War insisted that every matter, even of minor importance, should be referred to him. Zaghlul also announced publicly that Stack should be replaced by an Egyptian officer: 'It was not in keeping with the dignity of Egypt as an independent country that a foreigner living in the Sudan should hold that position.'[102] Zaghlul went even further and demanded that all officer posts should be held by Egyptian nationals. While Stack could see the reasonableness of Zaghlul's aspiration, he also believed that by making it public it had destroyed his own authority as *Sirdar* and that of all other British officers in the Egyptian army. In Stack's opinion, this state of affairs was already influencing the attitude and discipline of Egyptian officers and this would then spread to Sudanese officers and down into the rank and file, thereby making the position of British officers intolerable.[103]

In any future settlement Stack recommended the military garrison of the Sudan be placed under the sole control of the Governor-General. He also recommended that the Egyptian army should be divided into two distinct parts – an army for Egypt and a Sudanese army, each under its own *Sirdar* – and that the Governor-General of the Sudan should be in command only of the latter. Stack appreciated the inherent difficulties in achieving this but urged that 'half measures will not meet the case, and that the time has come frankly to face the situation'.[104]

Of course, the main difficulty lay in the financing of a Sudanese army. It was highly unlikely that Egypt would continue to finance an army that was completely removed from its control. Consequently, Stack proposed a solution whereby the Sudan could have an army suited to its own needs, costing about half of the existing Egyptian army in the Sudan, to which Egypt would make an annual contribution in order to benefit from the peaceful administration of the Sudan and security of Egypt's water rights.[105] Stack calculated that the maintenance of the Egyptian army in the Sudan cost the Egyptian government £E1,200,000 annually. An army sufficient for the internal requirements of the Sudan could be maintained for half that sum at £E600,000 annually. Stack believed that the financial difficulties could be overcome if Egypt, instead of spending £E1,200,000 annually on maintaining her own troops in the military garrison of the Sudan, made an annual contribution to the Sudan government of £E500,000. The balance of £E100,000 would be met from the Sudan government's own resources.[106] While Stack conceded that the 'period of transition would be a matter of some difficulty [...] the prospect of an ultimate annual saving of £E700,000 combined with the unequivocal guarantee of her water supplies ought, provided that a reasonable atmosphere can be created, to prove not unattractive to the Egyptians'.[107] This was certainly an optimistic assessment!

Allenby generally supported Stack's proposals with regard to the future status of the Sudan and endorsed them to the Foreign Office. Nonetheless, he perceived a number of difficulties ahead. As regards the financial aspects of the question, Allenby believed that Stack's recommendations should not deter a reasonable Egyptian negotiator. In exchange for a loss in direct control, Egypt would gain money and a right of inspection of accounts. However, Allenby did point out that the Egyptian government would prefer Cairo and not London as the seat of the proposed Anglo-Egyptian Finance Commission 'a point on which we might find it convenient to give way'.[108] On the question of the Sudanese Defence Force, Allenby believed this would be:

> Highly distasteful to the Egyptian Government, for reasons of sentiment and chauvinism, and that is will be a matter of extreme difficulty to persuade them to agree both to surrender their existing measure of control, and to pay £E500,000 a year towards the upkeep of the defence force.[109]

Allenby also perceived that the guarantees offered to Egypt over the integrity of her southern frontier would be estimated by the Egyptians at far less than their real value. Moreover, the water guarantee would lose much of its attractiveness if the proposed Nile Control Board were not so composed as to convince Egyptian opinion of its impartiality. Allenby saw the chances of an Anglo-Egyptian settlement over the Sudan as slim. That said, he also believed that 'the advantages of an agreement would be so great that even a slight chance should not be neglected'.[110] Allenby was also concerned that Egyptian propaganda over the Sudan had begun to take on a life of its own and was becoming a permanent feature of the Anglo-Egyptian relationship:

It is true that the intense agitation which is being conducted in Egypt about the Sudan had its origin in the desire of Zaghlul Pasha's opponents to embarrass him, and that it is moved at present by sentimental rather than material considerations, but he has himself been carried away by it, to all appearances, and we shall be fortunate, should negotiations be unsuccessful or not take place, if it does not continue, and if propaganda in the Sudan does not tend to increase.[111]

Indeed, in view of this Egyptian propaganda Allenby raised the question of whether Stack's proposals actually went 'far enough in the direction of securing our interests in the Sudan, and the peaceful and prosperous progress of the inhabitants'.[112]

The Foreign Office tended to share Allenby's assessment. Whilst Murray praised the 'practical and reasonable spirit' of Stack's proposals, he doubted their acceptance by Zaghlul 'who is not a free agent and who has committed himself to the most extravagant claims in respect of the Sudan'.[113] Stack's emphasis that British compromise was out of the question was accepted by the Foreign Office. Murray therefore advocated that Britain had to be prepared to contemplate the situation which would arise if the negotiations with Zaghlul failed. 'It will be necessary for HMG to take some kind of unilateral action in respect of the army, financial control, and, in the fairly near future, the distribution of water'.[114] Indeed, Murray later commented that 'the Egyptian Army as at present constituted should disappear so far as the Sudan is concerned and be replaced by a locally raised gendarmerie containing no Egyptian officers'.[115] That this proposal was becoming a real possibility is shown by the Foreign Office's readiness to advocate that the Treasury meet the £500,000 cost of this as calculated by Stack. Copies of Stack's memorandum were distributed to the Treasury and War Office who were urged to meet with the Sudan Government's Financial Secretary and other members of the Governor-General's Council, who were in London, to explore in more detail the financial and military aspects of the Sudan question.[116]

The Sudan's political landscape

As the possibility of the Anglo-Egyptian negotiations between the British Prime Minister Ramsay MacDonald and Saad Zaghlul over the reserved points grew so did political tension. Indeed, from as early as May 1924, Stack reported to Allenby a considerable increase in Egyptian propaganda in supporting their claims to the Sudan.[117] Initially, the effect of this propaganda was confined to the more populous towns of the North, such as Khartoum, Khartoum North, Omdurman, Medani and El Obeid, but its influence was gradually moving southwards towards Gezira. This propaganda, supported by a vigorous press campaign in Egypt, was aimed at the 'younger and more impressionable Sudanese, more particularly those in Government employment'.[118] It promoted the idea that Britain would surrender her control over the Sudan as 'she [Britain] will find she had no right to the country', as she had in the case of Egypt.[119] In contrast, Egyptian rule promised a larger share for the Sudanese in the government of the Sudan, political careers within the Egyptian Parliament, improved prospects of promotion in government service and the abolition of taxes.[120]

Stack pointed out that even those Sudanese who supported the British administration regarded the lack of a British response as ominous and were 'eager for an indication from official quarters to remove their uncertainty'.[121] Thus, while Stack did not perceive this propaganda as posing a serious threat for the moment, he warned that 'definite steps may be necessary to counteract it in the near future'.[122]

Allenby was in general agreement with Stack. He reported that the reiteration of Egypt's claim to the Sudan had recently occupied a large part of the energies of the Chamber and the press. This activity was judged to have lent encouragement to the minor Egyptian officers, and to others who comprised the element most susceptible to Egyptian propaganda.[123] The Foreign Office was unsurprised at Stack's reports of increased Egyptian propaganda in the Sudan. Murray minuted that 'this development has long been foreseen and it is to be anticipated that the natives of the Sudan will be subjected to an ever increasing torrent of Egyptian propaganda'.[124] It was believed that whilst a categorical statement from the British Government over Britain's intention to remain in the Sudan would be enough to steady the Sudanese it would not stop the Egyptian propaganda itself.[125] Murray even raised the possibility that, in time, the situation would become so serious that 'HMG will have to pass from words to acts [...] leading to the elimination of Egyptian influence and Egyptian officials as a result of British annexation'.[126] Nevertheless, the Foreign Office followed Stack's advice and Lord Parmoor, Lord President of the Council and joint leader of the House of Lords with Viscount Haldane, made a statement in the House of Lords declaring Britain's intention of remaining in the Sudan and upholding the *status quo*.[127]

The Sudanese government strongly believed that they possessed a ground swell of support amongst 'reasonable Soudanese opinion'. Indeed, the Khartoum intelligence Department reported a meeting at the house of Sayed Abdel Rahman-el-Mahdi (the Mahdi's son) at which a leading number of Sudanese government officials and notables of Khartoum Province declared their support for British rule.[128] C A Willis, head of the Khartoum Intelligence Department, further believed that the majority of the young provincial *kadis*, district *kadis*, schoolmasters, officers of Arab origin and most well-to-do merchants belonged to this group or the so-called *intelligentsia* party. According to Willis, this party, although to a certain degree influenced by Egyptian newspapers and propaganda, had no direct relations with Egyptians. Their motto was: 'the Sudan for the Sudanese'.[129] In the run-up to the MacDonald-Zaghlul negotiations of 1924, the Khartoum Intelligence Department interpreted the *intelligentsia* party's actions as rejecting completely the notion of Egyptian rule, preferring instead British rule so long as Sudanese institutions were developed and a time limit was set on British instruction. Popular in the northern and central provinces the *intelligentsia* party attempted to spread its principles among the better educated class and were perceived as being the party to take notice of as the current generation of provincial rulers passed away.

The second opposition party in the Sudan took a much tougher stance against the British. The two main leaders were Sid Ahmed Osman-el-Gadi and Abd al-Latif. They advocated that 'on no account should the Sudan people ask [for] guardianship from the English, who would, when unchecked in the Sudan reduce the Sudan and Sudanese to servitude'.[130] They believed that the existence of the Egyptians as partners would at least become a check to British designs. A former graduate of Gordon College, Abd al-Latif was understood to be the nominal leader of the League of the White Flag. This organization was thought to have been formed in July 1920 and that it supported some form of Nile Valley unity.[131] The League called for 'all Egyptian parties struggling for the independence of the Nile Valley to consolidate their efforts and direct them towards the grand aim. The Sudan is for Egypt and Egypt is for the Sudan'.[132] Khartoum intelligence believed the League possessed links with the Egyptian nationalists in the form of monetary aid and contacts at both *al-Akhbar* and *al-Liwa* (pro-Nationalist Egyptian newspapers) in order to promote their cause. Although it was impossible to prove the League's Egyptian connection legally, the British authorities viewed its methods as an exact replica of those adopted in Egypt.[133] For example, demonstrations by a nucleus of students, and the hiring of young boys to break the windows of European cafes, were previously unheard of in the Sudan and all bore Egyptian hallmarks. British intelligence in the Sudan also pointed to the frequent exchanges between Egyptian officers and officials with the leader of the League or other relevant people. Also, the publication in the Egyptian press of subscriptions for the families of imprisoned Sudanese was held as evidence of Egyptian support for the League.[134]

The composition of the League was different to that of the *intelligentsia* party. Its members were largely composed of employees in the lowest two grades of the Sudan administration or discharged and discontented officers. Attempts were made to widen the basis of the party by attracting sons of 'good' families to join their ranks. Although this was largely unsuccessful, Willis believed that it would continue to grow and form the 'noisy' party within the country.[135] Therefore, although the Intelligence Department and Stack reported a great sense of loyalty among the Sudanese towards Britain, it was wary and alive to the danger posed by Egyptian agitation. This was a view that Allenby supported and communicated to the Foreign Office.[136]

Willis's assessment of the White Flag League was accepted by the Foreign Office in its entirety. 'There seems no doubt whatever that Egypt is primarily responsible for the inception and maintenance of [and] have signed on a budding Sudanese nationality movement to lend a spontaneous appearance to the business for the benefit of the outside observer'.[137] In order to keep a careful watch on the development of the White Flag League, the Residency in Cairo requested the Governor-General to file his appreciation of reports compiled by the Sudan Intelligence Agency. Indeed, without an overview, the Residency complained that 'it is impossible for us here to know how much importance to attach to such reports'.[138] Thus, a clear line of assessment of the development of the League movement was not established until after a series of disturbances during the summer of 1924. British policy was yet again shown to be reactive in what was judged in Cairo and London to be a largely quiescent Sudan.[139]

In fact, Allenby was nervous over the Anglo-Egyptian negotiations and how their failure and even success would impact the Sudan. The most worrying feature was that the disturbances of 1924 'owed their inspiration, and probably their direction to Egyptian agency'.[140] What concerned Allenby was what this new development held for the future and the prospect of a settlement. Allenby was concerned that even if Zaghlul returned with an Anglo-Egyptian treaty it could not be regarded as certain that the existing Egyptian movement in favour of recovery of the Sudan, and consequent Egyptian efforts to influence the course of events in that country by every available means, would come to an end. The chief opposition to any Anglo-Egyptian treaty would be over the Sudan. On the other hand, the failure of the Anglo-Egyptian talks would probably result in an increase of Egyptian propaganda within the Sudan. Allenby also pointed out that the 'strength and scope' of such opposition was impossible to estimate, warning that:

> The 'Sudan' movement in Egypt [...] is an unhealthy growth, in that it is based upon no sincere national feeling of long standing. It owes its recent prominence, indeed, largely to political manoeuvre by the Opposition. Nevertheless, it would, in my view, be premature to assume that it has not produced a deep impression upon the minds of the inexperienced and half-educated, who play such a considerable part in the politics of this country.[141]

It was not only the politics of 'chauvinism or fraternity' which motivated the Egyptians' concern for their relations with the Sudan, but more practical, political and economic considerations. These revolved around a potential shortage of Nile water due to the increased economic development of the Sudan, British interference in the flow of the Nile as a political lever, increased production of Sudanese cotton in direct competition with Egyptian cotton, an Egyptian share in the profits of the Sudan's development, security of Egypt's southern border as the population of the Sudan increased and the Sudan as an outlet for Egyptian emigration. As a result, Allenby advocated close links to, and encouragement of, the *intelligentsia* party, as identified by Willis, to ensure that Britain's current position as temporary guardian was not usurped by Egypt. For British policymakers, encouraging Sudanese nationalism was an essential check to Egyptian calls for a united Nile Valley. Since Egyptian efforts to influence the Sudan relied largely on the agency of Egyptians stationed within the country – officers of the army, and officials of the civil administration – Allenby recommended that Stack's proposals for a Sudanese Defence Force should be effected even if an agreement could not be reached with Egyptian negotiators on this point and that the policy of de-Egyptianization of the civil administration should be accelerated, even at a cost to administrative efficiency.[142] As a counter to Egyptian influence, Allenby suggested special emissaries, or a propagandist press. Moreover, the growing community of religion between Egypt and the Sudanese was also seen to be a potential threat to Britain's position, especially in the possible event of the return of the Caliphate to Egypt.[143] Indeed, Stack, Allenby and the Foreign Office were in full agreement that whether or not a negotiated settlement could be reached over the Sudan, the Egyptian officers and officials 'have got to go'.[144]

The disturbances of June–August 1924

The tensions created by the Anglo-Egyptian negotiations in the Sudan finally erupted into a series of demonstrations between June and August 1924. These had the effect of pushing the Sudan up the political agenda. The Sudan Government largely believed that Egyptian nationalists were behind these demonstrations providing support and finance to disaffected Sudanese. Further demonstrations also occurred at the beginning of August with disturbances at Atbara and Port Sudan and a demonstration by the military cadets at Khartoum Military School. Although the disturbances and demonstrations at Atbara and Port Sudan were serious, they were not judged as having any lasting impact. A A W Skrine, Governor of Mongalla, remarked 'their discipline has never been good'.[145]

The demonstration by the cadets, however, was judged to have far-reaching consequences. Refusing to go on parade, the cadets instead marched through Khartoum with rifles and equipment proclaiming their loyalty and support for King Fuad, Saad Zaghlul and Abd al-Latif. From the British perspective, this mutiny called into question the future officering of the Arab and Sudanese units of the army.[146] Colonel Huddleston, Adjutant-General of the Egyptian army, suggested that 'whatever new formation replaces the Egyptian army in the Sudan must, to ensure its reliability, be officered mainly by British officers assisted by a certain number of very carefully selected ranker officers'.[147] Huddleston also recommended that the military school be reorganized with the immediate removal of disloyal ex-cadet officers.[148] London went further, suggesting that 'at first sight the obvious course would seem to be to try the ringleaders and close the military school *for good* pending the reorganisation of the Sudan Defence Force'.[149]

Since the military school belonged to the Egyptian War Office, closure would bring about a direct conflict between the Governor-General as *Sirdar* and the Egyptian Minister of War. This and the involvement of the Egyptian railway battalion (which consisted of 2,400 Egyptian conscripts) in the disturbances at Atbara gave further weight to Stack's suggestion of creating a Sudanese Defence Force and separating his dual role of *Sirdar* of the Egyptian Army and the Governor-Generalship of the Sudan. Stack clearly feared that increasing Egyptian propaganda would influence the attitude and discipline of the Egyptian army in the Sudan. His concern centred around his belief that 'practically all the younger Sudanese and Arab officers of the army are now more or less disaffected, and it is only a matter of time for the contagion to spread from the officers to the rank and file. Once this occurs a mutiny is inevitable'.[150]

Although these disturbances did not pose a fatal threat to the British position, it was because the British believed it demonstrated a growing Egyptian connection at a time of concerted British attempts to regularize the Anglo-Egyptian relationship.[151] In London to advise on the forthcoming Anglo-Egyptian negotiations with MacDonald and the Foreign Office, Allenby and Stack were able to drive home their point:

> I feel that the time has come to emphasise the very serious danger involved in deferring steps to clear up the situation. The Egyptians are already taking active steps to undermine British authority and particularly to stir up dissatisfaction in the army [...] I must make my opinion quite clear that unless a definite policy is effectively adopted in the immediate future by the British Government, which will enable me to have the garrison of the Sudan under my sole control and freed from Egyptian influences, I cannot guarantee the maintenance of order.[152]

MacDonald understood that Stack's position was 'obviously excessively awkward'.[153] He also accepted that if the Egyptian government were not going to play the game in the Sudan, he was prepared to tell them that they must evacuate the Sudan altogether.

'We must preserve a steady and quiet demeanour, and carefully guard ourselves against fussy and unnecessary action. However, we must act vigorously when necessity required it.'[154]

MacDonald highlighted the decisive steps already taken to demonstrate and ensure British dominance. These included the despatch of a battleship to Alexandria, the arrival of a cruiser at Port Sudan, the immediate transfer of a British battalion from Egypt to the Sudan and its replacement by a further battalion from Malta. MacDonald also agreed with, and even encouraged, the accelerated disbandment of the Egyptian railway battalion to be completed by the end of the year. In the meantime, MacDonald agreed with Stack's suggestion that any large bodies of the railway battalion concentrated at any one place, such as at Atbara where over 1,000 men were stationed, should be immediately sent back to Egypt. MacDonald, repeating the advice of the Foreign Office,[155] was clearly anxious to show Zaghlul the tough stance of his Labour administration and silence any Conservative critics. Stack believed that further measures were necessary and recommended the closure of the Khartoum Military School because of the manifestation of disaffection there. Since this would also entail a financial saving for the Egyptian government, MacDonald agreed and assured Stack that he would 'give him his support and would not let him down'.[156] As to further action, MacDonald felt that the 'time had come to speak very plainly to the Egyptian Government',[157] and suggested making a representation to the Egyptian government reiterating that the British government was committed to the Sudan. Allenby agreed that a statement such as this would be useful but only if it was delivered at a 'psychological moment', and that the present movement of British battalions into the area was 'worth half a dozen speeches'.[158] Allenby pointed out that statements had already been made by both Lord Parmoor, Lord President of the Council, and MacDonald and that the Egyptians had 'merely laughed […] and said that whenever the British government were frightened they always talked about what they intended to do'.[159] Nonetheless, it was agreed that a telegram to the Egyptian government regarding their responsibility would be drafted.[160]

The Sudanese disturbances forced Whitehall to consider and decide on its policy for the Sudan, something which the men-on-the-spot had been urging them to do since 1919. As regards the relationship between Stack and Allenby, it is apparent that the High Commissioner was prepared to allow Stack latitude in his policy considerations for the Sudan and to provide backing for them in London. Despite warnings from the Egyptian government of outbreaks of violence in support of the Sudanese against their British oppressors,[161] it is clear that MacDonald was not going to relinquish Britain's place in the Sudan, thereby demonstrating the continuity of Conservative and Labour policy in the Nile Valley.

Nevertheless, for those in Khartoum this declaration did not go far enough. In communicating the results of the conference with MacDonald in Khartoum, Wasey Sterry, Legal Secretary and Acting Governor-General, complained that this resolve was not enough.

> Unless British Government prepared [sic] to settle definitely Army question consider [sic] proclamation useless and probably only provide counter propaganda.

Drifting seems impossible policy as it merely means Army gets worse with young Sudanese officers, removed from Battalions, doing nothing here and probability Egyptian officers being sent up specially selected to make mischief; and further with intensive propaganda from Egypt being started.[162]

Stack sympathized with this view but advocated that 'we must accept the facts and make the best of very difficult circumstances'.[163] Stack explained that MacDonald, and supported by Allenby, was unable to take the very drastic step of ejecting the Egyptian army from the Sudan at this point as it would have practically amounted to a declaration of war on Egypt. However, if the Egyptian government disregarded the explicit warning issued by the British Government, then severe action would be used. Stack maintained that 'although it is less than what we wanted it is at the same time a decisive defeat of Egyptian claims and confirmation of [the] existing administration'.[164]

Zaghlul's visit to London looked as though it would merely confirm Anglo-Egyptian differences, but Stack did not miss the opportunity to emphasize the feeling of impending crisis within the Sudan. Having received a telegram from the Acting *Sirdar* on 3 September 1924 highlighting the anti-British attitude of the Arab and Sudanese officers, Stack urged that a complete change in the garrison of the Sudan was essential in 'the very near future unless the risk is to be deliberately taken of the situation getting altogether out of hand'.[165] Stack was certainly aware of the grave implications associated with the removal of all Egyptian officers from the Sudanese and Arab units of the Egyptian army in the Sudan. For Stack, the justification was that he saw the Egyptian government as responsible for the situation and that no alternative which offered a satisfactory solution was possible. Stack pointed to the public and official utterances of Zaghlul himself which made any form of active partnership between the British and Egyptian government in the internal administration of the Sudan impossible. Since the British government was responsible for that administration, it had to take steps to ensure that its administration would not be interfered with by the Egyptian government.[166]

Stack had the full support of the Foreign Office. In fact, his letter to MacDonald on 16 September was drafted in consultation with the Foreign Office. As a Foreign Office memorandum pointed out, the condition under which the Condominium had worked successfully was due to a unity of direction and control of policy secured by the British representative in Cairo acting as though he held a proxy on behalf of Egypt; and Egyptians were willing to trust British officers and British officials. An independent and openly hostile Egypt made this partnership 'impossible'.[167] The Foreign Office believed that 'the British position in the Sudan is being steadily undermined, and any action to consolidate or protect it can only be taken at the expense of the Egyptian position'.[168] The only condition that the Foreign Office envisaged in which Egyptian participation in the internal administration of the Sudan could be permitted would be a public repudiation by Zaghlul of Egyptian claims to 'rights' and accusations of British 'usurpation'. This was deemed as highly unlikely since 'his [Zaghlul's] political position in Egypt, already far less strong than it was six months ago, would make it impossible for him to do this'.[169] Indeed, the Foreign Office believed that Zaghlul was coming to England, partly with the idea of gaining time to allow anti-British influences in the

Sudan to continue their work uninterrupted, and partly with the hope, not so much of effecting an amicable Anglo-Egyptian settlement, as of deriving some personal and political advantage from his visit.[170] The Foreign Office certainly took a very pessimistic view of Zaghlul and his motives:

> He must know that His Majesty's Government are not prepared to yield to Egyptian pretensions in the Sudan, and consequently that he will not obtain such concessions as would enable him to claim a diplomatic triumph before his own people. In these circumstances, while he may be expected to attempt to justify the attitude which he and his Government have taken up over the Sudan, he will probably count on Egyptian propaganda and the agitation which it has engendered producing a situation which will oblige His Majesty's Government either to allow their position to become untenable, or else to take drastic action. Such action he may attempt to depict as a violation of the 1899 Convention, and although Egyptians have been taught to regard that instrument as a monstrous injustice imposed upon Egypt, Zaghlul has, so far, been careful to avoid all direct repudiation of it. He probably realises that by repudiation he would free our hands and place the Egyptian Government in the wrong. His game will [...] probably take the form of relying on developments in the Sudan to force our hand.[171]

The Foreign Office painted Zaghlul as a cunning fox, playing the diplomatic game to his advantage by forcing Britain to take drastic measures and abrogate the 1899 Convention themselves. The forthcoming negotiations were seen therefore as an opportunity to extract 'at all costs' a clear definition of his position towards the 1899 Anglo-Egyptian agreement. It was held by the Foreign Office that if he stood by his June statements he could not be surprised at the steps which the British Government would have to take to safeguard public order in the Sudan,[172] and thereby Britain would be absolved of any contravention of the Condominium Agreement. If, on the other hand, Zaghlul admitted that Egypt was bound by the agreement, the Foreign Office saw that it would be impossible for him not to withdraw these statements and thereby forfeit a large part of his following in Egypt. The Foreign Office was prepared to take a strong line, using force if necessary. Indeed, the Foreign Office was even prepared to recommend the readiness of two battalions to be sent to the Sudan. 'The despatch of reinforcements is a lengthy business [...] The longer action is delayed the more necessary it will be to ensure that the reinforcements sent are ample and the larger they are the less the danger and the greater the moral effect.'[173]

Egypt, the Sudan and the League of Nations

One factor which concerned MacDonald was that Zaghlul might take the whole Sudan question to the League of Nations in the guise of an 'honest broker'. These concerns were dealt with by Colonel Schuster, Financial Secretary to the Sudan Government, in consultation with William Malkin, a legal adviser at the Foreign Office. Since

Egypt was not a member of the League, the question could only be raised if another member brought the dispute to the attention of the assembly or council. This was without precedent and Malkin could only speculate on the course and form of any such discussions. Following the registration of such a dispute, it would be up to Britain either to show that there was no dispute in existence, or to persuade the council that the dispute had arisen out of a matter which, by international law, was solely within Britain's domestic jurisdiction. Malkin proposed that in either case the argument would be much the same: that Egypt was a British Protectorate; that the Protectorate was only to be terminated by an instrument in which Britain reserved the question of the Sudan to be settled between Britain and Egypt and therefore could not be regarded as an international question for submission to the League. According to Malkin, whilst this argument was not 'without weight', he doubted whether it would be sufficient to 'prevail in the atmosphere of Geneva'. Malkin continued that: 'it must be remembered that it would not be a case of our refusing to allow the matter to be brought before the League on the grounds suggested, but of our persuading the council that the matter which was before it was not one with which it could properly deal'.[174] Whilst Malkin was less sanguine over Britain's defence he also believed that if Zaghlul succeeded in getting the matter before the League he would also be in a rather difficult position. Zaghlul would be forced to admit either that the 1899 agreement existed, and to remain the governing instrument and that his complaint was against the way in which that instrument had been interpreted and administered, or would attempt to demonstrate that the agreement ought to be terminated and replaced by some other system. Malkin rightly pointed out that either course would lead to difficulties for Zaghlul. The first would be unacceptable to Nationalists within Egypt; whilst in pursuing the second course, he would find it difficult to persuade the League to deprive Britain of her rights under the 1899 agreement. In this regard, Malkin advised that 'it is important to avoid any action which would enable Zaghlul to contend with some show of reason that we ourselves had in effect terminated the convention or made its future operation impossible'.[175] Malkin emphasized that 'we want to leave Zaghlul with the onus of making a case for the termination of the present system'. Thus whilst there would be a discussion in Geneva, embarrassing in itself, Malkin believed that the 'odds are always against the party which is challenging the jurisdiction of the League; and in such cases it is always open to the Council to refer the preliminary report to the Permanent Court for an advisory opinion'.[176] From the British perspective it would be preferable that Zaghlul adopt the second course and advocate the termination of the convention. It would make the British position a good deal easier as he would be trying to induce the League to terminate a system established under a treaty, still in force, and, if his bid appeared successful, Britain would be able to make it clear that the Anglo-Egyptian partnership had broken down and it was necessary to establish a new workable system. To Malkin the alternatives were clear: either the British government would alone fulfil the function of a trustee, perhaps even under League control; or Zaghlul's contention would be accepted, and the Sudan handed over to Egypt. Malkin was certainly confident that Britain would be able to prevent any intermediate solution under which it would be possible for Egypt to 'interfere in and hinder our [Britain's] administration'.[177]

This line was supported by the Prime Minister who declared that the Sudan question was a 'domestic problem'.[178] The Foreign Office was concerned that reference to the League would be interpreted as a sign of British weakness, thereby providing further fodder for Egyptian propaganda in the Sudan and 'designed to create the impression that Britain, having surrendered her position in Egypt, might be induced to abandon the Sudan'.[179] Reference to the League would only add to this uncertainty and make the Sudanese even more receptive to Egyptian propaganda, creating a 'most dangerous situation'.[180] The Foreign Office view was very much in line with that expressed by Stack who also saw that any reference to the League would appear inconsistent with the declarations already made by the British government to the effect that under no circumstances would the British government retire from the *status quo* or hand over to others its trust for the good government of the Sudan. Moreover, Stack argued that even if the question was handed over to the League, the delay created whilst evidence was gathered as to the wishes of the people, perhaps six to twelve months, would provide 'the most fertile opportunities for a Mahdist movement or a religious uprising'.[181]

As a result, the aim of the Foreign Office was submitted as being to resolve the Sudan question without delay one way or the other, even if Zaghlul wished to avoid any conclusive issue, since time and uncertainty were working in his favour. The Foreign Office advocated that if an agreed settlement was impossible, Britain would be forced to take action, and that no other course than that recommended by Stack appeared possible, short of a complete abandonment of the British position in the Sudan. How this would be perceived in Egypt, the Foreign Office could only speculate, but it hoped that the firm attitude adopted by the British government over the Sudan in July and August which did not excite any reaction or disturbance would be the same under the measures then being considered. Moreover, it would be 'unlikely to produce anything in the nature of an upheaval in Egypt'.[182] If this proved to be erroneous better then, while the British garrison remained in the Egyptian interior in order to provide adequate protection of foreign lives and property.

The army question

Despite concerns over the legal nature of Britain's position in the Sudan, and any embarrassment at its being raised in the League of Nations, the Foreign Office was prepared to drive home the threat that Egyptian propaganda and army officers posed to the British position. The crux of the matter was the position of the Egyptian army. The Foreign Office argued that while Stack might find it inexpedient to carry out orders from the War Minister in his capacity as Governor-General, a more worrying development was that indigenous officers, whether Egyptian or Sudanese, now looked to the Egyptian War Office for promotion instead of to the *Sirdar*. Stack's hold on the army 'has already largely disappeared'.[183] Of course, with the advent of Zaghlul's government this no doubt added a sense of urgency to discussions over policy formulation for the Anglo-Egyptian Sudan. Indeed, the Foreign Office believed that the 'Egyptian officers serving in the Sudan are, with the exception of a very few of the senior men, more or less ardent nationalists, and they have converted practically all of the young Sudanese officers'. Related to this was the question of replacing British officers whose period of secondment to the Egyptian army had expired. It was assumed that these, along with any Egyptian officers sent back to Egypt who showed symptoms of being particularly active agitators, were merely being replaced by similarly ardent nationalists in the Anglophobe eyes of the Egyptian Minister of War. The Foreign Office therefore urgently called for 'more drastic measures', if the 'spread of disaffection in the army is to be prevented'.[184] Again, the Foreign Office advocated the creation of a Sudanese Defence Force by taking over the locally recruited units. It saw this as the 'only practicable solution', but it also recognized that it was 'essentially a high handed proceeding, which could only be adopted if His Majesty's Government were determined to insist upon a radical and permanent settlement of the Sudan question'.[185]

Financially, the consequences of this move would entail a subsidy from the British government of between four and eight years. It was difficult to forecast the extent of this assistance as it was dependent upon factors such as the price of cotton, which was impossible to forecast with any accuracy. As regards the civil administration, a number of nationalist Egyptians had already been removed and once the position of the army was resolved, the Foreign Office believed that the Sudan government would not face any great difficulty in dealing with the civil element:

> With so much inflammable material about it is obvious that a policy of drift is bound to end in a disastrous upheaval, the consequences of which it is impossible to predict, but which would make a far greater call upon the British Treasury than the relatively trifling financial assistance with the Sudan Government will require if it is called upon to take over responsibility for its own defence.[186]

Indeed, as the Foreign Office emphasized, Britain had over 8½ million pounds in capital liabilities and over £750, 000 per annum in respect of interest which the Treasury would have to meet if things were to go seriously wrong in the Sudan.[187] Moreover, British loss of the Sudan would also mean the 'loss of the most promising source of high grade cotton yet in sight'.[188] The Foreign Office and the Sudan Government were at one in their ideas of how British policy should develop. It is certainly interesting to note that the Foreign Office was largely in agreement with its men-on-the-spot in advocating such a forward and definite policy under a Labour Prime Minister and in a climate traditionally viewed as one in which Britain attempted to limit her responsibilities. Moreover, it is in this context that the actions of Allenby following the assassination of Sir Lee Stack (see Chapter 5) must be viewed and it is clear that he was continuing this forward policy as advocated by the Foreign Office and Sudan Government on numerous occasions.

The assassination of Sir Lee Stack and the Sudanese Mutiny, 27–28 November 1924

The assassination of Sir Lee Stack on 19 November 1924 was, unsurprisingly, viewed as a culmination of an intensive anti-British propaganda and subversion within the Sudan. His assassination could therefore not go unpunished.[139] As a consequence, the measures taken – the creation of a Sudanese Defence Force, the evacuation of the Egyptian Army from the Sudan and even the possibility of extending the area of irrigation by the Blue Nile dam – cannot be seen as a knee jerk reaction by Britain but as a set of policies that had been under discussion since 1919. These events also took place as Austen Chamberlain replaced Ramsay MacDonald as Foreign Secretary in October 1924.

The evacuation of the Egyptian Army from the Sudan did not pass without incident.[190] The most significant of these developments was the mutiny of the 11th Sudanese Battalion on 27–28 November 1924. After marching through Khartoum the mutineers were surrounded in a nearby hospital and compound and, after sustained resistance, were finally brought under British control. Of the mutineers, fifteen were killed, thirteen wounded and nine missing. Of the officers, one escaped and the other four surrendered.[191] In other disturbances, the officers and men of the transport corps, located in a barracks south of Khartoum, 'pushed out' a considerable section of the railway, and a mutiny broke out in the central Prison at Khartoum North where a number of political prisoners were held.[192]

To the authorities these disturbances were largely the result of Egyptian agitation. Indeed, the Director of Prisons reported that signals between the prison rioters and Egyptian troops, the 3rd Egyptian Battalion was stationed nearby and had just received their evacuation orders, were constantly being exchanged. 'I am convinced that help from Egyptian troops was expected and may have been promised. I am firmly of the opinion that the mutiny was engineered from outside.'[193] W Berridge has shown that this riot demonstrated the failure of the colonial state's prison regime 'to restrain an influential set of political prisoners'.[194] It took the actions of British troops and their continued presence to bring the situation under control. 'The very necessity of a permanent British troop presence in [the] Sudan, which was not a feature of other colonial states in sub-Saharan Africa, indicated the lack of confidence of the colonial state'[195] in the existing prison regime. Indeed, the continued presence of a British battalion had significant consequences for the Anglo-Egyptian treaty negotiations of the latter 1920s.

In terms of official opinion, Willis understood that the Wafd party regarded it as 'urgently desirable to convince the world in general, by a demonstration on an unprecedented scale, that the Sudanese desired union with Egypt and detested the British yoke'.[196] This opinion was repeated by Allenby to the Foreign Office in the Annual report on the Sudan which called the movement for the 'Union of the Sudan with Egypt' 'fictitious' and 'artificially stimulated by demonstrations, circulars and propaganda'.[197] Responsible Sudanese opinion was believed to have 'unanimously condemned the misguided action of the few who allowed themselves to be duped into folly'.[198] Indeed, in appraising the importance and significance of the political events affecting the Sudan in 1924 the Report asserted that the political agitation had been confined to certain classes in the main urban areas of the country:

> The mass of people, the tribes and their sheikhs, remained entirely unaffected. Throughout the disturbances their attitude has been one of steadfast loyalty to the Government, of sorrow and anger at the murder of their Governor-General, and,

finally, of satisfaction at the evacuation of the Egyptian troops and the deportation of a number of ill-disposed Egyptian officials.[199]

In official minds the assassination of Stack and the mutiny in the Sudan possessed all the hallmarks of Egyptian complicity and instigation. It was seen as the latest and most serious manifestation of the 'Union of the Sudan with Egypt movement' with students being the primary vehicle for transporting nationalist ideals and sentiments.[200] British investigations into the mutiny all laid the blame on Egyptian complicity, but since much of this evidence came from statements by condemned men its reliability was somewhat questionable.[201] British Sudanese officials were desperate to prove the Egyptian connection in order to justify their previous warnings over Egyptian activity in the Sudan and as reason for continuing the de-Egyptianization of the Sudan government.

Conclusion

The Sudan played an important role in the Anglo-Egyptian relationship. Not only from a prestige point of view but heavy Treasury investment in irrigation schemes accorded the Sudan a growing prominence within the Empire. This importance was brought home with the advent of a Nationalist Egyptian government in 1924 and its own desire for a unified Nile Valley. The profile of the Sudan was also raised in London by prominent officials, such as Wingate and Stack. This was a double-edged sword; however, as the more they advocated a separation of the Sudan from Egypt, the more the Sudan came to be seen as subject to the vicissitudes of Egyptian politics. The fact that all communication between Khartoum and London was filtered through Cairo only compounded this difficulty.

It is interesting that as the Anglo-Egyptian Condominium was becoming increasingly untenable, because of perceived Egyptian propaganda and intrigues against the British, the Foreign Office, under MacDonald, was prepared to support the suggestions of the Sudanese government by ejecting the Egyptians from the Sudan, finally severing any anti-British links between the burgeoning nationalist movement within Egypt and the Sudan. It is in this light that Allenby's ultimatum following Stack's assassination must be seen and the reaction of Chamberlain was in marked contrast to what the Foreign Office and men-on-the-spot had been preparing for under MacDonald. As we shall observe with the Egyptian treaty negotiations, it is possible to see in the case of the Sudan a transfer of power from the Khartoum-Cairo axis back to London.

5

The Assassination of Sir Lee Stack: The British Lion's Final Roar?

Since the turn of the twentieth century, and as a direct result of Britain's occupation of Egypt, political violence played a growing and deadly role within Egyptian political life. A variety of secret societies targeted not only British officials but also Egyptian politicians who were deemed to be in the pockets of their British overlords and thereby failing to advance the nationalist calls of 'Egypt for the Egyptians'. The most significant of these attacks was the murder of Sir Lee Stack, Governor-General of the Sudan and *Sirdar* of the Egyptian Army, in November 1924. The assassination of Stack presented an opportunity for British officials to secure a whole slate of advantages at the expense of Egyptian nationalists that would have otherwise been impossible. As a result, it exposed tensions that existed between the Foreign Office and their High Commissioner, the much vaunted and decorated Sir Edmund Allenby, conqueror of Palestine and High Commissioner of Egypt and the Sudan (1919–25). Of equal importance, the assassination and subsequent events provide a greater insight into the complex relationship between the Egyptian ministers, the Cairo Residency and the Foreign Office, demonstrating that London was consistently out of step with its officials on the ground; men who were being forced to deal with a real and sustained nationalist threat in Egypt that professed its ambitions to expand its reach into the neighbouring Sudan.

Secret societies and political violence

At the turn of the twentieth century, no less than twenty-six secret societies existed within Egypt.[1] The deepening British occupation through the domination of the Sudan, the Dinshaway incident of 1906,[2] British preponderance in government positions coupled with the perceived failings of the Egyptian Government, including the absence of a constitution, a Press law that restricted freedom of speech and the decision to extend the Suez Canal concession, provided fodder for the growth and extension of these secret societies. The original aim of these organizations was to work for the interests of Egypt by creating strong political ties amongst Egyptians in order to demand a constitutional government for the country.[3]

Such sedition against British colonialism was not merely confined to Egypt. Noor-Aiman I Khan has demonstrated the growing connection between Indian and Egyptian nationalists at the beginning of the twentieth century. One such connection was that between the assassination of Sir William Curzon-Wylie, a political *aide-de-camp* to the Secretary of State for India, by Madanlal Dhingra in London in 1909 and that of Butros Pasha Ghali, Egyptian Prime Minister, by Ibrahim Nassif al-Wardani in Cairo less than nine months later. Both assassins were from upper-middle-class families and both had spent time in Europe studying, possibly even meeting whilst in London during 1908. Through their experiences in Europe, where their personal and political freedom was much greater, they were exposed to influences and debates in the press and among the students on imperial questions that could not be suppressed in the European metropoles.[4] The connection between the two assassinations was not lost on both officials and the press at the time. The *Egyptian Gazette*, the organ of the British community in Egypt, complained:

> [O]f late the Anglophobe native journals have made a specialty of setting before their readers every detail they could get about the unrest in India [...] when Sir Curzon-Wylie was murdered in London last summer, "*al-Liwa*" the official organ of the Nationalist Party published a poem glorifying Dhingra, his murderer.[5]

Wardani, a pharmacist and graduate of the University of Lausanne, had joined the Nationalist Watani party on his return from Europe.[6] As Ghali exited the Ministry of Justice, Wardani shot the Prime Minister six times and made no effort to escape. He was apprehended immediately, confessed to the crime and, ultimately, sentenced to death. Wardani maintained he had acted alone and described his assassination of Ghali as a 'patriotic act'.[7] Nevertheless, the subsequent investigation into the assassination revealed that Wardani also belonged to a secret society, *Jam'iyyat al-Tadamun al-Akhawi*, the Society of Brotherly Solidarity. The Society was composed of lawyers, engineers and teachers, and it was at the time of Wardani's joining, in 1907, that the Society began to assume a political character by introducing several innovations and advanced European ideas. A company was founded – the Brotherly Solidarity Company – so that the funds collected would be spent on promoting the various activities of the Society, including charitable works, such as helping orphans and educating the poor.[8] The members themselves were expected to make contributions. The Society had formally drawn up a programme of action and in 1909 these plans began to be executed with the establishment of branches of the Society in almost every school and ministry.[9]

Following the murder of Ghali, political violence increasingly became a feature of Egyptian political life. Other attempts on the lives of Egyptian ministers included: Sultan Husayn Kamil in July 1915; Ibrahim Pasha Fathi, Minister of *Waqfs*, who had encouraged the denunciation of the Society of Brotherly Solidarity, in 1916; and, Yusuf Pasha Wahba, Finance Minister in Muhammad Sa'id's Cabinet and later Premier.[10] Of course, British officials did not escape this political violence unscathed. Attempts were carried out by a particular group of students and workmen of whom the Enayat brothers were the most notorious. Their victims included: Aldred Brown, Controller-

General at the Central Administration in the Ministry of Education, on 18 February 1922; Bimbashi Cave, Deputy Commandant in the Cairo Police, in May 1922; Colonel Piggott, Paymaster-General of the British army, in July 1922; Thomas Brown, responsible for the horticultural section at the Ministry of Agriculture, in August 1922; and W N Robson, professor at the School of Law, on 27 December 1922.[11]

The Society of Brotherly Solidarity demonstrated a clearly organized and far-reaching association that comprised well-defined roles for its members prior to the First World War. Although the Foreign Office grasped the intellectual composition of the Society, it fundamentally underestimated the level of organization and capability at its disposal. While the Foreign Office was keen to emphasize the role the First World War and its aftermath played in the development of nationalism by promoting Egyptian political ideas,[12] it failed to account for the pre-war political violence and how the nationalist movement was gaining its own momentum even before the outbreak of the war. This was a fatal mistake considering the violent upheaval of the March 1919 revolution.[13] The war merely acted as a catalyst to an already nascent movement.

The assassination of Sir Lee Stack

Despite the establishment of the Special Section within the Public Security Department and the best efforts of the police,[14] Sir Lee Stack, *Sirdar* and Governor-General of the Sudan, was attacked on 19 November 1924. Stack was travelling to the Residency to attend a small luncheon party for the visiting former Liberal Prime Minister, Herbert Asquith. The *Sirdar* was travelling with his *aide-de-camp* and chauffeur when they were ambushed by several assailants, dressed as effendis and armed with revolvers, near the Ministry of Education at about 1.30 pm. According to reports, a bomb was thrown at the car, which failed to detonate followed by at least thirty shots fired at the car. Stack received three wounds in the hand, leg and abdomen, and although his chauffeur was also hit in the leg and arm he managed to drive to the Residency. The assailants escaped by taxi.[15]

The Residency was first alerted when Archibald Clark Kerr, Counsellor to the Residency, preparing to leave for lunch at home, heard a commotion in the hallway. As he went out to investigate, a wounded *Sirdar* and chauffeur confronted him. Clark Kerr saw to it that Stack was quickly made comfortable on the sofa in the drawing room and the guests alerted. However, Clark Kerr complained that 'as seems inevitable on such occasions here, at the moment when important decisions had to be taken HC [Allenby] was emphatically under the influence of gin, [Sir Sheldon] Amos [Judicial Advisor], was still more alcoholic and [Sir Reginald] Patterson [Financial Advisor], was grumpy drunk.'[16] Clark Kerr immediately realized the political significance this incident would have in Britain, Egypt and the Sudan. 'It is quite clear that we can hold our hand no longer. We shall be obliged to take vigorous action against [Saad] Zaghlul, for morally he and his government are responsible and they cannot be allowed to escape responsibility.'[17] Clark Kerr wanted to act immediately and felt constrained by having to consult with the Foreign Office first. He believed that vigorous action would secure the greatest advantage for Britain.

Reactions to the attack on the *Sirdar*

About an hour after the crime, Saad Zaghlul, Premier and leader of the Nationalist Wafd Party, called at the Residency. According to Allenby, 'he had every appearance of being horror struck and seemed unable to express himself coherently'.[18] The Grand Chamberlain, ministers, ex-ministers, notables and officers of the Egyptian army quickly followed Zaghlul. London was immediately informed of the attack and Allenby included a list of demands to be presented to the Egyptian Government for Cabinet approval. These included: an apology; the apprehension and punishment of the assailants; the payment of a large indemnity; the withdrawal from the Sudan of all Egyptian officers and purely Egyptian units of the Egyptian army; the Egyptian Government to consent to the increase, as need arose, of the land to be irrigated under the Gezira irrigation scheme[19]; that the rules and conditions governing foreign officials within the Egyptian Government should be revised according to the wishes of the British Government; and that the traditional powers and privileges of the Judicial and Financial Adviser posts should be maintained. Allenby added that if the Egyptian Government failed to comply, Britain would 'take appropriate action to safeguard their interests in Egypt and the Sudan'.[20] Stack died from his wounds the next day, 20 November, in the Anglo-American hospital in Cairo.

To Allenby, the attack on Stack was the final straw in a period of increasing violence against the British community. He believed that the demands should be made 'without delay'.[21] In Allenby's opinion, Zaghlul and the Wafd were the chief culprits of this upsurge in violence. 'The spirit of indiscipline and hatred which the present Egyptian Government have incited by public speeches and through the activities of the Wafd cannot but be regarded as contributory to the crime.'[22] Allenby wanted the consequences of this political violence to be brought home to Zaghlul's ministry.

> I do not know whether Zaghlul will resign or not, but if he does he should be given by us grounds to do so, which will be in the eyes of the world a signal proof of his incapacity and failure to conduct the affairs of the country. My object has been to make demands consonant with the present and not with a future Ministry.[23]

In London, and in the same month as the attack upon Stack, the second Baldwin administration came to power.[24] Baldwin's government moved swiftly and agreed with Allenby's calls for decisive action and his assessment of the role played by Zaghlul. Austen Chamberlain, the Foreign Secretary, generally agreed with Allenby and emphasized Britain's object of 'completely [...] separat[ing] the military forces of Egypt from those of the Sudan'.[25] The Cabinet instructed Allenby to prepare a communication along the lines of Chamberlain's response. Once approved by the Cabinet, Chamberlain would publish it in Britain simultaneously with its presentation to the Egyptian Government.

However, a divergence of opinion between Chamberlain and his High Commissioner began to emerge. Although Allenby saw the payment of an indemnity as an important part of British demands, Chamberlain was unconvinced. 'Payment of an indemnity seems to be the least part of reparation to be expected.'[26] Even after the *Sirdar*'s death, Chamberlain instructed Allenby to omit anything relating to the cash indemnity. 'The reparation required by HMG is the adoption of such measures as will protect our officers and interests for the future against the incitements and crimes of the past.'[27] Allenby disagreed. He believed that although it may seem undignified, a heavy fine should be imposed. 'I have increased my proposed figure to half a million. Even a million might be preferable. This is the sort of humiliation which is understood here.'[28]

The proposed increase in irrigation at Gezira also provoked a divergence in views between the Foreign Secretary and his High Commissioner. Chamberlain proposed the appointment of an Egyptian member to a commission convened to examine the possibility of extending the area of irrigation provided by the Nile. Allenby, however, perceived this to be inadequate. 'It secures the object but does not produce the moral effect.'[29] Instead, Allenby recommended that the demand read: 'Consent to the increase of the irrigated area in the Sudan as need may arise.'[30] Allenby believed that 'without the inclusion of these two demands the force of the communication would be vastly impaired'. The High Commissioner continued:

> The reasons for our Egyptian policy have been so liable to misunderstandings by vain and ignorant minds, and we have during the last few months been so far obliged to hold our hand and apparently acquiesce in breaches of the status quo, that we must not fail to use this opportunity to bring Egypt to her senses, to assert our power to harm her, and to stigmatise the regime of the present Government.[31]

Allenby obviously felt that the failed negotiations between Zaghlul and Ramsay MacDonald's Labour Government between September and October had done much damage to the Residency's and, by extension, to Britain's prestige within Egypt.[32]

Whatever the disagreements over the wording of the communication, it was understood by all that time was of the essence. Indeed, Wasey Sterry, Acting Governor-General of the Sudan, emphasized that:

> the state of public feeling is such that nothing but immediate, firm and drastic action as regards the Sudan will be understood here. Any parlaying or delay would create an impression which time would never eradicate. The symbol of [the] Egyptian part of control is [the] Egyptian flag which flies on all Army and Government buildings, and as long as it remains there native opinion – especially in the Provinces – will be doubtful of our determination to see this matter through in [the] only way that appears to be consonant with national dignity.[33]

Allenby expressed his wish to present the demands immediately after Stack's funeral. Thus, not only did Allenby fail to concur with the proposals made by the Foreign Office and approved by the Cabinet, but he also proceeded to send to Zaghlul on 22 November his list of demands prior to securing Cabinet approval as clearly instructed. In presenting these demands, Allenby was accompanied by Clark Kerr and was escorted by a full regiment of cavalry through the streets of Cairo to the offices of the Council of Ministers so creating a 'striking spectacle'.[34]

Chamberlain was understandably perturbed by Allenby's actions. All the more so when the Foreign Office had emphasized to Allenby that while the

British Government appreciated the local considerations that influenced his draft communication, it was felt that:

> the importance of taking into consideration public opinion abroad and at home was so great that it outweighed the considerations which you urged and led them to confine the demands upon the Egyptian Government to those which could be shown to be no more than adequate reparation to the Sudan for the injury inflicted upon that country by Egypt.[35]

Chamberlain, with the Prime Minister's support, demanded an explanation.[36] It was made clear to Allenby that while the Cabinet would support the action he had already taken it 'may be necessary for them [the Cabinet] after the immediate crisis is over to restate their position'.[37] In his defence, Allenby emphasized the importance of acting swiftly and decisively. 'Three complete days had already elapsed after the commission of the outrage, without any public sign from His Majesty's Government [...] Any delay after that [Sir Lee Stack's funeral] would inevitably be interpreted as indicating hesitation.'[38] Furthermore, Allenby asserted that time was running out as:

1. it was necessary to act upon Zaghlul personally before he had had further time to consider his position, and possibly to resign;
2. Egyptian opinion was prepared for severe measures, but was likely very rapidly to become less so as the first shock of the murder passed off;
3. the foreign colonies were much excited, and were being increasingly worked up by the foreign press. There was reason to apprehend the possibility of European manifestations hostile both to Egyptians and to His Majesty's Government. The Italians had already organized an unofficial defence force.[39]

Allenby had the full support of Clark Kerr in the essence and timing of these demands: 'we must do something that will strike the public mind in a signal way'.[40] Allenby was also under increasing pressure to act from Sterry in Khartoum. According to Sterry, a large representative delegation of sheikhs, merchants, *kadis* and *ulema* insisted that the British must make a clean cut. 'If we do not clear out the Egyptians and their flag the only possible inference is that we are not strong enough.'[41]

As the exchange of opinions continued between the Residency and London, Zaghlul replied to Allenby's demands. Zaghlul expressed the Egyptian Government's horror at the murder of the *Sirdar* but maintained the innocence of his government in encouraging political dissent. Zaghlul asserted that the Egyptian Government had 'in claiming the rights of the country, always invoked and proclaimed the use of legal and peaceful methods and has never had any contact whatsoever with organisations which advocate the use of violence'.[42] As an act of good faith the Egyptian Government accepted the first four of Allenby's demands. However, Zaghlul rejected the demand to evacuate the Sudan as it was perceived as a modification of the *status quo* and thereby in direct conflict with Article 46 of the Egyptian Constitution whereby the King occupied the position of Supreme Commander of the Army. Zaghlul maintained that any increase in the irrigation at Gezira was premature and agreement could be reached by further discussion. Finally, it was emphasized that the last demand concerning the position of foreign officials was determined by diplomatic agreements, which could not be modified without the intervention of the Egyptian Parliament.[43]

Allenby's response was immediate and unequivocal. Without consulting his superiors, he informed Zaghlul that instructions were being sent to the Sudan to effect the withdrawal of Egyptian officers and units and that the British were at liberty to increase the irrigated area at Gezira from 300,000 *feddans* to an unlimited size as the need arose.[44] On communication of Zaghlul's response to Chamberlain and the steps he had already taken to bring the Egyptian Government to heel, Allenby proposed three further measures to gain Egyptian acquiescence concerning foreign officials and the protection of foreign interests. These were: a display of military might at Cairo, Alexandria, Port Said and Suez coupled with the seizure of tobacco customs to provide a source of revenue; the rupture of diplomatic relations; and if another British or foreign resident was murdered, hostages would be taken and shot if the violence continued. 'This is repugnant but [...] it is the only sure way of stopping murders [...] If only to avoid the danger of the foreign colonies taking matters into their own hands.'[45]

Allenby requested an urgent reply since he had learned that Zaghlul's resignation would be accepted by the King and for 'political reasons I am especially desirous to break off relations before it is accepted and resume them with [the] new Government'.[46] Without waiting for Chamberlain's response, Allenby ordered the immediate seizure and occupation of the Alexandria customs on 24 November. Zaghlul's resignation was accepted on the same day.

The Foreign Office was understandably alarmed at the steps the High Commissioner proposed, which appeared as rash and hasty. Indeed, Chamberlain was disturbed by Allenby's disregard for protocol, especially since he discovered that the Alexandria customs had been occupied through reports from Reuters without providing Chamberlain the opportunity to reply! 'I leave to you who are on the spot fullest discretion as to [the] measure required to preserve order [...] but I must insist that political measure of grave import not affecting the internal situation of Egypt alone shall not be undertaken till I have approved them.'[47] Chamberlain stated that he did not perceive any advantage in the rupture of diplomatic relations especially if they were to be immediately resumed with another ministry. He also rejected any plans for the taking of hostages warning that 'it is a measure so repugnant to British traditions that only in the last extremity of all would public opinion here and in the British Dominions support you'.[48] Indeed, Chamberlain reminded Allenby that the situation in Egypt was watched closely by foreign powers, a concern that was only heightened by the hostile outcry in some quarters of the French press against the 'brutal Imperialism which recalls the worst days of Lord Curzon'.[49] Both the *Journal des Débats* and *Le Temps* questioned the wisdom of coercion and argued that in the long run 'nothing would be more dangerous than a permanent centre of discontent in Egypt, and that any over-hasty action should be avoided'.[50]

Britain's actions had also roused the wrath of the Third International (Comintern) in Moscow. The Comintern issued a manifesto to all workers denouncing the 'Conservative Government of England, which has begun its active career with a predatory attack on Egypt and the Sudan'.[51] Moreover, it was reported that a 'Hands off Egypt' movement had emerged in the Soviet Union with mass meetings of protest being organized, particularly in Muslim districts, such as the Crimean Republic.[52]

On the domestic front, MacDonald sympathized with Chamberlain's position, but believed that the crisis could have been managed a little more carefully, thereby avoiding any lessening of British prestige in the eyes of the world.[53] 'The democratic genius and experience of Labour would have led it to handle the situation so that an agreement would have been issued and not a successful ultimatum.'[54] Moreover, he regretted the inclusion of the extension of the Gezira scheme within the ultimatum, believing it to be unnecessary, a point that John Murray emphasized since Allenby had ignored British Government instructions. Nevertheless, perhaps reflecting upon his unsuccessful negotiations with Zaghlul over the Sudan, MacDonald condemned Zaghlul's uncompromising attitude in refusing to accept the *status quo* and admitted that Egypt was deliberately hampering the British Government in the Sudan:

> Every Egyptian officer was tending to become a centre of propaganda for the destruction of law and administration in the Sudan. That could not go on. It was absolutely impossible for Britain to agree to Egypt treating the Sudan as though it was her own property, because it was not. If Egypt did not care to carry on the joint trusteeship the time would have to come sooner or later when we should have had to say to Egypt: 'Really, if you cannot help us, you must go'.[55]

As a result of this and as a way to place Britain's position in the Sudan on a firm footing in the eyes of the world, MacDonald suggested asking the League of Nations for a mandate over the Sudan and thereby Britain would remain responsible for its administration. This was not a new suggestion to the Foreign Office and contained much to recommend it. As Murray minuted:

> A mandate would exactly define our position as trustees which is the one which we profess to hold towards the Sudanese. It would be a solace to those politically minded elements in the Sudan who are already beginning to think, if not talk, about 'the Sudan for the Sudanese'. Though it would be a bitter disappointment to Egyptian imperialism, it would at least give the material guarantee of League supervision over the irrigation policy of the Sudan Government.[56]

However, the problem was how to square a British mandate with the continued existence of the 1899 Anglo-Egyptian Condominium Agreement.[57] Sir William Tyrell, Assistant Under-Secretary at the Foreign Office, and Chamberlain both shared this concern, with Chamberlain minuting: 'I am not disposed to *invite* interference in any form.'[58] This point was emphasized in Chamberlain's speech to the newly elected Nonconformist Unionist League MPs on 3 December.[59]

The Cabinet itself echoed Chamberlain's misgivings and its lack of confidence in Allenby was illustrated in its authorization of the High Commissioner to show Herbert Asquith, who was staying at the Cairo Residency, all communications and to keep him fully informed. More significantly, the Cabinet ordered the appointment of diplomat Nevile Henderson, a friend of Austen Chamberlain, to Allenby's staff. He would be able to explain the views of the British Government and thereby overcome the difficulty of keeping Allenby informed of the Cabinet's views on a day-to-day basis by telegram alone.[60]

It was now the turn of the Foreign Office to act, Henderson's appointment was announced by the Foreign Office without any prior consultation with Allenby over his role or the nature of his mission.[61] Chamberlain declared that:

> He [Henderson] is an official of exceptional experience, and I have explained to him verbally with a completeness which is not possible in telegraphic communication the objects at which His Majesty's Government are aiming and the difficulties which they wish to avoid. He has my fullest confidence.[62]

The reality, however, was much different. Henderson had actually been 'recalled hurriedly from holiday, had no prior knowledge or experience of Egypt, and had only had a mere half-hour briefing from Austen Chamberlain before being packed off to Egypt'.[63] According to Walford Selby, Principal Private Secretary to the Foreign Secretary, and writing in 1950, it was Tyrrell's comment to Chamberlain that Allenby was being 'badly advised' that precipitated the despatch of Henderson in order to 'strengthen' Allenby's staff. Selby notes that both he and Murray were dismayed at Tyrrell's comment. 'Neither Mr Murray nor I felt it was the moment to give any such warning to Sir Austen. I made this clear to Sir William with some vigour, but the damage had been done'.[64] At Henderson's appointment Selby later commented that:

> Here I blundered: I should have resigned knowing all I did of Allenby's loyalty to those who served him. Instead I allowed myself to be party to sending our Mr Nevile Henderson over Mr Clark Kerr's head. It is an action I have ever regretted, since the decision of the Cabinet precipitated Lord Allenby's resignation which he refused to withdraw unless Sir Austen would agree to withdraw Mr Henderson. This Sir Austen, backed by Crowe and Tyrrell, refused to do, despite my subsequent entreaties.[65]

It now became a trial of strength between the Foreign Office and the Residency as it was hoped that Henderson's presence could be utilized to rein in the errant High Commissioner.

Initially, Allenby failed to grasp the significance of Henderson's imminent arrival. The appointment of Henderson as Minister Plenipotentiary meant that he ranked alongside Allenby as High Commissioner, effectively demoting Clark Kerr to number three at the Residency. Possibly at the prompting of Clark Kerr himself, Allenby sought reassurance from London that Henderson was 'not intended to supersede my Counsellor, in whom, as in the other members of my staff, I have complete confidence'.[66] However, upon further reflection on the implications of Henderson's appointment, coupled with Chamberlain's rather blunt reply, the unsettled Allenby began to appreciate the effect upon his own position.[67] Allenby complained that the appointment of Henderson as Minister Plenipotentiary had been perceived as 'amounting to my practical supersession, [and] has seriously weakened my position'.[68]

Probably also mindful of how his own appointment as Special High Commissioner five years earlier had had the effect of ousting Sir Reginald Wingate, Allenby requested that a public announcement be made, without delay, stating that Henderson was coming solely for the purpose of discussing the situation and facilitating the exchange of views between Cairo and London and that he would leave within a week.[69]

Chamberlain's response was unequivocal. He assured Allenby of the 'fullest measure of support', but he also stated that 'I have my own responsibility which you must allow me to discharge. In no circumstances can I allow arrangements deliberately made after careful consideration to be questioned'.[70] Thereafter a flurry of telegrams passed between Allenby and Chamberlain. Allenby constantly complained that Chamberlain's ill-considered actions had 'a deplorable effect', on his position within Egypt.[71] Since it was apparent that he no longer enjoyed the confidence of the British Government Allenby made it clear that, as soon as circumstances permitted, he wished to resign.[72] In response, Chamberlain tried to explain that Henderson merely filled an existing vacancy at the Residency following the departure of Ernest Scott, Minister Plenipotentiary, in 1923 and assured Allenby that 'we have given and will continue to give you the fullest support in dealing with this critical situation'.[73]

Chamberlain's failure to grasp the unease created at the Residency and the effect Henderson's appointment would have upon Allenby's standing within Egypt was a firm reprimand for blatantly disobeying Foreign Office and Cabinet instructions. The furore certainly did not go unnoticed by Chamberlain's Cabinet colleagues. Winston Churchill, Chancellor of the Exchequer, complained to Lord Birkenhead, Secretary of State for India, that 'Austen [...] has sent exactly the wrong answer and as usual is making the heaviest weather over a personal point'.[74]

In Egypt itself, Henderson's appointment was interpreted as showing that something was 'going on behind the scenes in England and in Egypt'.[75] Newspapers, such as *al-Balagh*, the chief organ of the Zaghlulist party, speculated that the appointment was either in preparation for official negotiations with the new ministry, which in reality had been created to conclude a secret treaty, or for mounting opposition to Allenby's policy in England with Henderson sent as a check on the High Commissioner's actions.[76]

Chamberlain repeatedly attempted to persuade Allenby to withdraw his resignation but Chamberlain's refusal to make a decision on the duration of Henderson's stay continued to frustrate Allenby:

> Either you have confidence in me or you have not. Since you have made a striking appointment to my staff in the midst of a crisis without consulting me, and published it without giving me an opportunity of expressing my opinion, I presume you have not. It is therefore my duty to resign. You must know that in a country like this the only interpretation of such an appointment is infirmity of purpose and this at such a moment is disastrous.[77]

Allenby's position was clear. He even interpreted the Egyptian Cabinet's hesitation over the acceptance of Clause VII[78] of the ultimatum as proof of the difficulties caused by Henderson's appointment. Chamberlain, however, remained resolute:

The ungrudging support given to you by His Majesty's Government, even when you had acted contrary to my instructions that the terms of the declaration must be approved by them before presentation to Zaghlul, does not justify your reiterated allegations that they have not given you their confidence.[79]

The uncompromising stance of both Chamberlain and Allenby left the Foreign Secretary no other alternative but to agree with regret, on 29 November, to pass on Allenby's resignation to the Cabinet for consideration. According to Clark Kerr, 'what happened was that HM Government lost their heads and panicked and discovered too late that we have had the situation well in hand and then they were too small-minded to undo the foolish thing they have done.'[80]

Upon Henderson's disembarkation at Alexandria and his arrival in Cairo in early December, he received a somewhat frosty reception. 'Talk about the cook's hair in the *consommé*: If she had moulted entirely into the soup it would scarcely have been as unwelcome as my arrival in Cairo.'[81] However, Chamberlain's hope that Henderson would impress the view of the Foreign Office upon the Residency was quickly scotched once Henderson and Allenby had cleared the air. Indeed, Henderson agreed that his appointment had created an 'unfortunate impression and effect here [...] Although that phase is already passing out of its acute form, its taint will remain for a long while and I much doubt if it will ever pass altogether, unless and until I once more fade off the stage here.'[82] In fact, Henderson believed that three months would be sufficient as 'Lord Allenby will persist in his resignation – unless I go [and] Lord Allenby is from certain points of view [...] ideally suited to this post. Therefore it is in the public interest to keep him here.'[83]

Once Henderson had familiarized himself with all the facts, he fully supported Allenby's ultimatum to Zaghlul, stating that 'Lord Allenby did the only thing possible.'[84] This view was also shared by Asquith. Henderson even went so far as to say that the full urgency of handing the ultimatum to Zaghlul before he declared his resignation was not fully appreciated by the Cabinet, perhaps because the Residency had not been sufficiently clear in their telegrams. Although he was at pains to point out that 'he need not have inserted some of the clauses which he (or his staff) knew would be unwelcome to HMG.'[85]

Henderson and Asquith differed with Allenby on only two points. Firstly, the text of Allenby's ultimatum in respect of the £500,000 fine and, secondly, the tendency to confuse the demands resulting directly from the crime and the demands which could not logically be regarded as satisfactory reparation for the crime. These were minor criticisms and, in fact, Henderson actually praised Allenby's wording of the Gezira irrigation clause 'since it has in it a menace which the Egyptian can understand as well as a basis for a useful concession.'[86]

Henderson's praise of the Residency's response to Stack's assassination undoubtedly came as a surprise to the Foreign Office, especially Henderson's expression of confidence in Clark Kerr and the belief that 'it is in the best interests of the public to keep him here [... he] knows the situation inside out and is in close personal touch with all the actors on the Cairo stage.'[87] However, this was all to no avail. Allenby stuck to his resignation and in March, with Henderson still in post, Clark Kerr was informed that he would be moved to a new positing, a transfer that he had anticipated back in December 1924.[88]

Even with the appointment of Henderson, Allenby was again forced to justify his actions and, once again, he used the issue of timing as his reason. With the resignation of

Zaghlul imminent, Allenby believed that it was of the 'highest importance for the future position here that the fullest possible measure of odium should fall upon his Ministry'.[89] Indeed, this tactic appeared to have had the desired effect as *The Times'* correspondent reported: 'the promptness with which Great Britain has acted, together with the indications that the necessary force is at hand, has greatly impressed the Egyptians and is inducing the conviction that Britain now means business'.[90] Although the High Commissioner expressed regret that circumstances had compelled him to take action before receiving Chamberlain's instructions, Allenby felt that Zaghlul should have the least possible ground for claiming to have defied His Majesty's Government and thereby maintain Britain's projection of strength and prestige within the region. In support of Allenby's actions Lord Lloyd, Allenby's successor as High Commissioner, later commented that the High Commissioner was the only person who could accurately estimate the degree of urgency:

> The courage and capacity for swift decision which he [Allenby] displayed were beyond praise: and these are qualities which are apt to be undervalued by those in the safe and sequestered atmosphere of Whitehall, who have never experienced the heat and burden of Egyptian conditions, or felt the strain of desperate issues encountered daily face to face.[91]

Lord Lloyd's comments are perhaps unsurprising following his own run-in with the Foreign Office during his appointment as High Commissioner. However, there is a deeper point to be appreciated and that is the High Commissioners were attempting to reconcile both foreign, imperial and defence policy which often worked at cross purposes in a country such as Egypt. Egypt stood not only at the cross-roads of empire for the defence of the Far East and the Antipodean nations but also on the periphery of Europe where European powers such as Italy possessed interests in North Africa that abutted the British in Egypt and whose interests British diplomacy had to be mindful.

In order to avoid an open breach with his High Commissioner, Chamberlain upheld Allenby's action at Alexandria Customs. However, he reminded Allenby that Britain's primary aim was to make British authority secure in the Sudan and to interfere as little as possible in Egypt with the Egyptian Government taking responsibility for measures required to meet the British Government's demands.[92]

Following Zaghlul's resignation and his appeal for peace and good order, the poisoned chalice was now handed to Ahmed Ziwar Pasha, who assured Allenby of his 'intention to co-operate with us [Britain], and [...] to take strenuously in hand public security and the students'.[93] Allenby did not waste any time in pushing forward Britain's three remaining demands and proposed two alternatives. Firstly, he suggested that Britain should formulate a complete policy towards Egypt and the Sudan, which would be published simultaneously in Cairo and London. His second proposal suggested negotiation on each point.[94] Chamberlain favoured the latter option as it was least likely to arouse Zaghlulist opposition and 'having at last secured a reasonably well-disposed Egyptian Government it is to our interest to make compliance by them as easy as possible'.[95] It is interesting to note that while Chamberlain reminded Allenby to bear in mind the political situation at home and abroad, Chamberlain also understood the value and sway that Allenby's opinion held:

I desire however to be guided by your advice in my choice of the course to be pursued, for you are in the best position to judge the probable effect of either [proposal] on our prospects of succeeding in Cairo.[96]

Thus, while Chamberlain probably had doubts over Allenby's abilities in undertaking delicate diplomatic manoeuvres, he still held confidence in the High Commissioner's ability to extract the best possible deal for Britain. Allenby presented the Egyptian Government with the demands necessary to ensure the evacuation of the Alexandria Customs and on the evening of 30 November, the assent of the Egyptian Government was secured.[97]

In a mere eleven days, Britain achieved its goal of supremacy in the Sudan. This had been an objective of the British Government since 1919.[98] At first glance Britain's demands following the attack upon Stack do certainly appear as a pretext for tightening the imperial noose around Egypt. Not only was Egypt unceremoniously evicted from its aspirations to empire with the evacuation of Egyptian troops from the Sudan, but Zaghlul's resignation and Ziwar's complete acceptance of Allenby's demands meant that Egyptian nationalism was momentarily checked by the reassertion of British authority. Furthermore, British dominance was assured, for the time being at least, as its one trump card was its control over the irrigation at Gezira and the latent threat this posed to Egyptian water supplies further up the Nile.

However, Allenby's reaction to Stack's assassination may also be viewed as an increasing frustration at his inability to halt attacks upon pro-British Egyptian officials and British personnel. Allenby was coming under mounting pressure from the British community to reassert order and halt this violence, something that extra precautions and increased police patrols in Cairo had failed to achieve. As a result of these compelling motives, it does appear that Allenby was directing Egyptian policy regardless of the Cabinet or Foreign Office. From the exchanges between Chamberlain and Allenby, it emerges that London was playing catch-up with the actions undertaken by Allenby, Chamberlain complaining that Allenby 'did keep me very short of information'.[99] Was he a High Commissioner out of control? He certainly blatantly disregarded instructions from London regardless it seems of public opinion at home or abroad. This obviously became such a concern for his political masters that Nevile Henderson was despatched to Cairo undoubtedly to rein in the errant High Commissioner. Nonetheless, to Allenby his motives were clear: to reassert British authority, and to place as much responsibility as possible on Zaghlul and his nationalist associates for Stack's death in order to discredit the nationalist movement.[100] This also came at a cost to Allenby. Despite pleas from Chamberlain, and seconded by Baldwin, to reconsider his threat of resignation, Allenby left the Residency in June 1925.[101]

The trial

The trial of Stack's assailants naturally attracted much press attention with detailed daily reports appearing in the newspapers.[102] In total, nine assailants were prosecuted. The trail concluded on 1 June 1925 and Abdel Hamid Enayat, Abdel Fattah Enayat,

Ibrahim Moussa, Mahmoud Rashid, Aly Ibrahim Mohammed, Raghib Hassan, Shafik Mansur and Mahmoud Ismail were all sentenced to death. The taxi driver Mahmoud Hassan Saleh was sentenced to three years' imprisonment with penal servitude.[103] However, following further confessions the sentences were reviewed. G H Hughes, Chief Inspector of the Parquet, recommended that Abdel Fattah Enayat's sentence be reduced to lifetime imprisonment with penal servitude for several reasons:

a) it is entirely due to his confession that the whole gang have been apprehended [...]
b) as far as can be judged, his statements have been true throughout;
c) clemency extended to a criminal whose avowals have been full and accurate is likely to encourage similar confessions in future crimes;
d) the evidence of Abdel Fattah Enayat [...] will be required in the trial of Mohammed Fahmy.[104]

Hughes also added that he did not consider that the commutation of the death penalty in the case of Abdel Fattah Enayat would be looked upon by the Egyptian public as a sign of weakness but rather as indicating that 'we are just and not vindictive'.[105] This recommendation for clemency was to be delivered by the Egyptian King as 'it is better that the Residency and His Majesty's Government should not appear to have played any part in the matter',[106] and risk an early return of Zaghlul.

The executions of the remaining seven condemned men took place on Sunday 23 August 1925, a date that was kept secret to avoid inflaming nationalist opinion. R Graves, Acting Director-General of the Ministry of the Interior, commented: 'The spirit of Islam is well brought out by the fact that not one of them uttered a word of regret for killing a Christian'.[107]

Consequences: The Anglo-Egyptian relationship

Britain's actions over the murder of Sir Lee Stack were called into question in a number of quarters, not least in the Houses of Parliament. In response, Chamberlain emphasized that the assassination was not an isolated incident but rather the 'natural outcome of that campaign of hatred of Great Britain which had been fomented by Egyptian politicians, and which Zaghlul Pasha had singularly failed to discourage'.[108] Thus, the British Government was guided by two considerations when devising its demands. Firstly, it was necessary to bring to an end the subversive activities that threatened to jeopardize peaceful progress in the Sudan. This conveniently included removing the restriction over irrigation at Gezira. This action was defended as being necessary to ensure the continued economic development of the Sudan. In other words, it shored up Britain's dominant position by providing a bulwark against any Egyptian nationalist expansionist ideas within the Sudan. Secondly, the British Government maintained that the demands took into consideration 'the machinery devised in 1922 for the protection of foreign interests [which] should be allowed to perform its functions'.[109] In practice this meant that foreign officials in the Egyptian service 'should be protected from acts of spite and vindictiveness [... and] that the pensions of retired officials should be protected against confiscation by the manipulation of depreciation of the Egyptian currency'.[110]

The assassination of Stack presented Britain with an opportunity of punishing the Egyptian nationalists and in the context of increasing political violence Allenby was not about to pass this up. However, cutting off the head of Egyptian nationalism and alienating those who had any nationalist credentials and the support of the people meant that Britain ensured a Wafd victory in the elections of June 1926. This was the final time that Britain could act with such impunity.

6

'I Wish Austen Were Less of an Old Woman and Less Occupied with His Tea Parties in Geneva': The Conservative Government and the Anglo-Egyptian Treaty Negotiations

Negotiations for an Anglo-Egyptian settlement were not attempted again until 1927 under a very different set of circumstances from that of 1924. Britain was governed by a Conservative administration under Stanley Baldwin, with Austen Chamberlain at the helm of the Foreign Office. Egypt, on the other hand, was led by Abd al Khaliq Sarwat Pasha.[1] Following the resignation of Lord Allenby over the handling of Sir Lee Stack's assassination, George Lloyd was appointed to the post of High Commissioner. Lloyd's appointment to this post was not without difficulties.[2] Despite a promise from Baldwin to Lloyd that Egypt's High Commissionership was his, he was actually offered the governorship of Kenya where the white settlers had been 'clamouring for him'.[3] Chamberlain commented to Baldwin that 'some of our colleagues seemed to think that G[eorge] L[loyd] was not sufficiently imposing'.[4] Leo Amery, now Colonial Secretary, made it clear to Lloyd that there had been a change of mind about sending him to Egypt as they had found a more suitable candidate. Although Amery promised Lloyd would be considered as a possible Viceroy for India, Lloyd's long-held ambition, he would not be the first choice for the position. Amery therefore implied that 'unless G[eorge] took Kenya, there would be nothing for him at all'.[5] Since Lloyd had turned down the Governorship of Kenya seven years previously, before heading for Bombay, this came as 'a staggering blow and utterly bewildering'.[6]

Nevertheless, undeterred by this news, both Lloyd and his wife, Blanche, continued to press his right to the High Commissionership of Egypt and the Sudan throughout March, lobbying individuals, such as Stanley Baldwin, Edward Wood and Austen Chamberlain. This finally paid off and, despite receiving short shrift from Austen Chamberlain over a letter Lloyd had written to him,[7] Lloyd received a phone call from Baldwin assuring him that 'it is all right [...] the post will be offered to him'.[8] The offer was made on 30 March 1925. However, it was a hollow victory as Chamberlain informed Lloyd that 'his pressing his claim in the way he did had done him harm both with himself, Austen and with the prime minister – and had left an unfortunate impression on their minds'.[9] A sign of things to come! The Lloyds departed for Egypt in October 1925 in full knowledge of the difficulty involved in making a striking success as a British administrator in Egypt. 'That is the big gamble of taking the post', remarked Lloyd.[10]

The Lloyds' arrival in Egypt

On 21 October the Lloyds landed at Port Said and were met by Ralph Wiggin, First Secretary of the Chancery, and Robert Furness, Oriental Secretary, and a number of Egyptian officials. They then completed their journey to Cairo by train and were met by Nevile Henderson and a number of Egyptian notables and members of the British community. Incidentally, on the day of their arrival it had rained in Cairo, which was looked upon as a good omen. The Lloyds' first impression was not altogether favourable. They were immediately struck by the 'rather higgledy piggledy formation of the people at the station – not nearly so well arranged as they would have been in India and introductions were therefore very difficult'.[11] The Lloyds proceeded to the Residency – about a mile and a half – in an open-top Rolls Royce and were '*very much struck by the number of people in the streets, and by the cordiality of their welcome* – far better than either of us had expected'.[12] The Zaghlulists had also joined in welcoming the Lloyds 'considering that at the outset discretion was the better part of valour'.[13] The warmth of their reception in Egypt was taken to reflect an 'expression of their weariness' with the overbearing rule of the King and of a 'hope that England might now relieve them of it'.[14] Although impressed by this welcome, the Lloyds' were also realistic about its meaning: 'one knows that it means little or nothing'.[15]

Lord Lloyd arrived in Egypt with a determination to make 'the policy of 1922 a real policy – to leave no doubt in any minds that whilst the measure of independence granted under the Declaration must be real, the reservations and Egypt's respect for them must be equally real and our intention to see them respected made evident'.[16] However, almost as soon as the Lloyds had arrived in Egypt, the maelstrom of Egyptian political life engulfed them. Indeed, in one of Lloyd's first letters to Chamberlain, he noted: 'I feel as if I had walked into a political Bedlam where everything is strident and nothing is real – the most complete tangle I think I ever saw'.[17] While a successful tenure in Egypt would certainly strengthen 'George's elbow'[18] for his Indian ambition, it was not going to be an easy task.

Lord Lloyd's first steps in Egypt began rather tentatively, but this timidity was short-lived and throughout 1926 and 1927 relations between the Foreign Office and the Residency became somewhat strained due to his dogged persistence over the number of honours for Egypt and the Sudan and the handling of the Army Crisis.[19] This led Chamberlain to comment:

> You do occasionally hold rather severe language to your Secretary of State and speak to him more imperatively than our other representatives abroad are accustomed to do [...] You and I understand one another too well for mischief to arise between us on this account [...] But beware of this tone in public telegrams for some criticism was made to me about this in high quarters a little time back where it had produced an unfortunate impression.[20]

Indeed, Lord Lloyd was warned that his private letters to Chamberlain were tending to replace those of official despatches in conveying the political situation. Chamberlain tersely asked Lloyd to 'regard any private letters which you may have occasion to send me as supplementary to and not in substitution for official despatches'.[21] With the mounting pressure of the Chinese crisis throughout 1927, the Foreign Office deemed it imperative that Egypt was kept quiet. 'Its repercussion will no doubt make itself felt in Cairo according to the success we obtain in the Far East'.[22]

King Fuad and Sarwat's visit to Britain

Lord Lloyd and the Foreign Office certainly strove for the same aim – a quiescent Egypt – but their methods were very much at odds.[23] It was during the summer of 1927, as Lloyd returned to England on leave, that King Fuad's long projected visit to London took place. King Fuad was accompanied by Sarwat, and Lloyd was hopeful that demonstrations of goodwill on both sides would consolidate Sarwat's position and thereby allow the dust to settle following the favourable settlement of the Army Crisis.

Once the opening ceremonies of King Fuad's visit were over, Sarwat met Chamberlain at the Foreign Office on 12 July. During this meeting Chamberlain urged Sarwat to consider the necessity of reaching a permanent agreement between Britain and Egypt and to 'perhaps prepare the way for conversations between himself [Sarwat] and Lord Lloyd when they had both returned to Egypt'.[24] It remains unclear whether Chamberlain intended some form of draft agreement to emerge from Sarwat's visit. He certainly protested that 'I had no idea of entering into a negotiation with [Sarwat] during his visit', but acknowledged that it would be 'useful if before Lord Lloyd left, I could give him rather more precise indications on the lines on which we might proceed'.[25] In a letter to Ida, Chamberlain's sister, Chamberlain commented that his conversation with Sarwat was:

> extraordinarily interesting and important. What if anything will eventually come of them is in the lap of the Gods – very probably nothing, but even so they are most useful, for they have enabled me to win his confidence and he has shown a more serious desire for agreement and in private a clearer understanding of the facts of the situation than any Egyptian has yet done.[26]

According to Chamberlain's account, it was after this initial conversation that Sarwat produced a draft treaty of perpetual friendship and alliance. Whatever Chamberlain's intentions were, permanent officials at the Foreign Office began negotiations with Sarwat on 13 July 1927, without recourse to Lord Lloyd who was in London on leave.[27]

At a lunch meeting with Walford Selby, principal private secretary to the foreign secretary, and William Tyrrell, permanent under-secretary of state for foreign affairs, Sarwat was told that the British desired a settlement which centred around three points: (1) the army, (2) the British advisers and (3) the safeguarding of foreigners and their property.[28] In producing the Egyptian draft, Sarwat stated he had communicated the draft to Kind Fuad, who was in general agreement with the idea.[29] While it would be impossible for Britain to accept Sarwat's draft, Chamberlain believed that it 'marked a great advance in the attitude of any previous Egyptian Government since 1922. It seemed to show that Sarwat Pasha had been attracted by Sir Austen's idea, and that he hoped to do business'.³⁰ On 20 July Chamberlain informed the Cabinet that in response to Sarwat's draft he had formed a committee in the Foreign Office, which included Lord Lloyd, to examine the draft and prepare alternative clauses where necessary. Once this was completed the Cabinet agreed that Sarwat's draft and the comments of the Foreign Office should be considered by a ten-man Cabinet committee.³¹

On 28 July the Cabinet considered Sarwat's draft treaty together with the alternative Foreign Office draft approved by the above committee.³² Concern was expressed over three issues: Britain's position if Egypt became a member of the League of Nations; the lack of provision for the British protection of minorities, which formed the third reserved point in the 1922 Declaration; and the growth of maladministration and corruption in line with a diminution of British control and guidance. In reference to the League question, a report, undertaken by Sir Douglas Hogg, actually suggested Egypt's accession to the League as any disputes referred to the League would improve Britain's position 'more especially owing to the regularisation of the position of the British Army in Egypt'.³³ For the protection of minorities, it was suggested that Britain would be deprived of all power to come to their aid, especially if minorities were oppressed to the point where serious trouble might arise. In the last resort, an appeal to the League could be made. The Foreign Office emphasized the fact that 'if we [HMG] were unwilling to make any concessions of this kind it was useless to hope for an Agreement'.³⁴ In relation to the increase of maladministration and the decrease in British power within the Egyptian administration, the Cabinet was again reminded: 'To insist on further British control of the Administration involved a policy inconsistent with the Declaration and would render any treaty out of the question'.³⁵ With these terse words from the Foreign Office, the Cabinet agreed to the continuation of negotiations with Sarwat on the basis of the Committee-approved treaty but that no concessions should be made without reference to the Cabinet. Furthermore, the Cabinet wanted the Treaty to be a permanent one rather than one for a period of fifteen or twenty years as suggested.

Chamberlain found a great deal of support from the Foreign Office for his Egyptian policy. According to Chamberlain, Tyrrell commented: 'You put your European policy on the right footing by Locarno, you did the same for China with your December declaration, now you have done the same for Egypt. You are on firm ground in all three.'³⁶ Selby also supported Chamberlain's Egyptian stance. 'Do you remember saying some time ago that you had won your niche in the temple of foreign affairs by your work in Europe and ought to get out before you lost in China or Egypt? Well, you won't lose it now in Egypt. I can't tell how delighted I am, for I have been anxious about Egypt.'³⁷ It is interesting to note that despite Chamberlain's assurance that Lloyd had been associated with the Cabinet committee charged with examining the draft treaty, according to Lloyd this was not the case. 'Had I been consulted – and as I was in London, consultation with me was not difficult – I should have urged […] that in the present temper of Egypt there was absolutely no hope of any treaty which maintained the interests that we considered vital being accepted by that country.'³⁸ It would certainly appear that the Foreign Office wished to place Anglo-Egyptian relations on a solid footing and felt that it could not rely on the imperious Lloyd to undertake this initiative. Indeed, when it was suggested that he should attend a Cabinet meeting to express his views prior to his departure for Egypt, the Prime Minister responded that this was premature. The CID was not even consulted over the security of imperial communications until October/November 1927. Chamberlain was satisfied that Sarwat wished to reach a settlement and it was agreed that he would return in October to continue treaty discussions.[39]

Zaghlul's death

Meanwhile, news of the unexpected death of Zaghlul on 23 August 1927, from blood poisoning, was received with caution at the Residency. The timing of his death was certainly opportune from a public security angle. The Egyptian Parliament was in recess, and many of those likely to foment excitement were on their country estates or abroad. The students themselves were on their summer holidays whilst the critical season of the Nile flood kept the *fellahin* busy in their fields. The great heat of August was itself a deterrent to enthusiasm.[40] Although Zaghlul's death did not occasion unrest, the Residency did not believe that with his passing British difficulties would disappear:

> With his death he passes into a silence which preserves him from any possibility of weakness or error, and may give to the record of his spoken words an iron flexibility. The tradition of a dead past is sometimes more powerful than the logic and arguments of the living, or than the present expediency of altered circumstances.[41]

Indeed, as the *Manchester Guardian* remarked, 'Zaghlul Pasha was the only man whose signature to an Anglo-Egyptian settlement would have bound his countrymen, almost without exception'. The primary concern for the British was who would succeed Zaghlul as leader of the Wafd. Henderson questioned 'whether there is an Egyptian of moral courage great enough to recommend his country to accept what the dead man had hitherto, and perhaps would never have, dared to recommend'.[42] Although it was hoped that Zaghlul's death would mean the disappearance of a number of mischievous individuals and a general disorganization of the Wafd, concern was expressed over the running of Egypt without Zaghlul's steadying influence. 'Younger men than he may well not shrink from, or even welcome, the martyrdom which is often an essential part in the making of national leaders and heroes.'[43]

In essence, the whole balance of power had been disturbed by Zaghlul's death. With nationalist power temporarily in abeyance, Henderson believed that this would provide King Fuad with a very definite opportunity. 'Of all Egyptians, the King of Egypt is the only one who might have some prospect of succeeding Saad as the universally recognised leader of the nation. Under his aegis alone is real unity practicable.'[44] Of course, this situation would not be entirely unproblematic, especially in relation to Sarwat's forthcoming conversations with Chamberlain in October. Therefore, Henderson urged a wait and see approach for the moment. 'The only useful role which the Residency can at present play is that of an interested spectator, whose participation in development will be sought the more eagerly by Egyptians if it is in no way thrust upon them.'[45]

Anglo-Egyptian relations were certainly at a crossroads. Zaghlul's death complicated matters for the British. If Zaghlul had survived, Sarwat would have had only one person to report to, whose decision would have virtually decided the acceptance or rejection of any Anglo-Egyptian terms. Zaghlul was viewed as having the power and authority to have silenced the extremists. Now, however, Sarwat needed the support of all the moderate elements of the Egyptian Parliament in order to make an agreement with Britain.[46] Mustafa al-Nahas Pasha was elected as the new Wafd leader. A man, who, although 'sincere, eloquent and honest', was 'hysterical, fanatic and unbalanced, with a warped mind that gives to his every thought since his early close association with Mustapha Kemel Pasha a definitely Anglophobe twist'.[47] The Wafd manifesto, published on 20 September, was as hostile to Sarwat and the Liberals as to England. Henderson warned that 'there is thus cause to apprehend that the future councils of the Wafd will be controlled by its firebrands, and that the moderation which Zaghlul inspired in recent crises with Great Britain will henceforward be lacking'.[48] Indeed, as storm clouds were gathering in the Egyptian political sky, Henderson predicted that the growing influence of extremists within the Wafd made some sort of British intervention in the near future highly likely unless some firm ground could be found where the moderates could challenge the extremists with a good chance of success. To this end, the Foreign Office allowed Henderson to give Sarwat encouragement for further conversations with Britain over the treaty if only to split the Egyptian nationalist opinion still further.[49]

Nahas's advent to power certainly made Sarwat's task harder as the Egyptian Parliament was dominated by Wafd extremists. Henderson believed that Sarwat hoped to obtain from Britain an agreement that was largely a compromise between his original and the Foreign Office's counter draft, thus seeking to obtain in London an idea of the limits of concessions from the British government. Henderson certainly placed great faith in Sarwat's abilities. 'He is such a thorough master of political intricacies that any line of action adopted by him is likely to contain considerable chance of success.'[50] Indeed, John Murray emphasized that Zaghlul's death and the election of Nahas as leader of the Wafd 'should not affect our policy'.[51] This aimed at creating a party of moderate men who would, in time, be able to speak for Egypt and with whom it would then be possible to do business. Of course this required a British representative who possessed 'patience and forebearance', as without these 'there is every prospect of a very early clash which may easily involve us much more deeply than we want to go'.[52] Chamberlain agreed and noted:

1. Whether we are moving slowly towards peace or quickly towards trouble, we must walk with extreme caution.
2. We must play out the hand which I have dealt, i.e. work for an accord, whether treaty or not, until it has been proved impossible by action of the Egyptians. There are possibilities, probabilities some would say of failure, but our only possible policy is to do everything in our power to secure its success. And if we fail – 'patience and shuffle the cards'.[53]

This raised the question of whether, in light of Lord Lloyd's difficult relationship with the Foreign Office, was he their man to fulfil this policy? In a memorandum reluctantly submitted by Murray, the divergence of opinion between Tyrrell and Murray on the one hand and Lord Lloyd on the other was exposed, in particular over the 1922 Declaration of Independence and the policy which inspired it:

> Lord Lloyd remains as firmly determined as ever to emphasise the 'negative and prohibitive' side of the 1922 Declaration, and to aim at 'decisive action' in Egypt. The Department, on the other hand, are convinced that Lord Lloyd is mistaken in both respects and that if he is allowed to work on these lines the result can only be disastrous; they believe that a not unsatisfactory working arrangement, compatible with reasonable British and Egyptian requirements, can ultimately be obtained and can only be obtained by continuing to apply the 1922 policy.[54]

Sarwat departed for London without having taken either the Egyptian Cabinet or the Wafd into his confidence. Yet, Henderson noted that he still enjoyed widespread political support. With this in mind, Henderson continued his cautiously optimistic assessment.

> This attitude indicates a real desire, which has for some time past been steadily growing, on the part of Egyptians generally, to come to some definite agreement with us [...] It does not, of course, follow that Egyptian politicians are yet ready for an agreement such as would give satisfaction to our vital interests, but the ground may at least be cleared for future constructive work.[55]

Henderson also emphasized the precarious nature of Nahas's position:

> Nahas and his friends are inexperienced in the more practical and responsible side of politics. They have, no doubt, a healthy fear of us and some apprehension of Sarwat, sphinx-like, waiting for his opportunity, and the master of political arts in Egypt. All these circumstances no doubt incline Nahas to think it advisable to endeavour to allay the apprehensions of possibly dangerous adversaries, until, at any rate, he has had time to strengthen his position, both within and without his party. Time, however, is just as likely to work against him as for him.[56]

The Chamberlain-Sarwat discussions

Even though Henderson's despatches swung like a pendulum from cautionary remarks to outright optimism,[57] the Foreign Office interpreted them as reasons to push for an agreement when Sarwat arrived in London at the end of October. The idea was that further negotiations would make it easier for Sarwat to form a pro-treaty faction, which could lessen the influence, and perhaps, in time, out vote the extremists. Chamberlain informed the Cabinet that Sarwat had shown the draft treaty to Fatallah Barakat, a member of the Wafd, Adli and other Liberals, and that he had some hope of obtaining support in the Egyptian Parliament for a treaty. If acceptance could not be secured, Sarwat would recommend the dissolution of Parliament.[58] This does appear to be stretching the facts somewhat on the Foreign Office's part. There was never any firm confirmation that Sarwat had divulged the details of his discussions with Chamberlain prior to his departure for a second round of talks, certainly to Adli and Barakat. It also seems fantastic that Sarwat was willing to propose dissolution of the Chamber bearing in mind his pessimism prior to his departure over the loss of Zaghlul and the impact of this in securing acceptance of a settlement. The interpretation of Henderson's despatches was certainly optimistic.

Once Chamberlain had had his first meeting with Sarwat, there was again some discrepancy between Cairo and the Foreign Office. According to Chamberlain, Sarwat believed that the prospect of obtaining Egypt's assent to an agreement was 'rather improved by Zaghlul's death'.[59] This was obviously in direct contrast to Henderson's discussions with Sarwat prior to his departure. While Sarwat may have had an unexpected change of mind once he met Chamberlain, it is clear that the Foreign Office was emphasizing only the positive aspects of Henderson's despatches to the Cabinet. As regards the treaty itself, Chamberlain made it clear to Sarwat that it was impossible to fix a date for the evacuation of British troops from Cairo. He was unable to go beyond a promise to re-examine the question after ten years. In relation to the Sudan, Chamberlain emphasized that any change to the *status quo ante* was also impossible. Three years after the murder of Sir Lee Stack and the creation of the Sudan Defence Force, the Sudan was inevitably a difficult issue and Sarwat was willing to omit all mention of the Sudan. In some matters Chamberlain thought it might be possible to accommodate Sarwat, either by omitting particular words from the draft or by providing explanations. The details and the form of the Treaty were to be worked out between Sarwat, Sir Cecil Hurst, Britain's Principal Legal Adviser, and Murray after which discussions would be held within the Foreign Office with Lord Lloyd.[60]

Sarwat Pasha left London for Paris on 8 November with a Cabinet-approved Treaty, subject to two additional conditions:

1. that in the event of the transfer of British troops to the Canal Zone as a result of a decision by the League of Nations, alternate accommodation would be provided at the expense of the Egyptian Government;
2. that the Egyptian Army should be limited to 12,250.[61]

Selby was dispatched to Paris later on the same day in order to reach agreement on these points as it was desired to avoid any reopening of the negotiations with Sarwat by telegram following his return to Cairo.[62] It is interesting that Lord Lloyd was not party to this, although he was in Paris. Nevertheless, Selby managed to reach an agreement with Sarwat over the limitation of the Egyptian army by linking it with admission to the League of Nations. However, agreement over alternative accommodation in the event of British troops being transferred to the Canal Zone was more problematic and it remained the single point on which a final agreement could not be reached. According to Selby, Sarwat left Paris on the understanding that 'he must make it clear to those in Egypt with whom he would discuss the question that the arrangement on which he had agreed must be taken as it stood or left'.[63] Sarwat, appreciating Selby's point, replied that he would 'oppose any idea of reopening the question by telegraph'.[64]

The full extent of the negotiations was finally disclosed to Lord Lloyd at the end of October. Lord Lloyd believed these negotiations to be not only 'impolitic, and useless, but actually full of harmful possibilities to our own interests, and to those of our Egyptian supporters [...] The one thing that was certain to destroy the influence of reasonable opinion was to throw into the present situation the torch of agreement with England, with its inevitable result of inflaming emotional unreason'.[65] When asked to comment on the draft treaty, Lloyd felt that Britain was not securing fully her vital imperial and commercial interests. This was a view echoed by the Chiefs of Staff. Any diminution in the security of this strategic link would not only have consequences in or near Egypt alone but would affect almost every portion of the Empire:

> Should there be any risk of free communication through the Canal being severed or menaced, it follows that our Naval forces on each side of the Suez Isthmus may have to be regarded as self contained and separate entities; for example, Singapore may have to strengthened to render it less dependent on home supplies and support.
>
> Apart from the actual dispositions of our Naval forces, it will be necessary to reconsider our cruiser, destroyer and submarine strength.
>
> Further, the alternative route to the East via the Cape will immediately assume greater importance, with consequent increases to the garrisons and armaments of essential bases lying along this route. For example, it may become necessary to review the recent decision in regard to the defended port of Sierra Leone.
>
> Lastly, the possible reactions on the scale of defences on the Overseas Dominions of South Africa, Australia, New Zealand and in India must not be overlooked.
>
> It is for His Majesty's Government to decide whether the increased risk to the security of the Canal and the possible consequences [...] outweigh the political advantages which are claimed for the Treaty.[66]

Military considerations versus the political advantages were the crux of the issue. With the full support of the Egyptian Department,[67] Chamberlain argued that 'there was now an unprecedented opportunity of placing our relations with Egypt on a footing more permanent and secure than any basis we have had since our first occupation of the country'.[68] According to Chamberlain, the proposed treaty secured a military alliance; barred foreigners, other than British subjects, from the service of the Egyptian state; laid down Britain's right to maintain troops as necessary and in perpetuity; and in the event of Britain being engaged in a war, Egypt would afford Britain all her assistance, including harbours, waterways and communications.[69] In response to the Chiefs of Staff's fears over the security of the Suez Canal, Chamberlain believed that the risks would be less by substituting an alliance for the present 'ambiguous and unsatisfactory position'.[70]

The Home Secretary, William Joynson-Hicks, expressed grave anxiety over the wisdom of concluding the proposed treaty as he 'feared the only result would be demand for further concessions and the gradual whittling down of our power in Egypt'.[71] The Secretary of State for War, Laming Worthington-Evans, also voiced opposition to the treaty on grounds of public policy and imperial defence. Nevertheless, and despite the opposition of Churchill, Joynson-Hicks and Worthington-Evans, the Cabinet approved the draft treaty.[72]

Sarwat and the treaty in Egypt

With Cabinet and Dominion approval secured, the truly difficult task began when Sarwat took the treaty to Egypt. Chamberlain wasted no time in communicating the approved draft to Lloyd on Lloyd's return to Egypt, seeing it as the logical outcome of British policy that had been followed for the last seven years. Aware of Lord Lloyd's reservations over the negotiations, Chamberlain instructed Lord Lloyd to

> take every opportunity of assisting Sarwat in his endeavour to obtain the ratification of this treaty [...] by the exercise of particular patience and forbearance in the treatment of any questions pending between the two Governments [...] I count with confidence on you for those qualities of patience, tact and moderation which will be required for the safe conduct of our enterprise, [...] the greater the achievement if successful the graver the consequences which would follow on failure'.[73]

Initially, Sarwat seemed 'extremely optimistic and cheerful [...] Nahas was behaving himself fairly well – and [...] he had every hope that all would go smoothly', so long as he had as much time as necessary in order to secure the assent of the Egyptian Parliament. This was to become the major sticking point. Murray noted that 'I do not think that either Sarwat or Lord Lloyd realise that we were expecting the signature of the treaty to take place within the next few days'.[74] Unsurprisingly, Lloyd dissented somewhat from Sarwat's sanguinity. 'I am a little puzzled at the degree of this [Sarwat's] optimism in so far as it conflicts to a certain extent with all our private information – for however well things may be going there can be no question that Sarwat has many difficulties to face'.[75] Lloyd found it extremely hard to believe that the extreme element in the Wafd would accept any treaty without a fight, and all depended on whether Sarwat could succeed in detaching sufficient Wafd moderates to his side to enable him to face Parliament.[76] As instructed by Chamberlain, Lloyd proposed to remain in the background as much as possible and encourage Sarwat from behind the scenes until the terms of the treaty became public, at which point he would be able to take on a more active role.[77]

Chamberlain was clearly anxious for the treaty to be signed as soon as possible. The Foreign Office was painfully aware that the longer the treaty remained unsigned, and therefore unpublished, the greater the danger that garbled versions of its provisions would leak out. This could harm and, possibly wreck, any prospect of its acceptance. As early as 30 November, Lloyd began sounding alarm bells over Sarwat's attitude. 'There are [...] indications that Sarwat is shrinking from the final plunge [...] He is anxiously testing the temperature of the water and the direction of the wind'.[78] Sarwat was 'surprised and perturbed',[79] when handing Sarwat Chamberlain's telegram inviting his prompt signature of the treaty. He reminded the High Commissioner that Chamberlain had assured him he could have whatever time was necessary to ensure success. Still bristling from his exclusion from the negotiations, Lloyd commented:

> I do not of course know what you said to him about this [time …] There is no doubt he wants to gain time in view of the very real difficulties with which he is faced. A divided Cabinet and no majority of his own are not the only difficulties he has to face, for he has a press which constantly calls upon him to take the nation at once into his confidence.[80]

Chamberlain backed off, declaring that 'I am content to wait patiently for what he may consider the opportune moment and to leave him to do his work in his own way. He has obviously got a difficult and delicate task before him and he is in the best position to judge in what way he is most likely to secure the necessary support'.[81]

In an interview with Lloyd, Sarwat stated that he was unable to show the draft treaty to his Cabinet colleagues and Nahas until a number of outstanding points were resolved. These were:

1. A more precise understanding as to what were to be the functions of British officers in the Egyptian Army after the treaty;
2. Certain points in regard to Nile 'control'; and
3. General questions arising out of article 9 in regard to the Capitulations.[82]

In Lloyd's assessment there was a real concern that Sarwat might attempt to broaden the scope of the conversations. Whilst the High Commissioner advocated listening to Sarwat's proposals, he confined them to subsidiary notes in order to avoid calling into question the text of the actual treaty:

> Sarwat's difficulties are very real, and undue hastening on our part may not only drive him to a false step for which we shall be blamed, but may be construed as excessive anxiety in our own interests to secure a Treaty, which should be regarded by Egyptians as an offer which we may not repeat, and which, if declined, we can afford to drop without imperilling those British interests which, treaty or no treaty, we intend to safeguard.
> I propose to hurry on as much as possible the further conversations which Sarwat desires and then to wait until he can speak to me for his Cabinet as a whole and until he has consulted Nahas Pasha.[83]

Lloyd's picture appeared even gloomier just prior to Christmas as Sarwat proceeded to examine the treaty clause by clause seeking Lloyd's adherence to his interpretation of the meaning of each clause. Lloyd refused to express any opinion to Sarwat but Sarwat clearly took advantage of Lloyd's original exclusion from the negotiations in London, by exploiting the High Commissioner's inability to accept or refute Sarwat's interpretation.[84] Indeed, by excluding Lord Lloyd from the original talks in London, the Foreign Office had effectively circumscribed the power of the Residency in one fell swoop ensuring that London controlled the course of Anglo-Egyptian relations. This was certainly shown by instances such as the failure to consult Lord Lloyd over the appointment of an Iraqi Consul-General in Cairo.

It was becoming increasingly clear that the treaty would not be published until after Christmas, already over a month since Sarwat had returned to Egypt. Sarwat made excuses such as awaiting the British government's response to his interpretations of the clauses as recorded and communicated by the High Commissioner, and waiting until the King of Afghanistan's visit to Egypt was completed on 5 January 1928.[85] The Foreign Office was unhappy over the way matters were moving in Egypt and largely blamed Lloyd for this. Tyrrell wrote to Chamberlain complaining that if Lloyd's telegrams were taken at face value they 'would appear to indicate that Sarwat was going to prove both slippery and unreliable. This you will recollect was the impression of him which Lloyd was anxious to create when he was over here this summer'.[86] Moreover, doubt was again cast upon Lloyd's reading of the Egyptian situation: 'I find it difficult to reconcile Sarwat's apparent wish to reopen discussions with Lloyd on a number of points of detail with the very genuine anxiety he displayed a few weeks ago to clear up everything during his negotiations with you [Chamberlain] and to leave as little as possible for settlement in Cairo'.[87] Tyrrell and Godfrey Locker-Lampson, Parliamentary Under-Secretary of State for Foreign Affairs, clearly did not have any confidence in Lloyd's completion of the instructions from the Foreign Office and even suggested that Hurst and Murray be sent to Egypt in order to continue and complete the London conversations.[88]

Despite Sarwat's vacillations, Chamberlain continued to hold faith in him. 'It is not that I suspect him of wishing to go back on the arrangement to which we came, but I am a little afraid of his losing his opportunity by too much delay.'[89] As a result, the Foreign Office advocated employing a stronger line with Egyptian politicians in order to rally support for Sarwat and the treaty. It warned that since Egypt formed a vital line of communication for the British Empire, Britain would not hesitate to use force for the protection of her interests or the discharge of her obligations from which 'Egypt, not Great Britain, would emerge the loser'.[90] Nonetheless, the New Year only brought new questions from Sarwat. Lord Lloyd complained that:

> Sarwat continues to raise difficulties at every step [...] Our [Henderson and Lord Lloyd's] united efforts to get Sarwat to take the treaty to his Cabinet have so far completely failed. It is very difficult to find any justification for his attitude. He quite definitely accepted that text in London. Since his arrival here he has in effect done nothing but question it.[91]

Even the Foreign Office was beginning to realize that an Anglo-Egyptian treaty was not going to be as straightforward as first thought.[92] A frustrated Murray minuted: 'We showed the Egyptians that there was a whip in the cupboard; if we want to get the Treaty signed the time has come to take it out and crack it.'[93]

Lloyd, however, already felt that he and the Foreign Office had gone far enough. 'I cannot conceal from you that I think that the interpretations already given tend to some weakening of the text to our disadvantage.'[94] He was certainly frustrated with

Sarwat and urged Chamberlin to force Sarwat's hand. 'It is now several weeks since Sarwat's return during which he has had every possible encouragement and support from us, and I think the time has come when we must tell him that he must take the treaty to his Cabinet.'⁹⁵ Lloyd believed that further interpretations or modification would render the text and Britain's position 'almost ridiculous'. Chamberlain tended to agree. 'I have gone, I think, as far as is wise or indeed possible to help Sarwat.'⁹⁶ Moreover, it was highly probable that once the treaty went to the Egyptian Cabinet further demands would be made. Letting the matter drift endlessly was also hurting the treaty's prospects as the moderates were becoming increasingly frustrated at Sarwat's lack of communication and the administration's increasing paralysis whilst the Wafd were busily engaged in passing certain laws in Parliament aimed at strengthening their organization in the country as a whole.

Labour Party speeches, notably Trevelyan's and Ronald McNeill's, were also seized upon by the Egyptian press as proving that if only Egypt could wait until the British general election better terms could be secured from a Labour administration than from any Conservative government.⁹⁷ The position of the Egyptian King was also increasingly difficult to gauge with charges against the King of anti-Sarwat intrigue. So much so that Chamberlain instructed Lloyd to warn King Fuad that the British government 'do not intend to allow themselves to be used by him as his instrument to effect the drastic reduction of the powers of Parliament on the one hand and of the Wafd on the other'.⁹⁸ Chamberlain continued: 'The King's position in the last resort depends on our support, and this he can only have by conforming to our policy.'⁹⁹ Chamberlain was not about to let 'the worst elements in Egyptian politics, with the King's connivance if not his encouragement, wreck a favourable opportunity for a settlement'.¹⁰⁰

By the end of January 1928, Lloyd had completely given up hope on Sarwat securing Egyptian political support for the treaty. 'What is really the case, I am afraid, is that Sarwat cannot muster the courage either to go forward or to go back – and is completely indecisive'.¹⁰¹ Since his return to Egypt, Sarwat had been diagnosed with diabetes and kidney trouble which might have also diminished his political energy. According to Lloyd, 'Sarwat is undoubtedly terrified of the Wafd [...] Even if he eventually sums up courage to take the Treaty to his Cabinet I doubt if he will advocate it, or tell them that he had accepted it in London, he is more likely to lay it before them saying that it was the most he could get out of us'.¹⁰² Perhaps mindful of his detractors within the Foreign Office, Lloyd was at pains to point out that during his conversations with Sarwat, Henderson was always present and in his recommendations to the Foreign Office he had 'gone further towards meeting Sarwat's requests than you yourself deemed prudent, simply because I felt pledged to you to leave no stone unturned to get the treaty signed'.¹⁰³ However, Lloyd drew the line at further concessions over the army or police, raising the Bolshevik threat as his reason.

According to the High Commissioner, dangerous Bolshevik activity extended from Palestine, through Egypt – with the re-introduction of their commercial propaganda – to Jeddah and the Red Sea littoral. 'Their successful infection of these areas will yield them results far beyond the Middle East itself, for every pilgrim will carry the virus back to India, Ceylon and Java, as well as to East Africa, the Sudan and even to the Hausa country in West Africa.'[104] A combination of Egyptian fear and the short-sightedness of the Wafd in refusing to ally themselves with other forces who depended upon the same methods of political agitation as themselves would allow the Soviets to succeed in establishing their influence in Egypt in a formidable manner. 'What we do in Egypt at this juncture is, in my opinion, not only of local strategic importance and cannot in our consideration of the problem be confined to the mere protection of the canal, but must be envisaged in regard to its effect upon the whole Middle East and India itself.'[105]

Despite making further representations to Sarwat, as instructed by Chamberlain, the Egyptian prime minister remained 'almost hopelessly elusive'.[106] Sarwat clearly perceived the negotiations as continuing and was reluctant to show the draft treaty to his Cabinet colleagues until points over the army, police, Nile waters and the Capitulations were resolved. Sarwat faced enormous difficulties in attempting to overcome the anti-treaty forces within every section of the Egyptian public:

> (1) The property owners because they fear that a treaty will mean reduction of our power to interfere with incompetent and corrupt administration, (2) the minorities who want our protective power to remain, (3) the Wafd because they feel an alliance would rob them of their chief platform for agitation, and (4) Sarwat because he is afraid of the Wafd and desires to remain in office. As to the King, it is impossible to say what he wants. All these sections of opinion are playing for delay. It is clear that the King wants to avoid any risk of the Wafd getting into power until his budget is through. Nahas and the extremists want delay because they need time to perfect their organisation [...] And Sarwat seems clearly to be playing for delay because he is afraid either to go forward or go back as regards the Treaty.
>
> I tell you all this in order that you may realise the enormous difficulty with which I am confronted in getting Sarwat to face the music. It is all very discouraging and indeed I think there is no parallel for this situation except perhaps Ireland.[107]

From Sarwat's perspective, while he dangled the carrot of a treaty in front of the British, he knew he could count on the Residency's support against the King and the majority Wafd. It was in his interest to play for time in the belief that either Britain would agree to further concessions or quietly abandon the whole project. Any extensive publication of the discussions and agreed terms would probably mean his resignation as prime minister. What Sarwat had failed to appreciate was that although an imperially overstretched Foreign Office wished to shore up its position in Egypt as soon as possible following the crisis in China and the continued wrangling in Europe, it was neither willing nor able to accept a treaty at any price. Lloyd's position was clear. He believed that Britain had shown 'infinite patience', considering Sarwat had accepted the treaty in London, and they had done 'our level best [...] to meet him [Sarwat] on every possible point of easement'.[108]

As the treaty issue continued without any clear moves forward, Chamberlain could not but agree:

> I have never been over sanguine about the success of the Treaty, but I will admit that I am disappointed about Sarwat's attitude. He spoke with so much confidence

when he was here and declared such a fixed determination to put the treaty through that I am puzzled by his waverings and hesitations since his return [...] At any rate as far as concession is concerned, the Government have now spoken their last word and he must either take the Treaty or accept the consequences of refusal.[109]

Sarwat, warned that a full account of the Anglo-Egyptian negotiations to the Egyptian Parliament could no longer be postponed, finally divulged the treaty's contents to Nahas and several of his Cabinet colleagues in mid-February. Chamberlain immediately instructed Lloyd to visit Nahas and convey the 'solid advantages' contained within the Treaty and emphasize the 'grave responsibility which lay upon him to lead Egypt down the right road at so important a turning point in her fortunes'.[110] However, Nahas's response was unfavourable. Although he desired friendly relations with Britain, unless a Treaty provided for the complete evacuation of British soldiers from Egyptian territory, the Wafd would never agree.[111]

In the face of uncompromising Wafd opposition to the treaty, Sarwat had little choice but to reject the draft treaty on 4 March 1928 and tender his resignation. For Lloyd this was unsurprising and an outcome he had predicted when he was first informed of the negotiations. In fact, Lloyd believed that Sarwat had never intended to negotiate a settlement on his first visit to London in July 1927 but merely to ascertain the British attitude and report back to Zaghlul. Committed perhaps further than he intended, and in view of the death of Zaghlul, Sarwat gained a certain amount of prestige in the Egyptian public eye from continued negotiations with Chamberlain. Moreover, continued negotiations would also 'stifle and silence' attacks upon Sarwat as prime minister and give him time to consolidate his position in the confused times following the death of Zaghlul 'who was the lynch-pin holding together the various and divergent political forces in Cairo'.[112] His persistence in pursuing interpretations of the articles was an attempt to gain time in the hope that a rift would appear in the Wafd or in the Cabinet. This would allow time either to win over sections of parliamentary opinion to his side, or to resign over some other issue leaving him 'untainted by the crime of negotiation'.[113] Chamberlain largely agreed with Lloyd's analysis but made no apology for attempting an Anglo-Egyptian settlement. 'I do not regret the London negotiations or the formulation of our conclusions in the draft Treaty for I think they have strengthened our hands at home and abroad and I permit myself to doubt whether they have really rendered your position in Egypt any more difficult'.[114]

The whole treaty debacle had brought Residency-Foreign Office relations to a new low as exemplified by the Lloyds' 'thankfulness' that Tyrrell was leaving the Foreign Office for Paris. Lady Lloyd even commented: 'I wish Austen were less of an old woman and less occupied with his tea parties at Geneva'.[115] It is worth noting, however, that disagreement over the future of British policy in Egypt between the Foreign Office and Lord Lloyd should not have come as a surprise and that, perhaps, the Foreign Office's treatment of Lord Lloyd was unfair. John Charmley, in his biography of Lord Lloyd, notes that in a meeting with Chamberlain on 12 May 1925, prior to his departure for Egypt, Lloyd spelt out his view on what the future British policy towards Egypt should be – 'not, in my opinion, "Cromerism" but annexation'. This statement went unchallenged by Chamberlain.[116]

The discord between the Residency and the Foreign Office only continued as Egypt reached crisis point at the end of April 1928 over a bill to permit seditious assemblies and Chamberlain even called into question Lloyd's loyalty over the Paterno affair.[117] This strained relationship did not go unnoticed by the new Labour Foreign Secretary, Arthur Henderson in 1929.[118]

Conclusion

From these negotiations it is clear that in a period of imperial overstretch Britain was attempting to reduce her liabilities or points of weakness by entering into a treaty with Egypt. Rex Hoare commented at the time that the Wafd sensed the 'tremendous anxiety on our side to reach an Anglo-Egyptian settlement'.[119] The Foreign Office's desire to secure a settlement led to a marked decrease in the power and influence of the High Commissioner. Lord Allenby practically led the Foreign Office in the 1924 negotiations. Lord Lloyd, however, was distrusted by the Foreign Office. Officials assembled a portfolio of evidence against him, thereby guaranteeing his replacement with a High Commissioner willing to undertake Foreign Office bidding.

The British stood little chance of success in negotiating a settlement with Egypt and what they failed to appreciate on every other occasion was that a Treaty was impossible without Wafd involvement. So long as Britain encouraged Egypt along the path of democracy, the Wafd's presence was always going to be a factor. Herein lay the contradiction of British policy in Egypt. It was not until faced with a serious external threat from Italy in the mid-1930s that the Wafd desired British protection and, as a result, an alliance was concluded in 1936.

7

'The Two Ends Just Didn't Meet':

The Labour Government and Anglo-Egyptian Treaty Negotiations

The return of a Labour minority government in May 1929 came as a 'complete surprise', to some. Chamberlain commented: 'I had expected the reduction but not the extinction of our majority, and [...] I am now feeling the disappointment which is natural when one sees work which was maturing brought to an end or transferred to other hands.'[1] The new Foreign Secretary, Arthur Henderson made it clear that an agreement would be sought with Egypt. Learning that the Foreign Office viewed Lord Lloyd as 'high-handed, ill-liberal and unwilling to carry out instructions',[2] Henderson voiced serious concerns over Lloyd's position. Henderson examined the previous correspondence between Lord Lloyd and Chamberlain and, in writing to the High Commissioner, commented:

> I should not be frank if I did not say I have been struck by the divergence of views between Your Lordship and my predecessor [...] a difference so wide that I cannot but ask myself whether it is not irreconcilable.[3]

Henderson maintained that Labour's policy would not be any less liberal and would therefore require British government representatives to interpret it with 'sympathy and understanding'.[4] The horizon certainly looked ominous as Henderson wished to discuss the situation when Lloyd returned to England on leave:

> I should not be candid with you were I not to warn you that it is difficult for me in light of these despatches to feel confident that your ideas can be harmonised with those either of my predecessor or myself.[5]

The stage was set and despite the largely 'friendly nature' of Lloyd's interview with Henderson he felt he had no other option but to resign as 'I realised that I had not the confidence of His Majesty's Government'.[6] Henderson's announcement of Lloyd's resignation caused a stir in both Houses of Parliament, most notably with Winston Churchill, to whom Lloyd had appealed directly. Stanley Baldwin, however, was concerned that any confrontation with the government over this issue would unite the Liberals with the Labour Party and leave the Conservatives in a marked minority. As

Churchill rose to interrogate Henderson, it became clear that the Whips had been hard at work to make it clear to the opposition that Baldwin did not think Lloyd's removal was a good point to press. And, apart from a few murmurs from the Conservative benches, it was evident that Churchill was 'almost alone in the House'.[7] In his speech, Henderson emphasized the 'stream of dissatisfaction in the relations between his predecessor and a High Commissioner who had shown a marked determination to misinterpret, or ungenerously to misapply policy from London'.[8] Hugh Dalton, the junior Labour Foreign Minister, recalled:

> Winston in a terrible state. Rose without a Tory cheer. Attacked the F[oreign] O[ffice]. Got the worst of it in exchanges with Uncle [Henderson]. Even began to lose the House. J R M [John Ramsey MacDonald, Labour Prime Minister] attacked him very effectively. Samuel [Herbert Samuel, Liberal leader] supported us. Baldwin quite half-hearted. Austen very wisely kept right out of it![9]

Chamberlain himself commented:

> I had not decided what I should have done myself [with Lloyd] but the office was pressing strongly that Lloyd's appointment should not be renewed at the end of its five years & I was hoping that a place might be found for him as High Comr in East Africa under the new arrangements. He has courage, energy & ability, but his qualities are more suited to an administrative post or a time of crisis rather than to the more diplomatic duties which he was called upon to discharge in Egypt. I had advised Henderson not to recall him whatever I might have done myself, on the grounds that for a new Govt to change the High Comr as soon as they came in would be to needlessly arouse suspicion & fear in certain quarters here & to excite hopes, which must be disappointed, in Egypt & would add to his difficulties there. As to the manner of his dismissal & its announcement I think Henderson and his colleagues blundered as much as it was possible for men to do.[10]

Lloyd's resignation met the objectives of both Henderson and the Foreign Office. For Henderson, the removal of a stout Conservative imperialist on the eve of attempting a more favourable Anglo-Egyptian settlement represented a cheap victory for the minister and placed his stamp of authority on foreign policy. At the Foreign Office, Ronald Lindsay and Walford Selby were the prime intriguers. They disliked Lloyd's 'exceptional position' as an outsider and 'wanted the post to be held by an ordinary member of the Diplomatic Service'.[11] Indeed, through a number of Residency informants that included C A G MacKintosh, former British official in the Egyptian Public Security Department and Cairo correspondent for the *Morning Post*, Gerald Delaney, Reuters correspondent, and Cecil Campbell, the Financial Adviser, Selby was kept informed of Lloyd's movements as well as Egyptian and foreign perceptions of him.[12] These letters reinforced the Foreign Office view that Lloyd was unsuitable for the post of High Commissioner in Egypt and that the Foreign Office required someone who was prepared to take orders from the British Government if it was going to shore up Britain's imperial position and place Anglo-Egyptian relations on a secure footing.

In considering Lloyd's replacement Henderson wanted to change the character of the Cairo Residency back to one of a diplomatic nature rather than administrative. In this vein Henderson advocated that all of the military appendages of the Residency that had been 'unduly emphasised under Lord Lloyd's regime' should disappear.[13]

Lloyd's successor was Sir Percy Loraine, a close friend of both George and Blanche. Loraine was a member of the Diplomatic Service and had served as Head of Mission in Persia between 1921 and 1926 and in Greece between 1926 and 1929. Loraine was prepared to follow Foreign Office instructions, noting that 'diplomacy is not a policy maker but an agency, which takes its orders and its guidance from the Government that it serves'.[14] The Foreign Office had their man.

The Henderson-Mahmoud negotiations, 1929

To Britain, Mohammed Pasha Mahmoud appeared a good candidate with whom to secure an Anglo-Egyptian treaty. A graduate of Balliol College Oxford, he nonetheless seemed to have sound nationalist credentials, having been one of the seven delegates chosen by Saad Zaghlul to go to Paris in 1919. Although he later quarrelled with Zaghlul, he joined a Wafdist coalition in 1925 and again in March 1928.[15] Mahmoud came to the fore in June 1928 when King Fuad dismissed Mustafa al-Nahas Pasha and called upon Mahmoud to form a Cabinet. Mahmoud's ministry was predominantly Liberal-Constitutionalist in political colour, containing several *Ittehadists* (Palace Party) members. Mahmoud dissolved Parliament on 19 July and suspended the Constitution and continued to rule by decree with King Fuad's, at times, grudging consent. Mahmoud pledged himself to the internal reform of Egypt through irrigation works, electrification, the supply of clean drinking water to the provinces, land reform and legislation for the protection of labour. Mahmoud also committed himself to the restoration of the Constitution. Mahmoud's programme was acceptable to the British but one fundamental problem remained: it lacked any great following within the country. The Liberal-Constitutionalists did not have any leader of comparable popularity to that of Zaghlul. It may have included 'many of the best brains in the country and a considerable proportion of its wealthier and more influential inhabitants [but it was] aptly described as a General Staff without an army'.[16] The Foreign Office fully recognized this. The country was politically apathetic at this juncture, but the Foreign Office appreciated that 'a good deal of the Zaghlul tradition remains. What was his party represents in most Egyptian minds the sentiments of nationality and patriotism'.[17] In any election, the Foreign Office estimated that the Wafd would again be returned with a considerable majority.

The other political player, King Fuad, was perceived by the Foreign Office to be a 'recurrent nuisance. Energetic, and by no means unintelligent, he is an inveterate and devious intriguer who is detested by many of his subjects and liked by few'.[18] The King's overriding aim was to increase his political power. 'His ambition is to rule Egypt as an autocrat and to this end he works against whatever personage or party is in the ascendant.'[19] Accordingly, the British government sought a middle ground between a recalcitrant Wafd and an autocratic monarch, a figurehead who commanded a certain amount of support from both Parliament and ordinary Egyptians. Such a person, they believed, they had found in Mahmoud. They were prepared to intervene and prevent his deposition in September 1928 by the King, despite declaring when Fuad ousted Nahas in June 1928 that the British government would intervene in internal affairs only if it concerned the reserved points of 1922. However, this faith in Mahmoud was fragile – could he really command the necessary support to pass the treaty? Could the Egyptian circle really be squared? Even MacDonald voiced his concern to Henderson believing that Mahmoud to be 'drowning man and if we do try to help him it must not be at the expense of our own lives'.[20] Mahmoud's prolonged illness in late 1928 certainly did not bode well.

In June 1929 Mahmoud presented the terms on which he was prepared to negotiate an Anglo-Egyptian settlement. These were largely the same as Milner's 1920 recommendations. The Foreign Office always believed that a settlement on the lines recommended by Milner would have adequately protected essential British interests. Therefore, there was nothing in Mahmoud's proposals which should have proved to be an insuperable obstacle to the conclusion of a satisfactory treaty.[21] As details of the proposed treaty terms began to leak back to Cairo, the Egyptian press, rather than analysing the merits and demerits of the treaty, tended to concentrate more upon the general question of whether or not a treaty negotiated by Mahmoud, whatever its terms, could be accepted by Egypt. It was clear that to have any treaty accepted would be difficult, if not impossible, whilst the Constitution remained suspended. Apart from the Liberal-Constitutional *al-Siassa*, Mahmoud was largely condemned across the Egyptian political spectrum. Again, it was the same question that had blighted the 1921 Adli-Curzon negotiations and the 1927 Chamberlain-Sarwat talks: how could a treaty be negotiated by a Prime Minister who lacked popular backing, was opposed by the populist Wafd and was undemocratic? This last point was somewhat ironic since it was a Labour administration that undertook the negotiations. As a minority administration the Labour Government was on shifting sands domestically too. MacDonald wrote to Henderson:

> Surveying the position from Chequers, that leakage, whoever is responsible for it, seems to me to have enormously lessened the chances of the F[oreign] O[ffice] being able to carry through its expectation that a good treaty would result in the establishment of a good government in Egypt. Rather, we shall have said our last word and that last word will be rejected. A troublesome and dangerous period of unrest will have then to be faced and we shall be in the end opposed by the Tories, Liberals and a section of our own people. We must try and avoid this.[22]

Moreover, MacDonald was mindful of Egyptian domestic realities and warned against making the Wafd into our 'deadly enemy' and therefore an 'essential consideration in our policy must be the possibility of a Wafd Government in a few months'.[23] Loraine commented:

> The cardinal mistake was for the Labour Government ever to have embarked on treaty negotiations with Mahmoud at all. Any treaty signed by Mahmoud would

be repudiated, not by reason of its terms, but because the Wafd was a powerful and popular party, and Wafdists held that they alone could negotiate on Egypt's behalf.[24]

This view was repeated by Rex Hoare, Acting High Commissioner, to the Foreign Office: 'I have expressed a very definite opinion that the prospects of Mohammed Mahmoud Pasha being able to ratify the contemplated treaty are highly precarious.'[25] The Residency warned the Foreign Office not to be blinded by the assurances of Mahmoud:

It is easy and natural to be pessimistic when dealing with Egyptian affairs, in Egypt. It is equally easy, especially for an Egyptian – Zaghlul, Sarwat and Mahmoud have all gone the same way – to be optimistic in London. I therefore have little doubt that he is fairly confident of obtaining his "broad coalition" and of winning an election on it. Such a coalition *must*, in view of an election, contain a strong Wafd element, supported by the predominant elements of the Wafd organisation.

In London Mohammed Mahmoud may believe that it suffices for him to restore Parliament and bring with him a treaty (admittedly so generous that many Wafdists are rather taken aback) for the past to be forgotten and for his political opponents to receive him with open arms. Were he in Egypt he would be more likely to realise that the Wafd will say 'we always knew that the Labour Government would give us back our Parliament, and as they have removed Lord Lloyd, they obviously cannot expect us to accept his puppet [Mahmoud]'. I do not believe that Mohammed Mahmoud has any chance of obtaining Wafdist support. In those circumstances the result of the elections is a foregone conclusion.[26]

How the elections were to be held was the crux of the matter. Under the 1923 Constitution the electoral law was based on indirect election on the grounds that 90 per cent of the population was illiterate. Following the Wafd's success in 1924 and in order to ensure Wafd predominance at the polls, Zaghlul had persuaded Parliament to ratify an amended electoral law which provided for universal suffrage and direct elections.[27] In order to ensure the passage of the treaty, Mahmoud planned a new electoral law which would limit the electorate to those who were literate and paid a certain amount in government taxes. This equated to about 25 per cent of Egyptians. It would be intended that each *mudir*, village leader, would be sent a list of approved candidates and the administration used to support these candidates and prevent the election of rivals.[28] Lawrence Grafftey-Smith, Counsellor at the Residency, noted: 'This incidentally would be worse than anything Zaghlul ever did, for no elections have ever been held in Egypt with a Zaghlulist Cabinet controlling the Administration. Zaghlul used to nominate his partisans, but opposition to them was always possible and occasionally successful'.[29] Nonetheless, while the Egyptian Department appeared happy to acquiesce in Mahmoud's plans, citing the watchword of non-interference in internal Egyptian politics,[30] the Labour government balked at this obvious attempt to rig the elections. Instead, Mahmoud was urged to pave the way for a coalition government under Adli. Once a coalition was formed, pledged to the safe passage of the treaty, the Foreign Office advocated Mahmoud's withdrawal 'from the limelight to the wings before the elections take place'.[31]

Mahmoud suffered further humiliation when he learned that the Wafd Secretary, Makram Ebeid, had been received by Henderson on 31 July and by Hugh Dalton, Parliamentary Under-Secretary of State for Foreign Affairs, on 7 August. Rex Hoare commented that the interview placed 'all the cards in Wafdist hands'.[32] MacDonald also commented that 'the trust reposed upon Makram was extraordinary on the part of those who ought to have known him'.[33] The inexperience of the Labour Government was further exemplified by Dalton's speech at Welwyn on 9 August in which he stated that Henderson had made negotiations *conditional* upon a return to constitutional government in Egypt. In fact, it had been Mahmoud who had declared his intention to restore the Egyptian Parliament upon the opening of negotiations. Moreover, according to an agreement with Mahmoud that should have remained confidential, Dalton assured his listeners that there was to be no change in the existing electoral law.[34] This was immediately seized upon by the Egyptian press and placed Mahmoud in a highly awkward position, with Dalton later commenting: 'I was, perhaps rather innocently, quite astonished at the fuss which was made in many quarters'.[35]

Nevertheless, Dalton was unapologetic about this episode, even after 'a rather chilly correspondence', between himself and Ronald Lindsay, permanent Under-Secretary of State at the Foreign Office.[36] Dalton believed that Mahmoud 'in spite of the influence of Balliol, was not much less of a twister than certain other Egyptian politicians'.[37] Mahmoud perceived Dalton's speech as a clear breach of faith by the British Government and believed that Britain was going to replace him with Nahas, thereby placing the Wafd in the 'position of arbiters of the treaty's fate'. If the Wafd were given the impression that the British Government were determined to see Mahmoud go, the Wafd would be unlikely to accept the treaty or even a coalition under Adli and, instead, would merely wait for office which any changing of the electoral law would give them. If, on the other hand, Mahmoud, and possibly Adli, remained in the picture for the time being, the Wafd would be bound to show at least some moderation, which would correspondingly enhance the treaty's prospects. Lindsay commented: 'There is, I think, much force in this argument'.[38] Mahmoud informed Loraine that despite British statements that the treaty represented the limits of the British position, the Wafd had already decided upon modifications to the treaty that they would demand once in power.[39] Although this contained an element of accuracy, it must also be seen as an attempt by Mahmoud to protect his position as long as possible by retaining British support.

Throughout this constitutional toing and froing the Wafd maintained a non-committal stance on the treaty proposal. Indeed, the official organ of the Wafd, *al-Balagh*, declared that it would not express its opinion on the proposals until the parliamentary regime was restored. The Wafd's intransigence concerned MacDonald:

> My fears regarding the attitude of the Wafd are being realised, especially those which proceeded on the assumption that as a matter of fact the Wafd leaders would never pursue a policy on the assumption that any Anglo-Egyptian agreement was of such overwhelming importance as to justify a suspension of their partisan

policy. You must assume, in all your dealings with Egypt, that the Wafd is purely partisan, and that its leaders are to do nothing whatever that will rob them of the laurels of vanity and victory.[40]

The view of the Committee of Imperial Defence

On presenting the draft treaty to the Committee of Imperial Defence (CID), the Foreign Office declared that it embodied the recommendations of the 1920 Milner proposals. In that respect the new draft treaty provided for the concentration of British troops in the Canal Zone, rather than in Cairo and Alexandria, to protect imperial communications. The Foreign Office had always refuted War Office concerns over the withdrawal of British troops from these cities as 'unwarranted' and warned that 'unless we agree to this there is humanly speaking, no possibility of any settlement being accepted by Egypt'.[41] With Egypt about to assume the responsibility of protecting foreign interests, the Foreign Office argued that there remained little point in British troops remaining in Cairo and Alexandria. In fact, in the event of British involvement in hostilities in the Mediterranean with say France or Italy, the Foreign Office judged it to be of greater advantage that Egypt was tied to Britain through an alliance and thereby 'should at least cease actually to weaken us, by compelling us to retain our garrison or even to increase it considerably for repressive purposes'.[42] Moreover, Egypt would be bound to use British military officials for advice and assistance. With the League of Nations, the Kellogg Pact of 1928 and an Anglo-Egyptian Alliance, the Foreign Office perceived Britain's position in Egypt secure and urged the CID to view their role as one of determining what military air forces would be required in the Canal Zone: firstly, to secure the Canal's safety and, secondly, for use as a strategic reserve in an emergency outside Egypt.[43]

The draft treaty also dealt with the difficult subject of the Sudan, something that was omitted in the Chamberlain-Sarwat draft. The Anglo-Egyptian Convention of 1899 was to be reaffirmed and, whilst all reference to Egyptian participation in the administration of the Sudan was to be omitted, the return of an Egyptian battalion was conceded as a face saving device and one that was likely to carry considerable weight amongst Egyptian public opinion.[44] The return of an Egyptian battalion to the Sudan had not been a straightforward accomplishment. MacDonald had questioned whether its return was even essential. He was concerned that the return of an Egyptian battalion to the Sudan would mean the indefinite retention of a British unit in Khartoum. Henderson disagreed. He assured MacDonald that the British battalion would remain in the Sudan for the present time but its further retention would be examined 'in the light of the new spirit which the coming into effect of the proposals will produce'. Henderson reasoned that 'Egypt will have nothing to gain and much to lose by trouble in the Sudan. Besides what can one isolated battalion do?'[45] For his part, King George V voiced his opposition to any gesture affecting the Sudan and which centred upon 'very personal aspects'. John Loader Maffey, Governor-General of the Sudan, reported that 'it irks him [King George V] that he cannot sign the commissions of British Military Officers serving in the Sudan, and how he is always hoping that the condominium is yielding to something more healthily red'.[46] Praised for his 'courage and statesmanship' by Henderson, Maffey placed the Sudan within 'its proper perspective'.[47]

> It is strange for me to find myself on what, at first sight, might appear to be the side of surrender. But as a real die-hard where British interests are concerned I am convinced that it is by maintaining the condominium that the British will remain in the Sudan. They have no other justification and no other future.
>
> I have always held that when England succeeds in concluding a treaty with Egypt, securing our vital imperial needs on the Suez Canal and putting our relations on a new basis, the new chapter would never be opened unless some gesture were made to soothe the amour-propre of the Egyptian people on the subject of the Sudan and to obliterate the memories of 1924.
>
> At this juncture when, owing to conditions which can never recur, the stage is wonderfully set for an attempt to settle the Anglo-Egyptian question, when we all know that with every year that passes international jealousy will make it increasingly difficult for us to secure our vital imperial needs in Egypt, at this point is everything to be jeopardised because we cannot swallow an Egyptian battalion in the Sudan?[48]

Maffey pointed out that accepting an Egyptian battalion was small fry compared to the Egyptian Irrigation Department that was already established within the Sudan and whose proposed vast works would mean the widespread activity of Egyptian officialdom within the Sudan. As Maffey eloquently phrased it, 'we are straining at a gnat [the Egyptian battalion] when we have to swallow a camel [the Egyptian Irrigation Department]'. In Maffey's opinion a battalion was 'nothing in the scale compared to this'. He concluded that 'though I should take the medicine with something of a wry face, I know in my bones that in the long run it is the thing to do, and that in taking the long view it is essential to a new and happier chapter of Anglo-Egyptian relations before the world and in the Sudan. But it must be the last thing we grant'.[49]

In Foreign Office eyes, therefore, the British government 'have nothing to lose and much to gain',[50] in this treaty proposal and felt that nothing was given away that had not been given away when Milner's proposals were published in 1920:

> For the past ten years our relations with Egypt have been of an unsatisfactory character. They have been marked by recurring periods of tension, which more than once have necessitated the use or threat of force on our side, followed by intervals of somewhat uneasy and sullen quiet. This state of things is conspicuously and increasingly out of harmony with our imperial and foreign policy in general [...] The present Government is the most capable from the internal point of view and the most moderate in external affairs which has yet held office in Egypt, and, in spite of unreasoning agitation by extreme elements in the Wafd, there is a sentiment in favour of settling with us.[51]

That this treaty was of primary importance to the Foreign Office is demonstrated by their failure to consult the Chiefs of Staff prior to discussions with Mahmoud. They only sought their opinion once a draft had been formulated and initialled, thereby agreeing to its terms regardless of CID opinion. This did not go un-noticed by the Chief of the Imperial General Staff, Field Marshal G F Milne:

> I find some difficulty in approaching the subject [...] it appears that some considerable measure of agreement has already been reached; without knowledge of the exact extent of this agreement I feel some diffidence in offering remarks which may be construed as criticisms of decisions already arrived at.[52]

According to the Chief of the Imperial General Staff, the draft treaty posed a serious threat to British interests on two counts: the removal of British control over the Egyptian army, and the evacuation of British troops from Cairo and Alexandria. Referring to the removal of British control of the Egyptian army and especially over its munitions, Milne maintained that the danger lay not in so much as it represented a grave military menace but in the Egyptians' 'lack of real discipline leading the soldiery to join in with the mob in any anti-foreign demonstration [which] may, in the future, assume a violent form'.[53] The relocation of British troops to the Canal Zone was also greeted with unease. The need for maintaining British troops in Cairo and Alexandria and their environs was threefold. Firstly, any internal trouble in Egypt would mean the endangering of communications through the Canal. The Chiefs of Staff believed Cairo was the breeding ground of any trouble and therefore its military control was the surest safeguard against trouble breaking out. Secondly, in relation to this, an Egyptian garrison of 4,000 to 5,000 men was based in Cairo and concerns existed that in certain conditions they would join the forces of disorder. Finally locating British troops in the Canal Zone would leave them completely dependent on a water supply entirely in Egyptian hands. Moreover, they would have at their rear a potentially hostile Egyptian army whose number under the draft treaty was liable to an undefined increase.[54]

Nevertheless, the Chiefs of Staff were prepared to make some concessions, which was a significant step considering their stance during the previous negotiations. Now prepared to evacuate Cairo they still wanted to retain the cantonments of Helmieh and Abbassia, located six and three miles to the east of Cairo respectively. Although the views of the Chiefs of Staff were to be referred to the Egyptian Committee, consultation with them appeared to be more of a procedure rather than a serious discussion of military requirements, since the Chiefs of Staff were not permitted sufficient time to submit their views to the 244th meeting of the CID on 25 July 1929. Importantly, they were instructed to elaborate their views on the arrangements for the defence of the Canal Zone alone, rather than provide a strategic overview.

The policy of the Foreign Office and the Residency

Loraine arrived as High Commissioner on 2 September 1929. His arrival was a rather muted affair and was not accompanied by any of the pomp and ceremony usually associated with the arrival of the High Commissioner – the Egyptian Prime Minister was not even present. Loraine spoke to Mahmoud later the same day and found that he was unhappy with the train of negotiations. Mahmoud complained that:

The one understood condition on which he entered into the discussions which led to the treaty proposals was that his hands would not be tied as regards [the] method of reintroducing the Constitution and matters of electoral law. This understanding had been broken by Mr Dalton's speech.[55]

Dalton's speech had served only to encourage the Wafd to believe, not erroneously, that the British government wished to deal with them. Nonetheless, Mahmoud was prepared to place himself entirely at Loraine's disposal.[56] In his first audience with the King, Loraine found him to be quite friendly and the interview was more satisfactory than he had anticipated. Loraine outlined three possible alternatives for pursuing the treaty question: to continue with the present government; to form a broad coalition, including Wafd representation, to decide by agreement the time and manner of establishing a Constitution and holding elections; or a Wafdist Government. The King's dislike of Mahmoud and the Wafd was evident in his dismissal of the first and last options, but he declared his support for securing a coalition government.[57]

However, the central problem remained: cajoling the Wafd into a coalition government without appearing to interfere in Egyptian internal affairs. This was to become an intractable problem and, as Lindsay noted on 6 September, the Wafd 'want to have it both ways'[58] – universal manhood suffrage and then further negotiations in the hope of greater concessions on the treaty. Loraine's contact with the Wafd through Cecil Campbell, Assistant Financial Adviser to the Egyptian Government, put paid to any ideas of a Coalition Cabinet. Makram, speaking on behalf of the Wafd, stated that any hopes of forming a coalition were 'utterly unattainable and disadvantageous to the cause of Anglo-Egyptian friendship'. Furthermore, Makram maintained: 'No treaty would have any finality unless signed by Nahas as Prime Minister.'[59] Therefore, by 12 September it was clear to Loraine that an impasse had been reached. The policy of the Wafd was in no way compatible with the policy of the British government either in spirit or letter:

> They refuse definitely to enter a coalition under any conditions, to lay the treaty issue before the electorate, or to reply to the proposals of His Majesty's Government. They are thus lying athwart of every one of the main or immediate objectives of our policy in professed confident reliance that you will accept their terms and on self-satisfied pretext that they are the best judges of what is most advantageous to Anglo-Egyptian relations and friendship. They thus confirm description made of their attitude as 'power or no treaty', and will not even tell us what sort of treaty they will accept if they get power. They merely ask us to change King Log for King Stork and see what happens.[60]

Loraine's assessment was accepted by the Foreign Office; Murray minuted: 'The attitude of the Wafd is profoundly unsatisfactory [...] It is clear that we cannot do business with them until they come to a saner appreciation of realities.'[61] In light of Wafd intransigence, Loraine advocated maintaining Mahmoud in power rather than allowing the Wafd to come to power totally uncommitted to the treaty, thereby gambling on their goodwill. 'It would be a stiff job, but there is no apparent reason to anticipate failure provided there is no weakening at home [London]. A firm Government, if we can eliminate the abuses of the last nine months, may effect radical change. In any case my impression is that this course is a less dangerous one than to gamble on goodwill of a homogenous Wafdist Government.'[62] As Murray commented, it was a 'choice of evils'.[63] Loraine reasoned that 'over Mahmoud we can exercise friendly and beneficent control; over a triumphant Wafd in power we can exercise none'.[64] Loraine himself complained that he'd had 'enough worry to kill a cat'. He continued:

> Had to telegraph simply reams since arriving here and every word has to be weighed with the utmost care. Wretched old think-tank going full blast all the time. And we're getting nowhere. The fact is that the Egyptians and we are not talking about the same thing. We want to talk about a treaty, and they, according to their party, about whether they are going to get or lose office. The Wafd merely refuse to express any opinion on all treaty proposals and they merely want to have Mahmoud kicked out, to have elections, get a big majority, form a Wafdist Govt. and then perhaps talk about a treaty, and condescend to start a fresh negotiation over the whole field of our proposals. It is really quite preposterous.[65]

Time was becoming a crucial factor. Henderson had wanted the verdict of the Egyptian people through a referendum on the treaty proposals before the British Parliament reconvened in October. However, this looked unlikely and was completely ruled out when it was discovered that the Egyptian electoral lists had not been updated from the latest census and would have to be completely revised.[66] The position of Foreign Office and the Residency was not helped either by the Secretary of State's involvement in League business in Geneva and the Prime Minister's 'engagements all over the place'.[67] This meant that British policymaking became paralysed. Loraine had to wait days before a firm line of policy was issued from London. 'It's very difficult to guess what is happening at home and what the Cabinet are thinking. I've had some guidance, but it is neither very clear nor very consistent.'[68] As the Egyptian situation became more fluid London's instructions were now hopelessly outdated.[69] In the meantime, Ramsay MacDonald, concerned over the developing situation, waded into the debate in a letter to Lindsay on 13 September. In it he declared:

> Mahmoud's position in Egypt quite plainly prevented him from carrying out the programme which seemed to him a possible one when he was in London. It was the Sarwat mistake all over again [...] The formula of our Egyptian policy is a very simple one, and I advise you strongly not to depart from it by a hair's breadth. We want to come to an agreement which will put an end to the reservations; the agreement will be liberal, but when it is made we wish it to be permanent. In the meantime, we shall not interfere with Egyptian affairs which do not involve any of the four points, and, with those reservations in mind, we throw the responsibility for governing their own country upon Egyptian political parties.[70]

The Prime Minister's intervention put paid to any further attempts to back a referendum. 'If this [a referendum] were agreed to by the political parties it might be a way out but I have very little hope of it. If it is forced upon Egypt in the teeth of opposition, especially from the Wafd, its results will then be ineffective and even might amount to a farce.'[71] However, while MacDonald's letter provided a statement on British policy, it did not provide any specific instruction and was contradictory in places. In the absence of any further comment form Henderson in Geneva, MacDonald's letter constituted the despatch to Loraine. The extent of paralysis on Whitehall was demonstrated by Murray's letters accompanying his despatches; they apologized for the lack of direction:

> It has at least the merit of being a perfectly clear statement of policy, but how it will work out in practice I do not know and hesitate to guess [...] For all we know these instructions may only serve to render you impotent at a moment when you would have liked to put out your maximum effort. I have written this indiscreet and possibly improper letter because I want you to know that we not only understand and sympathise with your difficulties but honestly did our best to return your lead.[72]

Meanwhile, Rex Hoare attempted to interpret the Foreign Office's latest despatch and referred to it as a 'farrago of inconsequent nonsense'.[73] According to Hoare's analysis, if Britain sat back the political initiative would lie with King Fuad:
We shall have achieved a series of astounding successes.

(1) The fall of a friendly Government in circumstances of the utmost discredit to ourselves.
(2) A free choice to the King between virtually Palace Government and a Wafdist Government.
(3) The Treaty left to be picked up by a Wafdist Government if it is graciously pleased to do so.

Even if our 'plotting' had failed conspicuously we could not have done worse.[74] Loraine largely concurred with Hoare's assessment, forecasting that 'it will end with a homogenous Wafdist Government, at the best willing to take its stand on the treaty proposals before and during elections; at worst maintaining its adamantine non-committal attitude as defined by Nahas and especially Makram'.[75] Loraine refuted the suggestion in the Foreign Office despatch that his actions had entangled the British government in Egyptian internal affairs; he recalled that the Egyptian Department had sent him to Egypt with instructions to 'guide them [Egyptian politicians] into the right path'.[76]

Although Loraine demonstrated an appreciation for the bigger picture and the obstacles that the Secretary of State's absence in Geneva placed on policy formulation, he did feel that he lacked immediate positive guidance from London:

> I read into your telegram that the Government sees rocks ahead on the parliamentary front at home and that the telegram represents a gallant effort to reconcile the navigation of these rocks with the desire to give me all the support that is possible [...] It is most unfortunate from my point of view that owing to Geneva the consideration of the Egyptian problem has been so geographically

dispersed [...] You have given me an extremely awkward mount, and I have little or no time to study and become used to his tricks, or to find out counters to them. It would have helped me enormously if stage by stage as I have reported action you had been able to tell me whether my style of equitation was approved.[77]

This lack of firm guidance was not about to change as Lindsay went on leave on 27 September and the Prime Minister left for the United States on 28 September. Murray commented: 'Ronald has been such a tower of strength and could manage to bring the Secty [sic] of State up to the scratch in a way that I cannot hope to rival: besides I shall be working through Lancelot and I doubt whether he and Uncle Arthur speak the same language.'[78] The departure of the Prime Minister was a mixed blessing for the Foreign Office. On the one hand it meant they would have 'only one master', but on the other it deprived them of a 'guiding and controlling hand'. The perplexing situation that faced the Foreign Office was summarized by Murray:

The PM has the hang of Egypt, has no illusions about the Wafd – (he described Nahas as unprincipled and unbalanced) and my experience of him in 1924 gives me confidence in his instinct where Egypt is concerned. Now Uncle A doesn't know the first thing about Egypt, is slow and hesitant and can't understand the frequently vital importance of an immediate decision, and his mind is so utterly different from that of the Egyptian that it will probably take him months to realise that the mass mentality of the Wafd isn't a bit like the mass mentality of, say, the boilermakers union.[79]

Although MacDonald may have possessed a better understanding of the Wafd, his deliberations over policy also posed difficulties for the Foreign Office. Murray complained that 'he expresses himself with a curious woolliness and I find his minutes almost impossible to paraphrase: when I attempt to dissect his sentences with a view to expressing the meaning in our official jargon, the meaning that I thought I had grasped has disappeared. Hence when the PM writes anything that one has to pass on, I embody it whole whenever possible.'[80] Loraine noted alongside this complaint of Murray's 'which gets himself but not me out of the difficulty.'[81]

On 25 September Henderson finally communicated to Loraine that he regarded the return of the Wafd to power as inevitable. Loraine commented to Murray that it would have been 'distinctly useful' to have known this at an earlier stage![82] Again, Henderson demonstrated a distinct lack of understanding over the Egyptian situation:

They [the Wafd] must not get it into their heads that you are involved in a conspiracy to keep them out of office. It is, I feel largely a question of handling. Let them and others realise that they will get their elections and will get office, but there is no reason to lose their tempers about it [...] I should like the change over to be gentle so as to avoid further inflaming political feeling.[83]

Of course, this was all to be accomplished at the same time as adopting an attitude of complete detachment! Although Henderson praised Mahmoud for his 'reasonable and conciliatory' attitude, he advocated Mahmoud's resignation, which Mahmoud duly gave on 1 October 1929.[84] For 'throwing him to the wolves' and to make the blow a little less bitter for Mahmoud, he was awarded a GCMG.[85]

In the meantime, Nahas had made contact with the Residency on 27 September. According to Loraine, the lunchtime meeting passed off well and Nahas departed 'as pleased as Punch',[86] even though Loraine had refused to discuss the current political situation with him. A neutral caretaker government was appointed under Adli Yakan Pasha in order to oversee the restoration of the Constitution and a universal suffrage election. Loraine continued to meet with Nahas in an attempt to gauge Wafd opinion over the treaty proposals. He described his personal relations with Nahas as 'excellent', commenting that 'he obviously enjoys coming along to the Residency and having a little chat'. Loraine continued that at a State banquet 'Nahas seemed to be drawn to my side by some irresistible magnetic influence'. Although there were some rumblings over installing Wafd *mudirs* and *omdahs* and a virulent press campaign called for Mahmoud's impeachment, the atmosphere was 'very much clearer and very much lighter'.[87] The question was whether this more relaxed atmosphere could be turned towards the successful conclusion of the treaty issue. Nahas, however, remained reluctant to submit the treaty proposals to the electorate at the forthcoming election or to say whether he accepted the proposals in substance or not. Henderson reminded Nahas that while he was anxious to avoid anything that would create unnecessary difficulties for Nahas and the Wafd, he also desired the same regard for his own difficulties:

> He [Nahas] must remember that I am likely to encounter strenuous opposition in the House of Commons to concessions made to Egypt in our offer, which are regarded in many quarters as over generous.[88]

Henderson wanted a more explicit assurance as to the Wafd's attitude and a promise to sign the treaty and secure its ratification. To Nahas, this was unacceptable and would undermine the authority and prestige of himself and the Wafd if he accepted proposals that were drawn up with a former prime minister. 'They would stand convicted of having clamoured against Mahmoud's regime merely in order to secure power for themselves.'[89] Instead, Nahas proposed that the Wafd's refusal to comment until after free elections did not imply hostility towards a treaty; on the contrary, they were anxious for a settlement. Loraine believed that Nahas was being sincere and proposed accepting Nahas's stance. The 'real question is whether we have faith in his sincerity or not. If not, we may lose the treaty now; if yes, we keep it alive and may get it yet'.[90] Although disappointed by Nahas's position, Henderson was prepared to accept the formula, agreeing with Loraine's line of strengthening the confidence and goodwill between Nahas and the British government. The Residency and the Foreign Office had now to wait until the outcome of the elections before any further treaty moves could be made. As Murray wrote to Loraine:

> May I congratulate you on your extraordinarily successful accomplishment of the feat of changing horses in mid stream without wetting your or our feet, accompanied as the achievement was by the more difficult gesture of throwing

our friends to the wolves (we have had heaps of practice at this) without exciting more than a modicum of bitterness. In doing all this the dice were pretty heavily weighted against you. In the department we realised all this very acutely and appreciated your success the more.[91]

The Henderson-Nahas negotiations, 1930

Unsurprisingly the Wafd won an overwhelming victory in the December 1929 elections and Nahas took office as Prime Minister on 1 January 1930. Despite protests from the British government, Mahmud Fahmi al-Nuqrashi, associated with the assassination of Sir Lee Stack, was included in the Cabinet and, along with Makram, represented the 'more extreme elements', of the Wafd.[92] Although this represented a compromise since Ahmed Maher, also linked with the murder of the *Sirdar*, was excluded from power, Rex Hoare warned that this gave a 'false impression of the squeezability of HMG'.[93]

On 3 February Nahas sought a mandate from the newly assembled Egyptian parliament to enter into negotiations with the British government to reach a complete settlement in a 'spirit of friendliness and conciliation'.[94] It was agreed that negotiations would be held in London at the end of March following the international Naval Conference. However, Henderson wanted some sort of indication of the Wafd's opinion and Nahas's modifications on the British proposals previously agreed with Mahmud. 'While I am anxious to facilitate his task in every way possible, I must once again make it clear to the him that, generally speaking, the proposals I have made represent the extreme limit of concessions which His Majesty's Government are prepared to make in existing circumstances. We must be assured beforehand that in using the words "no hard negotiation" he intends only modification of form and detail.'[95] Henderson continued that while he appreciated Nahas's difficulties and had done his best to accommodate them, 'he must realise that I have difficulties on my side. A wide and influential section of public opinion here is opposed to concession already indicated which it regards as excessive'.[96]

Nonetheless, Nahas would not be drawn, believing that any formulation of Egyptian desiderata prior to the London talks would involve the consultation of technical and expert opinion and thereby arouse curiosity. 'The result would be an immediate attempt by persons well and ill-disposed to force or tie [Nahas's] hands'.[97] Loraine trusted the sincerity of Nahas's intentions and advocated: 'If you can possibly afford to give Nahas the rope he now pleads for I believe it wise to let him have it.'[98] Loraine believed that if Nahas were compelled to formulate Egyptian desiderata in Cairo they would be far less flexible and easier for Nahas to draw back from than any formulated in London. Moreover, since Nahas refused to articulate any modifications 'it is impossible for him to go to London only to return empty-handed'.[99] Loraine supported his argument by pointing to a favourable public opinion towards Britain and the conclusion of a settlement: 'Atmosphere here towards us is at the moment unusually cordial, and there seems to me a sort of general feeling that at last understanding and co-operation with us is going to replace misunderstanding or friction'.[100] With Loraine's support, Henderson let the matter drop. According to Loraine, 'my idea is that the iron is hot, the atmosphere more favourable than I had thought possible to get it in the time and that the less time we're afforded for either to cool off the better.'[101] Furthermore, Loraine believed that the Egyptian government wanted to get the treaty passed by parliament by the end of April or at the very latest before the summer break.

King Fuad also appeared to be happy with the course of events, believing that '90% of the difficulties in the way of an Anglo-Egyptian settlement have been overcome and is a confirmed optimist as regards result'.[102] Loraine certainly felt that his excellent relations with the King and Wafd and a continued absence of friction with either quarter would be helpful in the pending negotiations.

The Egyptian delegation was composed of four ministers: Nahas; Wassif Ghali, the Foreign Minister; Makram Ebeid; and Osman Moharram Pasha, Minister of Public Works. A number of advisers also accompanied the delegation. Among these was Ahmed Maher, much to the chagrin of the British Government. Loraine was also to attend the negotiations. The Egyptian delegation arrived in London on 26 March 1930 and were met by Henderson and Loraine 'Nahas seemed much touched by the attention'.[103] A dinner party was held at Claridges the same evening. Loraine commented that 'Nahas [was] in good form and with Uncle A it went with quite a swish. They sat next to each other at supper, cracked jokes and were almost digging each other in the ribs'.[104] Henderson himself remarked that 'Nahas was quite a good fellow. Straight and really meant to have an agreement'. Loraine wryly observed that 'it will soon be forgotten that I had any share in bringing him [Nahas] to that frame of mind'.[105]

Negotiations began on 31 March in 'quite a friendly atmosphere'.[106] The British team comprised the Secretaries of State for Foreign Affairs, Dominion Affairs, War and Air Office, with representatives from Australia, New Zealand and India as observers. The provisions agreed with Mahmoud formed the basis of the discussions. In the first week of negotiation, agreement on many of the non-controversial provisions was reached. Arthur Henderson appeared to be the driving force. Dalton recorded that Henderson 'frightened all our officials by going so fast and refusing to worry about small points or all the little notes they passed to him'.[107] Loraine was somewhat uneasy, however, at Henderson's trail-blazing.

> Everyone is on good terms, but Uncle A has matters very much in his own hands and I can't always be sure of knowing everything that is being said or done. Perhaps I am over-anxious about it, but it would be unpleasant to find one morning that something had been settled, which I could not reconcile with my own ideas on the subject.[108]

Nevertheless, Loraine was optimistic that an agreement was possible although he was not convinced that it would be 'as satisfactory as I could wish. Maybe it's a question of more or less, because there are snags in any agreement and snags equally if we fail to reach one'.[109] However, although the Wafd eventually conceded that British troops could be stationed on the west bank of the Suez Canal – a huge concession considering they had consistently rejected the presence of the British army in any part of Egypt – the major stumbling block, as predicted by the Residency prior to negotiations, was the Sudan. Following consultation with the Governor-General, Britain's position was to maintain the *status quo*. The Egyptian delegation, however, demanded a 'share in the civil administration, unrestricted Egyptian immigration and an assertion of Egypt's sovereignty'.[110] This was unacceptable to the British Cabinet. The Governor-General, Sir John Maffey, had been ordered to remain in Khartoum during the negotiations in order to dissuade any Egyptian hopes of a compromise.[111] A draft treaty was handed to the Egyptian delegation on 17 April, but Nahas refused to sign it until an agreement could be reached over the Sudan. At Nahas's request the negotiations were adjourned to allow Cairo to consider the proposals. For Loraine, these negotiations were an opportunity to show the Foreign Office what he had been up against in Cairo. 'Our Labour people are getting a bit fed up with the Wafdists and no wonder! Anyway they will understand now – and I wanted 'em to – what one has to deal with and put up with out there.'[112]

Once the negotiations reconvened Loraine believed the recess had diminished the chances of a treaty. He complained: 'The Egyptians' heads are so confused and it takes hours and hours to find out what they are really talking about [...] They are simply incapable of going straight at a problem and trying to solve it.'[113] Nahas handed a counter-draft treaty to Henderson but, again, the Sudan proved to be the stumbling block. Without prospect of a compromise, and the Egyptian refusal to sign any treaty that did not address the Sudan issue, the negotiations closed on 8 May, both parties 'very sober and dignified. There was no acrimony [...] and we separated as quite good friends'.[114] Loraine commented:

> Several times we seemed within an ace of agreement [...] It is certainly a relief that the matter has ended one way or another though from my own point of view and having to go back to Cairo I am by no means sure which ending was the frying pan and which the fire! But it is a pity that so much effort should have remained without result and fruitless. Perhaps we have gone a little further in some ways than the 1929 proposals, though not in my opinion materially so: but the Wafdists have certainly come a longish way in our direction by comparison with the attitude taken up by Saad Zaghlul in 1924 during his brief and abortive negotiations with Ramsay MacDonald. But there it is: the two ends just didn't meet.[115]

The vast majority of the Egyptian press applauded the Egyptian delegation's decision to refuse to come to an agreement over the Sudan. *Al-Ahram* exclaimed: 'Egyptians do not regret the failure of the negotiations. Negotiations are entered upon to establish rights, not to lose them. Egyptians are solidly with Nahas Pasha on this. What Egyptian would sign away with his own hands the Sudan after the sacrifices in men and money made during the last 130 years?'[116] The Egyptian press attributed the failure of the negotiations to a last minute stiffening of the British Cabinet due to external pressures on the Labour Party. They contended that the Liberals, who held a large proportion of shares in the Sudan Plantation Syndicate, had threatened to withdraw their support from the MacDonald Government if further concessions were made over the Sudan.[117] Although the 'patriotic diatribes' of previous attempts did not accompany this breakdown of negotiations, it was noted that the most serious feature of this rupture was the 'prominence, which is naturally being given in Egypt to the Sudan issue'.[118] The Wafd were now able to present the Sudan issue as a 'matter of life or death, on which no compromise is possible'.[119] Indeed, Loraine echoed this sentiment, for Egypt, the Sudan was sacred, the two countries being bound by religion, language and the Nile. Britain, however, perceived herself as the Sudan's guardian as it progressed towards independence:

> In his [Loraine's] opinion the problem was not one that could be settled by a compromise, and Henderson had been unwise in attempting it. Having made the initial error of inviting the Wafd to state their claims, Henderson should then have rejected them outright; by laying them before the Cabinet he led the delegation to believe that he was himself prepared to give ground.[120]

The Egyptian delegation may also have felt that they had already gone 'too far'.[121] In meeting Henderson, the Egyptians saw how the Sudan issue provided a convenient point over which to break off talks. Indeed, Mahmoud Fahmy-el-Nokrashi Bey, Minister of Communications, had told *The Times* that 'Nahas had made too many concessions'. Meanwhile Rex Hoare reported rumours in Cairo that threats had been made against Makram and Wasif Ghali, Minister for Foreign Affairs, if the treaty was agreed.[122]

In Britain, Henderson was criticized for having gone further than the 1929 proposals. He was also attacked for ignoring the advice of the Chiefs of Staff and acquiescing in the dismissal of a number of British officials from the Egyptian administration and the police. Hoare commented on Henderson's 'ostentatious inability to conceal his passionate desire to sign something'.[123]

The Palace-Sidky regime

As the Anglo-Egyptian treaty negotiations broke down, a power struggle between the Wafd and the King developed over the Constitution. The Wafd wished to introduce a Bill in order to protect the Constitution whereby any Minister found 'suspending or sinning' against the Constitution would be tried for high treason and could be condemned to penalties ranging from hard labour to a fine of £8,000.[124] Loraine perceived this Bill as a 'grave mistake' and a 'fruitful source in future of political vengeance and proscription'. He believed that it would render the Wafdist Government 'virtually irremovable' whilst, simultaneously, strengthening the position of that Government both against the King and also their refusal to accept any settlement with Britain except on their own terms. The latter point Loraine perceived as indirectly constituting a threat to Britain's position within Egypt and would provide a justification to 'fulfil the role we have frequently played in the past of endeavouring to keep the peace between the contending sections of Egyptian people'. Hoare believed that the Wafd had 'concluded from the course of the negotiations that there is a tremendous anxiety on our side to reach an Anglo-Egyptian settlement and that His Majesty's Government will be extremely reluctant to make their weight felt in the internal affairs of Egypt'.[125] Indeed, MacDonald warned that 'we may be manoeuvred into a very awkward position'. He suggested a stance that 'whilst neutral as to immediate action' it would be made clear to Nahas that Britain was not unaware of the possible effects of his Bill and 'that if that were to happen we might be compelled to interest ourselves as all our policy is based upon the *status quo* until agreement is reached'.[126] The Foreign Office, however, was more cautious and felt that any intimation to Nahas in the sense of MacDonald's minute would be 'interpreted by him as something very like a threat'. Instead the Foreign Office advised patience. 'We may have to utter such a threat and, having uttered it, if necessary live up to it; but until need for threatening is more acute than it appears to be the inclination of the Foreign Office would be to mark time'. More particularly since the Egyptian Parliament was due to rise for the summer recess shortly and 'every day that passes without the introduction of these foolish bills increases the chances of their postponement – perhaps indefinitely'.[127]

In the observance of neutrality over this crisis it was inevitable that the King would have the upper-hand since all Egyptian Government Bills had to be endorsed by him before they were presented to the Egyptian Chamber of Deputies. Indeed, Loraine postulated that the King would not ask for the Residency's support but merely for its neutrality. The logical result of which would be for the Residency to remain equally neutral if the King dismissed the Government before the Bill was placed on the statute book, or dissolved Parliament in the event of the resignation of the present government and an inability to find any alternative government. In the event, Fuad refused his signature on the grounds that this Bill was too important to rush through towards the end of a Parliamentary session.

Despite Henderson's informal attempts to broker a compromise between Nahas and the King, Nahas tendered the resignation of his Cabinet on 17 June 1930 in the hope of breaking down the King's opposition to the Bill. The Egyptian Chamber attempted to strengthen Nahas's hand by granting their confidence to no one but him, thereby making it impossible for the King to appoint another Prime Minister without suspending parliamentary government. Nonetheless, Fuad responded to this challenge by accepting Nahas's resignation and appointed Ismail Sidky Pasha as Prime Minister. Parliament was then adjourned on 21 June for a month. Henderson was clearly frustrated at this turn of events when the opportunity for a treaty had appeared so propitious only a few months earlier.

> I need not dilate on the unfortunate and untimely character of this crisis. If it is an example of the manner in which Egyptians manage their own affairs when left free to do so it is not an encouraging one. Each side has placed itself in a position whence withdrawal is impossible without loss of face.
>
> In my own opinion Wafd have forced the pace. They contend, however, that the King brought the matter to a head by failing to sanction presentation of the Bill to Chamber. As usual, each side is thoroughly mistrustful of the other.
>
> [...] Wafd were clearly determined to get the law for protection of the Constitution put through during the present session. They have shown that they regard the treaty issue as secondary to consolidation of their own supremacy.[128]

Loraine shared in his frustration:

> Nahas has really behaved idiotically. Never has a hand so full of trumps been so vilely played and squandered [...] Of course, the Wafd wanted me to intervene and produced the argument that if we were really sincere about the treaty, we should have told the King that he must keep the Wafd because they were the only people who could deliver the goods we wanted.[129]

To Loraine, the failure of negotiations was a disappointment. He also felt that Nahas had let him down.

Ismail Sidky, once a Wafdist, had been interned with Zaghlul at Malta and was one of the Egyptian delegates at the Paris Peace Conference in 1919 where his moral behaviour was described as 'scandalous'. His relationship with Zaghlul was somewhat fractious and had served in a number of Cabinet positions of various Ministries and as a member of the commission that drafted the Constitution of 1923. Sidky was described as:

> A man of very quick intelligence, great ingenuity and administrative ability, industry and courage. Loves intrigue – has, I should think, no scruples of any sort. Very ambitious. I think his chief failing, apart from a certain inability to inspire confidence, is that he is occasionally apt (under the ambition or resentment, or, I might add, concupiscence) to keep his nose so close on the scent of his object that he fails to notice what is going on around him. It is to be observed about Sidky that, though he is not a truthful person, and, unlike Sarwat, seeks to mislead by what he says, and not by what he leaves unsaid, he makes a practice of keeping his promises. He has a remarkable clarity and activity of mind, and is the only Egyptian I know whose conversation is a real intellectual excitement.[130]

On 22 October Sidky promulgated a new Constitution and an electoral law without submitting them for the approval of the Senate or Chamber of Deputies. The Constitution of 1923 expressly provided that no constitutional amendments should become effective until they had received approval by a two-thirds vote in each Chamber, no vote being permissible unless at least two-thirds of the members were present. The accompanying electoral law substituted direct universal suffrage for a system of two-degree voting. The new Constitution and electoral law would, in effect, enhance the prerogatives of the King, strengthen the position of the Cabinet and reduce the power of the Wafdist party.[131] Sidky, unsurprisingly, objected to his Ministry being termed as a Palace Cabinet and pointed out that 'he himself has never been regarded as being enfeoffed to the Palace'. Henderson highlighted that 'apart from Sidky Pasha, who must by the force of circumstances depend entirely on the King, all the Ministers are exceedingly well disposed to His Majesty'.[132] Sidky's regime was described by the Residency as 'semi-dictatorial' but that he had 'shown great astuteness and ability in handling both the administrative and political problems'.[133]

British observance of neutrality represented a change in the position of the British *vis-à-vis* the Palace and the Wafd. Rather than siding with one or the other, the British now proclaimed neutrality in the contest between Fuad and Sidky on the one hand and the Wafd on the other.[134] This was all the more striking with a Labour Government in power in London. Indeed, Loraine commented that the Foreign Office appeared rather 'woolly headed' about the situation. Henderson admitted to Loraine that an Anglo-Egyptian treaty could only be successfully negotiated with a popularly elected party. 'This being the case, our strategic objective must be to get the late Government [the Wafd] back into office in a sober and chastened temper, and the Sidky Government out without penalty or subsequent persecution. The King's face must be saved, but he no less than the Wafd must learn his lesson.'[135] In writing to his wife, Loraine complained:

> I sniff pretty strongly that Uncle A and Mr D[alton] want Nahas put back again. If they'd said so before the King accepted his resignation I might have done something about it, but it is a little trying if they expect me to step in & clear up a mess in wh. I'd been definitely told to keep neutral after careful consideration of the circumstances [...] One would have thought the Labour people would be a bit sick of the Wafd after that dreary business in London but apparently no. There is evidently some curious affinity between them, which one could suspect of being purely erotic if it were between man & woman. Very odd![136]

Loraine was not convinced that British actions to precipitate a Wafd return to power were as clear-cut as Henderson made out. Loraine outlined to Henderson that any attempts to manoeuvre the Wafdist party back into power 'would constitute a far-reaching involvement in Egyptian party conflict' and involve a considerable departure from the path of neutrality. Loraine warned that 'once we intervene we must carry the matter through'. Any intervention along Henderson's lines would paralyse the King, who was just as much an integral part of the Constitution as Parliament, and maybe even precipitate his abdication. It would also eliminate from Egyptian public life the more sober element as well as removing nearly all the trained administrative talent of the country and ensure the hegemony of the Wafd.[137] Loraine warned that 'we must not, I think, lose sight of the fact that present crisis is fundamentally constitutional'. Loraine perceived the present crisis as one between a one-party parliamentary dictatorship and a limited monarchy with a tendency towards unparliamentary dictatorship. It was a struggle for existence between the King and the Wafd and, if it became understood that the British Government supported a Wafd return to power, it would acquire a revolutionary character.[138] Loraine believed that the action Henderson proposed was an intervention and he did his utmost to dissuade Henderson from this line of policy. To encourage a Wafd return to power 'would connote a pregnant change of policy; it would mean and be understood throughout Egypt to mean that His Majesty's Government had taken sides on a major internal issue, and, in my opinion, we should morally be pinned down to that partisanship for the future'.[139] Loraine advocated mediation over intervention, to play the waiting game, for both the Palace and Sidky on the one hand and Nahas and the Wafd on the other, to reach a more sober realization of attainable objectives.

> A Fabian attitude on our part for the present would, I conceive, be more effective in bringing Wafd to a more sober and chastened frame of mind than an attitude

which [the] Wafd would rightly understand as ensuring their victory over the King. If experiment which the King and Sidky contemplate proves to be unrealisable, save at cost of revolution, it will give them time to appreciate fact. It should, moreover, help to disabuse the Wafd and public opinion generally in this country of the idea now widely diffused that His Majesty's Government are so bent on reaching a treaty settlement with Egypt that they are prepared to support the Wafd in order to get it and to the exclusion of all other considerations.[140]

Loraine's advice certainly made an impact within the Foreign Office. Murray's memorandum on 5 July noted that whilst it remained the ultimate objective of the British Government to achieve a treaty settlement with Egypt, that settlement now looked 'relatively remote, and consequently less valuable as a day-to-day guide for our policy'.[141] British policy was caught between two undesirable alternatives 'both of them thoroughly unpleasant'. On the one hand, benevolent neutrality exercised in favour of the present Palace Government, i.e. King Fuad, or, on the other, the triumphant return to power of a Wafdist Government.[142] 'So unpleasant are these', Murray recommended working towards what he termed a 'diluted Wafdist Government'. Examples of a diluted Wafdist Government were those of the Adli Government in 1926 and the Sarwat Government of 1927–28. The Foreign Office perceived that with these governments negotiation had been at least possible and compromise solutions of various problems had been achieved, such as the issue over British officials in 1926 and British officers in the Egyptian Army in 1927. Murray recognized that these types of Government were possible only when the Wafd felt uncertain of themselves or of British intentions. 'Paradoxical, therefore, though it may appear, it looks as if our best chance of an early return to a workable constitutional Government lies in encouraging this feeling of uncertainty in the Wafd.' Murray therefore supported Loraine's suggestion of an 'emphatic endorsement of the absolutely unbiased character of our neutrality and refusal to discuss our attitude in hypothetical contingencies, [it] appears the right one'.[143] Indeed, Loraine recognized that 'what I say is being listened to with real attention and sympathy: they recognise that the views I express are utterly unbiased [...] and at least we have got to the stage of being able to discuss brass tacks [...] without suspicion'.[144] Loraine emphasized that this time he wanted to wait until he was quite sure over the correct path to follow and then do so 'as fearlessly as I can'. Loraine continued: 'There is no course now, I think, but the negative one of neutrality, watchfulness and sympathy. It is a very difficult course to follow and keep on an even keel, but I see danger in every alternative, both actual danger of consequences and possible danger of being dragged a long way further along the road than I am willing to go.'[145]

Nevertheless, this Fabian approach advocated by Loraine and seemingly endorsed by the Foreign Office was always going to be a tricky tightrope to walk. This latest political crisis coupled with the news of Sidky's plans resulted in a number of turbulent demonstrations throughout July 1930. These demonstrations resulted in both loss of life and damage to property. More worryingly, it appeared that these Wafd demonstrations were undertaken in order to drive the Sidky Government into enforcing repressive measures, a challenge from which the Palace Government did not shrink. Henderson therefore believed that it would be 'optimistic to hope for emergence of "diluted Wafdist Government" or even of an early opportunity for effective mediation'.[146] Henderson posed the question: 'Would it [...] be any more unreasonable for the Wafd to demand our silence whilst they dethroned the King than for Sidky to expect us to refrain from expressing our opinion whilst he and the King revise the Constitution in order to dethrone the Wafd?' Henderson recognized that Egypt under a republic or under a ruler of the Wafd's choice would be more difficult to deal with, but those difficulties would be enormously enhanced if the Wafd had reason to believe that their opponents had been able to rely upon British support. Henderson predicted that Sidky would fail irrespective of whether he tampered with the Constitution. The British Government could not conceal her disapproval of any tampering with the Electoral Law, even though actual intervention was precluded by the terms of the 1922 Declaration. In the final assessment, Henderson believed that 'whatever course Sidky may decide to adopt, it will at least produce an Egyptian solution of what is essentially an Egyptian question, however intimately it may affect us'.[147] This seemingly tangled policy stance was repeated to the House of Commons on 17 July by the Prime Minister, Ramsay MacDonald. MacDonald reaffirmed Britain's attitude of neutrality and non-intervention in Egyptian internal affairs. However, his statement also declared that 'His Majesty's Government did not intend to be used as an instrument for an attack on the Egyptian Constitution. In consequence they could not be party to an alteration to the Electoral Law even if it precluded, by their declaration in 1922, from actual intervention in an internal issue of this nature'.[148] Loraine was disappointed by MacDonald's statement. He regarded it as of the 'utmost importance' that the Egyptians should resolve the issue themselves. 'Then we shall really know on what keel we are floating, and then there is a real chance of getting the situation to settle down. If only the F[oreign] O[ffice] could perceive and understand this! Perhaps with patience and perseverance I shall be able to run the thing in the way I'm sure it ought to be run – or rather allowed to – [...] it's a very tough job.'[149]

In response to MacDonald's statement Sidky was 'upset' and perceived the statement given to the House of Commons as in of itself 'an intervention in Egyptian internal affairs'.[150] The King reacted in much the same vein.[151] Loraine attempted to convince Henderson of the utility of the Sidky Government and that its potential for securing British ends should not be, as yet, entirely discounted. 'In the space of a few weeks the increased efficiency of the administrative machine is remarkable. The political grit thrown into the wheels by the Wafd is being quickly cleaned out [...] the British cogs in the machine are fulfilling smoothly their proper functions as Egyptian officials instead of being side-tracked and embarrassed at every turn.' Loraine spelled out the situation to Henderson:

Wafd represent to us that unless they are in power we cannot have our treaty.

Sidky represents to us that if the Wafd have power we cannot have a well-governed Egypt, but that as soon as there is a well-governed Egypt our treaty will follow logically. But that it is no use from anyone's point of view having a treaty with a divided and disordered Egypt.

There is truth in both views. We naturally do not like to see Egypt governed by an Administration that has no parliamentary support; but we have had convincing evidence of the political immaturity, the administrative inefficiency and the deficiency of statecraft of the Wafd.

Wafd denied the right of anyone else in Egypt but themselves to sign a treaty with England. Other elements, of which the Sidky Government is momentarily the symbol, deny the capacity of the Wafd to govern Egypt in general interests of population and State.

Last year we redressed the balance with a declared bias in favour of the Wafd.

We reaped no effective result except, perhaps, taking the anti-foreign plank out of the Wafdist platform, but we nevertheless did nothing to dislodge them. They blundered miserably, and there is no obligation on us to fight their battles or rescue their chestnuts.[152]

Murray noted that 'this review is certainly objective but it does not disclose the road to our goal and for the excellent reason that the road is at present blocked by the inability of the Wafd to recognise the necessity of compromise in politics'.[153] Murray continued that until the Wafd learn this lesson, it would be impossible to achieve the goal of securing an Anglo-Egyptian treaty.

Loraine's frustration at Henderson and the Labour Government was clear. In a letter to his wife on 22 July, three days prior to the above telegram to London, Loraine wrote:

I'm more afraid of London's policy than Egypt's vagaries. We must either take charge of the situation wh. H.M.G. hate the idea of doing: or let the Egyptians work out their own salvation – provided of course they do not touch foreign lives and property in the process. But Uncle A. don't [sic] seem to like that either for fear – so far as I can make out – lest the Wafd should lose the battle: for he still seems to think we can only get a treaty with the Wafd. So I want things to find their own level here – wh. I am sure is sound and they apparently want the situation influenced without the appearance of intervening. This I consider impossible. Can't have cakes and eat 'em![154]

Nevertheless, Loraine was wary of disagreeing too outwardly and openly with the Foreign Office. 'I shouldn't nag Lancelot [Oliphant] or Walford [Selby] too much about things here – they are very sensitive about Egypt and you know what unhappy memories there were of bickerings etc. between the Residency and F.O. during the last regime.'[155] Indeed, the debate in the House of Commons on 29 July 1930 tended to support Loraine's policy of wait and see. Winston Churchill, not having forgotten his friend Lord Lloyd, accused the Labour Government of interference in the Egyptian situation despite its declaration of neutrality. In its attempts to negotiate a treaty settlement since coming to power, Churchill accused the Labour Government of merely segregating Egyptian politics into two extreme categories. 'There is an oriental court entrenched by the practical necessities of law and order, facing a corrupt and fanatical caucus which is armed with a Parliament falsely professing to represent some definite expression of the wishes and interests of the people. That is the situation which His Majesty's Government have managed to create. They have declared absolute impartiality, but it is not passive impartiality.'[156] Churchill presciently pointed out that 'you cannot withdraw to the Canal and to the Sudan, and shrug your shoulders and allow matters to take what course they will in the intervening areas'.[157] Churchill perceived that British influence had disappeared and now interference was all that the British Government had to rely upon. Loraine noted that Churchill's speech was 'as usual disconcerting, especially as regards the Sudan'.[158] In the absence of Henderson, away ill, MacDonald provided a robust defence. He underlined that in any attempt to change the constitution, Britain would not be used as a tool for its alteration, nor would it be promulgated that it was done with British consent, connivance or approving knowledge. 'It is purely an Egyptian question. It belongs to that field of Egyptian political activities where the Egyptians rule without interference by us; it is their own affairs, and they can do what they like.'[159] However, were a change in the constitution to result in the deterioration in the conditions of law and order that resulted in a threat to foreign life and property, then British responsibility under that reserved subject of the 1922 Declaration would be enacted. During the debate David Lloyd George expressed his relief that the Labour Government were fully versed in their responsibilities to protect the lives and property of foreign nationals. However, Lloyd George pointed out that perhaps some of MacDonald's declarations 'will not land him in interference'. MacDonald's statement on 17 July to the House of Commons declaring that the Government could not be party to an alteration in the Egyptian Electoral Law was, in Lloyd George's opinion, 'a very serious interference with the internal rights of the Egyptians. After all, the kind of franchise, and the basis on which you elect your Parliament, is one of the primary rights of any country'.[160] For Lloyd George, he believed that it was a 'great mistake' to use British power in a way that would increase the rivalry between the two parties in Egypt. 'We must not give the impression that we are taking sides upon the question of the franchise, or upon the question of how you should elect the Parliament of Egypt.'[161] Loraine commented that 'I actually feel positive warmth towards Ll[oyd] G[eorge]. He put exactly my point about non-intervention, and put it extremely well'.[162] Without any sense of irony considering his involvement in the re-drawing of the map of the Near and Middle East during the Paris Peace Conference, Lloyd George warned MacDonald:

> I do not know to what extent we have a right to force western ideas of democracy and Government upon the East. It is very much older than Europe, and the biggest ideas in the world have come from the East. There is a great deal in what the Easterner thinks about the Occidental, namely, that, although we are wise in practical affairs, the deepest things of life he understands better than we do. We say to him, 'We are so much wiser than you, although we are much younger in experience of Government, and, therefore, you must take our ideas of Government'. That seems to me to be a vice which is extending.[163]

Loraine commented that, on the whole, it had been a good and useful debate. 'It brings us nearer to a consensus policy towards Egypt.'[164]

The central issue, therefore, was how to resolve this impasse. Within Egypt itself, Sidky had appeared to win the first round against the Wafd over the point of law and order and Egypt continued to be 'extraordinarily quiet'. Rumours that Mohammed Mahmoud had been intriguing with the Wafd with a view to re-forming a coalition as in 1925–26 appeared to strike a cord with Foreign Office. Murray commented that whilst he did not believe Mahmoud's time was just yet, the idea of a coalition 'may yet prove the best way out of the present arrangement'.[165] Dalton added that this was 'an interesting cross current'.[166] In a private letter to Loraine, Murray took up this suggestion and proposed Loraine mediate a Coalition Cabinet. Loraine, about to depart for his overdue leave, made his point of view clear. Any attempt at mediation, Loraine believed, would be a 'very serious blunder'.[167] For mediation to be effective, it must be acceptable to both sides. In the present circumstances, Loraine judged it to be acceptable to neither. Nahas had recently categorically refused to entertain participation in a Coalition government of any sort whilst Sidky was prepared to stand or fall by his constitutional and electoral reform scheme, reforms of which precluded Wafdist co-operation. 'If we "mediate" with Nahas on the basis of a coalition, we shall be repulsed. If we act similarly with Sidky we shall be rebuffed, on the ground of interference in internal affairs which we have publicly eschewed.' Loraine again counselled a wait and see approach, to allow Sidky to introduce his reforms, hold an election and bring a parliament into session. At this juncture Sidky 'may produce your rabbit out of his tarboush, and that even if he don't [sic], you will be none the worse off'. The Foreign Office was happy to accept Loraine's assessment of the political situation, a demonstration of both their confidence in him and the improvement in relations between the Residency and Foreign Office, unlike Loraine's predecessors. 'We are agreed', Murray minuted, 'an untamed and undiluted Wafd' will not produce the conditions ripe for the conclusion of a treaty whilst 'a minority Govt. like Sidky's certainly won't do so'.[168] What Murray found unsettling was the introduction of another 'if' into Anglo-Egyptian relations with Sidky's proposed reforms and subsequent elections.

Loraine's consistent calls for a policy of neutrality, a wait and see approach, were rooted in the fact that it would bring all parties to a truer appreciation of the importance of the conclusion of a treaty rather than Egyptian politicians merely utilizing the treaty as a lever in the internal struggle between the Egyptian political parties.

> Granting the immaturity of Egyptian nationalism, the mental heritage of deceit and tortuousness which centuries of oppressive rule cannot fail to breed, and the "underdog complex which still haunts the rather strident manifestations of modern oriental nationalism, I am inclined to regard this tendency fairly leniently. But I am obliged to notice it and, though I am unable to condone it, regret its presence as militating against the genuineness of Egypt's comprehension of the obligations which the treaty will lay on her, as well as of the advantages which it will bestow.[169]

Sidky published his new Constitution, which reduced the number of Deputies by over a third, and the amendments to the Electoral Law at the end of October 1930. The British Government maintained an attitude of 'watchful reserve and neutrality' as a tactical expedient. They were left to await Egyptian developments and whether Sidky possessed the confidence of the majority of the electorate in the forthcoming elections. Dalton commented that 'we should not, I think, contemplate any departure from our present attitude until after the elections. And perhaps not even then'.[170] It was judged that Britain could afford to wait, British prestige was not suffering. Indeed, it was perceived that 'their [the Wafd's] impotence, in the absence of a treaty, to deal with the King and a palace Government is teaching the Wafd and the Liberals a lesson which nothing else would have made them learn'.[171] Furthermore, the worldwide economic slowdown and subsequent depression lent itself to a wait and see policy. At the beginning of 1931 land that until a year ago was changing hands at £200 an acre was either now unsaleable or only fetching £80.[172] Agricultural rents had also collapsed by approximately 50 per cent for cotton land or were uncollectable whilst cotton prices had also fallen by 40 per cent from 1930 levels.

With the announcement of elections imminent, Henderson acknowledged that:

> If elections are conducted with reasonable propriety, if a respectable proportion of the electorate gives its vote, and if Sidky Pasha enjoys a substantial majority in the resulting Parliament, it will be difficult, if not impossible, to refuse to negotiate with him. If, on the other hand, any of these three conditions are not fulfilled, and if, in consequence, His Majesty's Government have to decline to negotiate, the blow to Sidky's prestige will be severe and, possibly, overwhelming.[173]

Again, the British adopted a wait and see attitude. In the meantime, and despite the lack of support from any Egyptian statesmen of standing, Sidky continued to prepare the ground for the forthcoming elections largely through repressive measures, including control of the Press and the refusal to allow Wafdist and Liberal leaders to tour the country in order to advocate the boycott of the impending elections, which aimed to destroy liberty of opinion and bring the Opposition to heel. In response, a petition to King Fuad by Adli, Mahmoud, Nahas, Ziwer and a number of ex-Ministers of different parties called for the restitution of the 1923 Constitution and declared that the forthcoming elections would not express the opinion of the country whilst any treaty concluded by this Parliament would not bind the nation. London became nervous. Murray minuted: 'The signature of this petition by Adli and Ziwer who are non-party men, not to mention the twenty odd ex-Ministers, it is a very important development. I do not believe that Sidky and King Fuad can successfully flout the wishes of the country [...] in my opinion Sidky's chances begin to look extremely doubtful.' The idea of a national coalition was again raised. 'Neutrality if pushed too far may leave us carrying the baby in the event of serious disturbances and a collapse of the present regime.'[174] Henderson could not see how the Sidky Government would be able to carry out their plans without recourse to further measures of repression. His concern lay in the fact that this may inflame popular feeling and lead to clashes that would involve Britain's physical intervention in order to protect foreign lives and property and thereby impose upon Britain the direct responsibility for finding a way out of this impasse. Henderson posed the question to Loraine as to whether he was 'satisfied that the complete absence of that Residency guidance and advice which has in the past prepared the way for so much political evolution and which a strict adherence to neutrality and aloofness would preclude will in time promote a national coalition with a definite programme of constitutional compromise and treaty settlement'.[175] Henderson feared that recent developments would successfully create a national coalition but one that would be implacably opposed to Britain and thereby any future political settlement. Loraine, however, was adamant that nothing should be done. It is a testament to the Foreign Office's confidence in Loraine that this was accepted without reservation. W M B Mack minuted: 'Loraine's views are so definite that it seems that there is nothing to be done at the moment'.[176] It was agreed to wait until the results of the elections that 'may give us a new situation and another opening'.[177]

Despite Wafd attempts to enforce a boycott of the elections the primary election round began on 14 May and continued until 18 May. Figures from the Ministry of Interior showed that 66.8 per cent of the 2 million electorate had voted whilst during the secondary election of 1 June over 90 per cent of the 50,000 eligible had voted. The Foreign Office noted that 'Sidky has reduced to impotence – for the moment at any rate – the hitherto efficient Wafd organisation throughout Egypt'.[178] Was the way forward for British policy any clearer? Loraine reserved judgement. It was still too difficult to assess the significance of the recent elections for the future Anglo-Egyptian relationship. If the election result was accepted at face value, then it certainly represented a considerable victory for Sidky. However, the Opposition movement was 'loud and angry' in its denunciation of the election and countered that it was conducted by 'force and fraud'. From the Egyptian point of view, Loraine perceived that his position would depend upon his ability to consolidate the authority of the new Parliament and to attract support from those at present hostile towards him. From the British perspective, Loraine believed that 'we have not [...] yet got a conclusive Egyptian answer to Egyptian question'. Loraine believed that it was not yet possible to negotiate with Sidky due to those political heavyweights who remained hostile to him coupled with tying British morality to a possibly fraudulent election. Loraine therefore advocated compromise and conciliation between the two rival forces since 'it is a form of pressure on both sides in Egypt, it involves no departure from our settled policy, it enables me to stand on the same ground [...] whether I am speaking to Sidky, Mahmoud or Nahas'.[179] Indeed, Henderson added that 'until there is a much greater degree of political stability [...] fresh treaty negotiations would not be expedient, and in these circumstances I think it would be inadvisable from our side even to hint at their possibility'.[180] Parliament was opened by the King on 20 June 1931 and Loraine commented that 'I think the summer is going to be quite calm: and I am not feeling at all guilty about going away [on his summer leave]'.[181]

On Loraine's arrival in London in August 1931 he was to be embroiled in a whirlwind of a different kind. The Wall Street Crash of October and November 1929 caught Britain, in what MacDonald referred to as the 'economic blizzard' from America. Britain's exports were hit by the double-whammy of a sharp decline in world trade and a collapse in commodity prices. Britain's balance of payments deteriorated whilst confidence in sterling declined. As a result, unemployment increased rapidly from 1.164 million in June 1929 to 2.5 million in December 1930 whilst the rate of unemployment rose from 9.9 per cent in September 1929 to 22.4 per cent in September 1931.[182] In August 1931 the economic crisis peaked. Philip Snowden, Chancellor of the Exchequer, proposed the cutting of some public sector pay as well as a 10 per cent reduction in unemployment benefit. The cut in unemployment benefit was in direct contravention to the Labour election manifesto pledge and it divided the Cabinet. The possible resignation of Ministers, such as Henderson, over this issue led the Cabinet to conclude that it was impossible to continue and the Labour Government resigned. A temporary National Government of individuals rather than party representatives was formed to deal with the immediate economic crisis. MacDonald remained as Prime Minister with Stanley Baldwin as Lord President of the Council and Herbert Samuel as Secretary of State for Home Affairs. Lord Reading became the Secretary of State for Foreign Affairs. A General Election was called for 31 October 1931 in which the National Government coalition announced that it should continue in power. In opposing the National Government, Labour was reduced to a mere 52 MPs from its 1929 high of 288. Arthur Henderson himself lost his seat. The National Government itself won an enormous landslide, 554 seats. MacDonald remained as Prime Minister and Lord Reading was replaced by Sir John Simon as Foreign Secretary.

Conclusion

The conclusion of an Anglo-Egyptian settlement was the goal of both Conservative and Labour administrations. A treaty would place Britain's economic and strategic interests in the Nile Valley on a much more secure footing in this era of imperial overstretch that had resulted from the gargantuan effort of the First World War. To this end there was little difference in the foreign policy pursued between the Conservative and Labour governments of the 1920s, both prepared to disregard military concerns during the 1927, 1929, 1930 and 1931 discussions, in order to achieve their aims. Importantly, whilst an overarching shift in power from Cairo to London does occur during this period, Loraine's restoration in the confidence of the position of High Commissioner allowed an influence over policy that had not been enjoyed since Lord Allenby. And, even then, Allenby's influence stemmed from his military successes in Palestine during the First World War, and was much more of an overt and bombast nature as compared to Loraine's quiet persuasion. Nowhere was this made more plain than over Henderson's desire to see a return of the Wafd to power whilst Loraine was content with the Palace-Sidky bloc to run its course. In essence, Loraine understood that Britain had to stand back from the internal political struggle that marked Egyptian politics. So long as the prospect of a treaty could be used as a lever in this internal struggle, Britain would be drawn into the political minutiae of the competing Egyptian interest groups. Indeed, it was not until Egypt faced a serious external threat in the form of Benito Mussolini's Italy in the wake of his Abyssinian adventure, and since Egypt shared a border with Italian Libya, that the Wafd and other Egyptian political interest groups desired British protection. Accordingly, an Anglo-Egyptian alliance was finally concluded in 1936, fifteen years after the abortive Curzon-Adli negotiations.

Conclusion

Britain's occupation of Egypt was to be of an ephemeral nature. However, wider imperial rivalries encapsulated in the Scramble for Africa ensured that British involvement in Egypt, in particular to protect free passage of the Suez Canal – her 'jugular vein' of empire, became a long-standing commitment in an area where Britain's economic and strategic interests converged. The First World War and the use of Egypt as a military and intelligence centre for both the Egyptian Expeditionary Force and the Arab Bureau served only to underline the importance of Egypt within Britain's imperial network. Egypt's rising status was no more amply demonstrated than in the debates over its possible annexation to the British Empire in 1917. Ronald Graham at the Foreign Office recognized that Egypt provided a bulwark against pan-Islamic propaganda, French and Italian intrigues, but that it also provided a centre from which British influence could radiate throughout the Muslim world. This was a factor of great significance bearing in mind Britain's rule over the Indian sub-continent.[1] These discussions illustrate that Egypt was at the crossroads of empire, between the closely administered states of West Africa and the, as yet, undefined regions of the Near and Middle East where Britain's type of administration over Egypt would have far-reaching consequences.

The strains of war took a particularly heavy toll upon Egypt. This, coupled with a Foreign Office overwhelmed in dealing with the post-war world and divided between London and the Paris Peace conference, contributed not only to the growth of nationalism which exploded onto the Egyptian streets in March 1919 but also to the way in which the Foreign Office responded to this dangerous development. Despite warnings from the British High Commissioner over the effect of Woodrow Wilson's calls for self-determination on Saad Zaghlul's Wafd party, the Foreign Office was caught on the back foot. Reginald Wingate undoubtedly took the brunt of the Foreign Office's slow reaction to developments within Egypt. Wingate had alerted his superiors in the Foreign Office as early as November 1918 that if the future of Egypt *vis-à-vis* the Protectorate and Britain remained unresolved 'we are likely to have considerable difficulty in the future'.[2] That the Foreign Office chose to ignore Wingate's warnings was symptomatic of an overworked Foreign Office which lacked, in the case of Egypt, decisive leadership during the heady days of the immediate post-war settlement.

The supplanting of Wingate by Field Marshal Sir Edmund Allenby and the despatch of a mission under the imperialist Alfred Milner were undertaken by the Foreign Office with a view to reinforce the authority of London over the Cairo Residency and

Egypt generally, particularly with the growth of Cairo as a vital military and political hub during the First World War. Much to the Foreign Office's dismay, however, both Allenby and Milner advocated a policy that would recognise Egypt's independence in return for her acquiescence in remaining Britain's satellite in diplomatic and strategic terms. Despite the ultimate failure of the Milner-Zaghlul negotiations, the mission as a whole represented a significant milestone in Anglo-Egyptian relations. In attempting to regularise the relationship, Britain was endeavouring to withdraw from those aspects of internal administration most likely to cause conflict between British officials and local politicians as well as aiming to secure London's wider strategic interests. The Curzon and Adli Yakan Pasha talks in the summer of 1921 marked a convergence of Residency and Foreign Office aims in attempting to satisfy Egyptian demands. It also demonstrated that the Foreign Office was prepared to go further than the British Cabinet in meeting Egyptian demands. Allenby's threatened resignation forced David Lloyd George's reluctant acquiescence in the proposed unilateral declaration of Egyptian independence, pending the negotiation of the four reserved points. The declaration embodied the idea that had been in existence since the Milner Mission: a British withdrawal from Egypt's internal affairs whilst reserving Britain's right to intervene over imperial and strategic interests until a permanent agreement could be reached. That Allenby was able to force through the declaration on an unwilling Prime Minister and Cabinet demonstrated not only his personal authority and the command that the Residency continued to hold in an era of coalition politics but can also be considered as part of wider concerns within Whitehall relating to the perceived threat of a 'revisionist alliance between Germany, the USSR, Turkey, anti-British nationalist movements, and perhaps Japan'. Although these fears began to dissipate by late 1922, these concerns 'shaped British policy toward political reform in Egypt'.[3]

Following Britain's unilateral declaration of Egypt's independence in 1922, the Anglo-Egyptian relationship was punctuated by a number of attempts to negotiate a treaty in order to resolve the four reserved points. What emerged during these negotiations was Britain's attempt to balance the principle of non-intervention in the internal affairs of another country with the vital necessity of protecting imperial communications. For the Foreign Office, the conflicting demands of the British military establishment and the nationalist ideal, as embodied by the Wafd party, proved an intractable problem. The Foreign Office, even under a Labour administration, struggled to reduce the Chiefs of Staff military demands in order to make the negotiation of a treaty a realistic possibility. Not only did the Foreign Office have to contend with recalcitrant Chiefs of Staff, but the relationship between the Foreign Office and the Residency in Cairo, in particular, the High Commissioner was pivotal to the negotiation process. Until now, this relationship has been little understood.

During the 1924 negotiations the Chiefs of Staff gave MacDonald and the Foreign Office very little room for manoeuvre, thus making any chance of negotiating a treaty slim. Allenby generally enjoyed a wide latitude in directing the course of negotiations. This emphasized the strength of his position and the influence of the Residency over a politically inexperienced and minority Labour administration and whose Prime Minister also held the position of Foreign Secretary. As a direct consequence, Allenby and the Residency in Cairo largely drove the pace of the discussions. Nevertheless, as the community of interest between Britain and Egypt weakened, particularly over the Sudan, MacDonald was not prepared to barter away Britain's strategic interests within the Nile Valley. The settlement of the Anglo-Egyptian relationship in 1924 proved to be too large a mountain to climb: obstinate Chiefs of Staff, an inexperienced and politically precarious Labour Government, an explosive situation in the Sudan and an Egyptian nationalist leader unprepared to give any room for manoeuvre proved, unsurprisingly, to be insurmountable. By the end of 1924, any idea of a treaty had evaporated.

Of course, the Sudan formed an integral part of the Anglo-Egyptian relationship, especially in terms of the development of nationalism. Although the Sudan was governed by a joint Anglo-Egyptian Condominium Agreement, Britain's aim was to separate the two nations as much as possible. The Sudan had emerged relatively unscathed from the First World War but the developing Egyptian nationalist movement heightened calls from Wingate and Sir Lee Stack, Wingate's successor as Governor-General of the Sudan and *Sirdar* of the Egyptian Army, to make a definite break in Egyptian-Sudanese ties. To this end, Wingate and Stack were successful in persuading the Foreign Office to pursue a policy de-Egyptianization of the Sudan administration whilst simultaneously encouraging the development of an indigenous Sudanese nationalism – 'Sudan for the Sudanese'.

It was not until 1924 and the projected Anglo-Egyptian negotiations that the Sudanese issue reached political prominence. For Stack, this once again allowed him to advocate British dominance in the Sudan and loosen Egyptian-Sudanese ties. The increase in Egyptian propaganda supporting Egypt's claims to the Sudan served only to underline Stack's concerns that the Egyptian nationalists were attempting to shake off the British yoke by promoting an Egyptian-Sudanese community of interest. The tensions created by the Anglo-Egyptian negotiations in the Sudan finally erupted into a series of demonstrations between June and August 1924. British administrators in Khartoum, Cairo and the Foreign Office were all convinced of Sudanese loyalty to Britain and the benefits of the de-Egyptianization policy of the Sudanese administration, and blamed the disturbances upon Egyptian agency believing that it demonstrated a growing Egyptian connection at a time of concerted British efforts to regularize the Anglo-Egyptian relationship. Whether the demonstrations were a consequence of Egyptian instigation or the result of Sudanese discontent, it forced the Foreign Office into a reconsideration of policy over the Sudan, something which the men-on-the-spot had been urging since 1919. One of the problems appeared to be the Egyptian officering of the Arab and Sudanese units of the Egyptian Army in the Sudan. These officers were believed to be fomenting Egyptian nationalism and therefore provided encouragement to Sudanese disaffection with British rule. In agreement with Stack, the Foreign Office therefore resolved to effect the accelerated disbandment of the Egyptian railway battalion stationed in the Sudan and added its voice to Stack's calls for the creation of a Sudanese Defence Force, thereby expelling once and for all Egyptian sedition from the Sudanese armed forces. At the same time, however, the Foreign Office recognized that this was a 'high-handed proceeding',[4] only to be adopted in the last resort since it would involve a financial subsidy from the Treasury.

That the Sudan formed an intrinsic part of the Anglo-Egyptian relationship in the 1920s was further demonstrated by the assassination of Sir Lee Stack by Egyptian nationalists in November 1924. Political violence had played a deadly role in the British occupation of Egypt since the turn of the century, but the assassination of Stack, despite the establishment of a Special Section within the Public Security Department in 1920 to collect information and deal with the movements or activities of a subversive nature, touched the British position directly. The relationship between the High Commissioner, Allenby, and the incoming Conservative Foreign Secretary, Austen Chamberlain, is fundamental to understanding the British reaction to the assassination. Allenby's ultimatum to Zaghlul, without waiting for official Cabinet sanction, can be viewed both as the culmination of an Anglo-Egyptian tussle for primacy in the Sudan that had been a feature of relations since 1919, and as evidence of increasing frustration on Allenby's part at being unable to halt attacks upon pro-British Egyptian officials and British personnel. Again, it was the Residency who took control of the situation with the Foreign Office playing catch-up. However, even though Allenby's ultimatum can be viewed as the natural development of British policy in reaction to Egyptian nationalist encroachments in the Sudan, Chamberlain, as Foreign Secretary of the first unified Conservative government since the First World War, reasserted his authority over policymaking by despatching Nevile Henderson as Minister Plenipotentiary in order to impose a degree of constraint upon the High Commissioner. This was undoubtedly the first step in drawing back power from the periphery – the Cairo Residency – to the centre – the Foreign Office in London, thereby rectifying a power imbalance that was a hangover from the First World War.

The assassination of Stack in Cairo by Egyptian nationalists a little over two weeks after the failure of the MacDonald-Zaghlul negotiations served as a pretext for a 'radical and permanent settlement of the Sudan question'.[5] The measures taken in reaction to Stack's assassination – the creation of a Sudanese Defence Force, the evacuation of the Egyptian Army from the Sudan and even the possibility of extending the area of irrigation facilitated by the Blue Nile dam – were not new and had been points of discussion between Cairo, Khartoum and the Foreign Office since 1919. The Foreign Office's initial resistance to Wingate's and Stack's urgings to bring the Sudan firmly within the orbit of the British Empire in 1919 can be seen to reflect the desire not to increase British commitments at a time when the international situation was particularly fluid, and to lessen the appearance of British interference in Egypt's or the Sudan's internal affairs, thereby avoiding unnecessary odium from the indigenous population. However, the rapid and decisive steps taken following Stack's assassination demonstrate that when Britain's imperial or strategic interests were directly threatened, Britain was prepared to protect its position by using whatever means necessary.

Both the assassination of Stack and the mutiny of the 11th Sudanese Battalion were perceived by the British authorities as possessing all the hallmarks of Egyptian complicity and instigation. British Sudanese officials were desperate to prove the Egyptian connection in order to validate their previous warnings over Egyptian activity in the Sudan and as justification for the continuation of the Sudanization of the Sudan government. Henderson himself visited the Sudan in January 1925 and his report served only to reinforce these opinions:

It was clear that such disloyalty as there was among the Sudanese troops was entirely due to Egyptian propaganda, which had been at work since 1919, and had been intensified during the past year. Under the circumstances, it was only remarkable that the results of that propaganda had not been more serious and widespread [...] Even in that mutiny, [28 November 1924] there would appear to have been more ignorance and childishness than real malice and disloyalty to the British.[6]

Henderson's visit was followed by a Committee of Enquiry in April 1925, which was commissioned by the Governor-General, Sir Geoffrey Archer. The aim of this committee was to review all the political developments that culminated in the mutiny of November 1924. Again, a number of familiar themes emerged: Egyptian instigation and manipulation were directly responsible for the Sudan disturbances and the extent of political activity in the Sudan bore a direct correlation to that of Egypt. The report endorsed the Egyptian evacuation of the Sudan but warned against complacency. It stated that the educated classes, who tended to occupy the lower civil service grades, had acquired definite conceptions over rights and national development and would therefore be particularly susceptible to promptings, subversive or otherwise, from anyone who would help them realize these aspirations. This concern was not merely confined to civilian officials, but also to those officers who comprised the Sudan Defence Force.

The report also pointed to the lack of any investigating agency or preventative system to tackle the problems identified in the official and military fields. No agency existed which could effectively check the flow of literature, money and other forms of propaganda material into the Sudan. Surveillance of the activities of political convicts or suspects was also lacking. Indeed, the organization and use of the Intelligence Department had already been criticized by Henderson during his visit to the Sudan. Henderson complained that the Intelligence Department appeared to usurp to a considerable extent the functions of the civil or chief secretary and to assume the position of advisor on indigenous affairs that should have been the prerogative of the civil secretary.[7] As a consequence, the committee recommended putting greater effort into sabotaging the machinery of future seditious movements and making the ground unfavourable for their growth. This would entail preventative action against possible outside agencies, such as an Irrigation Department dominated by Egyptian officials, and the infiltration of Bolshevik propaganda from Arabia, by tightening up departmental administration and the long-term surveillance of important Sudanese suspects. This line of action would also be complemented by a wider dissemination of publicity outlining the aims and intentions of the government, thereby counteracting the effects of disturbing rumours and forestalling agitation. A sympathetic consideration of the more honest and reasonable aspirations of the different classes of people and the formation of policy in light of such consideration were also recommended.

Again, the committee served only to reinforce existing beliefs that the 1924 agitation was 'solely a product of Egyptian politics', and that 'no other external source, whether Bolshevik or religious, had any effect whatever'. It was believed that no genuine pro-Egyptian sentiment had been created in the Sudan as 'all classes of true natives of the

Sudan dislike the Egyptians'. Indeed, in so far as an indigenous political sentiment existed, it was nationalist: 'The attitude towards Egyptian politics is subservient to national self-interest. The "Unity of the whole Nile Valley" is at most but a temporary expedient to get rid of the British before turning on the Egyptians.'[8]

The transfer of power from the Residency back to the Foreign Office continued apace even with the appointment of Allenby's imperialist successor, George Lloyd, in 1925. The importance of a solid working relationship between the High Commissioner and Foreign Secretary was nowhere more aptly demonstrated than during Lloyd's tenure. The soured relations between the High Commissioner and Chamberlain, first over Lloyd's appointment, then the number of honours for Egypt and the Sudan, and the handling of the army crisis of early 1927, resulted in the Foreign Office operating largely over Lloyd's head in the treaty discussions with Abd al Khaliq Sarwat Pasha during the summer of 1927. These negotiations, conducted largely without the guidance of Lloyd, demonstrated the Foreign Office's complete lack of faith in their man-on-the-spot. With the Sudan excluded from any settlement, Chamberlain was even prepared to overrule the Chiefs of Staff's military considerations in favour of the perceived political advantages which would accrue from a treaty with Egypt. The failure of the Chamberlain-Sarwat discussions marked a nadir in Residency-Foreign Office relations. This strained relationship also served as a pretext for the unceremonious ousting of Lloyd by the new Labour Foreign Secretary, Arthur Henderson. This move and Lloyd's replacement by a member of the Diplomatic Service, Percy Loraine, once again underlined the change in the balance of power from the periphery back to the centre. Furthermore, the fact that the Foreign Office was prepared, once again, to disregard military concerns during the negotiations with Mohammed Mahmoud and Mustafa al-Nahas, in June 1929 and January 1930 respectively, demonstrates that the Foreign Office was once again prepared to take the lead in matters of strategic importance. It is also important to note that in terms of policy formulation towards Egypt there was no significant difference between the Labour and Conservative administrations.

Herein lays the significance of the arguments threaded throughout this book. The nationalism of the populist Wafd - not Bolshevism, Pan-Arabism or Pan-Islamism - was the greatest threat to Britain's position within the Nile Valley during the 1920s. Indeed, Major G W Courtney, an MI5 officer appointed as head of a new Secret Intelligence Service Cairo station, repeatedly expressed the opinion that concerns over the Communist movement in Egypt were exaggerated. 'There was no evidence that the nationalist leader Saad Zaghlul and the Extremists were enlisting Bolshevik support in order to gain their ends. Rather the reverse is the case. All parties here, whatever their difference, are intensely national at the present moment, and will not entertain the idea of any foreign interference.'[9]

In attempting to normalise Anglo-Egyptian relations it became clear that, even in an era of retrenchment, Britain was not prepared to sacrifice its fundamental imperial principles, a fact bolstered by the realization in late 1922 that an unholy alliance between Bolshevism, Pan-Islamism and nationalism threatening British interests appeared increasingly unlikely. In fact, as John Ferris asserts, British policy pursued a 'Whig political strategy in the Empire, by letting Britain monitor and neutralise irreconcilable political threats while identifying which ones could be bought off and how'.[10] This was a fine and delicate line to tread, however, and one at which Percy Loraine became adept. Loraine fully realized that Britain had to assume the position of a watchful observer over the machinations of Egyptian politics. So long as the prospect of a treaty could be used as a lever in this internal struggle, Britain would be increasingly drawn into the political minutiae of competing Egyptian political interest groups. However, and here is the rub, without the nationalist Wafd's involvement every attempt at reaching a permanent settlement of relations would be doomed to failure. Thus, it was only when a very real external threat appeared in the form of Italian fascism that endangered the very borders of Egypt that the nationalist Wafd was prepared to get into bed with Britain and accept her imperial protection.

Notes

Introduction

1. K Kyle, *Suez* (London: Weidenfeld and Nicolson, 1991), p. 7.
2. See T G Otte and K Neilson (eds), *Railways and International Politics. Paths of Empire, 1848–1945* (Kings Lyn and Abingdon: Routledge, 2006); R Higham, *Britain's Imperial Air Routes, 1918 to 1939. The Story of Britain's Overseas Airlines* (London: GT Foulis & Co., 1960); and G Pirie, *Air Empire. British Imperial Civil Aviation 1919–1939* (Manchester: Manchester University Press, 2009).
3. J Darwin, 'Britain's Empires', in S Stockwell (ed.), *The British Empire. Themes and Perspectives* (Oxford: Blackwell Publishing, 2008), p. 1.
4. Ibid., p. 1.
5. Ibid., p. 1.
6. For an in-depth study of McMahon, Wingate, Allenby and Lloyd, see C W R Long, *Pro-Consuls in Egypt, 1914–1929. The Challenge of Nationalism* (Oxon: Routledge Curzon, 2005).
7. M Thomas, *Empires of Intelligence, Security Services and Colonial Disorder after 1914* (London: University of California Press, 2008), p. 73.
8. Ibid., p. 73.
9. Ibid., p. 91.
10. Mohammed Nuri El-Amin, 'International Communism, the Egyptian Wafd Party and the Sudan', *BRISMES Bulletin*, 16, 1 (1989), p. 29.
11. Ibid., p. 29.
12. See K Jeffery, *The British Army and the Crisis of Empire* (Manchester: Manchester University Press, 1984); R J Popplewell, *Intelligence and Imperial Defence. British Intelligence and the Defence of the Indian Empire, 1904–1924* (London: Frank Cass, 1995); C Townshend, *Britain's Civil Wars: Counterinsurgency in the Twentieth Century* (London: Faber and Faber, 1986).
13. The four reserved points comprised:
    a) The security of the communications of the British Empire in Egypt;
    b) The defence of Egypt against all foreign aggression or interference direct or indirect;
    c) The protection of foreign interests in Egypt and the protection of minorities; and
    d) The Sudan.

Chapter 1

1. M S Hussain, '*British Policy and the Nationalist Movement in Egypt 1914–24*' (unpublished DPhil thesis, University of Exeter, 1996), p. 15.
2. Ibid., p. 15.

3   Ibid., p. 15.
4   E Burns, *British Imperialism in Egypt* (Perth: The Labour Research Department, 1928), pp. 5–6.
5   See G Hicks, 'Disraeli, Derby and the Suez Canal, 1875: Some Myths Reassessed', *History*, 97, 2 (2012), pp. 182–203.
6   Arabi was a member of a secret society in the army dedicated to the abolition of favouritism for the Turco-Ciracassian officers and the deposition of Ismail. P Mansfield, *The British in Egypt* (Wiltshire: Readers Union, 1971), p. 19.
7   *The Times*, 16 April 1879.
8   Burns, *Imperialism in Egypt*, p. 9; and Mansfield, *British in Egypt*, pp. 19–20.
9   S Huffaker, 'Representations of Ahmed Urabi: Hegemony, Imperialism and the British Press, 1881–1882', *Victorian Periodicals Review*, 45, 4 (2012), p. 398.
10 Ibid., p. 375.
11 For a detailed investigation into the massacre, see M E Chamberlain, 'The Alexandria Massacre of 11 June 1882 and the British Occupation of Egypt', *Middle Eastern Studies*, 13, 1 (1997), pp. 14–39.
12 Huffaker, 'Representations of Ahmed Urabi', p. 398.
13 Chamberlain, 'The Alexandria Massacre of 11 June 1882', p. 14. For reports on the situation in Egypt from Gladstone to the King, see 15 June 1882, CAB 41/16/29.
14 Burns, *Imperialism in Egypt*, p. 12.
15 Hussain, *Nationalist Movement in Egypt*, p. 28.
16 Ibid., p. 29.
17 For a full discussion on whether Britain occupied Egypt in the interests of capitalists and industrialists or whether they were moved by their anxiety to keep step with France in case France gained command of the Suez route, see A Schölch, 'The "Men on the Spot" and the English Occupation of Egypt in 1882', *Historical Journal*, 3 (1996), pp. 73–785. Schölch concludes that when the Liberal government sent an army to Egypt, it had become neither a victim of the French Government 'nor of its own fear for the Canal, but of the "men on the spot", British controllers, officials and businessmen in the guise of journalists, however, feared primarily for finance, trade, investments and their own position. The Consul-General was both their ally and instrument [...] Like the sorcerer's apprentice, the British government was not really the master of the spirits it had evoked', pp. 784–85. The 1840 Treaty of London between the Ottoman government and the European powers, except France, offered Mehmet Ali, Egypt's leader, the hereditary pashalik but removed all of his state monopolies through applying all Ottoman laws and treaties to Egypt. The treaty also allowed Britain free access to Egyptian markets. This agreement superseded Egypt's regional laws of monopoly, but also, and more importantly 'this pact, like those developed earlier in India, the Punjab, Burma and the Persian Gulf, made Britain, in effect, the guarantor of the legal apparatus connecting Egypt juridically with the Porte, thus drawing her deeper into Egyptian affairs as a permanent stakeholder'. Traditionally this has been interpreted as 'informal' or indirect free trade imperialism, but Harrison argues that it was, in fact, a very 'formal' and direct mechanism of British control over Egypt. Egypt's political sovereignty was undermined by the terms of the treaty which thereby provided Britain with the legal device and precedent for the interference and, ultimately, the invasion of Egypt. R T Harrison, *Gladstone's Imperialism in Egypt. Techniques of Domination* (Westport CT: Greenwood Publishing, 1995), pp. 36–37.
18 S Morewood, 'Prelude to the Suez Crisis', in S Smith (ed.), *Reassessing Suez 1956. New Perspectives on the Crisis and Its Aftermath* (Hampshire: Ashgate, 2008), p. 14.

19 Edward Dicey became connected with the *Daily Telegraph* in 1861. His style and knowledge of foreign questions led him to become a permanent member of the staff in 1862. In 1869, whilst in the Near East, Dicey accepted the editorship of the *Daily News* which he held for three months in 1870. Upon leaving this post he became the editor of *The Observer*, a position he filled for the next nineteen years (1870–89). A consistent contributor to periodicals, such as *The Nineteenth Century* and the *Empire Review*, Dicey's interest in foreign affairs, particularly those of eastern Europe, remained keen. As a frequent visitor to Egypt, Dicey formed well-defined views of what Britain's position within Egypt should be, even advocating its annexation by Britain. H C G Matthew, 'Dicey, Edward James Stephen (1832–1911)', in H C G Matthew and B Harrison (eds) *Oxford Dictionary of National Biography* (Oxford: Oxford University Press, 2004). Online ed. Ed. Lawrence Goldman. May 2006. 29 April 2009. http://www.oxforddnb.com/view/article/32812. Huffaker also discusses the close association between journalists reporting on Egypt and the British Government. Huffaker, 'Representations of Ahmed Urabi', pp. 393–97.

20 J E Flint, 'Britain and the Scramble for Africa', in R W Winks (ed.), *The Oxford History of the British Empire, v Historiography* (Oxford: Oxford University Press, 1999), p. 450.

21 R C Mowat, 'From Liberalism to Imperialism: The Case of Egypt 1875–1887', *Historical Journal*, 16, 1 (1973), p. 109.

22 M Thomas and R Toye, 'Arguing about Intervention: A Comparison of British and French Rhetoric Surrounding the 1882 and 1956 Invasions of Egypt', *Historical Journal* 58, 4 (2015), pp. 1081–1113.

23 Ibid., p. 1086.
24 Ibid., p. 1086.
25 Ibid., p. 1086.
26 Ibid., pp. 1086–87.
27 Ibid., p. 1087.
28 Flint, 'Scramble for Africa', p. 450.
29 Ibid., p. 451.
30 Ibid., p. 451.
31 Alfred Milner was the British High Commissioner in South Africa during the Second Anglo-Boer War, a member of the Imperial War Cabinet and finished his official career in the Colonial Office, as Secretary of State for Colonies, with Leo Amery as his parliamentary under-secretary. For details of Milner's life and career, see Vladimar Halpérin's, *Lord Milner and the Empire: The Evolution of British Imperialism* (London: Odhams Press, 1952); Edward Crankshaw, *The Forsaken Idea: A Study of Viscount Milner* (London: Longmans, Green, 1952); John Evelyn Wrench, *Alfred, Lord Milner, the Man of No Illusions, 1854–1925* (London: Eyre & Spottiswoode, 1958); Alfred Gollin, *Proconsul in Politics: A Study of Lord Milner in Opposition and in Power* (Hertfordshire: Anthony Blond, 1964); and J Lee Thompson, *A Wider Patriotism: Alfred Milner and the British Empire* (London: Pickering & Chatto, 2007). A Milner, *England in Egypt* (London: Edward Arnold, 1899), pp. 5–6.

32 Milner, *England in Egypt*, p. 377.
33 Flint, 'Scramble for Africa', p. 452.
34 J A Hobson, *Imperialism: A Study* (London: George Allen and Unwin, 1938), p. 3.
35 In making this connection between nationalism, colonialism and imperialism, Hobson drew heavily upon John Stuart Mill's definition of nationalism. Hobson, *Imperialism* pp. 5–6, pp. 12–13 and p. 368.

36 For example, see Valentine Chirol, *The Egyptian Problem* (London: Macmillan, 1920) and Wilfred Scawen Blunt, *Secret History of the English Occupation of Egypt: Being a Personal Narrative of Events* (New York: Howard Fertig, 1967). The most recent biography of Chirol is L B Fritzinger, *Diplomat without Portfolio: Valentine Chirol, His Life and The Times* (London: I.B.Tauris, 2006).
37 A publication for the Labour Research Department that formed part of the Colonial Series which dealt with British imperialism in East Africa, Malaya, China and West Africa. Elinor Burns also wrote a similar publication on the British in Ireland. Burns, *Imperialism in Egypt*.
38 Burns, *British Imperialism in Egypt*, p. 72.
39 R Robinson and J Gallagher with A Denney, *Africa and the Victorians* (Hong Kong: Macmillian, 1981), p. xv.
40 Ibid., p. xxi.
41 Ibid., p. xxii.
42 Ibid., pp. 462–63.
43 Ibid., pp. 464–65.
44 Quoted in Wm Roger Louis, 'Introduction', in Wm Roger Louis (ed.), *Imperialism: The Robinson and Gallagher Controversy* (New York: New Viewpoints, 1976), p. 15.
45 P J Cain and A G Hopkins, *British Imperialism: Innovation and Expansion, 1688–1914* (Essex: Longman, 1993), p. 52.
46 Ibid., p. 363.
47 Ibid., p, 369.
48 Ibid., p. 369.
49 P J Cain, 'Character and Imperialism: The British Financial Administration of Egypt, 1878–1914', *Journal of Imperial and Commonwealth History*, 34, 2 (2006), p. 178.
50 Ibid., p. 178.
51 Ibid., p. 180.
52 Ibid., p. 194.
53 Strictly speaking these countries' fates were decided by the Allied leaders at San Remo in April 1920. France was given the mandates of Syria and the Lebanon, Britain that of Palestine and Mesopotamia. The dismemberment of mainland Anatolian Turkey soon forced the Turks into the signing of the Treaty of Sèvres in August 1920 which was to inflame Turkish opinion.
54 A J Toynbee, *The World after the Peace Conference: Being an Epilogue to the 'History of the Peace Conference of Paris' and a Prologue to the Survey of International Affairs, 1920–1923* (London: Oxford University Press, 1925), p. 43.
55 E Monroe, *Britain's Moment in the Middle East, 1914–71* (London: Chatto and Windus, 1981), p. 11.
56 Ibid., p. 11.
57 Ibid., p. 21.
58 Ibid., p. 83.
59 Ibid., p. 84.
60 E Kedourie, *The Chatham House Version and Other Middle-Eastern Studies* (London: Weidenfeld and Nicolson, 1970), p. x.
61 Ibid., p. xi.
62 Ibid., p. xi.
63 J Darwin, *Britain, Egypt and the Middle East. Imperial Policy in the Aftermath of War* (Hong Kong: Macmillan Press, 1981), p. xiii.
64 Ibid., p. xiii.

65 Ibid., pp. 267–68.
66 Ibid., p. 275. This is also reinforced by Jeffery, *The British Army and the Crisis of Empire*; J Darwin, 'Imperialism in Decline? Tendencies in British Imperial Policy between the Wars', *Historical Journal*, 23, 3 (1980), pp. 657–79; and J Darwin, 'An Undeclared Empire: The British in the Middle East, 1918–1939', *Journal of Imperial and Commonwealth History*, 27, 2 (1999), pp. 159–76.
67 Darwin, *Britain, Egypt and the Middle East*, p. 269.
68 Ibid., p. 278.
69 J Jankowski and I Gershoni, *Redefining the Egyptian Nation, 1930–45* (Cambridge: Cambridge University Press, 1995), p. xi.
70 Ibid., p. xii.
71 Ibid., pp. 212–13.
72 Ibid., p. 213.
73 Ibid., p. 213.
74 Ibid., p. 214.
75 Ibid., p. 216.
76 Ibid., p. 218.
77 J Jankowski and I Gershoni, *Rethinking Nationalism in the Arab Middle East* (New York: Columbia University Press, 1997), p. xiv.
78 Ibid., p. xxv.
79 Ibid., p. xiv.
80 Z Fahmy, *Ordinary Egyptians. Creating the Modern Nation through Popular Culture* (Stanford, CA: Stanford University Press, 2011), p. 167.
81 Ibid., p. 167.
82 Ibid., p. 168.
83 E A Haddad, 'Digging to India: Modernity, Imperialism and the Suez Canal', *Victorian Studies*, 47, 3 (2005), p. 376.
84 D M Reid, 'Cromer and the Classics: Imperialism, Nationalism and the Greco-Roman Past in Modern Egypt', *Middle Eastern Studies*, 32, 1 (1996), p. 7. See also E Barak, 'Egyptian Intellectuals in the Shadow of British Occupation', *British Journal of Middle Eastern Studies*, 35, 2 (2008), pp. 173–86. Taha Husayn, an important Egyptian thinker of the twentieth century argued that 'it was only natural that Egypt should lean toward Europe, for both cultures had undergone the same processes since the Pharaonic period, particularly their symbiosis with religious, Greek and Roman influences', Barak, 'Egyptian intellectuals', p. 180.
85 Reid, 'Cromer and the Classics', p. 8.
86 Ibid., p. 15.
87 Ibid., p. 22.
88 J Whidden, 'Expatriates in Cosmopolitan Egypt: 1864–1956,' in R Bickers (ed.), *Settlers and Expatriates: Britons over the Seas, Oxford History of the British Empire Companion Series* (Oxford: Oxford University Press, 2010), p. 19.
89 Ibid., p. 19.
90 H MacMichael, *The Anglo-Egyptian Sudan* (Plymouth: Faber and Faber, 1934), p. 272.
91 Prime Minister's Message, 'Broadcast to the Empire', 26 May 1930, *The Times*.
92 H J Sharkey, *Living with Colonialism, Nationalism and Culture in the Anglo-Egyptian Sudan* (Berkeley, CA: University of California Press, 2003), p. 1.
93 Ibid., p. 2.
94 Ibid., p. 138.

95 Ibid., p. 139.
96 Ibid., p. 3 and p. 139.
97 Communication and transport networks included roads, railways, car and steamboats. Telegraphs, telephones and postal systems. Sharkey, *Living with Colonialism*, p. 9.
98 Sharkey, *Living with Colonialism*, p. 3.
99 E M Troutt Powell, *A Different Shade of Colonialism. Egypt, Great Britain and the Mastery of the Sudan* (Berkeley, CA: University of California Press, 2003), p. 8.
100 M Daly, *Empire on the Nile. The Anglo-Egyptian Sudan 1898–1934* (Cambridge: Cambridge University Press, 1986). See also A Kirk-Greene, *Britain's Imperial Administrators 1858–1966* (Basingstoke: Macmillan Press, 2000), Chapter 6, pp. 164–201.
101 Kirk-Greene, *Britain's Imperial* Administrators, pp. 281–82.
102 G Kennedy, 'The Concept of Imperial Defence, 1856–1956', in G Kennedy (ed.), *Imperial Defence. The Old World Order, 1856–1956* (London: Routledge, 2008), p. 1.
103 The Washington Naval Conference opened in November 1921. It appeared impossible for Britain to retain the friendship of both America and Japan and the Anglo-Japanese Alliance was replaced by multilateral guarantees. Gordon, *British Seapower and Procurement*, p. 70. See also S Roskill, *Naval Policy between the Wars*, I (London: Collins, 1968) and C M Bell, *The Royal Navy, Seapower and Strategy between the Wars* (London: Macmillan, 2000), p. 13.
104 Memorandum by the Secretary of State for War, 'Military Policy in Egypt', CID 439-B, 30 July 1923, Cabinet Office papers, CAB 4/10.
105 J Ferris, *The Evolution of British Strategic Policy, 1919–1926* (Hong Kong: Macmillan Press, 1989), p. xii. The role of the Treasury in imperial defence during the inter-war years has always been a moot point for historians. Described as the 'most political of departments', the Treasury has often been held accountable for the defence spending of the armed services and its consequent impact upon imperial strategy throughout the 1920s. George C Peden largely agrees with Ferris's assessment in that it was only after 1924 that service policies came to be dominated by the Treasury. Treasury successes in affirming economies at this point were more a reflection of foreign policy as opposed to Treasury influence, such as the reduction in the Admiralty's plans for oil reserves and storage and the decision in March 1924 by the Labour Government to cancel the Singapore Naval base, later reversed by the Conservatives when they returned to power in November 1924. It was only in 1928 with the strengthening of the Ten Year Rule, with the acquiescence of the Foreign Office, that the Treasury 'at last secured an effective means of controlling defence expenditure', G C Peden, *The Treasury and British Public Policy, 1906–1959* (Oxford: Oxford University Press, 2000), p. 215. See also Peden, *Treasury and Public Policy*, pp. 170–74 and pp. 212–16.
106 For example, although G A H Gordon, *British Seapower and Procurement between the Wars: A Reappraisal of Rearmament* (London: Macmillan Press, 1988) admits that there was no formal continual supervision by the Treasury on the day-to-day running of the Services, it being the concern of each Department's civilian head, he perceives Treasury control as homogenous in contrast to Ferris' perception of it as evolving.
107 Ferris, *Evolution of British Strategic Policy*, p. 180.
108 Ibid., p. 181.
109 Ibid., p. 181.

110 For an opposing assessment of the 1930 London Naval Conference, see G Kennedy, 'The 1930 London Naval Conference and Anglo-American Maritime Strength, 1927–1930', in B J C McKercher (ed.), *Arms Limitation and Disarmament. Restraints on War, 1899–1939* (Westport, CT: Praeger, 1992), pp. 149–71.
111 G Kennedy, 'The Royal Navy and Imperial Defence, 1919–1956', in Kennedy (ed.), *Imperial Defence*, p. 133.
112 Ibid., p. 136.
113 Note by Naval Staff, 'Liability of the Suez Canal to Blocking Attack', CID 439-B, 2 July 1923, CAB 4/10.
114 Ibid.
115 Ibid.
116 Ibid.
117 D French, 'Big Wars and Small Wars between the Wars, 1919–39', in H Strachan (ed.), *Big Wars and Small Wars. The British Army and the Lessons of War in the 20th Century* (London: Routledge, 2006), p. 37.
118 D French, 'The British Army and Empire, 1856–1956', in Kennedy, *Imperial Defence*, p. 91.
119 Ibid., p. 91.
120 Memorandum by the Foreign Office, 'The Foreign Policy of His Majesty's Government', Appendix A, CID 700-B, CAB 4/14.
121 French, 'British Army', p. 99.
122 Ibid., p. 99.
123 See Jeffrey, *Crisis of Empire*, pp. 110–32.
124 B Bond, 'The Army between the Two World Wars, 1918–1939', in D Chandler (eds), *The Oxford Illustrated History of the British Army* (Oxford: Oxford University Press, 1994), p. 263.
125 Ibid., p. 263.
126 See K Jeffery, *Field Marshal Sir Henry Wilson. A Political Soldier* (Oxford: Oxford University Press, 2006), pp. 229–55.
127 Memorandum by the Secretary of State for War, 'Military Policy in Egypt', CID 439-B, 30 July 1923, CAB 4/10.
128 Ibid.
129 Ibid.
130 R Higham, *Britain's Imperial Air Routes, 1918–1939. The Story of Britain's Overseas Airlines* (London: G T Foulis, 1960), p. 310.
131 Ibid., p. 310.
132 Ibid., p. 310.
133 J Corum, 'The RAF in Imperial Defence, 1919–1956', in Kennedy, *Imperial Defence*, p. 152. Although the air force had developed from fairly small beginnings as reconnaissance forces, it had rapidly proved itself as a significant military arm 'capable of providing accurate intelligence, close support to ground troops, interdiction of enemy logistics and, finally, weapons with the capability of bombing cities and industries far behind the fighting front'. Ibid.
134 D Omissi, *Air Power and Colonial Control. The Royal Air Force, 1919–1939* (Manchester: Manchester University Press 1990), p. 11. In Egypt, the application of imperial policing through air control was limited to areas outside of the cities.
135 Corum, 'RAF in Imperial Defence', pp. 156–57.
136 M Smith, 'The Royal Air Force, Air Power and British Foreign Policy, 1932–37', *Journal of Contemporary History*, 12, 1 (1977), pp. 155–74.

137 Omissi, *Air Power*, p. ix.
138 S Morewood, 'The British Defence of Egypt, 1935–September 1939' (unpublished PhD thesis: University of Bristol, 1985), p. 11.
139 Memorandum by the Air Staff, 'Military Policy in Egypt: Status of the Royal Air Force', CID 462-B, November 1923, CAB 4/10.

Chapter 2

1 J Fisher, *Curzon and British Imperialism in the Middle East, 1916–19* (London: Frank Cass, 1999), p. 151.
2 Ibid., pp. 151–52.
3 A S Klieman, *Foundations of British Policy in the Arab World: The Cairo Conference of 1921* (Baltimore MD: Johns Hopkins Press, 1970), p. 17.
4 E Kedourie in *England the Middle East: The Destruction of the Ottoman Empire, 1914–1921* (London: Bowes & Bowes, 1956) interpreted the Sykes-Picot agreement as a piece of diplomacy in the European tradition. In essence, it represented a solution to the conundrum posed by the collapse of the Ottoman empire, a preoccupation of the European powers since the mid-nineteenth century, in order to avoid conflict between the great powers as well as to secure a reasonable future for the peoples of the region. M E Yapp, 'Elie Kedourie and the History of the Middle East', *Middle Eastern Studies*, 41, 5 (2005), p. 668. In Kedourie's view the Sykes-Picot agreement was 'in no way incompatible with the assurances given to the Arabs'. Britain's assumption of a leading role in the war, the withdrawal of Russia from the war due to revolution coupled with the entry of the United States into the conflict (albeit not in the Middle Eastern theatre) and the rise of ideas of self-determination overtook the Sykes-Picot agreement. Yapp, 'Elie Kedourie', pp. 668–69. Kedourie's examination of the McMahon-Husayn correspondence *In the Anglo-Arab Labyrinth. The McMahon-Husayn Correspondence and Its Interpretations* (1976) concludes that the correspondence was the result of a 'confusion of control over policymaking' between Lord Kitchener, Cairo, the Government of India, the India Office and Foreign Office, coupled with 'incompetence: neither [Sir Edward] Grey as Foreign Secretary nor McMahon as acting High Commissioner in Egypt were up to their duties'. This permitted an influential group of officials in Cairo [including Gilbert Clayton, David Hogarth, Ronald Storrs and Stewart Symes] a latitude in policy formulation. The aim of this group was to keep France out of Syria. Instructed by the Foreign Office that this was impossible they sought to use the Arab movement in order to achieve their objective. Yapp, 'Elie Kedourie', p. 671.
5 For greater detail, see J C Hurewitz, *Diplomacy in the Near and Middle East: A Documentary Record*, ii (New York: Octagon Books, 1972), pp. 18–22.
6 T J Paris, 'British Middle East Policy-Making after the First World War: The Lawrentian and Wilsonian Schools', *Historical Journal*, 41, 3 (1998), p. 775 and E Goldstein, 'British Peace Aims and the Eastern Question: The Political Intelligence Department and the Eastern Committee, 1918', *Middle Eastern Studies*, 23, 4 (1987), p. 424.
7 Hurewitz, *Diplomacy*, pp. 28–30.
8 Paris, 'British Middle East Policy-Making', p. 775.
9 For an examination of the Eastern Committee, see Goldstein, 'British Peace Aims and the Eastern Question', pp. 419–36. Goldstein argues that the preparation for

the post-war peace conference revealed two schools of thought in defining Britain's objectives. On the one hand, the Foreign Office's Political Intelligence Department (PID), which formed the centre of British preparations for peace-making and was primarily concerned with the European aspect, favoured a Wilsonian-style peace. On the other hand, a group centred around old-style imperialists, such as Lord Curzon and the imperial reformers who followed Lord Milner, perceived Britain's primary interests as lying overseas with the Empire, and were therefore mainly concerned with the non-European elements of the post-war settlement. According to Goldstein, this latter group effectively controlled the Eastern Committee. They perceived 'British control of the Middle East as an essential concern, on the one hand, for its strategic value as the gateway to India, and, on the other, for its potential petroleum resources', p. 419.

10 Unlike its predecessor, the Eastern Committee, the IDCE lacked executive powers even though it was chaired by the Foreign Secretary, Lord Curzon. Moreover, 'despite Curzon's personal knowledge of and expertise in matters pertaining to this region, his views often were not given due consideration by Lloyd George or by other senior political figures'. J Fisher, 'The Interdepartmental Committee on Eastern Unrest and British Responses to Bolshevik and Other Intrigues against the Empire during the 1920s', *Journal of Asian History*, 34, 1 (2000), p. 2.

11 For a full examination of attempts to create a Middle East Department, see J Fisher, 'Lord Robert Cecil and the Formation of a Middle East Department of the Foreign Office', *Middle Eastern Studies*, 42, 3 (2006), pp. 365–80. By the summer of 1921 the territories of Palestine, Mesopotamia, Arabia and Trans-Jordan formed a new Middle Eastern Department within the Colonial Office. Lord Robert Cecil (appointed as Parliamentary Under-Secretary of State for Foreign Affairs on 31 May 1915 and Assistant Secretary of State from 19 July 1918 to 14 January 1919), and supported by the India Office, was unhappy at this outcome believing that the 'splitting between departments of Britain's interests in the Middle East would lead to a fractured policy'. Fisher, 'Lord Robert Cecil and the Formation of a Middle East Department', p. 376. Writing in 1929, John Shuckburgh, previously Sir Arthur Hirtzel's deputy at the India Office, and now head of the Middle East Department at the Colonial Office, lamented that the situation resembled 'the old vicious groove of 1919–20 [...] control should rest with one department and, by default that must be the Foreign Office'. Fisher, 'Lord Robert Cecil and the Formation of a Middle East Department', p. 376.

12 Paris, 'British Middle East Policy-Making', p. 777.

13 B Westrate, *The Arab Bureau. British Policy in the Middle East, 1916–1920* (Pittsburgh: Pennsylvania State University Press, 1992), pp. 142–43.

14 Ibid., p. 142.

15 Ibid., p. 142.

16 P Woodward (ed.), *British Documents of Foreign Affairs. Reports and Papers from the Foreign Office Confidential Print, Part II, Series G Africa, 1914–1939*, I [hereafter BDFA] 9.

17 Wingate expressed these reservations to both Arthur Balfour, Foreign Secretary, and Arthur Hardinge, Permanent Under-Secretary at the Foreign Office, on 8 and 19 November respectively. 'I think it is not unlikely that self-determination policy [...] may have its repercussion among Egyptian nationalists who will, no doubt, desire similar treatment for Egypt'. Wingate to Balfour, 8 November 1918, doc 73, P Woodward (ed.), *British Documents of Foreign Affairs. Reports and Papers from*

the *Foreign Office Confidential Print, Part II, Series G Africa, 1914-1939*, I [hereafter *BDFA*] 9 (Washington DC: United Publications of America, 1995), p. 86. To Hardinge, Wingate complained that 'this Anglo-French Declaration has given the Nationalists their opportunity'. Labour Deputation, 'Situation in Egypt and Exile of Zaghlul', 1923, PREM 1/25.
18 Wingate to Hardinge, 14 November 1918, 237/10/8-10, Wingate papers, SAD.
19 Ibid.
20 Ibid.
21 Ibid.
22 Balfour to Wingate, 27 November 1918, doc 75, *BDFA, Series G Africa*, I, p. 87.
23 Hardinge to Wingate, 28 November 1918, Vol. 39 ff. 290-293, Hardinge papers, CUL.
24 Balfour to Wingate, 27 November 1918, doc 75, *BDFA, Series G Africa*, I, p. 88. See also Balfour to Wingate, 2 December 1918, doc 78, *BDFA, Series G Africa*, I, p. 89. 'I note that extremist leaders are exploiting fact of your having received them at Residency, which was unfortunate. You will of course, make it perfectly clear that you view this agitation and all those who participate in it with extreme disfavour [...] I understand that the leaders of the movement do not carry much weight, but it might easily become mischievous, and even seditious in character, if left unchecked. You will no doubt adopt all necessary measures to prevent any such developments'. Ibid.
25 Wingate to Balfour, 25 November 1918, doc 76, *BDFA, Series G Africa*, i, p. 88.
26 Ibid., p. 91.
27 Wingate to Balfour, 23 December, No. 1928, doc 100, *BDFA, Series G Africa*, i, p. 134. As Wingate reported to Balfour on 23 December 1918, Sirry Pasha, Minister next in seniority to the President of the Council, had appealed to Wingate to recommend that the British government treat the crisis in a manner which would permit the Ministers who had resigned to retain their posts.
28 Wingate to Balfour, 26 December 1918, doc 101, *BDFA, Series G Africa*, i, p. 135.
29 Ibid., p. 135.
30 Balfour to Wingate, 1 January 1919, doc 108, *BDFA, Series G Africa*, i, p. 142.
31 D Gilmour, *Curzon. Imperial Statesman 1859-1925* (Cambridge: John Murray, 1994). For a study of the Foreign Office and its structural changes, see Z Steiner and M Dockrill, 'The Foreign Office Reforms, 1919-1921', *Historical Journal*, 17, 1 (1974), pp. 131-56; and E Maisel, *The Foreign Office and Foreign Policy 1919-1921* (Brighton: Sussex Academic Press, 1994), particularly chapters 1-3.
32 Gilmour, *Curzon*, p. 502.
33 Wingate to Curzon, 16 January 1919, doc 114, *BDFA, Series G Africa*, i, p. 146.
34 Ibid., p. 146.
35 Ibid., p. 146.
36 Memorandum by Curzon for Balfour, 20 February 1919, doc 121, *BDFA, Series G Africa*, i, p. 153.
37 See Foreign Office to Cheetham, 26 February 1919, FO 371/3711/32665.
38 Ronald Graham to Hardinge, 22 January 1919, Vol. 40 ff. 49-51, Hardinge papers, CUL. Hardinge was in agreement with the line taken by Graham at the Foreign Office. 'I am quite certain that you are right in considering that the position ought to be faced squarely and that the movement should be treated as seditious. I only hope that if the [Egyptian] Ministers come over here and to London our own Ministers will not be afraid to be perfectly frank with them and that they will give them a good dressing-down. That is really what they want before we can listen to any scheme of

progressive development in Egypt. No doubt some progress must be made in Egypt, but it should be on steady lines, not on the lines now advocated for India, which in my opinion constitute too big a jump all at once'. Hardinge to Graham, 24 January 1919, Vol. 40 ff. 212–215, Hardinge papers, CUL.
39 Wingate to Hardinge, 18 October 1919, Vol. 41 ff. 70–78; and Hardinge to Wingate, 22 October 1919, Vol. 41 ff. 103–104, Hardinge papers, CUL. In this latter letter, Hardinge urged Wingate not to make public Wingate's side of the Egyptian question as he believed Wingate would not 'gain anything'.
40 Cheetham to Foreign Office, 4 February 1919, FO 371/3711/16055.
41 Cheetham to Foreign Office, 25 February 1919, FO 371/3711/31413.
42 Ibid.
43 Ronald Graham minuted 'I have always felt that time would work in our favour and it is evident from this that a political crisis, if it comes now, will be much less acute than if matters had been brought to a head six weeks ago'. Minute by Graham, 26 February 1919, FO 371/3711/31413.
44 Cheetham to Curzon, 6 March 1919, FO 371/3714/36312.
45 Ibid.
46 Ibid.
47 W J Berridge has shown in 'Imperialist and Nationalist Voices in the Struggle for Egyptian Independence, 1919–22', *Journal of Imperial and Commonwealth History*, 43, 3 (2014), pp. 420–39, that a shift occurred in imperialist rhetoric immediately after the end of the First World War. A shift from the scientific racism that had been used to justify European subjugation of indigenous populations to one of defining the 'otherness' of colonial subjects in purely cultural terms. As Berridge underlines, 'in an era still obsessed with the idea of "character", debates with regard to the personality of Egyptian nationalists were important'. Berridge, 'Imperialist and Nationalist Voices', p. 426. Cheetham's comments above are in marked contrast to Lord Cromer's approval of Zaghlul whilst the latter was Minister of Education.
48 Cheetham to Foreign Office, 10 March 1919, FO 371/3714/40278.
49 Minute by Graham, 14 March 1919, FO 371/3714/40278.
50 Cheetham to Foreign Office, 11, 13, 15 and 16 March 1919, docs 143, 146–48 and 151, *BDFA, Series G Africa*, i, pp. 182–87.
51 Cheetham to Foreign Office, 17 March 1919, FO 371/3714/42903.
52 Cheetham to Curzon, 19 March 1919, doc 157, *BDFA, Series G Africa*, i, p. 190.
53 In a telegram to Balfour in Paris it was noted that Cheetham's telegram (17 March) disclosed 'a more serious situation in Egypt than any previous reports had led us to expect'. Foreign Office to Balfour, 19 March 1919, FO 371/3714/42905.
54 Balfour to Curzon, 18 March 1919, FO 371/3714/42439.
55 War Office to GOC Egypt, 19 March 1919, FO 371/3714/44540.
56 See M Hughes, *Allenby and British Strategy in the Middle East, 1917–1919* (London: Frank Cass, 1999).
57 Hughes, *Allenby and British Strategy*, p. 16.
58 Allenby to his mother, 21 March 1919, AP 1/10/7, Field Marshal Lord Allenby papers, Liddell Hart Centre for Military Archives, Kings College London (LHCMA).
59 Memorandum by Wingate on the situation in Egypt, 21 March 1919, FO 371/3714/44711.
60 Ibid.
61 Cheetham to Curzon, 17 March 1919, FO 371/3714/42905.

62 Ibid.
63 Ibid.
64 Ronald Graham, 'Unrest in Egypt', 15 April 1919, CAB 1/28/17.
65 Wingate to Curzon, 25 March 1919, Vol. 40 ff. 148–151, Hardinge papers, CUL.
66 Graham, 'Unrest in Egypt', 15 April 1919, CAB 1/28/17.
67 Allenby to Curzon, 31 March 1919, FO 371/3714/50133.
68 Allenby to Curzon, 4 April 1919, FO 371/3714/52650.
69 Graham to Hardinge, 3 April 1919, Vol. 40 f. 52, Hardinge papers, CUL.
70 In a memorandum by Wingate, largely justifying his actions whilst in Egypt by the turn of subsequent events, strongly disagreed with the advice of Allenby. The removal of travel restrictions and thereby allowing Egyptians to travel to Europe without reference to their purpose would be, in Wingate's view, 'fraught with the gravest dangers, not only to the maintenance of our position in Egypt, but to the whole of our North Africa possessions.

The Nationalists will say, and not without justice, that by agitation and intimidation they have forced the hands of His Majesty's Government, and I do not think it is going too far to say that we shall have practically abandoned our position in Egypt which we have acquired after years of patient toil and labour'. Note from Wingate to the Foreign Office, 3 April 1919, doc 181, *BDFA, Series G Africa*, i, p. 206.
71 Foreign Office to Allenby, 18 April 1919, FO 371/3714/50133.
72 Ronald Graham, 'Unrest in Egypt', 15 April 1919, CAB 1/28/17.
73 Balfour to Foreign Office, 2 April 1919, FO 371/3714/51447.
74 Lloyd George to Allenby, 5 April 1919, FO 371/3714/50133.
75 Ibid.
76 Curzon to Wingate, 13 April 1919, 237/4/39, Wingate papers, SAD.
77 G S Symes to Wingate, 19 April 1919, 237/4/52–54, SAD.
78 Ibid.
79 Ronald Graham, 'Unrest in Egypt', 15 April 1919, CAB 1/28/17.
80 Ibid.
81 C Issawi, 'Asymmetrical Development and Transport in Egypt, 1800–1914', in W R Polk and R L Chambers (eds), *Beginnings of Modernisation in the Middle East* (Chicago: University of Chicago Press, 1968), pp. 391–92.
82 Ronald Graham, 'Unrest in Egypt', 15 April 1919, CAB 1/28/17.
83 Ibid.
84 A lecture paper on 'The Outbreak in Egypt', April 1919, AIR 1/2033/204/326/35. Indeed, ill-feeling over the employment of the Egyptian Labour Corps had already been noted in December 1918. Milner, writing to Balfour, informed him that: 'I am told too that they [Egyptian Labour Corps] were at one time not very well looked after – in the matter of equipment, food & c. This has now, I believe, been rectified, but a feeling of soreness is left. Some public acknowledgement of their services would certainly do good. Like all Orientals, the Egyptians are intensely sensitive, and a little praise goes a long way with them. Just now, when Egyptian "Nationalism" is again raising its head, it is just as well to keep on the right side of the Egyptian masses. Could a hint be given to Wingate? A pat on the back by the HC to the E Labour Corps would go a long way'. Milner to Balfour, 31 December 1918, fol. 224, Ms Eng hist c. 696, Viscount Milner papers, Bodleian Library, University of Oxford.
85 J Jankowski, 'The Egyptian Wafd and Arab Nationalism, 1918–1944', in E Ingram (ed.), *National and International Politics in the Middle East. Essays in Honour of Elie Kedourie* (London: Frank Cass, 1986), p. 164.

86 P J Vatikiotis, *The Modern History of Egypt* (London: Weidenfeld and Nicolson, 1969), p. 268.
87 J J Terry, *The Wafd 1919-1952* (London: Third World Centre, 1982), p. 71.
88 Ibid., p. 72.
89 Ibid., p. 72.
90 For a brief biography of Zaghlul, see A Goldschmidt Jr., *Biographical Dictionary of Modern Egypt* (Denver, CO: Lynne Rienner, 2000), pp. 234-35. Zaghlul's memoirs have been published by the Center for the Study of Documentation of Egypt's Contemporary History. There are currently no English language translations of biographies of Zaghlul.
91 Labour Deputation, 'Situation in Egypt and exile of Zaghlul', 1923, PREM 1/25.
92 Foreign Office to Balfour, 23 April 1919, FO 371/3715/60792.
93 Foreign Office to Balfour and Cairo, 22 April 1919, FO 371/3715/61233.
94 J D McIntyre Jr., *The Boycott of the Milner Mission. A Study in Egyptian Nationalism* (New York: Peter Lang, 1985), p. 33.
95 Ibid., pp. 35-36.
96 Milner to Curzon, 24 April 1919, fols. 101-102, Ms Eng hist c. 699, Milner papers, Bodleian Library.
97 Ibid. 'My own opinion is most strongly that a delay in the announcement is not only desirable but necessary. We are not agreed about the thing ourselves and I am perfectly certain that especially as Allenby is getting the better of the strikes there is nothing to be gained. Indeed, a great deal may be lost'.
98 Milner to Curzon, 24 April 1919, fols. 154-155, Ms Eng hist c. 699, Milner papers, Bodleian Library.
99 Ibid.
100 For a brief biographical entry, see A Goldschmidt Jr., *Biographical Dictionary of Modern Egypt*, pp. 178-79.
101 Foreign Office to Allenby, 10 May 1919, FO 371/3715/62672 and Allenby to Foreign Office, 24 May 1919, FO 371/3717/81932.
102 Lord Curzon's speech to the House of Lords, 25 November 1919, FO 371/3721/156041.
103 The Central Committee of the Wafd was established just prior to the Delegation's departure for Paris and London. Its primary concern was to collect donations and information on the situation in Egypt for those Wafd members in Paris. However, it rapidly grew beyond this remit and 'functioned as one of the main nerve centres for nationalist activities and worked very energetically with other significant centers [sic] of power in Egypt to undermine the British position'. McIntyre, *Boycott of the Milner Mission*, p. 41.
104 Labour Deputation, 'Situation in Egypt and Exile of Zaghlul', 1923, PREM 1/25.
105 Cheetham to Foreign Office, 9 October 1919, FO 371/3720/143801.
106 G F Clayton, 'Attitude of the Egyptian Press', 13 October 1919, FO 371/3720/147728.
107 Ibid.
108 Egypt and Red Sea Station, 'Intelligence – The Situation in Egypt', 22 August 1919, Admiralty papers, ADM 116/1872. According to Z Lockman the 'Wafd leadership, dominated by wealthy landowners, was socially quite conservative and had initially expressed no interest in social problems. But the capacity of the workers for sustained action and organisation during the revolution had impressed upon the Wafd the importance of incorporating the workers into the broad national

movement'. Z Lockman, 'British Policy toward Egyptian Labour Activism, 1882–1936', *International Journal of Middle Eastern Studies*, 20, 3 (1998), p. 272. In fact, intelligence reports suggested that donations from sympathisers to the Wafd cause were being used to encourage striking workers to stay away from work. Ibid.
109 Minute, 11 July 1919, ADM 116/1872.
110 Minute, 28 July 1919, ADM 116/1872.
111 Minute, 5 August 1919, ADM 116/1872. Jack Murray minuted that 'I cannot help feeling that the growth of the Labour movement has been unhealthily rapid in Egypt [...] I am sure that 80% of the present enthusiasm for unions is due to the belief in them as a political weapon'. Minute by Murray, 'Labour Syndicates in Egypt', 10 October 1919, FO 371/3728/139147. Cheetham felt it was difficult for the British authorities to regulate the growth of the trade union movement as it would be hailed as a victory by the political agitators and would therefore be regarded as so by the mass of the population and would consequently give fresh impetus to the movement of sedition. Note by Ministry of Labour, 14 October 1919, ibid.
112 Minute, 29 August 1919, ADM 116/1872. See also memorandum by General Staff Intelligence, 17 September 1919, FO 371/3719/130314. Concern was expressed that the indigenous Press was endeavouring to persuade the man on the street that true Bolshevism would be the saving of Egypt whereas, in the Provinces, it was represented to the *fellahin* as a means of obtaining free land, paying no taxes and driving out the British. Thus, Lockman argues that the strikes which accompanied the disturbances of March–April 1919 facilitated the formation of a number of trade unions which, in turn, allowed the forging of strong links between the emerging Egyptian labour movement and the nationalist Wafd movement. Allenby summarized official perception when he commented that 'the foreign and native working classes have apparently identified in their own minds the Syndicalist (i.e. trade union) movement and the Extremist (i.e. Nationalist) agitation'. Lockman, 'British Policy towards Egyptian Labour Activism', p. 273.
113 Minute, 29 August 1919, ADM 116/1872.
114 Minute, 5 August 1919, ADM 116/1872. M N El-Amin also argues that an alliance between the Wafd and International Communism did not exist, nor even between the Wafd and the Egyptian Communist Party. El-Amin, 'International Communism, the Egyptian Wafd Party and the Sudan', pp. 33–34. Thus British intelligence, in El-Amin's opinion, whether commenting on Egypt or the Sudan, raised the spectre of communism as a means for obtaining a freer hand for the men-on-the-spot.
115 For example, see A Calthorpe, Berne to Foreign Office, 4 May 1919, FO 371/3717/75883. The Metropolitan Police were also charged with keeping tabs on Egyptian Nationalists within Britain. The Egyptian Association, formed in Britain in 1919, was deemed to have links with the Indian nationalist movement and prominent Labour leaders, such as George Lansbury, Arthur Field and John Amall and agitators such as Sylvia Pankhurst and Arnold Lupton. John O'Sullivan, 'Report by the Metropolitan Police on the Activities of Egyptian Nationalists in the UK', 17 May 1919, FO 371/3717/78495.
116 Egypt and Red Sea Station, 'Intelligence – The Situation in Egypt', 12 September 1919, ADM 116/1872.
117 McIntyre, *Boycott of the Milner Mission*, p. 35.
118 A M Gollin, *Proconsul in Politics. A Study of Lord Milner in Opposition and in Power* (London: Anthony Blond, 1964), p. 16.

119 Ibid., p. 18.
120 Milner's other governmental appointments included: High Commissioner in South Africa (1897–1905), Governor of Cape Colony (1897–1901) and then Governor of the Transvaal and Orange River Colony, administering former Boer territories from 1901 to 1905; in 1916 he became a key member of Lloyd George's War Cabinet, Secretary of State for War (1918–19), and Colonial Secretary (1919–21).
121 Milner, *England in Egypt*, pp. 355–56.
122 McIntyre, *Boycott of the Milner Mission*, p. 34.
123 Ibid., pp. 34–35. In writing to Lady Edward Cecil on 8 December, Milner described the members of the Mission as getting on quite harmoniously. 'Maxwell is very entertaining and a focal social element. Owen Thomas, the dark horse, turns out to be quite a good fellow. Owen is no more a "Labour" man than I am – though perhaps this fact had better be kept dark – but a Welsh farmer, representing a purely agricultural constituency, who in his time has been a fighting man and a great traveller – he has large land interests in East Africa – and knows most parts of the Empire, *except Egypt!!* He is, however, I should say, a good sound Imperialist, and if such a thing is possible as a *straight Welshman*, he is a perfectly straight fellow'. As for Spender, Milner commented that 'apart from politics, he is the cultivated Liberal of your friend Trevelyan's type'. Milner to Lady Edward Cecil, 8 December 1919, VM 30/110/112, Violet Milner papers, Bodleian Library.
124 Labour Deputation, 'Situation in Egypt and Exile of Zaghlul', 1923, PREM 1/25.
125 Ibid.
126 Milner to the Prime Minister, 20 December 1919, fols. 122–128, MS Milner dep 449, Milner papers, Bodleian Library.
127 Lord Milner, 'Conversations on Egyptian Affairs while Chairman of the Special Mission to Egypt', 8 December 1919, FO 848/5.
128 Milner, 'Special Diaries: Egypt', December 1919, 8 December 1919, MS Milner dep 97, Milner papers, Bodleian Library.
129 Milner, 'Conversations', 10 December, FO 848/5.
130 Milner, 'Memoranda circulated to Members of the Mission', undated, fols. 5–9, MS Milner dep 449, Milner papers, Bodleian Library.
131 'We must walk warily here. We cannot give up the word altogether, for not only does it contain an absolutely necessary principle, viz. the exclusion from the affairs of Egypt of all foreign *political* influence except our own, but it is contained in the Peace Treaties, it has been acknowledged by several of the Great Allied Powers and we are pressing for its acknowledgment by Italy'. Milner, 'Memoranda circulated to Members of the Mission', undated, fols. 5–9, MS Milner dep 449, Milner papers, Bodleian Library.
132 Milner, 'Memoranda circulated to Members of the Mission', undated, fols. 5–9, MS Milner dep 449, Milner papers, Bodleian Library.
133 'In *private*, at their [Egyptian politicians'] own houses, the Club etc., anywhere *where they will not be seen*, they are delighted to talk to individual members of the Mission, and we, of course, are giving them every opportunity to do so. I believe that the contagion will rapidly spread, even to the Extremists, and that in a few weeks (during which we shall all be learning a great deal though not making any outward show of activity) the ice will be completely broken, and that it will be no longer possible for them to keep up even the *appearance* of a boycott; there is even now very little *reality* about it', Milner to Curzon, 10 December 1919, fols. 89–91, MS Milner dep 449, Milner papers, Bodleian Library.

134	Milner, 'Conversations', 13 December, FO 848/5. Milner also pointed to the negative influence of the Al-Azhar and its principal officials in its announcements demanding British withdrawal from Egypt also. He believed that their pronouncements against British authority greatly aggravated the situation with the danger of it leading to a 'fanatical outbreak of the people'. Ibid. See also Milner to Curzon, 18 December 1919, fols. 96–97, MS Milner dep 449, Milner papers, Bodleian Library.
135	Labour Deputation, 'Situation in Egypt and exile of Zaghlul', 1923, PREM 1/25.
136	Milner: 'Special Diaries Egypt', December 1919, 24 December 1919, MS Milner dep 97, Milner papers, Bodleian Library.
137	Milner to Curzon, 12 January 1920, fols. 106–109, MS Milner dep 449, Milner papers, Bodleian Library.
138	Labour Deputation, 'Situation in Egypt and Exile of Zaghlul', 1923, PREM 1/25.
139	Milner, 'Special Diaries: Egypt', December 1919–March 1920, 28 December 1919, MS Milner dep 98, Milner papers, Bodleian Library. Allenby was reluctant to sanction this as 'he [Allenby] argued, not without force, that when he had shown clemency in the past it had been taken as a sign of weakness'. Ibid.
140	Milner, 'Conversations', 6 January 1920, FO 848/5. See also Milner to Curzon, 12 January 1920, fols. 106–109, MS Milner dep 449, Milner papers, Bodleian Library.
141	Milner to Curzon, 12 January 1920, fols. 106–109, MS Milner dep 449, Milner papers, Bodleian Library.
142	Milner to Lloyd George, 25 February 1920, F/39/2/7, Lloyd George papers, Parliamentary archives.
143	Milner to Lady Edward Cecil, 23 January 1920, VM 30/110/117, Violet Milner papers, Bodleian Library.
144	Milner to Lady Edward Cecil, 1 February 1920, VM 30/110/118, Violet Milner papers, Bodleian Library.
145	Labour Deputation, 'Situation in Egypt and Exile of Zaghlul', 1923, PREM 1/25.
146	Milner, 'Special Diaries: Egypt, December 1919–March 1920, 8 March 1920', MS Milner dep 98, Milner papers, Bodleian Library.
147	Labour Deputation, 'Situation in Egypt and Exile of Zaghlul', 1923, PREM 1/25.
148	Curzon to Allenby, 21 May 1920, doc 43, *BDFA, Series G Africa*, ii, p. 60. C E Coles, former Inspector-General of Egyptian Prisons, wrote to Zaghlul prior to the conversations advising him 'not to be misled […] that because you find yourself in London, all your demands are about to be granted […] But although you cannot have all you want, I am very much mistaken if you do not find that Lord Milner is prepared to recommend that you have a great deal more in the matter of self-government than you enjoy at present. Your trouble will be to bridge the space between the maximum concession that the British Government will grant and the minimum of Home-rule which the extremists of the Nationalist Party consider their right and will endeavour to force you to insist on […] "Be reasonable and if you can't be reasonable be as reasonable as you can"!' C E Coles to Zaghlul Pasha, 7 June 1920, fols. 15–17, Add MS 46393, J A Spender papers, British Library.
149	Allenby to Curzon, 7 June 1920, doc 17, *BDFA, Series G Africa*, iii, p. 36.
150	Ibid., p. 36.
151	Ibid., p. 36.
152	Milner to Spender, 2 August 1920, fols. 21–23, Add MS 46393, J A Spender papers, British Library.
153	Ibid.

154 Memorandum by Lord Miner in Curzon to E Scott, 21 August 1920, doc 59, *BDFA, Series G Africa*, ii, pp. 223–24.
155 'Report on General Situation in Egypt, Aug 31–Sept 6 1920', doc 67, *Series G Africa*, ii, p. 237.
156 In a later report the activities of the delegates were criticized by the British as they had failed to call upon the Sultan, and their 'attitude towards the Egyptian Government and the British advisers was one of superior aloofness'. Labour Deputation, 'Situation in Egypt and Exile of Zaghlul', 1923, PREM 1/25.
157 'Report on General Situation in Egypt, Sept 14 to 21', doc 69, *Series G Africa*, ii, p. 242.
158 Ibid. Also, 'Report on General Situation in Egypt for period Sept 7 to 13 1920', doc 68, *BDFA, Series G Africa*, ii, p. 239.
159 See *The Times* 23, 24 and 25 August 1920. In an editorial on 25 August the Milner-Zaghlul scheme was received favourably since 'it was in accord with the spirit of the new age. The Egyptians have been restive under the yoke, and as in the case of other restive peoples, the yoke will now be lifted'. *The Times* editorial, 25 August 1920. See also M B Bishku, 'The British Press and the Future of Egypt, 1919–1922', *The International History Review*, 8, 4 (1986), pp. 604–12.
160 Churchill to David Lloyd George, no date, LG/C/3/15/13, Lloyd George papers, Parliamentary Archives. Indeed, reflecting in 1924 upon the publication of the Milner report Austen Chamberlain, then Chancellor of the Exchequer in Lloyd George's coalition government, 'seemed inclined to agree that the rejection of the report was a mistake, but [...] though in Cabinet, never said one word all through 1920 and then launched the Report on them [the Cabinet] like a bomb, and it was too much to expect any Cabinet to take it without preparation – especially when Milner himself told them he was never so surprised in his life as when he found his thoughts taking the form they did in the Report'. Spender to DDS and B, 6 October 1924, ff. 113–116, Add MS 46393, Spender papers, British Library.
161 Memorandum by the Secretary of State for War, 'The Egyptian Proposals', 24 August 1920, ADM 1/8610/139.
162 Ibid.
163 See also M J Cohen, 'Churchill and the Balfour Declaration: The Interpretation, 1920–22', in U Dann (ed.), *The Great Powers in the Middle East, 1919–1939* (New York: Holmes and Meier, 1988), pp. 91–108.
164 See M Gilbert, *Winston Churchill*, iv 1917–1922 (London: Heinemann, 1975), pp. 490–506.
165 Memo by CIGS to War Office, 25 August 1920, ADM 1/8610/139. For a biography of Sir Henry Wilson, see Jeffery, *Field Marshal Sir Henry Wilson*.
166 Memo by DCIGS and A/DMO to Alex Flint, Assistant Admiralty Secretary, 21 January 1921, ADM 1/8610/139.
167 Memo by CNS David Beatty, 'Naval Strategy as affected by the proposed future status of Egypt', 27 October 1920, ADM 1/8610/139.
168 Memorandum and minute by Flint to the Foreign Office, 'Egypt. Draft Article for insertion in Political Agreement and draft military Convention', 28 June 1921, ADM 1/8610/139.
169 Lancelot Oliphant, Under-Secretary of State at the Foreign Office to Secretary of the Admiralty, 19 July 1921, ADM 1/8610/139.
170 Ibid.

171 Trenchard to Secretary of State for the Foreign Office, 25 August 1920, ADM 1/8610/139. For a biography of Sir Hugh Trenchard, see A Boyle, *Trenchard Man of Vision* (London: Collins, 1962).
172 Air Staff notes on the effect of the new status of Egypt, ADM 1/8610/139.
173 Ibid.
174 Appendix to Conclusions of a Conference of Ministers, 1 November 1920, 62 (20), CAB 23/23,
175 Darwin, 'Imperialism in Decline? Tendencies in British Imperial Policy between the Wars', p. 674.
176 Hardinge to Spencer Harcourt Butler, Lieutenant-Governor of the United Provinces, 11 October 1920, Vol. 43 ff. 105–109, Hardinge papers, CUL. Hardinge continued: 'You may perhaps hardly believe me when I tell you that Milner has negotiated this scheme and launched it in Egypt without any members of the Government having the very slightest notion of its details; in fact the publication in the "Times" came to them as a great surprise! How are we to prevent the Indians making similar demands upon us, and why should such demands be conceded to the Egyptians and not to the Indians who are in reality more advanced and more able than the Egyptians'?
177 Memorandum by the Secretary of State for Colonies, 'The Egyptian Proposals', 16 September 1920, ADM 1/8610/139.
178 Ibid.
179 Ibid.
180 Ibid.
181 Ibid.
182 Milner to Lady Edward Cecil, 3 August 1920, VM 30/110/118, Violet Milner papers, Bodleian Library.
183 Ibid.
184 Ibid.
185 Bonar Law to Curzon, 20 August 1920, FO 371/4979/10237.
186 The ministerial conference was attended by the Prime Minister, Lloyd George; Bonar Law, Lord Privy Seal; Austen Chamberlain, Chancellor of the Exchequer; Milner, Secretary of State for Colonies; Churchill, Secretary of State for War and Air; R Munro, Secretary for Scotland; H A L Fisher, President of the Board of Education; Arthur Balfour, Lord President of the Council; Curzon, Secretary of State for Foreign Affairs; Montagu, Secretary of State for India; and Hamar Greenwood, President of the Board of Trade; Laming Worthington-Evans, Allenby and Philip Kerr were also present.
187 Appendix to Conclusions of a Conference of Ministers, 1 November 1920, 62 (20), CAB 23/23.
188 For example, if an engineer was required or an official to run the railways, or officers for the Egyptian Army, to what extent would Egyptian Ministers be beholden to use British personnel as opposed to French or American workers. Lord Milner replied that whilst this would not be expressly barred by his scheme it would be contrary to the spirit of the agreement and was sure that the Egyptians would readily agree to give a pledge to that effect. Lord Curzon used the example of India and its system of control over the Native States as regards their military forces and the employment of foreign officials. He suggested that the best way would be to lay down certain conditions and that if foreign officials were required they could

only be appointed with the concurrence of HMG. Appendix to Conclusions of a Conference of Ministers, 1 November 1920, 62 (20), CAB 23/23.
189   Ibid.
190   Ibid.
191   The Capitulations had originally been established in the sixteenth century whereby the Ottoman Sultan made special provision for the protection of non-Muslims who had established themselves within the Ottoman Empire for trade. These privileges exempted the foreign communities from taxes imposed on Muslim Ottoman subjects and gave them the right to be tried in their own consular courts. As Ottoman power declined, these privileges were reinforced and led to flagrant abuse, allowing the foreign communities in Egypt to be virtually above the law.
192   William M Hughes to Lloyd George, 18 November 1920, F/28/3/47, Lloyd George papers, Parliamentary archives.
193   Ibid.
194   Ibid.
195   Ibid.
196   Spender to 'dearest one', 10 December 1920, f. 26, Add MS 46393, J A Spender papers, British Library.
197   Spender, 'Some general observations' December 1920, ff. 27–38, Add MS 46393, J A Spender papers, British Library.
198   Milner to Spender, 16 January 1921, ff. 39–42, Add MS 46393, J A Spender papers, British Library.
199   Ibid.
200   Spender to his wife, January 1921, ff. 43–46, Add MS 46393, J A Spender papers, British Library.
201   Ibid.
202   Allenby's formula for a declaration to the Sultan read as follows: 'His Majesty's Government, after a study of the proposals made by Lord Milner, have arrived at the conclusion that the status of Protectorate is not a satisfactory relation in which Egypt should continue to stand to Great Britain. While they have not reached final decisions with regard to Lord Milner's recommendations, they desire to confer regarding them with an official delegation, nominated by the Sultan, with a view, if possible, to substitute for the Protectorate a treaty of alliance which would, while securing the special interests of Great Britain and enabling her to offer adequate guarantees to foreign Powers, meet the legitimate aspirations of Egypt and the Egyptian people'. Cabinet Conclusions 9 (21), 22 February 1921, CAB 23/24.
203   In a covering letter to Lloyd George, Curzon urged the Prime Minister to read his memorandum on Egypt prior to the forthcoming cabinet meeting.
204   Cabinet Conclusions 9 (21), 22 February 1921, CAB 23/24.
205   Curzon to Lloyd George, 16 February 1921, LG/F/13/2/4 Lloyd George papers, Parliamentary archive.
206   Darwin believes that Curzon's change of heart was largely down to the 'fiercer controversy in the Cabinet over the future of Persia'. Darwin argues that 'Curzon did not wish Churchill to become the arbiter of Britain's Eastern security'. As a direct consequence 'fresh tactics were required to limit the damage caused by Churchill's triumphs at the end of December, when it became clear that not only would British withdrawal from Persia be imposed by the Cabinet, but also that the responsibility for directing British policy in Mesopotamia, Trans-Jordan and Palestine would be vested in the Colonial Office', of which Churchill was to become the head.

Darwin, *Britain, Egypt and the Middle East*, p. 114. See also, Ministerial Conference, 1 December 1920, CAB 23/23. Curzon would also have had to consider that if HMG contemplated any drastic modifications to Milner's proposals then it would have been impossible for a representative delegation, able to carry through any agreement, to be formed. Allenby to Curzon, 12 January 1921, doc 83, *BDFA, Series G Africa*, ii, p. 271. Allenby warned that in his opinion 'any wide modification of conclusions reached by Lord Milner would bring extreme party [*sic*] once again into prominence and their hands would be strengthened in that such modifications would be regarded by all shades of opinion as a breach of faith on the part of His Majesty's Government'. Ibid. Moreover, it would also prohibit the formation of a stable, long-term moderate Ministry, under Adli Pasha, with whom Britain could do business.

207 The word 'official' was omitted before 'delegation' and 'relationship' was substituted for 'Treaty of Alliance'. Cabinet Conclusions 9 (21), 22 February 1921, CAB 23/24.
208 Cabinet Conclusions 9 (21), 22 February 1921, CAB 23/24.
209 Minute by Murray, 17 March 1921, FO 371/6294/3376.
210 Minute by R Lindsay, 17 March 1921, FO 371/6294/3376.
211 Allenby to Curzon, 21 March 1921, FO 371/6294/3529.
212 Minute by Lindsay, 22 March 1921, FO 371/6294/3529.
213 Ibid.
214 Ibid.
215 Curzon to Allenby, 24 March 1921, FO 371/6294/3549.
216 Murray, 'Summary of Political Movement in Egypt since the end of February', 24 May 1921, FO 371/6296/5985.
217 Allenby to Curzon, 8 April 1921, doc 133 *BDFA, Series G Africa*, ii, P. 366.
218 Minute by Murray, 16 April 1921; and Allenby to Curzon, 15 April 1921, FO 371/6295/4522.
219 Allenby to Curzon, 27 April 1921, FO 371/6295/5016.
220 Minute by Murray, 2 May 1921, FO 371/6295/5090.
221 Ibid. Milner noted in a letter to Spender: '[…] on the whole I am not dissatisfied with the Egyptian prospect. Winston nearly wrecked the whole thing in Cabinet, but I do not think that he did much harm in Egypt. Our principal danger now is that Zaghlul will get a swollen head, and having got so much more than he can ever reasonably have expected, will try to push us still further and so upset the coach'. Milner to Spender, 23 April 1921, ff. 51-52, Add MS 46393, Spender papers, British Library.
222 Milner to Spender, 23 April 1921, ff. 51-52, Add MS 46393, Spender papers, British Library.
223 Milner to Spender, 23 April 1921, ff. 55-56, Add MS 46393, Spender papers, British Library.
224 Allenby to Curzon, 7 May 1921, FO 371/6295/5352.
225 Ibid.
226 Curzon to Lloyd George, 13 June 1921, LG/F/13/2/30, Lloyd George papers, Parliamentary archives.
227 British troops would not be quartered outside of the towns; the employment of foreign officials and advisers by the Egyptian Government required the prior approval of the High Commissioner; and Egypt was to be permitted consuls where necessary but not diplomats. Cabinet Conclusions 9 (21), 22 February 1921, CAB 23/24.
228 The military clauses included: complete freedom of action to ensure the defence of Egypt against external aggression at all times; the numbers and distribution

of British troops to be decided in harmony with the circumstances; the Egyptian General Staff to work in close co-ordination with the British GOC in all military affairs; complete British freedom of action for the acquisition of land or buildings for military purposes. For a copy of the minutes of this meeting, see 'Proposed Anglo-Egyptian Treaty', 19 June 1921, FO 371/6297/6675.

229 Members of the Egyptian delegation included Adli Yakan, Husayn Rushdi, Ismail Sidqi, Mohammed Shafik, Ahmed Talaat, Youssef Soliman and Abdel Hamed. The British delegation consisted of Curzon, Ronald Lindsay, Robert Vansittart, Jack Murray and Alfred Duff Cooper.
230 See FO 371/6310 for the minutes of the Conferences and associated correspondence in connection with the Egyptian Official Delegation.
231 Cabinet Conclusions 81 (21), 20 October 1921, CAB 23/27.
232 H A L Fisher to Lloyd George, 28 October 1921, F/16/7/72, Lloyd George papers, Parliamentary archives.
233 Ibid.
234 Ibid.
235 Cabinet Conclusions 85 (21), 3 November 1921, CAB 23/27.
236 Ibid.
237 Ibid.
238 Ibid.
239 Cabinet Conclusions 86 (21), 4 November 1921, CAB 23/27.
240 Darwin, *Britain, Egypt and the Middle East*, pp. 124–25.
241 Labour Deputation, 'Situation in Egypt and Exile of Zaghlul', 1923, PREM 1/25.
242 J C B Richmond, Egypt 1798–1952 (London: Meuthuen & Co., 1977), p. 186.
243 Darwin, *Britain, Egypt and the Middle East*, p. 127.
244 Cabinet Conclusions 2 (22), 18 January 1922, CAB 23/29.
245 Cabinet Conclusions, 4 (22), 26 January 1922, CAB 23/29. The aim of this statement, approved by Austen Chamberlain, was to reassure public opinion and 'refute ill-informed and unfair criticism and make everyone wonder in Egypt and elsewhere why a policy so reasonable and on the whole generous as that we propose – is not accepted with gratitude instead of being refused with indignation'. Curzon to Lloyd George, no date, F/13/3/5, Lloyd George papers, Parliamentary archives.
246 Terry notes that 'Allenby had the full support of his hand-picked administrative staff', Terry, *The Wafd*, p. 143. We know only the names of two of the four British advisers who threatened to resign along with Allenby. Long, *Pro-Consuls in Egypt, 1914*-1929, p. 122; and Darwin, *Britain, Egypt and the Middle East*, pp. 128–29.
247 Cabinet Conclusions, 4 (22), 26 January 1922, CAB 23/29.
248 Foreign Office to Allenby, no date, F/13/3/5, Lloyd George papers, Parliamentary archives.
249 Hardinge to Curzon, 12 February 1922, Vol. 45 ff. 26–27, Hardinge papers, CUL.
250 Curzon to Lloyd George, 10 February 1922, F/13/3/6, Lloyd George papers, Parliamentary archives. Curzon also noted Allenby's reluctance to go before the Cabinet where he 'knows he does not cut a heroic figure'.
251 Richmond, *Egypt*, p. 186.
252 Ibid., p. 186.
253 Cabinet Conclusions, 5 (22), 27 January 1922, CAB 23/29. See also: Curzon to Lloyd George, 10 February 1922, F/13/3/6, Lloyd George papers, Parliamentary archives.
254 Darwin, *Britain, Egypt and the Middle East*, p. 129.
255 Richmond, *Egypt*, pp. 186–87.

Chapter 3

1. The Egyptian Department within the Foreign Office was formed in 1924. A result of organizational changes in the post-war period, this new Department comprised Egypt, transferred from the Eastern Department, and Abyssinia, from the African Department. For a detailed analysis of post-war reforms in the Foreign Office, see Steiner and Dockrill, 'The Foreign Office Reforms, 1919–1921', pp. 59–90; and Maisel, *The Foreign Office and Foreign Policy 1919–1926*.
2. 'Report on the General Situation in Egypt for the period from March 19–31 1924', doc 42, Woodward (ed.), *British Documents of Foreign Affairs*, vi, p. 95.
3. MacDonald to Allenby, 2 April 1924, doc 34, *Series G Africa*, vi, p. 78.
4. Allenby to MacDonald, 31 March 1924, FO 371/10040/2910.
5. Ibid.
6. Allenby to MacDonald, 31 March 1924, FO 371/10040/2911.
7. The Foreign Office was reluctant to acquiesce in Allenby's recommendations since it had originally been the Residency in Cairo which suggested that the 'spade work should be done by them [Cairo] [… and] to try preliminaries in Cairo quietly'. Moreover William Tyrrell, Assistant Under-Secretary of State at the Foreign Office, felt that the 'reluctance of Lord Allenby to carry on negotiations on the spot is very intelligible, but I think it is being pushed too far in these telegrams which suggest that nothing should be done in Cairo and everything in London [...] However, the Residency has changed its views and we have, I suppose, no alternative but to accept their statement that any serious negotiations cannot be carried out on the spot, but I do feel very strongly that we should make another effort to induce Lord Allenby to attempt to sound Zaghloul as to what prospects there are for reaching a satisfactory conclusion of our negotiations'. Minute by Tyrrell, 2 April 1924, FO 371/10040/2911 and MacDonald to Allenby, 2 April 1924, FO 371/10040/2910.
8. Allenby to MacDonald, 6 April 1924, FO 371/10040/3087.
9. Allenby to MacDonald, 14 April 1924, doc 43, *BDFA, Series G Africa*, vi, p. 101.
10. Allenby to MacDonald, 22 April 1924, doc 46, *BDFA, Series G Africa*, vi, pp. 104–11. See also Allenby to MacDonald, 6 April 1924, FO 371/10040/3114.
11. Residency opinion led the Foreign Office in London. Tyrrell noted that 'unless we are prepared to force the Residency to take any stand in these negotiations, we cannot expect assistance from them and must resign ourselves to face the other alternative of negotiation with Zaghlul in London'. Minute by Tyrrell, 8 April 1924, FO 371/10040/3113. This also forced London to examine what the policy of His Majesty's Government would be in relation to negotiations, particularly questions concerning the British garrison in Egypt and the position of the Sudan.
12. The CID was the most important standing committee charged with the defence of the Empire. It marked the apex of civil-military co-operation with representatives of all service ministries involved and chaired by the Prime Minister. One of the most important of these specialist committees was the Chiefs of Staff. The establishment of this sub-committee was the result of the 1924 Labour Government's acceptance and implementation of much of the Salisbury Committee Report. The Chiefs of Staff was composed of the three service chiefs whose dual role was to be individual advisers to their respective ministers and also to provide collective advice to the government on national military policy, not merely service policy. F A Johnson, *Defence by*

Committee. *The British Committee of Imperial Defence, 1885–1959* (London: Oxford University Press, 1960), p. 197.
13 Lord Derby to Stanley Baldwin, 12 April 1923, WO 137/2.
14 Ibid.
15 War Office memorandum, CID 439-B, 30 July 1923, CAB 4/10.
16 Ibid.
17 Ibid.
18 'The indefinite occupation by one country of the territory of another in time of peace is a phenomenon, rare and regrettable in itself, to which an honourable end should as soon as possible be found'. Foreign Office memorandum, CID 446-B, 9 August 1923, CAB 4/10.
19 Foreign Office memorandum, CID 446-B, 9 August 1923, CAB 4/10.
20 Ibid.
21 Report by the Naval Staff, 'Liability of the Suez Canal to Blocking Attack', CID 438-B, July 1923, CAB 4/10.
22 Lord Beatty, 188th meeting of the CID, 2 October 1924, CAB 2/4.
23 Colonial Office memorandum, 'Military Policy in Egypt', CID 448-B, 31 August 1923, CAB 4/10. Following the Ottoman attack on the Suez Canal in 1915, the Palestine mandate now provided defence in depth for the Canal. At this point, there was no notion that a threat to Egypt would manifest itself from another direction – the west – from the Italians in Libya.
24 Report by the COS, 'Military Policy in Egypt and Defence of the Suez Canal', CID 454-B, 29 September 1923, CAB 4/10.
25 Kenneth Lyon to Derby, 27 September 1923, WO 137/2. It had been suggested by the Foreign Office that the Egyptian garrison could be withdrawn to Cyprus.
26 Derby to Lyon, 28 September 1923, WO 137/2.
27 Report by the COS, 'Military Policy in Egypt and Defence of the Suez Canal', CID 454-B, 29 September 1923, CAB 4/10.
28 176th meeting of the CID, 2 October 1923, CAB 2/4.
29 Ibid. Despite Derby's hard-line position on the location of British troops at the Citadel, he had admitted to Lord Salisbury the day before that 'if hard pressed I would give up the Citadel, but I do not want to do so unless absolutely forced into that position'. Derby to Salisbury, 1 October 1923, WO 137/2.
30 Derby to Lord Stamfordham, the King's Private Secretary, 4 October 1923, WO 137/9.
31 J Barnes and D Nicolson (eds), *The Leo Amery Diaries. Volume I: 1896–1929* (London: Hutchinson, 1980), p. 348.
32 176th meeting of the CID, 2 October 1923, CAB 2/4.
33 Ibid.
34 Ibid.
35 Ibid.
36 Ibid.
37 180th Meeting of the CID, 4 February 1924, CAB 2/4.
38 Ibid.
39 Ibid.
40 Ibid.
41 Ibid. Stephen Walsh succeeded Lord Derby as Secretary of State for War in January 1924.
42 Minute by Tyrrell, 8 April 1924, FO 371/10040/3242.

43 Minute by Murray, 23 April 1924, FO 371/10020/3534.
44 Minute by MacDonald, 25 April 1924, FO 371/10020/3534
45 'Report on the General Situation in Egypt for the period 1 April – 15 April 1924', doc 50, *BDFA, Series G Africa*, vi, p. 116.
46 Cabinet Conclusion 29 (24), 1 May 1924, CAB 23/48. For an in-depth examination of the Sudan issue from the British perspective, see 'Memorandum on the Future Status of the Sudan', 25 May 1924, doc 61, *BDFA, Series G Africa*, vi, pp. 141–215.
47 See FO 371/10040/4078.
48 Allenby to MacDonald, 11 May 1924, FO 371/10040/4079.
49 Allenby to MacDonald, 23 May 1924, FO 371/10041/4550.
50 Ibid.
51 Minute by Murray, 26 May 1924, FO 371/10041/4570.
52 Allenby to Foreign Office, 9 June 1924, FO 371/10041/4995.
53 Allenby to MacDonald, 11 May 1924, FO 371/10040/4079.
54 MacDonald to Allenby, 27 May 1924, FO 371/10041/4570. MacDonald also received representations from the British Union in Egypt decrying any agreement with Zaghlul and the Wafd. But, as Philip Nichols minuted: 'I am not quite sure that the Council of the British Union quite realise that British policy in 1924 must necessarily differ from that which was pursued in the days of Lord Cromer.' Minute by Philip Nichols, 22 May 1924, FO 371/10040/4358.
55 MacDonald to Allenby, 27 May 1924, FO 371/10041/4570.
56 Question asked to the House of Commons, 30 June, doc 66, *BDFA, Series G Africa*, vi, p. 223.
57 Allenby the MacDonald, 29 June 1924, doc 71, *BDFA, Series G Africa*, vi, p. 228.
58 Ibid., p. 228.
59 Allenby to MacDonald, 7 July 1924, FO 371/10020/60680.
60 Minute by Nichols, 15 July 1924, FO 371/10020/60680.
61 Minute by Murray, 16 July 1924, 7 FO 371/10020/60680.
62 Stack to Allenby, 8 May 1924, FO 371/10049/4825.
63 Allenby to MacDonald, 13 July 1924, doc 95, *BDFA, Series G Africa*, vi, p. 274.
64 According to Willis, the League of the White Flag had been formed several years ago but had been of little importance until it was resuscitated through Egyptian influence in February 1924. E Vezzadini in *Lost Nationalism: Revolution, Memory and Anti-Colonial Resistance in Sudan* (Suffolk: James Currey, 2015) notes that it was formed sometime between 1923 and 1924, p. 2. The League's purpose was to agitate for unity of the Sudan with Egypt. Willis perceived its leader Ali Abdel Latif to be 'a person of moderate intellect and no standing'. Latif was supported by 'Egyptian officers and officials who supply him with money obtained from the Nationalist parties in Cairo' of whom 'provide advice and instruction'. Branches of the League were believed to exist in Medani, Makwar, El Obeid, Fasher and Shendi. C A Willis, 'Sudan Monthly Intelligence Report', May 1924, FO 371/10039/8189.
65 Demonstrations by Cadets of Khartoum Military School, doc 102, *BDFA, Series G Africa*, vi, p. 292.
66 Stack, 'Memorandum on the Future Status of the Sudan', 25 May 1924, FO 371/10049/5239.
67 Stack to MacDonald, 16 September 1924, FO 371/10053/8002.
68 Stack, 'Future Status of the Sudan', 25 May 1924, FO 371/10049/5239.
69 Ibid.

70 C A Willis, 'Memorandum on the League of the White Flag', 20 July 1924, FO 371/10051/6833.
71 Kerr to MacDonald, 25 August, doc 79, *BDFA, Series G Africa*, vi, p. 246.
72 Allenby to MacDonald, 26 July 1924, FO 371/10051/6659.
73 Certain practical changes would be made to favour Britain, such as an Anglo-Egyptian Finance Commission over which Britain would have direct control, and the newly created Sudan Defence Force.
74 Allenby to MacDonald, 29 June 1924, doc 106, *BDFA, Series G Africa*, vi, pp. 296–97.
75 House of Commons Debate, 10 July 1924, *Hansard*, Vol. 175 cc2503-52.
76 Minute by Murray, 21 June 1924, FO 371/10049/5239.
77 Murray, 'Memorandum respecting the Situation in the Sudan', 17 September 1924, FO 371/10053/8002.
78 MacDonald to Zaghlul, 23 August 1924, FO 371/10051/6937.
79 Allenby to MacDonald, 28 July 1924, FO 371/10041/6661.
80 Ibid.
81 Foreign Office, 'Memorandum respecting Anglo-Egyptian relations', 16 September 1924, FO 371/10042/7966.
82 Allenby to MacDonald, 28 July 1924, FO 371/10041/6661.
83 Ibid.
84 Stack to MacDonald, 11 August 1924, FO 371/10051/6937.
85 Foreign Office, 'Memorandum on the Forthcoming Conversations with Zaghlul Pasha', 20 September 1924, FO 371/10042/8114.
86 Ibid.
87 'Record of Conference held at 10 Downing Street', 25 September 1924, FO 371/10054/8325.
88 M Daly argues that by making the Sudan a reserved point in 1922 the British government had 'tacitly admitted the impermanence of the 1899 Agreement'. *Empire on the Nile*, p. 301.
89 'Record of Conference held at 10 Downing Street', 29 September 1924, *BDFA, Series G Africa*, vi, p. 335.
90 Ibid., p. 337.
91 Ibid., p. 337.
92 'Record of Third Conference at 10 Downing Street', 3 October 1924, *BDFA, Series G Africa*, vi, p. 343.
93 Ibid., p. 344.
94 Kerr to MacDonald, 5 October 1924, FO 371/10022/8882. David Marquand's biography of MacDonald suggests that he was prepared to 'give the Liberals an election [over the Anglo-Soviet treaty] if they force it'. D Marquand, *Ramsay MacDonald* (London: Jonathan Cape, 1977), p. 364.

Chapter 4

1 E M Troutt Powell, *A Different Shade of Colonialism: Egypt, Great Britain and the Mastery of the Sudan* (Stanford, CA: University of California Press, 2003), p. 6.
2 MacMichael, *The Anglo-Egyptian Sudan*, p. 64.
3 M Daly, *Empire on the Nile. The Anglo-Egyptian Sudan, 1898–1934* (Cambridge: Cambridge University Press, 2003), p. 12.

4   MacMichael, *Anglo-Egyptian Sudan*, pp. 67–69; also Daly, *Empire on the Nile*, pp. 17–18.
5   Sharkey, *Living with Colonialism*, p. 5. For a study of the Sudan Political Service, see A H M Kirk-Greene, *The Sudan Political Service: A Preliminary Profile* (Oxford: Oxford University Press, 1982); Kirk-Greene, *Britain's Imperial Administrators*, Chapter 6.
6   Daly, *Empire on the Nile*, p. 18.
7   Stack, 'Report on the Soudan for 1914–1919', doc 52, Woodward (ed.), *British Documents of Foreign Affairs*, ii, p 161.
8   Wingate to Fitzgerald, 30 December 1914, 192/3/268–270, Wingate papers, Sudan Archive, University of Durham [hereafter SAD].
9   Stack, 'Report on the Soudan', doc 52, *BDFA, Series G Africa*, ii, p. 162.
10 Wingate to Fitzgerald, 30 December 1914, 192/3/268–270, Wingate papers, SAD.
11 Ibid.
12 Clayton to Wingate, 30 November 1914, 192/2/221–224, Wingate papers, SAD.
13 After the re-conquest of the Sudan, the Sudan agent was based in Cairo and provided a liaison office between the Sudan Government and both the British representative in Cairo and the Egyptian Government. The Sudan Agency grew out of the Egyptian Army's department of military intelligence. The combined role of Agent General and Director of Intelligence was finally separated in 1920 when the Director of Intelligence was stationed permanently in Khartoum. Daly, *Empire on the Nile*, pp. 54–57.
14 Daly, *Anglo-Egyptian Sudan*, p. 153.
15 Ibid., p. 153.
16 Ibid., p. 153.
17 It remains unclear whether Slatin Pasha assisted the Central Powers to the detriment of Britain. Daly, *Anglo-Egyptian Sudan*, p. 154.
18 Ibid., p. 154.
19 Ibid., p. 154.
20 Clayton to Stack, 30 November 1914, 192/2/221–224, Wingate papers, SAD.
21 Wingate to Clayton, 19 November 1914, 193/4/120–121, Wingate papers, SAD.
22 Ibid.
23 G Warburg, 'Sudan, Egypt and Britain, 1919–24', in U Dann (ed.), *The Great Powers and the Middle East, 1919–1939* (New York: Holmes and Meier, 1988), p. 71.
24 Daly, *Empire on the Nile*, p. 155.
25 Ibid., p. 157.
26 R Wingate, *Wingate of the Sudan. The Life and Times of General Reginald Wingate, maker of the Anglo-Egyptian Sudan* (London: John Murray, 1955), p. 201. See also M Daly, *The Sirdar. Sir Reginald Wingate and the British Empire in the Middle East* (Philadelphia, American Philosophical Society, 1997); and G F Clayton, *An Arabian Diary* (ed.) R O Collins (Berkeley, CA: University of California Press, 1969).
27 Wingate, *Wingate of the Sudan*, p. 202.
28 Daly, *Empire on the Nile*, p. 157.
29 Ibid., p. 157.
30 As to Stack's appointment, he was the obvious choice as Wingate's successor. 'He had a reputation as an excellent staff officer, had a long experience of Sudan Government posts in Khartoum and Cairo, had served Wingate well and, as importantly, could be relied upon to continue to do so. He was a man of definite views who rarely tried to impose them. He preferred conciliation to confrontation and lacked decisiveness'. Daly, *Empire on the Nile*, p. 158.

31 Daly suggests that by keeping open his post in the Sudan – as Kitchener had done in Cairo – he seems to have had in mind a viceroyalty of the Nile Valley, mirroring that of the Raj, with the combined possession of the High Commissionership, Governor-Generalship and *Sirdar*ship. Daly, *Empire on the Nile*, p. 57. This idea had its genesis under Ronald Storrs, Oriental Secretary at the Cairo Residency, who 'cherished the idea of a near Eastern Vice-royalty under Kitchener, stretching from the Sudan to Alexandretta'. J Fisher, *Curzon and British Imperialism in the Middle East, 1916–19* (London: Frank Cass, 1999), p. 3. See also K Neilson, 'Kitchener: A Reputation Refurbished?' *Canadian Journal of History*, 15, 2 (1980), pp. 207–27.
32 Daly, *Empire on the Nile*, p. 158.
33 However, the one area that did test the Sudan government was the region of Darfur which, under the leadership of Ali Dinar, announced its independence and, with the assistance of the Turkish mission to the Sennoussi, began to plan an invasion of the Sudan at the same time as a Sennouissist attack upon Egypt. Concerns over the attitude and warlike preparations of Ali Dinar affecting the loyalty of the western tribes, and causing disaffection to run throughout the country, finally prompted the Sudan Government to act in early 1916 and resulted in the defeat of his forces on 22 May 1916 and his death on 6 November 1916. A further joint Anglo-French operation in neighbouring French Equatorial Africa against the marauding Guraan tribe and the later settlement of Darfur's western frontier at the Paris Peace Conference allowed Darfur to be ranked as one of the Sudan's provinces. Stack, 'Report on the Soudan', doc 52, *BDFA, Series G Africa*, ii, p. 162.
34 Stack, 'Report on the Soudan', doc 52, *BDFA, Series G Africa*, ii, p. 161.
35 Ibid., p. 163.
36 Ibid., p. 163.
37 Ibid., p. 163.
38 Ibid., p. 163.
39 Ibid., p. 163.
40 Ibid., p. 163.
41 Stack, 'Report on the Soudan', doc 52, *BDFA, Series G Africa*, ii, p. 163. See also, MacMichael, *Anglo-Egyptian Sudan*, pp. 121–23. These views were expressed in the memoirs of administrators such as H. MacMichael, who also perceived the benefits of the war upon the Sudan.
42 Warburg, 'Sudan, Egypt and Britain', p. 71.
43 Wingate to Hardinge, 27 December 1918, FO 371/3711/6537.
44 Ibid.
45 Ibid.
46 Minute by A T Loyd, 14 January 1919, FO 371/3711/6537.
47 Minute by Graham, 14 January 1919, FO 371/3711/6537.
48 Stack to Wingate, 22 December 1918, FO 371/3711/6537.
49 Wingate to Curzon, 26 March 1919, FO 371/3711/50265.
50 Ibid.
51 Stack, 'Note on Growth of National Aspirations in the Sudan', 23 February 1919, FO 371/3711/50265.
52 Ibid.
53 Ibid.
54 Ibid.
55 Ibid.
56 Wingate to Curzon, 3 April 1919, FO 371/3711/52714.
57 Ibid.

58 Wingate to Curzon, 4 June 1919, FO 371/3711/87127. Milner himself agreed with this policy and minuted that: 'It is desirable as far as possible to dissociate Egypt from the Sudan politically and administratively, and I am glad that Lord Curzon takes the same view'. Minute by Lord Milner, 21 June 1919, FO 371/3711/87127.
59 Stack to Wingate, 8 May 1919, FO 371/3711/87127.
60 It is also worth noting that a Sudanese delegation comprising religious men and officials was permitted to visit the Foreign Office once the peace treaties were signed. But this was only to be announced after the signature of the Peace conditions since Stack believed that 'it would be a great mistake [...] to point out the contrast at the moment between the loyalty of the Sudanese and the discontent of the Egyptians. It would only lead to bad feeling.' Stack to Wingate, 8 May 1919, FO 371/3711/8717. This action, on the part of the British government, can be viewed as an attempt to reassure the Sudanese of continued British support and to bring the Sudan closer into the orbit of the British Empire.
61 Cheetham to Curzon, 10 February 1920, doc 23 *BDFA, Series G Africa*, ii, p. 33.
62 Ibid., p. 33.
63 The Milner Mission was sent to Egypt to 'reconcile the aspirations of the Egyptian people with the special interests which Great Britain has in Egypt, and with the maintenance of the legitimate rights of all foreign residents in the country'. 'Statement by the British Mission', 29 December 1919, doc 9, *BDFA, Series G Africa*, ii, p. 17.
64 A W Keown-Boyd to Allenby, 14 March 1920, doc 36, *BDFA, Series G Africa*, ii, p. 50.
65 Milner to Curzon, 'Report of the Special Mission to Egypt: General Conclusions', 17 May 1920, doc 53, *BDFA, Series G Africa*, ii, p. 212.
66 Ibid., p. 212.
67 Ibid., p. 213.
68 Ibid., p. 213.
69 Ibid., p. 213.
70 Ibid., p. 213.
71 Ibid., p. 214.
72 Ibid., p. 214.
73 Allenby to Curzon, 18 February 1921, doc 107, *BDFA, Series G Africa*, ii, p. 318.
74 Ibid., p. 318.
75 Ibid., p. 318.
76 As a consequence of the mutiny of the Egyptian army in the Sudan in 1900, a number of purely Sudanese units were established to replace the Egyptian army of conquest. It was Mr Owen, Governor of Mongolla Province and the Lado Enclave, who had suggested in 1910 the creation of a British officered southern army. Wingate also appreciated that the creation of a non-Muslim army 'could be used more effectively to counter insurgencies among Muslims than could Muslim troops'. More importantly, these southern, pagan, tribes were seen as potential converts by missionaries and administrators (Wingate himself a devout Christian) alike and therefore as a bulwark against the spread of Islam. An Eastern Arab Corps, drawn largely from the tribes of the eastern Sudan, a Western Arab Corps formed after the occupation of Darfur in 1916 and an Equatorial Corps were to form the nucleus of the Sudan Defence Force. A Al-Awad Muhammad, *Sudan Defence Force: Origin and Role, 1925-1955* (Institute of African and Asian Studies, Occasional paper No. 18), pp. 14-15. See also H Abdin, *Early Sudanese Nationalism, 1919-1925* (Khartoum: Khartoum University Press/Sundanese Library Series 14, 1985), Chapter 4.
77 Clayton to Foreign Office, 21 March 1919, FO 371/3714/47997.
78 Allenby to Foreign Office, 4 May 1919, FO 371/3717/75218.

79 Ibid.
80 Allenby to Foreign Office, 4 May 1919, FO 371/3717/75218. Stack was confirmed as *Sirdar* and Governor-General in May 1919. However, as Abdin points out we must not set too much store by these British beliefs. The British idea in the Sudan was to create a 'veiled and tacit alliance between the colonial administration and traditional leaders in the country. Religious notables and tribal chiefs, most of whom enjoyed little or no real influence during the previous regime of the *Mahdiyah* [sic], were systematically encouraged and used to speak for the country in regard to its relations with Egypt. On numerous occasions, they were induced to emphasise the separateness of the Sudan and dissociate its political future from that of Egypt'. Abdin, *Sudanese Nationalism*, p. 18.
81 Stack to Allenby, 'Memorandum on the Future Status of the Sudan', 25 May 1924, FO 371/10049/5239.
82 See Sharkey, *Living with Colonialism*, pp. 76–77.
83 Stack to Allenby, 'Memorandum on the Future Status of the Sudan', 25 May 1924, FO 371/10049/5239.
84 Appendix 11, 'The Egyptian Claim for Political Control in the Sudan and Its Effects upon the Sudanese', doc 61, *BDFA, Series G Africa*, vi, p. 183.
85 Ibid., p. 183.
86 Ibid., p. 183.
87 Ibid., p. 183.
88 Stack to Allenby, 'Future Status of the Sudan', 25 May 1924, FO 371/10049/5239.
89 Ibid.
90 Ibid.
91 Ibid.
92 Daly, *Empire on the Nile*, pp. 421–24.
93 Stack to Allenby, 'Future Status of the Sudan', 25 May 1924, FO 371/10049/5239.
94 Daly, *Empire on the Nile*, p. 424.
95 William Himbury's Tour Diaries, India and the Sudan: Tour Diary of W H Himbury, 1923, British Cotton Growers Association [hereafter BCGA] 7/3/3, University of Birmingham Special Collections.
96 Murray to Himbury, 11 April 1923, BCGA/7/3/3, University of Birmingham Special Collections.
97 Minute by Murray, 'Future of the Sudan', 23 June 1924, FO 371/10049/5307.
98 Ibid. See also FO 371/10050/5328 containing a resolution from the Liverpool Chamber of Commerce emphasizing the importance of securing continued British control of the Sudan.
99 Stack to Allenby, 'Future Status of the Sudan', 25 May 1924, FO 371/10049/5239.
100 Ibid.
101 Ibid.
102 Ibid.
103 Ibid.
104 Ibid.
105 Ibid.
106 Ibid.
107 Ibid.
108 Allenby to MacDonald, 29 June 1924, FO 371/10050/5853.
109 Ibid.
110 Ibid.

111　Ibid.
112　Ibid.
113　Minute by Murray, 'Future Status of the Sudan', 21 June 1924, FO 371/10049/5239.
114　Ibid.
115　Ibid. Murray even mooted the idea that should the Egyptian government refuse to make the contribution of £500,000 towards the Sudan Defence Force, Egypt could not 'expect HMG or the Sudan Govt to be in any hurry to come to her assistance in regard to the payment of interest on and amortisation of the 5 millions advanced by Egypt in the past'. Minute by Murray, 4 July 1924, FO 371/10050/5739.
116　In the Committee of Imperial Defence (CID), the Sudan was only ever considered alongside Egypt. At the time of the conversations between MacDonald and Zaghlul, the Chiefs of Staff Sub-Committee was considering the strategic aspect of British policy towards Egypt. However, since the conversations were broken off before any agreement had been reached and owing to the changed political situation following the assassination of Stack, no report was submitted to the CID. In fact, Egypt, and by extension the Sudan, was not discussed by the CID between October 1924 and January 1925. Again, in January, the CID's primary focus was upon the strategic aspect of the situation in Egypt and it believed that the security of the Sudan lay in demonstrating 'no weakening of our position in Egypt'. Report by the Chiefs of Staff, 'Strategical Aspect of Situation in Egypt', CID 572-B, 27 January 1925, CAB 4/12.
117　Stack to Allenby, 8 May 1924, FO 371/10049/4825.
118　Ibid.
119　Ibid.
120　Ibid.
121　Ibid.
122　Ibid.
123　Allenby to MacDonald, 13 July 1924, doc 95, *BDFA, Series G Africa*, vi, p. 274.
124　Minute by Murray, FO 371/10049/4825.
125　Ibid.
126　Ibid.
127　Stack to MacDonald, 4 July 1924, FO 371/10050/5817.
128　Khartoum Intelligence Department memorandum, doc 95, 11 June 1924, *BDFA, Series G Africa*, vi, p. 277.
129　C A Willis, 'The Political Situation', doc 98, enclosure to doc 95, 16 June 1924, *BDFA, Series g Africa*, vi, p. 280. It was in the immediate post-war period that the politicization of groups and activities came to the fore. The earliest of these was the League of Sudanese Union formed sometime between 1919 and 1920 by a group of students and graduates of the Gordon College in Khartoum. Abdin, *Sudanese Nationalism*, pp. 37–44.
130　Willis, 'The Political Situation', doc 98, enclosure to doc 95, 16 June 1924, *BDFA, Series G Africa*, vi, p. 281.
131　Willis, 'Memorandum on the League of the White Flag', 20 July 1924, FO 371/10051/6864. See also Abdin, *Sudanese Nationalism*, chapter 3.
132　'Manifesto by the White Flag Society', undated, doc 83, *BDFA, Series G Africa*, vi, p. 252.
133　Ibid., p. 287.
134　Ibid., p. 288.

135 Ibid., p. 281. This is contested by Adbin who argues that the White Flag League was able to recruit from a cross-section of Sudanese society, the most important being the Sudanese officer corps. The League also managed to organize the artisans and workers of Khartoum, Omdurman, Port Sudan and Atbara in return for promises of 'economic and social advancement in an independent Sudan'. Abdin, *Sudanese Nationalism*, p. 60.
136 Allenby to MacDonald, 13 July 1924, doc 95, *BDFA, Series G Africa*, vi, p. 277. The reports and memoranda from Khartoum were sent to Cairo and Allenby forwarded them to the Foreign Office. He was generally prepared to accept the interpretations of Stack and Willis and support these in his dispatches to the Foreign Office.
137 Minute by Nichols, 13 August 1924, FO 371/10051/6864.
138 Minute, 15 August 1924, FO 141/805/2. However, the veracity of Willis's reports has been called into question. Daly has argued that in relation to analysing the development of *tariqas* (a *sufi* order or brotherhood) and in engaging with Sayyid 'Abd al-Rahman, Willis's expertise was unsurpassed as he relied upon his own experience and personal contacts. But, when it came to 'Ali 'Abd al'Latif, Willis was 'at a loss'. His 'agents were incompetent time servers or unreliable double-dealers, and leaders of the White Flag League could not [...] be engaged in tea-time repartee'. Daly, *Empire on the Nile*, pp. 329–30. Willis was accused of underestimating the strength of the White Flag League and of contributing to the revival of Mahdism. For an analysis of Willis's relationship with Sayyid 'Abd al-Rahman, see ibid., pp. 278–87. The production of the Sudan intelligence reports themselves was 'published and received so long after the news they reported as to be of little utility within the Sudan'. Ibid., p. 278. Indeed, the performance of the department in relation to political unrest became such a concern that Stack appointed J M Ewart of the Government of India Police at the head of a Committee charged with examining public security intelligence. The result, issued on 8 June 1925 and following the Sudanese mutiny, was a damning indictment of the department and served as a pretext for Willis's replacement by Reginald Davis in 1927. Ibid., pp. 330–33.
139 Indeed, many of these reports were merely initialled by officials in Cairo and London.
140 Allenby to MacDonald, 26 July 1924, FO 371/10051/6659.
141 Ibid.
142 Ibid.
143 Ibid.
144 Minute by Murray, 6 August 1924, FO 371/10051/6659.
145 A W Skrine, 'Appreciation of Situation. Atbara and Port Sudan Disturbances', August 1924, doc 105, *BDFA, Series G Africa*, vi, p. 295.
146 Colonel Huddleston et al., 'Demonstration of Cadets of Khartoum Military School', 10 August 1924, doc 105, *BDFA, Series G Africa*, vi, p. 292.
147 Ibid., p. 292.
148 Ibid., p. 292.
149 Minute by Murray, 11 August 1924, FO 371/10051/6833.
150 Stack to MacDonald, 16 September 1924, doc 108, *BDFA, Series G Africa*, vi, p. 301.
151 Abdin reminds us that although the White Flag League received both concealed and overt political support from Egyptian nationalist leaders in Cairo and Egyptian officials and residents in the Sudan, coupled with the League's call for Unity of the Nile Valley, we should be careful not to ascribe Sudanese discontent to Egyptian

	machination, as many British officials did. J M Ewart was a notable exception to this. Abdin, *Sudanese Nationalism*, pp. 63–64.
152	Stack to MacDonald, 11 August 1924, FO 371/10051/6937.
153	'Record of Conference in room of Secretary of State at the Foreign Office', 13 August 1924, FO 371/10051/6987.
154	Ibid.
155	Following the June demonstrations, Murray advocated that the Sudan situation 'must be handled firmly and promptly'. Minute by Murray, 11 August 1924, FO 371/10051/6833. The same minute is annotated by MacDonald with 'I agree', 11 August 1924. Again in reference to the Egyptian press campaign over its claim to the Sudan, it was minuted that the British 'remedy therefore must be in action rather than words'. Minute by Nichols, 13 August 1924, FO 371/10051/6865. 'The Sudan Govt. have got to hit hard and above all, hit quickly. Egyptians will realise that we mean business and that their intrigues have all but lost them the Sudan, but the swifter and more drastic our action in the Sudan the less likely it is that the situation in Egypt will become unmanageable.' Minute by Murray, 12 August 1924, FO 371/10051/6893.
156	'Record of Conference in room of Secretary of State at the Foreign Office', 13 August 1924, FO 371/10051/6987.
157	Ibid.
158	Ibid.
159	Ibid.
160	A telegram was drafted to Zaghlul on 23 August emphasizing the mutual observation of the *status quo* in the Sudan. 'Events have occurred in the Sudan which are the direct outcome of persistent propaganda engineered and financed from Egypt and designed to create disorder and embarrass the Sudan Government [...] The bad faith of these proceedings has painfully impressed me and disappointed my hope that I was dealing with honest men bent upon pursuing a peaceful settlement by straightforward and honourable means.' MacDonald ended his note with a warning. 'His Majesty's Government will not be intimidated but rather stiffened by such policy, for no British Government will ever consent to be moved by action or tactics of this kind'. MacDonald to Zaghlul, 23 August 1924, doc 118, *BDFA, Series G Africa*, vi, p. 321. Of course Zaghlul fervently denied any knowledge or connection with the Sudan disorders. 'Il va sans dire qu'il n'est pas à ma connaissance ni à la connaissance de mes collègues que les désordres au Soudan aient éte à aucun moment l'oeuvre d'une propaganda persistante de la part de l'Egypt ni finances par elle'. Zaghlul to MacDonald, 29 August 1924, doc 119, *BDFA, Series G Africa*, vi, p. 321.
161	See Clark Kerr to Foreign Office, 14 August 1924, FO 371/10051/6970. Indeed, the Egyptian ministry under acting Prime Minister Mohamed Said attempted to use the threat of violent outbursts as a lever with which to persuade the British to submit to a Court of Enquiry over the disturbances at Port Sudan and Atbara. The Foreign Office refused this proposal and in fact largely perceived the King as being behind 'all these sinister happenings'. Murray continued: 'He [King Fuad] has been a constant source of embarrassment and weakness. While posing as our friend he has never failed to add to our difficulties and much of the unpopularity which attaches to us in Egypt should by rights be his portion'. Minute by Murray, 14 August 1924, FO 371/10051/6970.
162	Sterry to Stack, 8 October 1924, FO 371/10054/8761.

163 Stack to Sterry, 8 October, FO 371/10054/8761.
164 Stack to Sterry, 8 October, FO 371/10054/8761.
165 Stack to MacDonald, 16 September 1924, FO 371/10053/8002.
166 Stack to MacDonald, 16 September 1924, FO 371/10053/8002. Stack provided examples of Zaghlul's public statements in what he saw as encouraging an anti-British attitude in the Sudan. 'It is not compatible with the self-respect of the Egyptian Government to have a foreigner as its Commander-in-Chief, nor foreigners as subordinate officers, but this is what has been the position hitherto, and this is what we ought to blot out'. – 17 May.
'The Sudan is ours, and we must have it, and we must dispose of it as a proprietor disposes of his property [...] Those whose hands are on the Sudan are strong, is therefore, the way to wrest the country from the hands of the usurpers to sit down here and say they have no right? Or is there another way to make them hear our voice and let them know our rights, and lay our proofs before them and show them that they are usurpers and that we are in the right?' – 7 June.
'I declare that the Egyptian nation will not surrender the Sudan as long as it lives. The nation will stick to its rights against any usurper, against any aggressor on every opportunity and at all times [...] If in our lifetime we do not attain this enjoyment we shall urge our children and our grandchildren to uphold it and not relinquish it one hair's breadth'. – 28 June. Stack to MacDonald, 16 September 1924, FO 371/10053/8002.
167 Foreign Office memorandum, 17 September 1924, FO 371/10053/8002.
168 Ibid.
169 Ibid.
170 Ibid.
171 Ibid.
172 Ibid.
173 Minute by Murray, undated, FO 371/10053/8002. MacDonald was however a little more cautious noting 'this is a serious step which ought not to be taken unless its need is abundantly clear'. Minute by MacDonald, 11 October 1924, FO 371/10053/8002.
174 Note by Mr Malkin to the Lord Chancellor, 1 October 1924, FO 371/10054/8839; also 'Note by Mr Malkin on the Sudan Question', 17 September 1924, doc 110, *BDFA, Series G Africa*, vi, pp. 304–05.
175 Ibid., pp. 304–05.
176 Ibid., pp. 304–05.
177 Ibid., pp. 304–05.
178 MacDonald, House of Commons statement, 10 July 1924, doc 109, *BDFA, Series G Africa*, vi, p. 302.
179 'Note by Mr Malkin on the Sudan Question', 17 September 1924, doc 110, *BDFA, Series G Africa*, vi, p. 302.
180 Ibid., p. 302.
181 Ibid., p. 303.
182 Ibid., p. 303.
183 'Memorandum on the position in the Sudan', 8 November 1924, FO 371/10054/9843.
184 Ibid.
185 Ibid.

186 'Memorandum on the position in the Sudan', 8 November 1924, FO 371/10054/9843. Murray minuted that although 'things are now quiet on the surface [...] Egyptian propagandists are bound to continue their agitation and as long as they can keep the political position uncertain they have a fruitful soil in which to sow the seed of discontent and disorder'. Minute by Murray, 8 November 1924, FO 371/10043/9713.

187 'Memorandum on the position in the Sudan', 8 November 1924, FO 371/10054/9843.

188 Ibid.

189 For a catalogue of evidence of semi-official and official Egyptian complicity in subversive propaganda in the Sudan, see 'Egyptian Propaganda in Sudan', FO 371/10054/10219.

190 The Egyptian officers evacuated from the Sudan and what to do with them caused the Cairo authorities a certain amount of concern. The natural feeling of resentment among the officers was seen as providing a fertile breeding ground for agitators. As a consequence, it was decided to distribute these officers across the provincial police and *Ghaffir* forces, coast guards and frontiers districts administration. This policy was generally approved by the Foreign Office, Murray adding that 'as they [Egyptian officers] always hated the Sudan they are unlikely to sigh for it provided that they are given comfortable and fairly lucrative jobs in Egypt'. Minute by Murray, 22 December 1924, FO 371/10022/11496. This policy does appear slightly at odds with previous ideas, largely within the Sudan Government, of avoiding the dissemination of nationalist ideas across a wider area. Nevertheless, it seems to have been agreed because of a lack of other options rather than as a positive policy choice. Chamberlain commented, 'I foresaw danger but c'd not see a safer solution'. Minute by Chamberlain, 22 December 1924, FO 371/10022/11496.

191 'Annual Report on the Sudan for 1924', doc 78, *BDFA, Series G Africa*, vii, pp. 134–35.

192 'Report by the Director of Intelligence on the Mutiny of Nov 27 and 28', doc 71, *BDFA, Series G Africa*, vii, p. 106. See also Mohammed Nuri El-Amin, 'Britain, the 1924 Sudanese Uprising, and the Impact of Egypt on the Sudan', *International Journal of African Historical Studies*, 19, 2 (1986), pp. 235–60; and 'Report by the Director of Prisons, Sudan Government, on the Mutiny in the Central Prison, Khartoum North, 6 December 1924', doc 72, *BDFA, Series G Africa*, vii, p. 107. Abdin believes that the primary political motive of the mutiny was a gesture of solidarity with the departing Egyptian battalions. He also suggests that perhaps the Sudanese officers hoped a *coup d'état* could be brought about by joining the Egyptian units. Abdin, *Sudanese Nationalism*, p. 94.

193 'Report by the Director of Prisons', doc 71, *BDFA, Series G Africa*, vii, p. 107.

194 W J Berridge, 'Ambivalent Ideologies and the Limitations of the Colonial Prison in Sudan, 1898–1956', *Journal of East African Studies*, 6, 3 (2012), p. 456.

195 Berridge, 'Ambivalent Ideologies', p. 456.

196 'Report by the Director of Prisons', doc 71, *BDFA, Series G Africa*, vii, p. 107.

197 'Annual Report for the Sudan', doc 71, *BDFA, Series G Africa*, vii, p. 107.

198 Ibid., p. 107.

199 Ibid., p. 107.

200 Sir Geoffrey Archer, 'Memorandum on Egyptian Complicity in the Mutiny of November 27 and 28 1924', undated, doc 75, *BDFA, Series G Africa*, vii, p. 112.

201   Ibid., p. 112. For example, statements had been obtained which described a meeting of Egyptian officers three or four days before the mutiny to which Sudanese officers were also invited. At this meeting Ahmed Bey Rifaat was elected to the supreme command of the Egyptian army. It was then alleged by Mulazim Awal Sueiman Mohammed of the Camel Corps (who was court marshalled and shot for his complicity in the mutiny), that a letter arrived at the musketry school on 26 November from Rifaat regarding the arrangements for the mutiny. 'I have issued this order to all Sudanese units of the Egyptian army; and as soon as I hear a shot fired, I will fire on the fort, the palace and the British barracks'. The letter also contained a false statement, presumably to convince waverers, that a Sudanese officer and twenty-five men, stationed at Khartoum North, had already joined the Egyptians. On 27 November, the day of the mutiny, further encouragement was received from the Egyptians promising support. This description of events was corroborated by Mulazim Tani Ali Mohammed-al-Banna, of the 12th Sudanese Battalion, condemned to death for participation in the mutiny but later reprieved, and Mulazim Tani Hassan Fadl-al-Mula of the Musketry School, who was court marshalled and shot. Also, statements from prisoners confined in the Central Prison at Khartoum North detailed signals exchanged while the mutiny was in progress between certain mutineering political prisoners, and the 3rd Egyptian Battalion and Egyptian Artillery. Within these messages the same suggestion of Egyptian promises to support a movement which the Sudanese were to initiate and which both had planned was seen.

Chapter 5

1   The Society of Vengeance is one such example. It was established during the Arabi Revolt in 1881 and Saad Zaghlul was alleged to have belonged to this group. M Badrawi, *Political Violence in Egypt, 1910–1925. Secret Societies, Plots and Assassinations* (Surrey: Curzon Press, 2000), p. 69. During 1920 a large trial was undertaken against the Society. Twenty-seven members were charged with: conspiracy in attempting to depose the Sultan and the government; disseminating sedition; inciting murder; distributing arms; and assassinating the Sultan, his ministers and others. Four of the accused were acquitted, seven were sentenced to death, including Abd al-Rahman Fahmi, eleven were sentenced to thirty lashes and the remainder to various terms of penal servitude, imprisonment and fines. Ernest Scott, Minister Plenipotentiary, to Secretary of Foreign Affairs, Lord Curzon, 10 October 1920, FO 371/4987/12447. These trials obviously represented police successes but the Foreign Office was often, unsurprisingly, far more sensitive to the wider political implications of such trials. For example, concern was raised that the death sentence on Fahmi was likely to have political ramifications at a time when Britain was attempting to re-define the Anglo-Egyptian relationship. See minute by John Tilley, Assistant Under-Secretary at the Foreign Office, 11 October 1920, FO 371/4987/12447. The Foreign Office therefore focussed upon the amelioration of the Anglo-Egyptian relationship. For a study on assassinations in Egypt between 1910 and 1954, see D M Reid, 'Political Assassination in Egypt, 1910–1954', *The International Journal of African Historical Studies*, 15 (1982), pp. 625–51.

2. The Dinshaway incident occurred in a small village near Tanta in the Nile Delta. It was a tragedy that had been caused primarily by British insensitivity and by subsequent misunderstanding on both sides. However, Lord Cromer, Consul-General of Egypt, and the overwhelming majority of the European community perceived the incident to be 'one more symptom of the dangerous xenophobic fanaticism, fanned by nationalists, then sweeping the countryside'. P Mansfield, *The British in Egypt* (New York: Holt, Rinehart, and Winston, 1971), p. 168.
3. Written confession of Shafik Mansur, *History of Secret Societies in Egypt*, 18 June 1925, FO 141/503/6, part 2. A covering letter from Nevile Henderson, Minister Plenipotentiary at Cairo, to Austen Chamberlain, British Foreign Secretary, stated that the 'police are satisfied from the information already in their possession that the substance of Shafik Mansur's written confession – except in so far as he describes his personal share in the various crimes – is accurate'.
4. Noor-Amin I Khan, *Egyptian-Indian Nationalist Collaboration and the British Empire* (New York: Palgrave Macmillan, 2011), p. 33. For a detailed examination of the assassination of Curzon-Wylie, see Khan, pp. 33–40.
5. Ibid., p. 42.
6. For an in-depth examination of Wardani, see Badrawi, *Political Violence*, chapters 2 and 3.
7. Wardani considered Ghali to be a traitor to Egyptian national interests for a number of reasons: his signing of the 1899 Anglo-Egyptian Condominium Agreement which asserted British control over the Sudan; presiding as a Native judge over the Dinshaway trials in 1906 and passing sentences that were perceived as unjustifiably harsh; his support for the renewal of the 1881 Press law that limited the freedom of the Press; and his recent support for the extension of the Suez Canal concession for a further fifty years. Badrawi, *Political Violence*, p. 22.
8. Ibid., p. 56.
9. Ibid., p. 56. Every branch was composed of ten members, one of which was elected as its representative to the 'Delegate's Committee'. The Delegate's Committee was then divided into groups, out of which one person was elected by each group as their representative on the Executive Committee. Alongside the Executive Committee existed the '*Fida'I*' Committee of which Wardani was President. This Committee was composed of three members and was entrusted with the commission of outrages and other acts of violence. Complete secrecy shrouded the membership of the *Fida'I* Committee and they were only acquainted with the President and not the Executive Committee. Badrawi, *Political Violence*, p. 66 and *n*. 81, p. 77.
10. Written confession of Shafik Mansur, FO 141/503/6, part 2, TNA. Two types of bombs were used in these assassination attempts. The Egyptian bombs were tubular in shape and contained a small bottle filled with Picric acid and surrounded with explosive substances. They were very dangerous and liable to explode if inclined one way or other. British-derived bombs were made by workmen who previously manufactured bombs for the military authorities during the war and Mahmud Ismail purchased these from either the British Army or Bedouin tribes. Ismail also purchased firearms from Alexandria that were then concealed at his house or elsewhere. The unstable nature of these bombs was demonstrated by the untimely death of Mustafa Effendi Hamdi while practising bomb throwing in the mountains near Helwan. The bomb exploded in his hand and despite the best efforts of his partner, Ahmed Bey Maher, he died of his injuries.
11. Ibid.

12   On 7 November 1918 a joint Anglo-French declaration stated that the 'Allied war aim in the East was to establish national governments and administrations deriving their authority from the initiative and free choice of the indigenous populations'. Paris, 'British Middle East Policy-Making', p. 775. Woodrow Wilson's pledge of self-determination, the above Anglo-French declaration coupled with the rise in prices during the war were perceived as the primary factors in the development of Egyptian nationalism.

13   For a discussion on the rise of Egyptian nationalism, see Toynbee, *The World after the Peace Conference*; E Kedourie, *The Chatham House Version and Other Middle Eastern Studies* (Hanover, NH and London: University Press of New England, 1984); Monroe, *Britain's Moment in the Middle East, 1914–71*; Darwin, *Britain, Egypt and the Middle East*; Jankowski and Gershoni, *Rethinking Nationalism in the Arab Middle East*; and Jankowski and Gershoni, *Redefining the Egyptian Nation, 1930–45*.

14   The continued attacks upon Egyptian ministers and members of the British community compelled the Cairo authorities to examine the organization of intelligence gathering locally within Egypt and the wider Middle East. Prior to the First World War the two offices that were chiefly concerned with supplying the Residency with political information were the Ministry of the Interior, through the Department of Public Security, and the Director of Sudan Intelligence (also known as the Sudan Agent), whose headquarters were in Cairo. The Public Security Department largely relied on the two city police forces of Cairo and Alexandria, but it was admitted that the Department was probably never strong enough to co-ordinate the work of the police properly and to utilize effectively the other sources of information available. The Director of Sudan Intelligence concentrated to a greater degree on the countries bordering Egypt. Since the war, however, the headquarters had been moved to Khartoum, and the office of the Sudan Agent in Cairo was no longer an intelligence office. During the war, General Staff Intelligence had not only acted as a central controlling authority of the police and other civil authorities in Egypt for intelligence purposes, but was also the control centre in this respect for the whole area covered by the Egyptian Expeditionary Force (EEF). By war's end, and the subsequent retrenchment of staff within the General Staff Intelligence at General Headquarters, nothing had taken its place and therefore no adequate central control organization existed for gathering civilian intelligence. Allenby to Curzon, 26 February 1920, doc 29, in Woodward (ed.), *British Documents of Foreign Affairs*. As a consequence, and to meet the immediate intelligence need within Egypt, Allenby established a temporary section within the Public Security Department which would co-ordinate the work of those local authorities who were charged with the collection of political information and to deal with the movements or activities of a subversive nature within Egypt itself. See C F Ryder, Report on the Special Section, 22 March 1922, FO 141/7993/7, TNA.

15   Account of evidence of Messrs. Wade and Long, 25 November 1924, FO 141/502/2, part 1. Also, *The Daily Mail*, 20 November 1924, P D Mulholland papers, Sudan Archive.

16   Clark Kerr to his mother, 19 November 1924, Lord Inverchapel papers, Bodleian Library, University of Oxford. Also, Frank C Madden, 'Medical Report on the Condition of His Excellency the *Sirdar* Sir Lee Stack', 20 November 1924, FO 141/502/2, part 1.

17   Clark Kerr to his mother, 19 November 1924, Inverchapel papers, Bodleian Library.

18   Allenby to Chamberlain, 19 November 1924, FO 141/502/2, part 1.

19 The Gezira Scheme was an agricultural project in the Sudan to increase the area under irrigation in order to allow greater cultivation of the cotton crop. Of course, any proposal which used Nile waters for vast agricultural projects in the Sudan was of direct concern to Egyptians. The issue of water rights and how it could be used as a nationalist lever amongst the *fellahin* had proved such a concern that Allenby had pledged in late 1919 and early 1920 that the Gezira Scheme would not irrigate any more than 300,000 feddans. (A feddan is a unit of land measurement; one feddan = 1.028 acres or 0.420 hectares). As M Daly points out this was a 'tactical error that was later to hobble the Sudan Government'. Daly, *Empire on the Nile*, p. 299. By placing the expansion of the scheme on his list of demands, Allenby was first extricating himself from this earlier error and, secondly, reminding Egyptians that Britain could starve Egypt of water if necessary.
20 Allenby to Chamberlain, 19 November 1924, FO 141/502/2, part 1. Once Egyptian officers and units had been evacuated, a Sudanese Defence Force would be created at the expense of the Egyptian Treasury. Allenby to Chamberlain, 20 November 1924, ibid.
21 Allenby to Chamberlain, 20 November 1924, FO 141/502/2, part 1.
22 Allenby to Chamberlain, 20 November 1924, FO 141/502/2, part 1. *The Times*' Cairo correspondent, Arthur Sidney Merton, repeated this view of the Wafd. 'The Wafd is, of course, at the root of all the trouble and ought to be dissolved as being an organisation detrimental to society and public security. It was originally founded for the purpose of supporting the national cause, but has degenerated into nothing but an instrument for the advancement of the interests of the members of its Executive Committee and their friends, and its propagandists are dangerous advocates of a policy of action [...]', *The Times* 27 November 1924.
23 Allenby to Chamberlain, 19 November 1924, FO 141/502/2, part 1.
24 R S Grayson argues that the 'Middle East and North Africa were important to Chamberlain and the Foreign Office chiefly in so far as they affected relations with other powers'. R S Grayson in *Austen Chamberlain and the Commitment to Europe. British Foreign Policy, 1924–1929* (London and Portland, OR: Frank Cass, 1997), p. 241. It was believed that 'giving more weight to relations with European than with local countries' was the most effective way of securing vital British interests'. Ibid.
25 Chamberlain to Allenby, 20 November 1924, 61 (24), CAB 23/49.
26 Ibid.
27 Chamberlain to Allenby, 21 November 1924, FO 141/502/2, part 1.
28 Allenby to Chamberlain, 21 November 1924, FO 141/502/2, part 1.
29 Ibid.
30 Ibid.
31 Ibid.
32 J Shepherd, 'A Gentleman at the Foreign Office: Influences Shaping Ramsay MacDonald's Internationalism in 1924', in P Copthorn and J Davis (eds), *The British Labour Party and the Wider World. Domestic Problems, Internationalism and Foreign Policy* (New York: Tauris Academic Studies, 2008), p. 45. This view is echoed in J Shepherd and K Laybourn, *Britain's First Labour Government* (Basingstoke: Palgrave Macmillan, 2006), pp. 152–53.
33 Khartoum to Allenby, 21 November 1924, FO 141/502/2, part 1.
34 *The Times*, 24 November 1924.
35 Foreign Office to Allenby, 22 November 1924, FO 141/502/2, part 1.
36 Chamberlain to Allenby, 22 November 1924, FO 141/502/2, part 1.

37 Ibid. See also, Conference of Ministers, 22 November 1924, CAB 23/49. Indeed, the Colonial Office immediately communicated to the Dominions that Allenby's actions were unilateral 'the demand addressed by Lord Allenby to the Egyptian Government today [22 November] had not been previously authorised by the Cabinet'. Leo Amery to the Dominion Governments, 24 November 1924, FO 141/502/2, part 1.
38 Allenby to FO, 23 November 1924, FO 141/502/2, part 1.
39 Ibid.
40 Clark Kerr to his mother, 21 November 1924, Inverchapel papers, Bodleian Library.
41 Acting Governor-General to Allenby, 22 November 1924, FO 141/502/2, part 1.
42 Zaghlul to Allenby, 23 November 1924, FO 141/502/2, part 1.
43 Ibid.
44 Ibid.
45 Allenby to Chamberlain, 23 November 1924, FO 141/502/2, part 1.
46 Ibid.
47 Chamberlain to Allenby, 24 November 1924, FO 141/502/2, part 1.
48 Ibid.
49 *The Times*, 24 November 1924.
50 Ibid. The Italian newspapers *Messagero* and *Nuovo Presse* pointed out that Britain's action in Egypt was a blow to the League of Nations. Graham to Foreign Office, 26 November 1924, FO 371/10073/10378.
51 *The Times*, 27 December 1924.
52 Ibid.
53 MacDonald's first Labour minority government had been ousted from office after just nine months in the General Election of 29 October 1924. Whilst in office MacDonald held the portfolio of Prime Minister and Foreign Secretary. See R Vickers, *The Labour Party and the World Volume 1 The Evolution of Labour's Foreign Policy 1900–1951* (Manchester: Manchester University Press, 2004), pp. 89–90.
54 *The Times*, 'Mr MacDonald on the Ultimatum', 29 November 1924.
55 Ibid.
56 Minute by Murray, 1 December 1924, FO 371/10046/10793.
57 The 1899 Anglo-Egyptian Condominium Agreement following the Anglo-Egyptian reconquest of the Sudan from Mahdist forces declared that the Khedive of Egypt and the Queen of England would jointly rule the Sudan. Britain's claim to share in the governing and future development of the Sudan was based upon the right of conquest. According to the agreement, the Sudan was defined as the territories south of the 22nd parallel which had either never been evacuated by Egyptian troops or had been previously administered by Egypt and now re-conquered by the Anglo-Egyptian force, or those which be re-conquered by the two government in the future.
58 Minute by Chamberlain, 1 December 1924, FO 371/10046/10793.
59 *The Times*, 4 December 1924.
60 Cabinet Conclusions 63 (240, 24 November 1924, CAB 23/49.
61 The appointment was announced publicly in *The Times* on 26 November 1924.
62 Chamberlain to Allenby, 24 November 1924, AP 2/3/1, Allenby papers, Liddell Hart Centre for Military Archives [hereafter LHCMA], King's College London.
63 D Gillies, *Radical Diplomat: The Life of Archibald Clark Kerr, Lord Inverchapel, 1882–1951* (London: I.B. Tauris, 1999), p. 62.
64 Diary letters, 28 November 1950, fols. 205–237, Ms Eng c. 6583, Sir Walford Selby papers, Bodleian Library.
65 Ibid.

66 Allenby to Chamberlain, 25 November 1924, AP 2/3/2, Allenby papers, LHCMA.
67 On a telegram from Allenby to Chamberlain on 26 November 1924, Clark Kerr noted: 'The second and the right reaction. N Henderson's arrival will be taken to be his supersession'. Inverchapel papers, Bodleian Library.
68 Allenby to Chamberlain, 26 November 1924, AP 2/3/4, Allenby papers, LHCMA.
69 Ibid.
70 Chamberlain to Allenby, 26 November 1924, AP 2/3/5, Allenby papers, LHCMA.
71 Allenby to Chamberlain, 27 November 1924, AP 2/3/9, Allenby papers, LHCMA.
72 Allenby to Chamberlain, 26 November 1924, AP 2/3/7, Allenby papers, LHCMA.
73 Chamberlain to Allenby, 27 November 1924, AP 2/3/8, Allenby papers, LHCMA.
74 Gillies, *Radical Diplomat*, p. 63.
75 Allenby to Chamberlain, 28 November 1924, AP 2/3/10, Allenby papers, LHCMA.
76 Ibid.
77 Ibid.
78 Clause VII referred to the withdrawal of all opposition to the special wishes of the British Government concerning the protection of foreign interests in Egypt.
79 Chamberlain to Allenby, 1 December 1924, AP 2/3/15, Allenby papers, LHCMA.
80 Clark Kerr to his mother, 3 December 1924, Inverchapel papers, Bodleian Library.
81 Henderson to Walford Selby, 6 December 1924, file 24/41, FO 800/264.
82 Ibid.
83 Ibid.
84 Ibid.
85 Henderson to Walford Selby, 6 December 1924, file 24/41, FO 800/264, handwritten annotation on the letter by Henderson.
86 Ibid.
87 Ibid.
88 'We have incurred the severe censure of the Foreign Office for what we did and how we did it and we have met with a certain amount of outside criticism in ill-informed quarters […] I do not wish in any way to escape full responsibility for any of these things. They may not improbably mean the disappearance of Lord A from Egypt and for me a long twilight at some port where thinking and acting and taking risks will be superfluous'. Clark Kerr to his mother, 15 December 1924, Inverchapel papers, Bodleian Library.
89 Allenby to Foreign Office, 24 November 1924, FO 141/501/2, part 1.
90 *The Times*, 25 November 1924.
91 Lord Lloyd, *Egypt since Cromer*, ii (Edinburgh: Macmillan, 1934), p. 99.
92 Chamberlain to Allenby, 24 November 1924, FO 141/502/2, part 1.
93 Allenby to the Foreign Office, 24 November 1924, FO 141/502/2, part 1. The British Government did not feel that Ziwar was strong enough to hold the nationalist forces in check and both Tyrrell and Sir Eyre Crowe, Permanent Under-Secretary at the Foreign Office 1920–25, believed that 'there is an urgent necessity of installing a stronger and more capable High Commissioner at Cairo. Under the present regime we are not in safe hands, and a great crisis may face us any day'. Minute by Crowe, 10 December 1924, FO 371/10059/11165.
94 Allenby to the Foreign Office, 27 November 1924, FO 141/502/2, part 1.
95 Chamberlain to Allenby, 29 November 1924, FO 141/502/2, part 1.
96 Ibid.
97 Allenby to Ziwar Pasha, 30 November 1924, FO 141/502/2, part 1 and Allenby to FO, 30 November 1924, FO 141/502/2, part 1.

98   In a memorandum written by Sir Lee Stack and endorsed by Sir Reginald Wingate, Stack raised the issue of 'readjusting the relations between the Soudan and Egypt on lines whereby Great Britain will gradually take over the part in the Government of the Soudan now played by the Egyptian Government'. Stack, 'Note on the Growth of National Aspirations in the Soudan', 23 February 1919, CAB 1/44. Wingate perceived that 'both Egypt and the Soudan – as well as the British Empire – will gain by loosening the tie which now binds the two countries together'. Wingate to Curzon, 26 March 1919, CAB 1/44.

99   Chamberlain to Allenby, 22 December 1924, AP 2/3/17, Allenby papers, LHCMA.

100   Perhaps Allenby was fortified by the instruction he had received from Sir Eyre Crowe before setting out for Egypt. 'We can't give you any instructions. Do what you think is best and we will back you up. You have a free hand'. Clark Kerr to his mother, 15 December 1924, Inverchapel papers, Bodleian Library.

101   'Together we have done great work – you in Cairo, H.M. Government here. On the great issues there has been no difference between us, and all the world at home and abroad, in spite of minor criticisms, has recognised our unity of purpose and the swiftness and sureness of our action, and has paid tribute to the success we have achieved.

Now once again I appeal to you. Do not, I beg, spoil this great national achievement by insisting that a momentary misunderstanding should be made public or that any failure of immediate comprehension of telegraphic messages, necessarily framed in hast or perhaps less clear to the recipient than they seemed to the sender, shall be made the subject of public controversy and so obscure our real unity of purpose and lessen our national triumph. That would indeed be a tragedy [...]

This letter is my personal appeal to you. I have shown it only the Prime Minister. He wishes me to say that it has his warm approval and that he feels confident that it will not be made in vain'. Chamberlain to Allenby, 22 December 1924, fol. 246, Vol. 114, Stanley Baldwin papers, CUL.

102   For a detailed report on how the assailants were apprehended, see file on the murder of Sir Lee Stack, 'Report of the Cairo Special Branch', February 1925, 1/6, Thomas Russell papers, St Antony's College, Middle East Centre Archive [hereafter MECA], University of Oxford; and G H Hughes, Chief Inspector, to Henderson, 'Murder of the Late *Sirdar*: Execution of Death Sentences', 12 August 1925, FO 141/503/6, part 2. For detailed daily reports of the trial, see '*al-Mokattam*', 1925, 1/8, Russell papers, MECA.

103   List of political crimes committed between 1910 and 1946, 1/10, Russell papers, MECA.

104   Henderson to Chamberlain, 14 August 1925, FO 141/503/6, part 2.

105   Report by Hughes, 'Murder of the Late *Sirdar*', FO 141/503/6, part 2.

106   Chamberlain to Henderson, 5 August 1925, FO 141/503/6, part 2.

107   Graves to Wiggin, Covering note on execution of the *Sirdar*'s murderers compiled by the Cairo City Police, 26 August 1925, FO 141/503/6, part 2.

108   Draft statement on Egypt, 2 December 1924, FO 141/502/2.

109   Ibid.

110   Ibid.

Chapter 6

1. 'A Turco-Egyptian, [Sarwat] was prosecutor in the trial of the assassins of Butros Ghali and a consistent upholder of the rule of law. He was in the Egyptian Cabinet throughout the First World War as Minister of Justice. Until reconciled late in the day, he was no admirer of Zaghlul. A close friend of Adli Yakan, he was Minister of Interior in his 1921 administration, in 1922 and in 1927–28. He was Hizb al Ahrar's prime minister and foreign minister in 1927–28, retiring on account of ill health. He was defeated by Zaghlul in his bid to be Speaker of Parliament in 1925'. C W R Long, *British Pro-Consuls in Egypt 1914–1929. The Challenge of Nationalism* (Oxford: Routledge/Curzon, 2005), p. 232.
2. See J Charmley, *Lord Lloyd and the Decline of the British Empire* (London: Wiedenfeld and Nicolson, 1987), chapters 16–23.
3. Blanche Lloyd's diary, 12 March 1925, George Lloyd's Papers [hereafter GLLD] 28-13, Churchill Archives Centre (CAC), University of Cambridge.
4. Austen Chamberlain to Stanley Baldwin, 29 November 1924, fol. 243, Stanley Baldwin papers, Cambridge University Library [hereafter CUL].
5. Blanche Lloyd's diary, 12 March 1925, GLLD 28-13, CAC.
6. Ibid.
7. 'A real schoolmaster's letter came from Austen, implying that G[eorge] had been impatient and unreasonable and warning him rather pompously against further "solicitations", or indeed action of any kind'. Blanche Lloyd's diary, 21 March 1925, GLLD 28-13, CAC.
8. Blanche Lloyd's diary, 21 March 1925, GLLD 28-13, CAC.
9. Blanche Lloyd's diary, 21 March 1925, GLLD 28-13, CAC, 31 March 1925, GLLD 28-13, CAC.
10. Just prior to the Lloyds' departure, Baldwin awarded George Lloyd a peerage. This pleased both of the Lloyds as it would also 'make George's job in Egypt a good deal easier for all Orientals think extra highly of a Lord and it puts him on a level with Lord Allenby, which is all to the good'. Blanche Lloyd's diary, October 1925, GLLD 28-13, CAC. See also Blanche Lloyd's diary, May 1925, GLLD 28-13, CAC.
11. Blanche Lloyd's diary, October 1925, GLLD 28-13, CAC.
12. Ibid.
13. George Lloyd to Austen Chamberlain, 25 October 1925, GLLD 13-4A, CAC.
14. Ibid.
15. Blanche Lloyd's diary, October 1925, GLLD 28-13, CAC.
16. Lord Lloyd, *Egypt since Cromer*, p. 143.
17. Lloyd to Chamberlain, 25 October 1925, GLLD 13-4A, CAC.
18. Blanche Lloyd to Percy Loraine, 9 November 1925, GLLD 4-34, CAC.
19. The Army Crisis of early 1927 centred upon the desire of a number of Egyptian politicians who wished to increase the size of the Egyptian army, strengthen its armament and transfer the British Inspector-General of the Egyptian Army's duties to the Minister of War. The Foreign Office perceived this to be primarily for the benefit of one political party: the Wafd, and as a challenge to British authority. Question asked in the House of Commons, 1 June 1927, FO 371/12356/1490. For a full discussion of the army crisis and its consequences for Lord Lloyd's relationship with the Foreign Office, see Charmley, *Lord Lloyd and the Decline of the British Empire*, chapter 19.

20 Chamberlain to Lloyd, 28 December 1926, GLLD 13-3, CAC.
21 Chamberlain to Lloyd, 25 January 1927, GLLD 13-3, CAC.
22 Tyrrell to Lloyd, 23 February 1927, GLLD 13-5, CAC. The Chinese Crisis centred on the Chinese Civil War which threatened foreign interests in China and became particularly acute between 1927 and 1929. Foreign interests had developed within China during the nineteenth century when the European colonial powers, Japan and the United States gradually acquired treaty ports and 'concessions', with the right to control customs revenues. These foreign concessions, such as special privileges, the establishment of law courts and some local administration, were obvious targets for criticisms and demonstrations by the nationalists. British concessions attracted the fiercest criticism since Britain was the dominant Power, and nationalists believed that if Britain was ousted, other foreigners would also have to withdraw. See Grayson, *Austen Chamberlain* chapter 7; and M Atkins, *Informal Empire in Crisis: British Diplomacy and the Chinese Customs Succession, 1927-1929* (Ithaca, NY: Cornell East Asia Program[me], 1995).
23 The relationship between Lloyd and the Foreign Office became increasingly strained and this can be seen throughout the army crisis. See FO 371/12358/1955.
24 Charmley, *Lord Lloyd and the Decline of the British Empire*, p. 227.
25 Ibid., pp. 227-28.
26 Austen Chamberlain to Ida Chamberlain, 1 August 1927, AC 5/1/426, Austen Chamberlain papers, University of Birmingham Special Collections. See also memorandum by Chamberlain, 13 July 1927, FO 371/12358/1934. In the conversation between Sarwat and Chamberlain, Sarwat admitted the 'necessary connection between our two countries [Britain and Egypt] and of the true interests of Egypt. There had been a great change in Egyptian opinion. The Egyptian parliament and public now recognised [as opposed to 1924] that there must be friendly collaboration between us and that the aid of Great Britain was necessary to Egypt. They were well aware of the dangers which would menace them from other quarters of they stood alone'. Memorandum by Chamberlain, 13 July 1927, FO 371/12358/1934.
27 Lloyd had even been encouraged by Tyrrell to 'give yourself, a period of thorough rest somewhere or other where the name of Egypt does not figure in the programme'. Tyrrell to Lloyd, 16 June 1927, GLLD 13-5, CAC.
28 See memorandum by Walford Selby, 13 July 1927, FO 371/12358/1943.
29 Cabinet Conclusions 4 (27), 20 July 1927, CAB 23/25. For a copy of the Egyptian draft treaty, see FO 371/12358/1985.
30 Ibid.
31 This Egyptian Committee would comprise: Chamberlain in the chair; the Lord Privy Seal, the Marquess of Salisbury; the Chancellor of the Exchequer, Winston Churchill; the Home Secretary, Sir William Joynson-Hicks; the Secretary of State for War, Sir Laming Worthington Evans; the Secretary of State for India, the Earl of Birkenhead; the Secretary of State for Air, Sir Samuel Hoare; the First Lord of the Admiralty, W Bridgeman; the Attorney-General, Sir Douglas Hogg ad Sir Maurice Hankey as Secretary. See FO 371/12358/2062, 26 July 1927 which contains in parallel columns Sarwat's draft treaty and the first alternative draft by the Foreign Office. The latter was considered the Egyptian Committee of the Cabinet and their modifications form the third column.
32 For a copy of the alternative Foreign Office draft treaty, see also FO 371/12358/2001. The Foreign Office in drafting this treaty followed 'as closely as practicable' the lines

of Sarwat's draft, whilst, at the same time, believing they had included 'safeguards necessary to us'. The result was a comprehensive and detailed document although not so over optimistic as to believe that Sarwat would accept all of it. Nevile Henderson, Acting High Commissioner, reported that, from the local point of view, some agreement was 'very desirable', and suggested that an ideal solution might be a 'Treaty of Alliance in one paragraph'. Mark Patrick of the Foreign Office noted that 'there is, I think, considerable force in this generalisation. If His Majesty's Government and Sarwat Pasha can agree upon some text, though it might be too general in character to be adequate from our point of view, we should have gained a good deal, even though negotiations subsequently broke down in the course of attempting to translate generalities into practical detail. The existence and terms of such a text would certainly become public in Egypt in [the] course of time, and would probably produce a sharp division of opinion, giving the moderates in the Wafd something over which to resist the extremists [...] The existence of some agreement in principle would make our task in settling details easier'. Minute by Patrick, 22 July 1927, FO 371/12358/2017.
33 Cabinet Conclusions 45 (27), 28 July 1927, CAB 23/55.
34 Ibid.
35 Ibid.
36 Austen Chamberlain to Ida Chamberlain, 1 August 1927, AC 5/1/426, Birmingham University. For a history of the China situation in 1927, see J F Fairbank and A Feuerwerker, *The Cambridge History of China. xiii Republican China, 1912–1949*, part 2 (Cambridge: Cambridge University Press, 1986).
37 Austen Chamberlain to Ida Chamberlain, 1 August 1927, AC 5/1/426, Birmingham University.
38 Lord Lloyd, *Egypt since Cromer*, p. 229.
39 Cabinet Conclusions 49 (27), 25 August 1927, CAB 23/55.
40 N Henderson to AC, 27 August 1927, FO 371/12359/2450. This despatch was well received within the Foreign Office.
41 Ibid.
42 Ibid.
43 Ibid.
44 Ibid.
45 Henderson to Chamberlain, 3 September 1927, FO 371/12359/2518.
46 Memorandum by Patrick, 1 October 1927, in 'Papers on the projected Anglo-Egyptian Treaty of Alliance', FP 371/12359/2777.
47 Henderson to Chamberlain, 24 September 1927, FO 371/12359/2715.
48 Ibid.
49 Note by Patrick, 27 September 1927, FO 371/12359/2660.
50 Henderson to Chamberlain, 30 September 1927, doc 62, *BDFA, Series G Africa*, ix, p. 175.
51 Minute by Murray, 5 October 1927, FO 371/12359/2730.
52 Ibid.
53 Minute by Chamberlain, 10 October 1927, FO 371/12359/2730.
54 Minute by Murray, 14 September 1927, FO 371/12359/2758.
55 Henderson to Chamberlain, 14 October 1927, FO 371/12360/2934.
56 Ibid.
57 For example, see Henderson to Chamberlain, 22 October 1927, FO 371/12360/3009.
58 Cabinet Conclusions 52 (27), 26 October 1927, CAB 23/55.

59 Cabinet Conclusions 52 (27), 2 November 1927, CAB 23/55.
60 Ibid.
61 Memorandum by Selby, undated, MS Eng c. 6581, fols. 159–175, Selby papers, Bodleian Library.
62 Ibid.
63 Ibid.
64 Ibid.
65 Lord Lloyd, *Egypt since Cromer*, pp. 232–33.
66 Report of COS Sub-Committee, 'Treaty of Alliance between Great Britain and Egypt', CID 842-B, 10 November 1927, CAB 4/17.
67 See, for example, comments by C Hurst, Mr Malkin and Mr Beckett on the memorandum by the Chief of Naval Staff, 11 November 1927, FO 371/12360/3175.
68 Cabinet Conclusions 55 (27), 11 November 1927, CAB 23/55.
69 Ibid.
70 Ibid.
71 Ibid.
72 Ibid.
73 Chamberlain to Lloyd, 17 November 1927, FO 371/12361/3257.
74 Lloyd to Chamberlain, 4 December 1927, GLLD 13-4B, CAC; and minutes by Murray, 6 December 1927, FO 371/12362/3473.
75 Lloyd to Chamberlain, 4 December 1927, GLLD 13-4B, CAC.
76 Ibid.
77 Ibid.
78 Lloyd to Chamberlain, 30 November 1927, FO 371/12362/3517.
79 Lloyd to Chamberlain, 11 December 1927, GLLD 13-4B, CAC.
80 Ibid.
81 Chamberlain to Lloyd, 8 December 1927, GLLD 13-3, CAC.
82 Lloyd to Chamberlain, 10 December 1927, doc 113, *BDFA, Series G Africa*, ix, p. 299.
83 Ibid., pp. 300–01.
84 Lloyd to Chamberlain, 17 December 1927, FO 371/12362/3625.
85 Sarwat claimed that King Fuad concurred, although Lloyd later discovered that the King was actually 'only too willing for the Treaty to be signed any day and that he had expressed no wish for delay on account of the Afghan visit'. Lloyd to Chamberlain, 18 December 1927, GLLD 13-4B, CAC.
86 Tyrrell to Chamberlain, 12 December 1927, FO 371/12362/3545.
87 Ibid.
88 Ibid.
89 Chamberlain to Lloyd, 15 December 1927, GLLD 13-3, CAC.
90 Chamberlain to Lloyd, 5 January 1928, FO 371/13114/78.
91 Lloyd to Chamberlain, 15 January 1928, GLLD 13-4B, CAC.
92 The Foreign Office suggested indirect methods of aiding Sarwat. For example, Murray suggested that if Sarwat carried out his threat of resignation, British support of any new government would be subject to its accepting the treaty. By playing arbiter between Egyptian politics and the King, it was hoped that this might discourage the disruptive activities of some of Sarwat's colleagues, such as Mohammed Mahmoud. Foreign Office to Lloyd, 11 January 1928, FO 371/13114/65.
93 Minute by Murray, 11 January 1928, FO 371/13114/65.
94 Lloyd to Chamberlain, 15 January 1928, GLLD 13-4B, CAC.
95 Ibid.

96   Minute by Chamberlain, 13 January 1928, FO 371/13114/169.
97   Lloyd to Chamberlain, 22 January 1928, GLLD 13-4B, CAC.
98   Chamberlain to Lloyd, 23 January 1928, FO 371/13114/247.
99   Ibid.
100 Ibid.
101 Lloyd to Chamberlain, 22 January 1928, GLLD 13-4B, CAC.
102 Lloyd to Chamberlain, 28 January 1928, GLLD 13-4B, CAC.
103 Ibid.
104 Ibid.
105 Ibid.
106 Lloyd to Chamberlain, 6 February 1928, GLLD 13-4B, CAC.
107 Lloyd to Chamberlain, 18 February 1928, GLLD 13-4B, CAC.
108 Ibid.
109 Chamberlain to Lloyd, 20 February 1928, GLLD 13-4B, CAC.
110 Lloyd to Chamberlain, 27 February 1928, doc 4, *BDFA, Series G Africa*, x, p. 87.
111 Ibid., p. 88.
112 Lloyd to Chamberlain, 4 March 1928, GLLD 13-4C, CAC.
113 Ibid.
114 Chamberlain to Lloyd, 19 March 1928, GLLD 13-3, CAC.
115 Blanche Lloyd's diary, 20 May 1928, GLLD 28-13, CAC. As Austen Chamberlain wrote to William Tyrrell on 19 September 1927 'I am much more of an "European" than most of my countrymen, for I have a clearer perception than they of the inextricable way in which our interests are bound up with every possibility of the European situation'. Grayson, *Austen Chamberlain*, p. xi.
116 Charmley, *Lord Lloyd and the Decline of the British Empire*, p. 116.
117 It was reported to Chamberlain by Paterno (the Italian Minister in Egypt) that Lloyd had expressed 'delight' at the breaking off of the Anglo-Egyptian negotiations and believed that British public opinion would now sanction a stronger policy, which he had been advocating for the past year. A member of the Foreign Office also reported a conversation between Lloyd and an American journalist, Karl von Wiegand, in which Lloyd emphasized his objections to the Anglo-Egyptian treaty, stating: 'I am for force both here and in India'. Lloyd denied the accounts of both episodes but received a severe ticking off from Chamberlain. Chamberlain to Lloyd, 28 March 1928, GLLD 13-3, CAC. This was not the first time that the Foreign Office had suspected Lloyd of undermining British policy through third parties. Murray learnt from Gerald Delaney, Reuters correspondent in Egypt, that Lloyd had visited both the *Morning Post* and *Daily Mail* to warn them that a crash was coming in Egypt and that he wanted them to prepare the ground for strong action by suitable articles, and support that action when taken. The article which appeared to bear out this story appeared on 30 September 1927. Again, the Foreign Office learned that Lloyd had dined with Howell Arthur Gwynne, editor of the *Morning Post* on 24 October 1927. The following day a *Morning Post* correspondent warned the Foreign Office that a 'drastic article' on Egypt was about to appear. It duly did so on 26 October leaving Tyrrell to comment 'it is a bad business'. Minute by Tyrrell, 27 October 1927, FO 371/12360/2956.
118 See D Carlton, *MacDonald versus Henderson. The Foreign Policy of the Second Labour Government* (Edinburgh: Macmillan Press, 1970); and M A Hamilton, *Arthur Henderson. A Biography* (Surrey: William Heinemann, 1938).
119 Hoare to Henderson, 17 May 1930, FO 371/14614/1747.

Chapter 7

1. Chamberlain to Lloyd, 25 June 1929, George Lloyd papers (hereafter GLLD) 17-12, Churchill Archives Centre (hereafter CAC), University of Cambridge.
2. Gordon Waterfield, *Professional Diplomat. Sir Percy Loraine of Kirkdale, 1880-1961* (London: John Murray, 1973), p. 148.
3. Arthur Henderson to Lloyd, 3 July 1929, GLLD 17-12, CAC.
4. Ibid.
5. Ibid.
6. Lord Lloyd, *Egypt since Cromer*, p. 309.
7. M Gilbert, *Winston Churchill, v 1922-1939* (London: Heinemann, 1976), p. 337.
8. R C Self (ed.), *The Austen Chamberlain Diary Letters. The Correspondence of Sir Austen Chamberlain with His Sisters Hilda and Ida, 1916-1937* (Cambridge: Cambridge University Press, 1995), p. 333. See also FO 371/1384/1694. For a record of the debate in the House of Commons, see FO 371/13844/2155.
9. H Dalton, *Call Back Yesterday. Memoirs 1887-1931* (London: Frederick Muller, 1953), pp. 225-26. Herbert Samuel, former Home Secretary (1916) and High Commissioner of Palestine (1920-1925) and leader of the Liberal party (1931-1935).
10. Austen Chamberlain to Ida Chamberlain, 1 August 1929, AC 5/1/479, University of Birmingham.
11. J Charmley, *Lord Lloyd and the Decline of the British Empire* (London: Weidenfeld and Nicolson, 1987), p. 156.
12. For example, see Delaney to Selby, 10 January 1929, MS Eng c 6581, fols. 317-321; and C A G MacKintosh to Selby, 14 February 1929, fols. 334-336, Selby papers, Bodleian Library, University of Oxford.
13. Henderson to MacDonald, 31 July 1929, PRO 30/69/272, MacDonald papers.
14. Waterfield, *Professional Diplomat*, p. 149.
15. Ibid., pp. 149-50.
16. 'Memorandum on Egypt', CP 181 (29), 13 June 1929, FO 1011/146, Percy Loraine papers.
17. Ibid.
18. Ibid.
19. Ibid.
20. MacDonald to Henderson, 27 July 1930, PRO 30/69/272. See also Dalton, *Call Back*, p. 226. Dalton recalled that Henderson did not appreciate MacDonald's forays into the Foreign Secretary's domain. 'If he [Henderson] is to be pulled about much more, he will suggest that J. R. M. should become Foreign Secretary himself, and be done with it'. Ibid., p. 227. Concern was also raised at Buckingham Palace where the King believed that Lloyd had been badly treated and that the Foreign Office had not kept the King fully informed of the treaty discussions between the British and Mahmoud. Henderson felt that the Palace and MacDonald appeared to be echoing one another and that it was 'difficult to fight such a combination'. Henderson confided to Dalton that he 'knows he's unpopular at the Palace, but that doesn't worry him. J.R.M., no doubt, is disowning him behind his back'. Ibid.
21. Minute by Murray, 25 June 1929, FO 371/13843/1897.
22. MacDonald to Henderson, 27 July 1929, PRO 30/69/272, MacDonald papers.
23. Ibid.

24 Waterfield, *Professional Diplomat*, p. 151.
25 Hoare to Henderson, 2 August 1929, FO 1011/146, Loraine papers. This was not the first time that Hoare had voiced misgivings to the Foreign Office. However, Murray was convinced that 'we are right, and, indeed, we have no choice but to go ahead with Mahmoud, and above all, to go ahead quickly. The day the treaty is published as having been initialled by His Majesty's Government the bottom is knocked out of Wafd propaganda – what better terms have they to offer? Who is going to give them better terms? Not a Labour Government who have said their last word and certainly not a Conservative Government.

If the treaty crashes it will be because the King, the Wafd and "constitutional fanatics" in this country have killed it – how could we go slow and give Mahmoud "steady support" against all these forces?

I don't say the treaty will be ratified by an Egyptian parliament at the first off: but with wise and sympathetic help assured by the Residency Mahmoud and the amorphous mass of moderate opinion who really want a fair settlement, should in the end prevail'. Murray to Hoare, 29 July 1929, FO 371/13844/2163.
26 Hoare to Henderson, 2 August 1929, FO 1011/146, Loraine papers.
27 Waterfield, *Professional Diplomat*, p. 152.
28 Minute by L B Grafftey-Smith, 'The Treaty and the Elections', 7 August 1929, FO 371/13845/2373.
29 Ibid.
30 It was noted: 'It is a delightful scheme with a simple unaffected brutality that is almost attractive. I suppose that it would have been quite impossible to work the election quite like this whatever the attitude of HMG'. Foreign Office minute, 21 August 1929, FO 371/13845/2373.
31 Lindsay to Hoare, 25 August 1929, FO 371/13845/2388.
32 Waterfield, *Professional Diplomat*, p. 154. For a record of the conversation between Makram Ebeid and Dalton see FO 371/13845/2293.
33 MacDonald to Lindsay, September 1929, PRO 30/69/272, Ramsay MacDonald papers.
34 Lindsay to Dalton, 14 August 1929, FO 371/13845/2303.
35 Dalton to Loraine, 22 October 1929, FO 1011/144, Loraine papers.
36 Dalton, *Call Back*, p. 229. Lindsay had been appointed Permanent Under-Secretary of State in July 1928 by Chamberlain. However, by March 1930 Lindsay was 'relieved to be allowed' to move to Washington as Ambassador to the United States since his relations with the new Labour Government 'quickly soured, chiefly over policy relating to European security'. B J C McKercher, 'Lindsay, Sir Ronald Charles (1877–1945)', in *Oxford Dictionary of National Biography* (Oxford University Press, September 2004); online edition, January 2008.
37 Dalton to Loraine, 22 October 1929, FO 1011/144, Loraine papers. Dalton commented: 'What I had said was true. And no Treaty without the Wafd's signature was worth a damn'. Dalton, *Call Back*, p. 229.
38 Lindsay to Dalton, 14 August 1929, FO 371/13845/2303.
39 Loraine to Henderson, 4 September 1929, FO 371/13846/2508.
40 MacDonald to Lindsay, 4 September 1929, PRO 30/69/272, MacDonald papers.
41 'Anglo-Egyptian Treaty', 15 July 1929, CID 954-B, July 1929, CAB 4/18.
42 Ibid.
43 Ibid.

44 This proposal caused MacDonald and the King much consternation. MacDonald's concerns were eased only by Sir John Maffey's, Governor-General of the Sudan, support of the draft treaty. Dalton commented: 'It is sardonic that the FO officials should be the objects of attack and abuse now, and that on Egypt they should be to the left of J R M'. Dalton, *Call Back*, p. 227.
45 Henderson to MacDonald, 30 July 1929, PRO 30/69/272, MacDonald papers.
46 Maffey to Murray, 29 July 1929, PRO 30/69/272, MacDonald papers.
47 Henderson to MacDonald, 30 July 1929, PRO 30/69/272, MacDonald papers.
48 Maffey to Murray, 29 July 1929, PRO 30/69/272, MacDonald papers.
49 Ibid.
50 'Anglo-Egyptian Treaty', 15 July 1929, CID 954-B, July 1929, CAB 4/18.
51 Ibid.
52 Memorandum by CIGS, 'Anglo-Egyptian Treaty', CID 954-B, 18 July 1929. The exclusion of the Chiefs of Staff prior to discussions with Mahmoud caused Dalton to complain: 'It is clear that not only Lloyd and Winston, but Admirals and Generals are in the habit of running to the Palace behind the backs of Ministers'. Dalton, *Call Back*, p. 227. This is hardly surprising since the Chiefs of Staff realized their views would receive a sympathetic hearing.
53 Memorandum by CIGS, 'Anglo-Egyptian Treaty', CID 954-B, 18 July 1929, CAB 4/18.
54 Ibid.
55 Loraine to Arthur Henderson, 4 September 1929, FO 371/13846/2508.
56 Murray minuted: 'Mahmoud is behaving even better than we could have expected [...] the Wafd under the influence of Nahas and Nokrashi are displaying characteristic inability to take the long view or to subordinate immediate personal ambition to the welfare of the country'. Minute by Murray, 6 September 1929, FO 371/13846/2511.
57 Loraine to Arthur Henderson, 4 September 1929, FO 371/13846/2511.
58 Lindsay to Loraine, 6 September 1929, FO 371/13846/2511.
59 Loraine to Arthur Henderson, 12 September 1929, FO 371/13847/2572.
60 Loraine to Arthur Henderson, 12 September 1929, FO 371/13847/2578.
61 Minute by Murray, 13 September 1929, FO 371/13847/2577.
62 Loraine to Arthur Henderson, 12 September 1929, FO 371/13847/2578.
63 Murray to Loraine, 11 September 1929, FO 1011/144, Loraine papers.
64 Loraine to Arthur Henderson, 13 September 1929, FO 371/13847/2596.
65 Loraine to his wife, 29 September 1929, MS Eng d. 3239, Bodleian Library, University of Oxford.
66 Waterfield, *Professional Diplomat*, p. 158.
67 Murray to Loraine, 11 September 1929, FO 1011/144, Loraine papers.
68 Loraine to his wife, 29 September 1929, MS Eng d. 3239, Bodleian Library, University of Oxford.
69 For example, Loraine recommended sustaining Mahmoud rather than allowing the Wafd into power, whereas London was still advocating the idea of an interim Cabinet to conduct elections.
70 MacDonald to Lindsay, 13 September 1929, PRO 30/69/272, MacDonald papers.
71 MacDonald to Lindsay, no date, PRO 30/69/272, MacDonald papers.
72 Murray to Loraine, 19 September 1929, FO 1011/144, Loraine papers.
73 Rex Hoare, 'Analysis and criticism of FO telegram No 278', FO 1011/144, Loraine papers.
74 Ibid.

75 Loraine to Lindsay, 20 September 1929, FO 1011/144, Loraine papers.
76 Ibid.
77 Ibid.
78 Murray to Loraine, 26 September 1929, FO 1011/144, Loraine papers. 'Uncle A' refers to Henderson. Lancelot Oliphant was appointed Assistant Under-Secretary of State in April 1929, after being Acting Assistant Under-Secretary of State since February 1928. Loraine, in a letter to his wife, added: 'the main lines are a Cabinet policy and so Ronald Lindsay is somewhat out of his depth for dealing with the show without reference to higher authority'. Loraine to his wife, 21 September 1929, MS Eng d. 3239, Loraine papers, Bodleian Library.
79 Murray to Loraine, 26 September 1929, FO 1011/144, Loraine papers.
80 Murray to Loraine, 2 October 1929, FO 1011/144, Loraine papers.
81 Ibid.
82 Loraine to Murray, 28 September 1929, FO 1011/144, Loraine papers.
83 Arthur Henderson to Loraine, 25 September 1929, FO 371/13847/2687.
84 Ibid. The Foreign Office agreed that Mahmoud 'is certainly quitting the stage like a sportsman'. FO 371/13848/2762.
85 The Knight Grand Cross.
86 Loraine to Murray, 28 September 1929, FO 1011/144, Loraine papers.
87 Loraine to Murray, 12 October 1929, FO 1011/144, Loraine papers.
88 Arthur Henderson to Loraine, 3 October 1929, FO 371/13848/2757.
89 Loraine to Arthur Henderson, 5 October 1929, FO 371/13848/2795.
90 Ibid. Nahas's attitude was not unexpected by the Foreign Office. 'The rather wooden and uncompromising attitude of Nahas is characteristic of the Wafd and is what makes it so difficult to do business with them'. Minute by Murray, 7 October 1929.
91 Murray to Loraine, 10 October 1929, FO 1011/144, Loraine papers.
92 Waterfield, *Professional Diplomat*, p. 174.
93 Ibid., p. 175.
94 Loraine to Arthur Henderson, 21 January 1930, FO 371/14605/246.
95 Arthur Henderson to Loraine, 27 January 1930, FO 371/14605/246.
96 Ibid.
97 Loraine to Arthur Henderson, 30 January 1930, FO 371/14606/353.
98 Loraine to Arthur Henderson, 30 January 1930, FO 371/14606/354.
99 Ibid.
100 Loraine to Arthur Henderson, 30 January 1930, FO 371/14606/361.
101 Loraine to Arthur Henderson, 2 February 1930, FO 141/623/5. The Foreign Office whole-heartedly supported Loraine. Furthermore, Murray minuted: 'From whatever angle we view the position I believe that the policy we have been pursuing is the right one and the fact that the Wafd, now that they are in power, are ready and anxious to negotiate as soon as possible is at least a healthy sign'. Minute by Murray, 3 February 1930, FO 371/14606/369.
102 Loraine to Arthur Henderson, 8 February 1930, FO 141/623/5.
103 Loraine to his wife, 27 March 1930, MS Eng d. 3239, Bodleian Library, University of Oxford.
104 Ibid.
105 Ibid.
106 Loraine to his wife, 2 April 1930, MS Eng d. 3239, Bodleian Library, University of Oxford.

107 Loraine to his wife, 9 April 1930, MS Eng d. 3239, Bodleian Library, University of Oxford.
108 Waterfield, *Professional Diplomat*, pp. 177–78.
109 Loraine to his wife, 9 April 1930, MS Eng d. 3239, Bodleian Library, University of Oxford.
110 Waterfield, *Professional Diplomat*, p. 178.
111 Henderson to Loraine, 22 February 1930, FO 141/623/5.
112 Loraine to his wife, 17 April 1930, MS Eng d. 3239, Bodleian Library, University of Oxford.
113 Loraine to his wife, 23 April 1930, MS Eng d. 3239, Bodleian Library, University of Oxford.
114 Loraine to his wife, 11 May 1930, MS Eng d. 3239, Bodleian Library, University of Oxford.
115 Ibid.
116 'Memorandum respecting the Egyptian Press, May 9 to 15 1930', doc 155, Woodward (ed.), *British Documents of Foreign Affairs*, p. 382.
117 'Memorandum respecting the Egyptian Press, May 9 to 15 1930', doc 155, *BDFA, Series G Africa*, xii, p. 382.
118 Hoare to Henderson, 17 May 1930, doc 156, *BDFA, Series G Africa*, xii, p. 385.
119 Ibid., p. 385.
120 Waterfield, *Professional Diplomat*, p. 181.
121 Hoare to Henderson, 17 May 1930, FO 371/14614/1747.
122 Waterfield, *Professional Diplomat*, p. 181. Nokrashi was perceived as 'administratively a good Minister, but politically as intransigent as ever'. Ghali was considered to possess an inclination to greater moderation. 'Extremely intelligent. Not so keenly interested in politics as he might be if he had not so many cultural interests, and rather more anti-English than he would be were it not for the strong influence of his [French] wife in that direction'. Report to the Foreign Office, 'Leading Personalities in Egypt', 1 January 1931, doc 1, *BDFA, Series G Africa*, xiii, pp. 14 and 31.
123 Waterfield, *Professional Diplomat*, p. 182.
124 Loraine to Henderson, 2 June 1930, doc 1, *BDFA, Series G Africa*, xi, p. 41.
125 Hoare to Henderson, 17 May 1930, FO 371/14614/1747.
126 Note by MacDonald, 9 June 1930, PRO 30/69/272, MacDonald papers.
127 Foreign Office to MacDonald, 12 June 1930, PRO 30/69/272, MacDonald papers.
128 Loraine to Henderson, 18 June 1930, doc 13, *BDFA, Series G Africa*, xi, p. 8.
129 Waterfield, *Professional Diplomat*, p. 183.
130 Report to the Foreign Office, 'Leading Personalities in Egypt', 1 January 1931, doc 1, *BDFA, Series G Africa*, xiii, p. 41.
131 Foreign Policy Association Information Service, 'Egypt: A Decade of Political Development', 7 January 1931, FO 371/15402/250. This article was noted by Foreign Office officials, including Walford Selby, as an accurate and comprehensive review of the period.
132 Loraine to Henderson, 27 June 1930, doc 83, *BDFA, Series G Africa*, xi, p. 106.
133 Report to the Foreign Office, 'Leading Personalities in Egypt', 1 January 1931, doc 1, *BDFA, Series G Africa*, xiii, p. 41.
134 M Deeb, *Party Politics in Egypt: The Wafd & Its Rivals, 1919–1939* (Essex: St Antony's Middle East Monographs, 1979), p. 238.
135 Henderson to Loraine, 24 June 1930, doc 22, *BDFA, Series G Africa*, xi, p. 13.

136 Loraine to his wife, 29 June 1930, MS. Eng d. 3239, Bodleian Library, University of Oxford.
137 Loraine to Henderson, 27 June 1930, doc 24, *BDFA, Series G Africa*, xi, p. 17.
138 Ibid., p. 17.
139 Ibid., p. 17.
140 Ibid., p. 18.
141 Murray, 'Memorandum on the Political Situation in Egypt', 5 July 1930, doc 82, *BDFA, Series G Africa*, xi, p. 106.
142 Ibid., p. 106. On King Fuad, Murray noted that 'unreliable and untruthful though he is, and despite the fact that in all his thirteen years on the throne he has been a liability rather than an asset to us, […] his schemes do not involve the elimination but rather the retention of British influence'.
143 Ibid., p. 106.
144 Loraine to his wife, 11 July 1930, MS. Eng d. 3239, Bodleian Library, University of Oxford. See also Loraine to Henderson, 7 July 1930, doc 87 and Loraine to Henderson, 8 July 1930, doc 88, *BDFA, Series G Africa*, xi, pp. 111–13.
145 Loraine to his wife, 11 July 1930, MS. Eng d. 3239, Bodleian Library, University of Oxford.
146 Henderson to Loraine, 15 July 1930, doc 96, *BDFA, Series G Africa*, xi, p. 119.
147 Ibid., p. 119.
148 *Hansard*, HC Deb 16 July 1930, Vol. 241 cc1284-6.
149 Loraine to his wife, 18 July 1930, MS. Eng d. 3239, Bodleian Library, University of Oxford.
150 Loraine to Henderson, 17 July 1930, doc 101, *BDFA, Series G Africa*, xi, p. 121.
151 Loraine to Henderson, 18 July 1930, doc 102, *BDFA Series G Africa*, xi, pp. 122–23.
152 Loraine to Henderson, 25 July 1930, doc 116, *BDFA Series G Africa*, xi, p. 135.
153 Minute by Murray, 28 July 1930, FO 371/14618/2519.
154 Loraine to his wife, 22 July 1930, MS. Eng d. 3239, Bodleian Library, University of Oxford.
155 Loraine to his wife, 30 July 1930, MS. Eng d. 3239, Bodleian Library, University of Oxford.
156 *Hansard*, HC Deb 29 July 1930, Vol. 242 cc. 330–412. In preparing a brief for MacDonald Murray noted that 'If the opposition force a debate it cannot be helped but if ever there was an occasion when silence is golden it is now'. Murray to Vansittart, 25 July 1930, FO 371/14618/2589. Dalton agreed. 'A debate at this stage is most unfortunate and unwise, and will handicap a policy that up to date has gone well and entirely justified itself. We must stick to our neutrality'. Minute by Dalton, 26 July 1930, FO 371/14618/2589.
157 *Hansard*, HC Deb 29 July 1930, Vol. 242 cc. 330–412.
158 Loraine to his wife, 1 August 1930, MS. Eng d. 3239, Bodleian Library, University of Oxford.
159 *Hansard*, HC Deb 29 July 1930, Vol. 242 cc. 330–412.
160 Ibid.
161 Ibid.
162 Loraine to his wife, 1 August 1930, MS. Eng d. 3239, Bodleian Library, University of Oxford.
163 *Hansard*, HC Deb 29 July 1930 col. 242 cc. 330–412.
164 Loraine to his wife, 1 August 1930, MS. Eng d. 3239, Bodleian Library, University of Oxford.

165 Minute by Murray, 30 July 1930, FO 371/14618/2545.
166 Minute by Dalton, 30 July 1930, FO 371/14618/2545.
167 Loraine to Murray, 22 August 1930, FO 371/14619/2914.
168 Minute by Murray, 30 August 1930, FO 371/14619/2914. See also memorandum of a conversation between Henderson and Loraine, 28 August 1930, FO 371/14621/3356.
169 Loraine to Henderson, 15 August 1930, doc 127, *BDFA, Series G Africa*, xi, p. 151.
170 Minute by Dalton, 3 January 1931, FO 371/14623/4150.
171 Memorandum by Murray, 'Egypt Revisited: January and February 1931', 20 February 1931, FO 371/15403/700.
172 Memorandum by Murray, 'Egypt Revisited: January and February 1931', 20 February 1931, FO 371/15403/700.
173 Henderson to Loraine, 27 March 1931, No. 296, FO 371/15403/851.
174 Minute by Murray, 8 May 1931, FO 371/15404/1448.
175 Henderson to Murray, 11 May 1931, doc 31, *BDFA, Series G Africa, xiii*, p. 94.
176 Minute by W M B Mack, 12 May 1931, FO 371/15404/1485.
177 Minute by Murray, 12 May 1931, FO 371/15404/1485.
178 Minute by Mack, 2 June 1931, FO 371/15405/1750.
179 Loraine to Henderson, 5 June 1931, No. 238, FO 371/154005/1819.
180 Henderson to Loraine, 9 June 1931, No. 169, FO 371/15405/1819.
181 Loraine to his wife, 27 June 1931, MS. Eng d. 3239, Bodleian Library, University of Oxford.
182 Vickers, *The Labour Party and the World Vol I*, p. 92.

Conclusion

1 Minute by Graham, 3 March 1917, FO 371/3722/173083.
2 Wingate to Hardinge, 14 November 1918, 237/10/8–10, Wingate papers, Sudan Archives, University of Durham [hereafter SAD].
3 J Ferris, 'The British Empire vs. The Hidden Hand: British Intelligence and Strategy and "The CUP-Jew-German-Bolshevik combination," 1918–1924', in K Neilson and G Kennedy (eds), *The British Way in Warfare: power and the international system, 1856–1856: Essays in honour of David French* (Surrey: Ashgate, 2010), pp. 338–40.
4 'Memorandum on the position in the Sudan', 8 November 1924, FO 371/10054/9843.
5 Ibid.
6 N Henderson, 'Notes on a visit to the Sudan, January 10–25 1925', 5 February 1924, doc 76, Woodward (ed.), *British Documents of Foreign Affairs*, vii, pp. 114–21.
7 Ibid., pp. 120–21.
8 'Report on the Political Agitation in the Sudan', doc 126, *BDFA, Series G Africa*, vii, p. 293.
9 K Jeffery, *MI6: The History of the Secret Intelligence Service, 1909–1949* (London: Bloomsbury, 2010), pp. 206–07.
10 Ferris, 'British Empire vs. The Hidden Hand', p. 346.

Bibliography

Unpublished Primary Sources

The National Archives (TNA), Kew, London:

Admiralty	ADM 1	Admiralty Secretariat Papers
	ADM 116	Admiralty Secretariat Papers
Air Ministry	AIR 1	Air Historical Branch Records: Series I
	AIR 5	Air Historical Branch Records: Series II
	AIR 9	Director of Plans, 1914–1939
	AIR 20	Papers accumulated by the Air Historical Branch
	AIR 23	Royal Air Force Overseas Commands: Reports and Correspondence
Cabinet Office	CAB 1	Cabinet Office: Miscellaneous Records
	CAB 2	Committee of Imperial Defence Minutes
	CAB 4	Committee of Imperial Defence Memoranda
	CAB 11	Colonial Defence Committee, and Committee of Imperial Defence, Colonial Defence Committee later Overseas Defence Committee: Defence Schemes
	CAB 17	Committee of Imperial Defence: Miscellaneous Correspondence and Memoranda
	CAB 21	Cabinet Registered Files
	CAB 23	Cabinet Minutes, 1916–1939
	CAB 24	Cabinet Memoranda, 1916–1939
	CAB 27	War Cabinet and Cabinet: Miscellaneous Committees: General Series
	CAB 41	Photographic Copies of Cabinet Letters in the Royal Archives Windsor
Colonial Office	CO 732	Colonial Office Middle East, 1921–1949
Dominions Office	DO 35	Original Correspondence
	DO 117	Supplementary Original Correspondence
Foreign Office	FO 141	Foreign Office and Foreign and Commonwealth Office: Embassy and Consulates, Egypt: General Correspondence
	FO 286	Foreign Office: Consulate and Legation, Greece (formerly Ottoman Empire): General Correspondence
	FO 366	Foreign Office and Diplomatic Service Administration Office: Chief Clerk's Department and successors: General Correspondence before 1906
	FO 371	Foreign Office: Political Departments: General Correspondence from 1906
	FO 407	Foreign Office: Confidential Print Egypt and the Sudan

	FO 608	Peace Conference: British Delegation, Correspondence and Papers
	FO 633	Cromer Papers
	FO 686	Foreign Office and predecessors: Jedda Agency Papers
	FO 794	Foreign Office: Private Office: Correspondence concerning Ambassadors and Senior Diplomats
	FO 800	Foreign Office, Private Offices: Various Ministers' and Officials' Papers
	FO 848	Foreign Office: Embassy and Consular Archives Egypt, Milner Mission
	FO 1011	Loraine Papers
Premier	PREM 1	Prime Minister's Office: Correspondence and papers, 1916–1940
Domestic Records	PRO 30/69	James Ramsay MacDonald papers
Treasury	T 160	Treasury: Finance files (F series)
War Office	WO 32	War Office: Registered files (General series)
	WO 33	War Office: Reports, Memoranda and papers (O and A series)
	WO 137	Earl of Derby, Secretary of State for War Private Office Papers

Private Papers

Bodleian Library, Oxford:
    Lord Inverchapel papers
    Sir Percy Loraine papers
    Lord Milner papers
    Violet Milner papers
    Walford Selby papers
    John Simon papers

The National Archives of Scotland:
    Lord Balfour papers
    Lord Lothian papers

British Library:
    J A Spender papers
    A T Wilson papers

British Library: Asia, Pacific and Africa Collections
    Lord Curzon papers
    Lord Chelmsford

University of Durham Library, Sudan Archive
    Gilbert F Clayton papers
    G R Bredin papers
    C G Dupuis papers
    E H Macintosh papers
    S L Milligan papers
    P D Mulholland papers
    Reginald Wingate papers

Cambridge University Library
    Stanley Baldwin papers
    Charles Hardinge papers

Churchill Archive Centre, Cambridge
    Leo Amery papers
    Sir Maurice Hankey papers
    Lord Lloyd papers
    Lady Lloyd papers

Liddell Hart Centre for Military Archives
    Sir Edmund Allenby papers

Middle East Centre Archive, Oxford
    Sir Edmund Allenby papers
    A Keown-Boyd papers
    Thomas Russell papers
    Ronald Storrs papers

House of Lords Record Office, London
    Andrew Bonar Law papers
    J Campbell Davidson papers
    David Lloyd George papers

Cadbury Research Library: Special Collections, University of Birmingham
    Austen Chamberlain papers
    British Cotton Growing Association

Rhodes House Library, University of Oxford
    Percy Coriat papers
    T R H Owen, *Sudan Days* (1960/1961) Mss Afr r. 201. Special Collections and Western Manuscripts, Bodleian Library of Commonwealth and African Studies, Rhodes House, University of Oxford.

Published Memoirs, Diaries, Letters and Contemporary Articles

J Barnes and D Nicolson (eds), *The Leo Amery Diaries. Volume I: 1896–1929* (London: Hutchinson, 1980).
J Barnes and D Nicholson (eds), *The Empire at Bay. The Leo Amery Diaries, 1929–45* (London: Hutchinson, 1988).
H Dalton, *Call Back Yesterday. Memoirs 1887–1931* (London: Frederick Muller, 1953).
M Gilbert, *Winston S Churchill, iii 1914–1916* (London: Heinemann, 1975).
M Gilbert, *Winston Churchill, iv 1917–1922* (London: Heinemann, 1975).
M Gilbert, *Winston Churchill, v 1922–1939* (London: Heinemann, 1976).
W E Gladstone, 'England's Mission', *The Nineteenth Century*, 19 (4 September 1878), pp. 560–84.
L Grafftey-Smith, *Bright Levant* (London: John Murray, 1970).
K Jeffery (ed.), *The Military Correspondence of Field Marshal Sir Henry Wilson, 1918–22* (London: Army Record Society, 1985).
T Jones, *Whitehall Diary*, 3 vols, in K Middlemas (ed.) (London: Oxford University Press, 1969–71).

E Kedourie, *In the Anglo-Arab Labyrinth. The McMahon-Husayn Correspondence and Its Interpretations, 1914–1939* (Cambridge: Cambridge University Press, 1976).
S Leslie, *Mark Sykes. His Life and Letters* (London: Cassell & Co, 1923).
E G Sarsfield-Hall, *From Cork to Khartoum. Memoirs of Southern Ireland and the Anglo-Egyptian Sudan, 1886–1936* (Kendal: T Wilson, 1975).
R C Self (ed.), *The Austen Chamberlain Diary Letters* (London: Cambridge University Press for the Royal Historical Society, 1995).
A J Toynbee, *The World after the Peace Conference: Being an Epilogue to the 'History of the Peace Conference of Paris' and a Prologue to the 'Survey of International Affairs, 1920–1923'* (London: Oxford University Press, 1925).
A J Toynbee, *Survey of International Affairs, 1924* (London: Oxford University Press, 1926).
A J Toynbee, *Survey of International Affairs, 1925. Volume I: The Islamic World since the Peace Settlement* (London: Oxford University Press, 1927).
P Woodward (ed.), *British Documents of Foreign Affairs. Reports and Papers from the Foreign Office Confidential Print, Part II, Series G Africa, 1914–1939* (Washington DC: United Publications of America, 1995).

Official Papers

Hansard
House of Commons Daily Debates (HC)
House of Lords Daily Debates (HL)

Newspapers

The Times
Manchester Guardian

Secondary Sources

Books

H Abdin, *Early Sudanese Nationalism, 1919–1925* (Khartoum: Institute of African & Asian Studies, Khartoum University Press, 1985).
R Adelson, *London and the Invention of the Middle East. Money, Power, and War, 1902–1922* (New Haven: Yale University Press, 1995).
Afaf Lutfi Al-Sayyid, *Egypt and Cromer. A Study in Anglo-Egyptian Relations* (London: John Murray, 1968).
L S Amery, *My Political Life. War and Peace, 1914–1929, ii* (London: Hutchison, 1953).
R Anderson, *The Forgotten Front. The East African Campaign, 1914–1918* (Stroud: Tempus, 2004).
C Andrews and D Dilks (eds), *A Missing Dimension. Governments and Intelligence Communities in the Twentieth Century* (Southampton: Macmillan Press, 1984).
A Al-Awad Muhammad, *Sudan Defence Force: Origin and Role, 1925–1955* (Institute of African and Asian Studies, Occasional Paper No. 18).

M Badrawi, *Isma'il Sidqi 1875-1950. Pragmatism and Vision in Twentieth Century Egypt* (Guildford and King's Lynn: Curzon Press, 1996).
M Badrawi, *Political Violence in Egypt 1910-1925. Secret Societies, Plots and Assassinations* (Richmond: Curzon Press, 2000).
C M Bell, *The Royal Navy, Seapower and Strategy between the Wars* (London: Macmillan Press, 2000).
M Beloff, *Britain's Liberal Empire 1897-1921. i Imperial Sunset* (Hong Kong: Macmillan Press, 1987).
G H Bennett, *British Foreign Policy during the Curzon Period, 1919-24* (Basingstoke: Macmillan, 1995).
J Berque, *Egypt. Imperialism and Revolution* (London: Faber and Faber Ltd., 1972).
W S Blunt, *Secret History of the English Occupation of Egypt: Being a Personal Narrative of Events* (New York: Howard Fertig, 1967).
B Bond, *British Military Policy between the Two World Wars* (London: Clarendon Press, 1980).
S Botman, *Egypt: From Independence to Revolution, 1919-1952* (Syracuse, NY: Syracuse University Press, 1991).
C Boyle, *Boyle of Cairo. A Diplomatists Adventures in the Middle East* (Kendal: Titus Wilson, 1965).
J Braunthal, *History of the International, 1914-1943* (London: Thomas Nelson & Sons, 1967).
J M Brown and W M Roger Louis, *The Oxford History of the British Empire, iv The Twentieth Century* (Oxford: Oxford University Press, 1999).
E Burns, *British Imperialism in Egypt* (Perth: The Labour Research Department, 1928).
B C Busch, *Britain, India and the Arabs, 1914-21* (Berkeley; London: University of California Press, 1971).
G Butt, *The Lion in the Sand. The British in the Middle East* (St. Ives: Bloomsbury, 1995).
P J Cain and A G Hopkins, *British Imperialism. Innovation and Expansion, 1688-1914* (London: Longman, 1993).
P J Cain and A G Hopkins, *British Imperialism. Crisis and Deconstruction, 1914-1990* (London: Longman, 1993).
D Carlton, *MacDonald versus Henderson. The Foreign Policy of the Second Labour Government* (Edinburgh: Macmillan Press, 1970).
B Carman and J McPherson, *Bimbashi McPherson. A Life in Egypt* (London: British Broadcasting Corporation, 1983).
D Chandler and I Beckett (eds), *The Oxford Illustrated History of the British Army* (Oxford: Oxford University Press, 1994).
J Charmley, *Lord Lloyd and the Decline of the British Empire* (London: Weidenfeld and Nicolson, 1987).
V Chirol, *The Egyptian Problem* (London: Macmillan, 1920).
J R I Cole, *Colonialism and Revolution in the Middle East. Social and Cultural Origins of Egypt's 'Urabi Movement* (Princeton (NJ): Princeton University Press, 1993).
R O Collins, *Shadows in the Grass. Britain in the Southern Sudan, 1918-1956* (New Haven and London: Yale University Press, 1983).
P Corthorn and J Davis (eds), *The British Labour Party and the Wider World. Domestic Problems, Internationalism and Foreign Policy* (New York: Tauris Academic Studies, 2008).
G A Craig and F Gilbert (eds), *The Diplomats, 1919-39* (New York: Atheneum, 1963).
E Crankshaw, *The Forsaken Idea: A Study of Viscount Milner* (London: Longmans, Green, 1952).

The Earl of Cromer, *Modern Egypt*, ii ([S.I.]: Macmillan & Co Ltd, 1908).
M Daly, *Empire on the Nile. The Anglo-Egyptian Sudan, 1898–1934* (Cambridge: Cambridge University Press, 1986).
M Daly, *The Sirdar. Sir Reginald Wingate and the British Empire in the Middle East* (Philadelphia: American Philosophical Society, 1997).
U Dann (ed.), *The Great Powers and the Middle East, 1919–39* (New York: Holmes and Meier, 1988).
J Darwin, *Britain, Egypt and the Middle East. Imperial Policy in the Aftermath of War* (Hong Kong: Macmillan Press, 1981).
J Darwin, *The Empire Project. The Rise and Fall of the British World System, 1830–1970* (Cambridge: Cambridge University Press, 2009).
P Dennis, *Decision by Default. Peacetime Conscription and British Defence 1919–39* (London: Routledge & Kegan Paul, 1972).
H H Dodwell (ed.), *Cambridge History of India*, vi (Cambridge: Cambridge University Press, 1932).
J F Fairbank and A Feuerwerker, *The Cambridge History of China. xiii Republican China, 1912–1949, part 2* (Cambridge: Cambridge University Press, 1986).
R W Ferrier, *The History of the British Petroleum Company. i The Developing Years, 1901–32* (Cambridge, Cambridge University Press, 2000).
J R Ferris, *The Evolution of British Strategic Policy, 1919–26* (Hong Kong: Macmillan Press, 1989).
D K Fieldhouse, *Economics and Empire, 1830–1914* (London: Weidenfeld and Nicolson, 1973).
D K Fieldhouse, *Western Imperialism in the Middle East, 1914–1958* (Oxford: Oxford University Press, 2006).
J Fisher, *Curzon and British Imperialism in the Middle East, 1916–19* (London: Frank Cass, 1999).
J Fisher, *Gentleman Spies. Intelligence Agents in the British Empire and Beyond* (Stroud: Sutton Publishing, 2002).
D French and B Holden-Reid (eds), *The British General Staff. Reform and Innovation, 1890–1939* (London: Frank Cass, 2002).
I Gershoni and J Jankowski (eds), *Redefining the Egyptian Nation, 1930–1945* (Cambridge: Cambridge University Press, 1995).
I Gershoni and J Jankowski (eds), *Rethinking Nationalism in the Arab Middle East* (New York: Columbia University Press, 1997).
D Gillies, *Radical Diplomat: The Life of Archibald Clark Kerr, Lord Inverchapel, 1882–1951* (London: IB Tauris, 1999).
A Goldschmidt, A Johnson and B Salmoni (eds), *Re-Envisioning Egypt, 1919–1952* (Cairo and New York: The American University in Cairo Press, 2005).
A M Gollin, *Pro-Consul in Politics. A Study of Lord Milner in Opposition and in Power* (London: Anthony Blond, 1964).
J F Goode, *Negotiation for the Past: Archaeology, Nationalism and Diplomacy in the Middle East, 1919–41* (Austin: University of Texas Press, 2007).
G A H Gordon, *British Seapower and Procurement between the Wars. A Reappraisal of Rearmament* (London: Macmillan Press, 1988).
B Görkay, *A Clash of Empires: Turkey between Russian Bolshevism and British Imperialism, 1918–1923* (London: Tauris Academic Studies, 1997).
W W Gottlieb, *Studies in Secret Diplomacy during the First World War* (London: Allen & Unwin, 1957).

R S Grayson, *Austen Chamberlain and the Commitment to Europe. British Foreign Policy, 1924-29* (London: Frank Cass, 1997).
M Greenberg, *British Trade and the Opening of China, 1800-42* (Cambridge: Cambridge University Press, 1951).
P Guinn, *British Strategy and Politics, 1914-1918* (Oxford: Clarendon Press, 1965).
Major-General Sir C W Gwynn, *Imperial Policing* (London: Macmillan, 1936).
W K Hancock, *Survey of British Commonwealth Affairs, ii Problems of Economic Policy, 1918-1939 part 1* (London: Oxford University Press, 1940).
J A Hail, *Britain's Foreign Policy in Egypt and Sudan, 1947-56* (Reading: Ithaca Press, 1996).
V Halpérin, *Lord Milner and the Empire: The Evolution of British Imperialism* (London: Odhams Press, 1952).
M A Hamilton, *Arthur Henderson. A Biography* (London: William Heinemann, 1938).
R T Harrison, *Gladstone's Imperialism in Egypt. Techniques of Domination* (London: Greenwood Publishing, 1995).
P Hardy, *The Muslims of British India* (London: Cambridge University Press, 1972).
M Herman, *Intelligence Power in Peace and War* (Cambridge: Cambridge University Press, 1996).
R Higham, *Britain's Imperial Air Routes, 1918 to 1939. The Story of Britain's Overseas Airlines* (London: G T Foulis & Co., 1960).
J A Hobson, *Imperialism. A Study* (London: George Allen and Unwin, 1938).
P M Holt, *Egypt and the Fertile Crescent, 1516-1922* (London: Longmans, 1966).
R Holland, *Blue-Water Empire: The British in the Mediterranean since 1800* (London: Allen Lane, 2012).
H L Hoskins, *British Routes to India* (New York: Longmans, Green and Co, 1928).
A Hourani, P S Khoury and M C Wilson (eds), *The Modern Middle East* (London: I.B. Tauris & Co. Ltd., 1993).
M Hughes, *Allenby and British Strategy in the Middle East, 1917-1919* (London: Frank Cass, 1999).
A Hunter, *Power and Passion in Egypt. A Life of Sir Eldon Gorst, 1861-1911* (London: I.B. Tauris, 2007).
J C Hurewitz, *Diplomacy in the Near and Middle East: A Documentary Record*, ii (Princeton: Van Nostrand, 1956).
R Hyam, *Elgin and Churchill at the Colonial Office 1905-1908* (London: St Martin's Press, 1968).
H Montgomery Hyde, *British Air Policy between the Wars, 1918-1939* (London: Heinemann, 1976).
E Ingram (eds), *National and International Politics in the Middle East. Essays in honour of Elie Kedourie* (Exeter: Frank Cass, 1986).
L James, *Imperial Warrior. The Life and Times of Field Marshal Viscount Allenby, 1861-1936* (London: Weidenfeld and Nicolson, 1993).
K Jeffery, *The British Army and the Crisis of Empire* (Manchester: Manchester University Press, 1984).
K Jeffery, *Field Marshal Sir Henry Wilson. A Political Soldier* (Oxford: Oxford University Press, 2006).
K Jeffery, *MI6: The History of the Secret Intelligence Service, 1909-1949* (London: Bloomsbury, 2010).
F A Johnson, *Defence by Committee. The British Committee of Imperial Defence, 1885-1959* (London: Oxford University Press, 1960).

D Judd, *Lord Reading. Rufus Isaacs, First Marquess of Reading, Lord Chief Justice and Viceroy of India 1860–1935* (London: Weidenfeld and Nicolson, 1982).
F Kazemzadeh, *Russia and Britain in Persia, 1864–1914* (New Haven; London: Yale University Press, 1968).
E Kedourie, *England and the Middle East: The Destruction of the Ottoman Empire, 1914–1921* (London: Bowes & Bowes, 1956).
E Kedourie, *Nationalism* (London: Hutchinson & Co., 1966).
E Kedourie, *Arabic Political Memoirs and Other Studies* (London: Franck Cass, 1974).
E Kedourie, *The Chatham House Version and Other Middle-Eastern Studies* (Hanover, NH; London: University Press of New England, 1984).
J E Kendle, *The Colonial and Imperial Conferences, 1887–1911* (London: Longmans, 1967).
M Kent, *Moguls and Mandarins. Oil Imperialism and the Middle East in British Foreign Policy, 1900–1940* (Bath: Frank Cass, 1993).
G Kennedy, *Imperial Defence. The Old World Order, 1856–1956* (London: Routledge, 2008).
A Kirk-Greene, *The Sudan Political Service: A Preliminary Profile* (Oxford: Oxford University Press, 1982).
A Kirk-Greene, *On Crown Service. A History of HM Colonial and Overseas Civil Service, 1837–97* (Bridgend: I.B. Tauris, 1999).
A Kirk-Greene, *Britain's Imperial Administrators 1858–1966* (Basingstoke: Macmillan Press, 2000).
A S Klieman, *Foundations of British Policy in the Arab World: The Cairo Conference of 1921* (Baltimore: The Johns Hopkins Press, 1970).
K Kyle, *Suez* (London: Weidenfield and Nicolson, 1991).
D Lavin, *From Empire to International Commonwealth. A Biography of Lionel Curtis* (Oxford: Oxford University Press, 1995).
J Lee Thompson, *A Wider Patriotism: Alfred Milner and the British Empire* (London: Pickering and Chatto, 2007).
C W R Long, *British Pro-Consuls in Egypt, 1914–29: The Challenge of Nationalism* (London: Routledge Curzon, 2005).
R D Long (ed.), *The Man on the Spot. Essays on British Empire History* (Westport: Greenwood Press, 1995).
P Lowe, *Great Britain and Japan 1911–1915* (London: St Martin's Press, 1969).
Sir H MacMichael, *The Anglo-Egyptian Sudan* (Plymouth: Faber and Faber Ltd, 1934).
J D McIntyre Jr., *The Boycott of the Milner Mission. A Study in Egyptian Nationalism* (New York: Peter Lang, 1985).
B J C McKercher, *Transition of Power. Britain's Loss of Global Pre-Eminence to the United States 1930–1945* (Cambridge: Cambridge University Press, 1999).
E Maisel, *The Foreign Office and Foreign Policy, 1919–1926* (Brighton: Sussex Academic Press, 1994).
P Mangold, *What the British Did: Two Centuries in the Middle East* (London: I.B. Tauris, 2016).
P Mansfield, *The British in Egypt* (New York: Holt, Rinehart and Winston, 1971).
J Marlowe, *Anglo-Egyptian Relations, 1800–1956* (London: Frank Cass, 1965).
H C G Matthew, *The Liberal Imperialists: The Ideas and Politics of a Post-Gladstonian Élite* (London: Oxford University Press, 1973).
P Mellini, *Sir Eldon Gorst. The Overshadowed Proconsul* (Stanford, CA: Hoover Institution Press, 1977).

A Milner, *England in Egypt* (London: Edward Arnold, 1899).
B R Mitchell, *Abstract of British Historical Statistics* (Cambridge: Cambridge University Press, 1971).
P A Mohs, *Military Intelligence and the Arab Revolt. The First Modern Intelligence War* (London: Routledge, 2008).
G Monger, *The End of Isolation: British Foreign Policy, 1900–1907* (Westport, CT: Greenwood Press, 1963).
E Monroe, *Britain's Moment in the Middle East, 1914–71* (London: Chatto and Windus, 1981).
S Morewood, *British Defence of Egypt, 1935–40: Conflict and Crisis in the Eastern Mediterranean* (London: Frank Cass, 2005).
C L Mowat, *Britain between the Wars, 1918–1940* (London: Methuen, 1968).
K Neilson and G Kennedy (eds), *Far Flung Lines. Studies in Imperial Defence* (London: Frank Cass, 1996).
K Neilson and T G Otte (eds), *The Permanent Under-Secretary for Foreign Affairs, 1854–1946* (Abingdon and New York: Routledge, 2009).
D E Omissi, *Air Power and Colonial Control. The Royal Air Force, 1919–1939* (Manchester: Manchester University Press, 1990).
T G Otte and K Neilson (eds), *Railways and International Politics. Paths of Empire, 1848–1945* (Abingdon: Routledge, 2006).
R Owen, *Lord Cromer: Victorian Imperialist, Edwardian Proconsul* (Kings Lynn: Oxford University Press, 2004).
G C Peden, *The Treasury and British Public Policy, 1906–1959* (Oxford: Oxford University Press, 2006).
G Pirie, *Air Empire. British Imperial Civil Aviation, 1919–39* (Manchester: Manchester University Press, 2009).
D Platt, *The Cinderella Service. British Consuls since 1825* (Harlow: Longman, 1971).
R J Popplewell, *Intelligence and Imperial Defence. British Intelligence and the Defence of the Indian Empire, 1904–1924* (London: Frank Cass & Co., 1995).
P A Reynolds, *British Foreign Policy in the Inter-War Years* (Westport: Greenwood Press, 1974).
J C B Richmond, *Egypt 1798–1952* (London: Meuthuen & Co., 1977).
K Robbins, *Sir Edward Grey* (London: Cassell, 1971).
R Robinson and J Gallagher, *Africa and the Victorians* (Hong Kong Macmillan, 1981).
W M Roger Louis (ed.), *Imperialism: The Robinson and Gallagher Controversy* (New York: New Viewpoints, 1976).
S Roskill, *Naval Policy between the Wars, i The Period of Anglo-American Antagonism, 1919–1929* (London: Collins, 1968).
E Rouard de Card, *Situation Internationale du Soudan Egyptien depuis l'Independence de l'Egypte* (Paris: A Pedone, 1932).
S B Saul, *Studies in British Overseas Trade 1870–1914* (Liverpool: Liverpool University Press, 1960).
Y Sheffy, *British Military Intelligence in the Palestine Campaign, 1914–1918* (London: Frank Cass, 1998).
J Shepherd and K Laybourn, *Britain's First Labour Government* (Basingstoke: Palgrave Macmillan, 2006).
H J Sharkey, *Living with Colonialism. Nationalism and Culture in the Anglo-Egyptian Sudan* (Berkeley: University of California Press, 2003).
P Smith (eds), *Government and the Armed Forces in Britain, 1856–1990* (Cambridge: The Hambledon Press, 1996).

S C Smith (ed.), *Reassessing Suez 1956. New Perspectives on the Crisis and its Aftermath* (Aldershot: Ashgate, 2008).
S Stockwell (ed.), *The British Empire. Themes and Perspectives* (Oxford: Blackwell, 2008).
H Strachan (ed.), *Big Wars and Small Wars. The British Army and the Lessons of War in the 20th Century*. (London: Routledge, 2006).
E Tauber, *The Emergence of the Arab Movements* (London: Frank Cass, 1993).
A J P Taylor (ed.), *Lloyd George: Twelve Essays* (London: Hamish Hamilton, 1971).
J J Terry, *The Wafd, 1919-1952* (London: Third World Centre, 1982).
M Thomas, *Empires of Intelligence. Security Services and Colonial Disorder after 1914* (London: University of California Press, 2008).
C Townshend, *Britain's Civil Wars: Counterinsurgency in the Twentieth Century* (London: Faber and Faber, 1986).
C Tripp (ed.), *Contemporary Egypt through Egyptian Eyes. Essays in Honour of P J Vatikiotis* (London: Routledge, 1993).
E M Troutt-Powell, *A Different Shade of Colonialism. Egypt, Great Britain and the Mastery of the Sudan* (Berkeley: University of California Press, 2003).
R Ullman, *Anglo-Soviet Relations, 1917-1921. iii The Anglo-Soviet Accord* (London: Oxford University Press, 1972).
F Venn, *Oil Diplomacy in the Twentieth Century* (Hong Kong: Macmillan, 1986).
R Vickers, *The Labour Party and the World. i The Evolution of Labour's Foreign Policy, 1900-1951* (Manchester: Manchester University Press, 2004).
P J Vatikiotis, *The Modern History of Egypt* (London: Weidenfeld and Nicolson, 1969).
G Warburg, *Islam, Nationalism and Communism in a Traditional Society. The Case of the Sudan* (London and Totowa: Frank Cass, 1978).
B Westrate, *The Arab Bureau. British Policy in the Middle East* (University Park, PA.: Pennsylvania State University Press, 1992).
J Whidden, *Monarchy and Modernity in Egypt. Politics, Islam and Neo-Colonialism between the Wars* (London and New York: I.B. Tauris, 2013).
M A Williams, *Mussolini's Propaganda Abroad. Subversion in the Mediterranean and the Middle East, 1935-1940* (Abingdon: Routledge, 2006).
K M Wilson (ed.), *Imperialism and Nationalism in the Middle East. The Anglo-Egyptian Experience, 1882-1982* (London: Mansell Publishing, 1983).
R Wingate, *Wingate of the Sudan. The Life and Times of General Reginald Wingate, Maker of the Anglo-Egyptian Sudan* (London: John Murray, 1955).
H V F Winstone, *Illicit Adventure. The Story of Political and Military Intelligence in the Middle East from 1898-1926* (Chatham: Jonathan Cape, 1982).
J E Wrench, *Alfred, Lord Milner, the Man of No Illusions, 1854-1925* (London: Eyre & Spottiswoode, 1958).
L K Young, *British Policy in China, 1895-1902* (Oxford: Clarendon, 1970).

Essays

G Baer, 'Urbanisation in Egypt, 1820-1907', in W R Polk and R Chambers (eds), *Beginnings of Modernisation in the Middle East* (Chicago: University of Chicago Press, 1968), pp. 155-69.
C M Bell, 'The Royal Navy, War Planning, and Intelligence Assessments of Japan, 1921-1941', in P Jackson and J Siegel (eds), *Intelligence and Statecraft. The Use and Limits of Intelligence in International Society* (London: Praeger, 2005), pp. 139-55.

R M Burrell, 'Britain, Iran and the Persian Gulf: Some Aspects of the Situation in the 1920s and 1930s', in D Hopwood (ed.), *The Arabian Peninsula: Society and Politics* (London: George Allen and Unwin, 1972), pp. 160–88.

G A Craig, 'The British Foreign Office from Grey to Austen Chamberlain', in G A Craig and F Gilbert, *The Diplomats, 1919–39* (Boston, MA: Princeton University Press, 1953).

D Dilks, 'The British Foreign Office between the Wars', in B J C McKercher and D J Moss (eds), *Shadow and Substance in British Foreign Policy 1895–1939* (Edmonton: University of Alberta Press, 1984), pp. 181–202.

J Ferris, 'The British Empire vs. The Hidden Hand: British Intelligence and Strategy and "The CUP-Jew-German-Bolshevik Combination," 1918–1924', in K Neilson and G Kennedy (eds) *The British Way in Warfare: Power and the International System, 1856–1956: Essays in Honour of David French* (Surrey: Ashgate, 2010), pp. 325–46.

J E Flint, 'Britain and the Scramble for Africa', in R W Winks (ed.), *The Oxford History of the British Empire. v Historiography* (Oxford: Oxford University Press, 1999), pp. 450–62.

A Hourani, 'Ottoman Reform and the Politics of Notables', in W R Polk and R Chambers (eds), *Beginnings of Modernisation in the Middle East* (Chicago: University of Chicago Press, 1968), pp. 41–68.

J Gooch, '"Building Buffers and Filling Vacuums": Great Britain and the Middle East, 1914–1922', in W Murray and J Lacy (eds), *The Making of Peace: Rulers, States and the Aftermath of War* (Cambridge: Cambridge University Press, 2009), pp. 240–64.

C Issawi, 'Asymmetrical Development and Transport in Egypt, 1800–1914', in W R Polk and R Chambers (eds), *Beginnings of Modernisation in the Middle East* (Chicago: University of Chicago Press, 1968), pp. 383–400.

A R Kelidar, 'The Arabian Peninsular in Arab and Power Politics', in D Hopwood (ed.), *The Arabian Peninsular: Society and Politics* (London: George Allen and Unwin, 1972), pp. 145–59.

G Kennedy, 'The 1930 London Naval Conference and Anglo-American Maritime Strength, 1927–1930', in B J C McKercher (ed.), *Arms Limitation and Disarmament. Restraints on War, 1899–1939* (Westport: Praeger, 1992), pp. 149–71.

M Kent, 'Guarding the Bandwagon: Great Britain, Italy, and Middle Eastern Oil, 1920–23', in E Ingram (eds), *National and International Politics in the Middle East. Essays in Honour of Elie Kedourie* (Exeter: Frank Cass, 1986).

A Luti Al-Sayyid Marsot, 'The Beginnings of Modernisation among the Rectors of Al-Azhar, 1798–1879', in W R Polk and R Chambers (eds), *Beginnings of Modernisation in the Middle East* (Chicago: University of Chicago Press, 1968), pp. 267–80.

J Whidden, 'Expatriates in Cosmopolitan Egypt: 1864–1956', in R Bickers (ed.), *Oxford History of the British Empire Companion: Britons over the Seas* (Oxford: Oxford University Press, 2010), pp. 45–73.

Journal Articles

A I Abushouk, 'The Anglo-Egyptian Sudan: From Collaboration Mechanism to Party Politics, 1898–1956', *Journal of Imperial and Commonwealth History*, 38, 2 (2010), pp. 207–36.

R Allen, 'Review Article: Cromer in Egypt', *International Journal of Middle Eastern Studies*, 4, 2 (1973), pp. 250–52.

A L Al Sayyid-Marsot, 'Religion or Opposition? Urban Protest Movements in Egypt', *International Journal of Middle Eastern Studies*, 16, 4 (1984), pp. 541–52.

C M Andrew and A S Kanya-Forstner, 'The French Colonial Party and French Colonial War Aims, 1914–1918', *Historical Journal*, 17, 1 (1974), pp. 79–106.

H N Ansari, 'The Islamic Militants in Egyptian Politics', *International Journal of Middle Eastern Studies*, 16, 1 (1984), pp. 123–44.

E Barak, 'Egyptian Intellectuals in the Shadow of British Occupation', *British Journal of Middle Eastern Studies*, 35, 2 (2008), pp. 173–86.

W Berridge, 'Ambivalent Ideologies and the Limitations of the Colonial Prison in Sudan, 1898-1956', *Journal of Eastern African Studies*, 6, 3 (2012), pp. 444–62.

W J Berridge, 'Sudan's Security Agencies: Fragmentation, Visibility and Mimicry, 1908–89', *Intelligence and National Security*, 28, 6 (2013), pp. 845–67.

W J Berridge, 'Imperialism and Nationalist Voices in the Struggle for Egyptian Independence', *Journal of Imperial and Commonwealth History*, 42, 3 (2014), pp. 420–39.

M B Bishku, 'The British Press and the Future of Egypt', *The International History Review*, 8, 4 (1986), pp. 604–09.

N Blewett, 'Free Fooders, Balfourites, Whole Hoggers: Factionalism within the Unionist Party, 1906–1910', *Historical Journal*, 11, 1 (1968), pp. 95–124.

N J Brown, 'The Precarious Life and Slow Death of the Mixed Courts of Egypt', *International Journal of Middle Eastern Studies*, 25, 1 (1993), pp. 33–52.

N J Brown, 'Who Abolished Corvée Labour in Egypt and Why?', *Past and Present*, 144 (1994), pp. 116–37.

P J Cain, 'Character and Imperialism: The British Financial Administration of Egypt, 1878–1914', *Journal of Imperial and Commonwealth History*, 34, 2 (2006), pp. 177–200.

B D Cannon, 'Nubar Pasha, Evelyn Baring and a Suppressed Article in the Drummond-Wolff Convention', *International Journal of Middle Eastern Studies*, 5, 4 (1974), pp. 468–83.

M A Chaichian, 'The Effects of World Capitalist Economy on Urbanisation in Egypt, 1800–1970', *International Journal of Middle Eastern Studies*, 20, 1 (1988), pp. 23–43.

M E Chamberlain, 'The Alexandria Massacre of 11 June 1882 and the British Occupation of Egypt', *Middle Eastern Studies*, 13 (1997), pp. 14–39.

P Charrier, 'The Evolution of a Stereotype: The Royal Navy and the Japanese "Martial Type" 1900–45', *War and Society*, 19, 1 (2001), pp. 23–46.

Y M Choueiri, 'Review Article: The Middle East: Colonialism, Islam and the Nation State', *Journal of Contemporary History*, 37, 4 (2002), pp. 649–63.

R O Collins, 'Review Article: The Mahdist State in the Sudan, 1881–1898', *International Journal of Middle Eastern Studies*, 6, 2 (1975), pp. 252–53.

R O Collins, 'Review Article: The Sirdar: Sir Reginald Wingate and the British Empire in the Middle East', *International Journal of Middle Eastern Studies*, 30, 4 (1998), pp. 580–82.

G L Cook, 'Sir Robert Borden, Lloyd George and British Military Policy 1917–1918', *Historical Journal*, 14, 2 (1971), pp. 371–95.

E Corp, 'Sir Eyre Crowe and Georges Clemenceau at the Paris Peace Conference', *Diplomacy and Statecraft*, 8, 1 (1997), pp. 10–19.

R M Coury, 'Who "Invented" Egyptian Nationalism? Part 1', *International Journal of Middle Eastern Studies*, 14, 3 (1982), pp. 249–81.

R M Coury, 'Who "Invented" Egyptian Arab Nationalism? Part 2', *International Journal of Middle Eastern Studies*, 16, 4 (1982), pp. 459–79.

C Earnest Dawn, 'Review Article: In the Anglo-Arab Labyrinth: The McMahon-Husayn Correspondence and Its Interpretations, 1914–1939', *International Journal of Middle Eastern Studies*, 9, 1 (1978), pp. 128–30.

C Earnest Dawn, 'The Formation of Pan Arab Ideology in the Inter-War Years', *International Journal of Middle Eastern Studies*, 20, 1 (1988), pp. 67–91.

J Darwin, 'Imperialism in Decline? Tendencies in British Imperial Policy between the Wars', *Historical Journal*, 23, 3 (1980), pp. 657–79.

J Darwin, 'An Undeclared Empire: The British in the Middle East, 1918–1939', *Journal of Imperial and Commonwealth History*, 27, 2 (1999), pp. 159–76.

M Deeb, 'The Socioeconomic Role of the Local Foreign Minorities in Modern Egypt, 1805–1961', *International Journal of Middle Eastern Studies*, 9, 1 (1978), pp. 11–22.

M Deeb, 'Labour Politics in Egypt, 1919–39', *International Journal of Middle Eastern Studies*, 10, 2 (1979), pp. 187–203.

M Deeb, 'Review Article: The Boycott of the Milner Mission: A Study in Egyptian Nationalism', *International Journal of Middle Eastern Studies*, 21, 2 (1989), p. 264.

R H Dekmejian, 'Review Article: The Emergence of Pan Arabism in Egypt', *International Journal of Middle Eastern Studies*, 17, 2 (1985), p. 267.

M N El-Amin, 'Britain, the 1924 Sudanese Uprising, and the Impact of Egypt on the Sudan', *International Journal of African Historical Studies*, 19, 2 (1986), pp. 235–60.

M N El-Amin, 'The Role of the Egyptian Communists in Introducing the Sudanese to Communism in the 1940s', *International Journal of Middle Eastern Studies*, 19, 4 (1987), pp. 433–54.

M N El-Amin, 'International Communism, the Egyptian Wafd Party and the Sudan', *BRISMES Bulletin*, 16, 1 (1989), pp. 27–48.

P G Elgood, 'The Situation in Egypt', *Journal of the Royal Institute of International Affairs*, 6, 5 (1927), pp. 299–313.

M Eppel, 'The Elite, the Effendiyya and the Growth of Nationalism and Pan-Arabism in Hashemite Iraq, 1921–1958', *International Journal of Middle Eastern Studies*, 30, 2 (1998), pp. 227–50.

J J Ewald, 'Review article: '"Bonds of Silk": The Human Factor in the British Administration of the Sudan', *International Journal of Middle Eastern Studies*, 24, 4 (1992), pp. 744–46.

Z Fahmy, 'Francophone Egyptian Nationalists, Anti-British Discourse, and European Public Opinion, 1885–1910: The Case of Mustafa Kamil and Ya'qub Sannu', *Comparative Studies of South Asia, Africa and the Middle East*, 28, 1 (2008), pp. 170–83.

J Ferris, '"Far Too Dangerous a Gamble"? British Intelligence and Policy during the Chanak Crisis, September–October 1922', *Diplomacy and Statecraft*, 14, 2 (2003), pp. 139–84.

J Ferris, '"The Internationalism of Islam": The British Perception of a Muslim Menace, 1840–1951', *Intelligence and National Security*, 24, 1 (2009), pp. 57–77.

J Fisher, 'The Interdepartmental Committee on Eastern Unrest and British Responses to Bolshevik and Other Intrigues against the Empire during the 1920s', *Journal of Asian History*, 34, 1 (2000), pp. 1–34.

J Fisher, 'Major Norman Bray and Eastern Unrest in the British Empire in the Aftermath of World War I', *Asian Affairs*, 31, 2 (2000), pp. 189–97.

J Fisher, 'British Responses to Mahdist and Other Unrest in North and West Africa, 1919–1930', *Australian Journal of Politics and History*, 52, 3 (2006), pp. 347–61.

J Fisher, 'Lord Robert Cecil and the Formation of a Middle East Department of the Foreign Office', *Middle Eastern Studies*, 42, 3 (2006), pp. 365–80.

E P Fitzgerald, 'France's Middle Eastern Ambitions, the Sykes-Picot Negotiations, and the Oilfields of Mosul, 1915-18', *Journal of Modern History*, 66, 4 (1994), pp. 697–725.

D French, 'The Dardenelles, Mecca and Kut: Prestige as a Factor in British Eastern Strategy, 1914–16', *War and Society*, 5, 1 (1987), pp. 45–62.

I Friedman, 'The McMahon-Hussein Correspondence and the Question of Palestine', *Journal of Contemporary History*, 5, 2 (1970), pp. 83–122.

J S Galbraith and A L Al-Sayyid-Marsot, 'The British Occupation of Egypt: Another View', *International Journal of Middle Eastern Studies*, 9, 4 (1978), pp. 471–88.

J Gallagher and R Robinson, 'The Imperialism of Free Trade', *The Economic History Review*, 6, 1 (1953), pp. 1–15.

I Gershoni, 'The Muslim Brothers and the Arab Revolt in Palestine, 1936–1939', *Middle Eastern Studies*, 22, 3 (1986), pp. 367–97.

N Ghorban, 'Review Article: The History of the British Petroleum Company, Volume I: The Developing Years', *International Journal of Middle Eastern Studies*, 16, 4 (1984), pp. 573–75.

Y Gil-Har, 'British Intelligence and the Role of Jewish Informers in Palestine', *Middle Eastern Studies*, 39, 1 (2003), pp. 117–49.

E Goldberg, 'Review Article: The Communist Movement in Egypt, 1920–1988', *International Journal of Middle Eastern Studies*, 24, 3 (1992), pp. 524–26.

E Goldberg, 'Peasants in Revolt—Egypt 1919', *International Journal of Middle Eastern Studies*, 24, 2 (1992), pp. 261–80.

E Goldstein, 'British Peace Aims and the Eastern Questions: The Political Intelligence Department and the Eastern Committee, 1918', *Middle Eastern Studies*, 23, 4 (1987), pp. 419–36.

J D Goold, 'Lord Hardinge as Ambassador to France and the Anglo-French Dilemma over Germany and the Near East, 1920-23', *Historical Journal*, 21, 4 (1978), pp. 913–37.

F M Gotheil, 'The Smoking Gun: Arab Immigration into Palestine, 1922–31', *Middle Eastern Quarterly*, 10, 1 (2003), pp. 53–64.

R S Grayson, 'Imperialism in Conservative Defence and Foreign Policy: Leo Amery and the Chamberlains, 1903–39', *Journal of Imperial and Commonwealth History*, 34, 4 (2006), pp. 505–27.

E Haddad, 'Digging to India: Modernity, Imperialism and the Suez Canal', *Victorian Studies* 47, 3 (2005), pp. 363–96.

C I Hamilton, 'Expanding Naval Powers: Admiralty Private Secretaries and Private Offices, 1800–1945', *War in History*, 10, 2 (2003), pp. 125–56.

C I Hamilton, 'British Naval Policy, Policy-Makers and Financial Control, 1860–1945', *War in History*, 12, 4 (2005), pp. 371–95.

R A Hinnebusch, 'The Reemergence of the Wafd Party: Glimpses of the Liberal Opposition in Egypt', *International Journal of Middle Eastern Studies*, 16, 1 (1984), pp. 99–121.

R A Hinnebusch, 'Review Article: Workers on the Nile: Nationalism, Communism, Islam and the Egyptian Working Class, 1882–54', *International Journal of Middle Eastern Studies*, 22, 4 (1990), pp. 473–74.

M J Hogan, 'Informal Entente: Public Policy and Private Management in Anglo-American Petroleum Affairs, 1918–1924', *Business History Review*, 48, 2 (1974), pp. 187–205.

A G Hopkins, 'The Victorians and Africa: A Reconsideration of the Occupation of Egypt, 1882', *The Journal of African History*, 27, 2 (1986), pp. 363-91.
A G Hopkins, 'Rethinking Decolonisation', *Past and Present*, 200 (2008), pp. 211-47.
D Hopwood, 'Earth's Proud Empires Pass Away: Britain's Moment in the Middle East', *British Journal of Middle Eastern Studies*, 29, 2 (2002), pp. 109-20.
V Huber, 'Connecting Colonial Seas: The "international colonisation" of Port Said and the Suez Canal', *European Review of History*, 19, 1 (2012), pp. 141-61.
S Huffaker, 'Representations of Ahmed Urabi: Hegemony, Imperialism and the British Press', *Victorian Periodicals Review*, 45, 4 (2012), pp. 375-405.
R F Hunter, 'Tourism and Empire: The Thomas Cook & Son Enterprise on the Nile, 1868-1914', *Middle Eastern Studies*, 40, 5 (2004), pp. 28-54.
C Issawi, 'Egypt since 1800: A Study in Lop-Sided Development', *Journal of Economic History*, 21, 1 (1961), pp. 1-25.
M Jack, 'The Purchase of the British Government Shares in the British Petroleum Company, 1912-1914', *Past and Present*, 39 (1968), pp. 139-68.
J Jankowski, 'Egyptian Responses to the Palestine Problem in the Interwar Period', *International Journal of Middle Eastern Studies*, 12, 1 (1980), pp 1-38.
J Jankowski, 'The Government of Egypt and the Palestine Question, 1936-1939', *Middle Eastern Studies*, 17, 4 (1981), pp. 427-53.
J Jankowski, 'Review Article: Egypt and the Palestine Question, 1936-45', *International Journal of Middle Eastern Studies*, 18, 4 (1985), pp. 544-46.
K Jeffrey, 'Sir Henry Wilson and the Defence of the British Empire, 1918-22', *Journal of Imperial and Commonwealth History*, 5, 3 (1977), pp. 270-93.
H H Johnston, 'Lord Cromer's "Modern Egypt"', *Journal of the Royal African Society*, 7, 27 (1908), pp. 239-48.
G G Jones, 'The British Government and the Oil Companies, 1912-24: The Search for an Oil Policy', *Historical Journal*, 20, 3 (1977), pp. 647-72.
E Kedourie and C E Dawn, 'In the Anglo-Arab Labyrinth', *International Journal of Middle Eastern Studies*, 10, 3 (1979), pp. 420-26.
G Kennedy, 'Review Article: C M Bell, "The Royal Navy Seapower and Strategy between the Wars"', *War in History*, 10, 4 (2003), pp. 494-96.
G Kirk, 'Review Article: The Chatham House Version and Other Middle Eastern Studies', *International Journal of Middle Eastern Studies*, 2, 1 (1971), pp. 91-92.
J M Landau, 'Review Article: Cairo University and the Making of Modern Egypt', *International Journal of Middle Eastern Studies*, 23, 4 (1991), pp. 632-33.
D E Lee, 'The Origins of Pan Islamism', *American Historical Review*, 47, 2 (1942), pp. 278-87.
R H Lieshout, '"Keeping Better Educated Moslems Busy": Sir Reginald Wingate and the Origins of the Husayn-McMahon Correspondence', *Historical Journal*, 27, 2 (1984), pp. 453-63.
Z Lockman, 'British Policy toward Egyptian Labour Activism, 1882-1936', *International Journal of Middle Eastern Studies*, 20, 3 (1988), pp. 265-85.
P A Lockwood, 'Milner's Entry into the War Cabinet, December 1916', *Historical Journal*, 7, 1 (1964), pp. 120-34.
J De V Loder, 'Egypt during and since the War', *The Edinburgh Review*, 248, 505 (1928), pp. 1-22.
K Luke, 'Order or Justice: The Denshawai Incident and British Imperialism', *History Compass*, 5, 2 (2007), pp. 278-87.

D McLean, 'Finance and Informal Empire before the First World War', *Economic History Review*, 29, 2 (1976), pp. 291-305.
A L Macfie, 'British Intelligence and the Causes of Unrest in Mesopotamia, 1919-21', *Middle Eastern Studies*, 35, 1 (1999), pp. 165-77.
J P Mackintosh, 'The Role of the Committee of Imperial Defence before 1914', *English Historical Review*, 77, 304 (1962), pp. 490-503.
L Mak, 'More than Officers and Officials: Britons in Occupied Egypt, 1882-1922', *Journal of Imperial and Commonwealth History*, 39, 1 (2011), pp. 21-46.
E Manela, 'The Wilsonian Moment and the Rise of Anticolonial Nationalism: The Case of Egypt', *Diplomacy & Statecraft*, 12, 4 (2001), pp. 99-122.
E Manela, 'Goodwill and Bad: Rethinking US-Egyptian Contacts in the Inter-War Years', *Middle Eastern Studies*, 38, 1 (2002), pp. 71-88.
S Matsumoto-Best, 'British and Italian Imperial Rivalry in the Mediterranean, 1912-1914', *Diplomacy and Statecraft* 18, 2 (2007), pp. 297-314.
W M Matthew, 'The Balfour Declaration and the Palestine Mandate, 1917-23: British Imperialist Imperatives', *British Journal of Middle Eastern Studies*, 40, 3 (2013), pp. 231-50.
T Mayer, 'Egypt and the 1936 Arab Revolt in Palestine', *Journal of Contemporary History*, 19, 2 (1984), pp. 275-87.
W D McIntyre, 'New Zealand and the Singapore Base between the Wars', *Journal of South East Asia Studies*, 2, 1 (1971), pp. 2-21.
H Mejcher, 'British Middle East Policy, 1917-22: The Interdepartmental Level', *Journal of Contemporary History*, 8, 4 (1973), pp. 81-101.
H Mejcher, 'Review Article: Britain, India and the Arab, 1914-21', *International Journal of Middle Eastern Studies*, 5, 3 (1974), pp. 363-65.
S M Mollan, 'Business Failure, Capital Investment and Information: Mining Companies in the Anglo-Egyptian Sudan, 1900-1913', *Journal of Imperial and Commonwealth History*, 37, 2 (2009), pp. 229-48.
A E Montgomery, 'The Making of the Treaty of Sevres 10 August 1920', *Historical Journal*, 15, 4 (1972), pp. 775-87.
K O Morgan, 'Lloyd George's Premiership: A Study in "Prime Ministerial Government"', *Historical Journal*, 13, 1 (1970), pp. 130-57.
L Morsy, 'Farouk in British Policy', *Middle Eastern Studies*, 20, 4 (1984), pp. 193-211.
R C Mowat, 'From Liberalism to Imperialism: The Case of Egypt 1875-1887', *Historical Journal*, 16, 1 (1973), pp. 109-24.
M H Murfett, 'Living in the Past: A Critical Re-Examination of the Singapore Naval Strategy, 1918-41', *War & Society*, 2, 1 (1993), pp. 73-103.
Y Nakash, 'Fiscal and Monetary Systems in the Mahdist Sudan, 1881-1898', *International Journal of Middle Eastern Studies*, 20, 3 (1988), pp. 365-85.
J F Naylor, 'The Establishment of the Cabinet Secretariat', *Historical Journal*, 14, 4 (1971), pp. 783-803.
K Neilson, 'Kitchener: A Reputation Refurbished?' *Canadian Journal of History*, 15, 2 (1980), pp. 207-77.
K Neilson, '"Pursued by a Bear": British Estimates of Soviet Military Strength and Anglo-Soviet Relations, 1922-39', *Canadian Journal of History*, 28, 1 (1993), pp. 189-221.
K Neilson, 'The Defence Requirements Sub-Committee, British Strategic Foreign Policy, Neville Chamberlain and the Path to Appeasement', *English Historical Review*, 118, 477 (2003), pp. 651-84.

J Q C Newell, 'Learning the Hard Way: Allenby in Egypt and Palestine, 1917–19', *Journal of Strategic Studies*, 14, 3 (1991), pp. 363–87.

J Newsinger, 'Liberal Imperialism and the Occupation of Egypt in 1882', *Race and Class*, 49, 3 (2008), pp. 54–75.

F Nicosia, 'Arab Nationalism and National Socialist Germany, 1933–39: Ideological and Strategic Incompatibility', *International Journal of Middle Eastern Studies*, 12, 3 (1980), pp. 351–72.

J A De Novo, 'The Movement for an Aggressive American Oil Policy Abroad, 1918–1920', *American Historical Review*, 61, 4 (1956), pp. 854–76.

R Owen, 'The Study of Middle Eastern Industrial History: Notes on the Interrelationship between Factories and Small-Scale Manufacturing with Special References to Lebanese Silk and Egyptian Sugar, 1900–30', *International Journal of Middle Eastern Studies*, 16, 4 (1984), pp. 475–87.

T J Paris, 'British Middle East Policy-Making after the First World War: The Lawrentian and Wilsonian Schools', *Historical Journal*, 41, 3 (1998), pp. 773–93.

K J Perkins, 'Colonial Administration in the Twilight of Imperialism: Great Britain and the Egyptian Frontier Districts Administration', *Middle Eastern Studies*, 18, 4 (1982), pp. 411–25.

D Malcolm Reid, 'Cairo University and the Orientalists', *International Journal of Middle Eastern Studies*, 19, 1 (1987), pp. 51–75.

D Malcolm Reid, 'Cromer and the Classics: Imperialism, Nationalism and the Greco-Roman Past in Modern Egypt', *Middle Eastern Studies*, 32, 1 (1996), pp. 1–29.

V H Rothwell, 'Mesopotamia in British War Aims, 1914–18', *Historical Journal*, 13, 2 (1970), pp. 273–94.

M M Ruiz, 'Manly Spectacles and Imperial Soldiers in Wartime Egypt, 1914–1919', *Middle Eastern Studies*, 45, 3 (2009), pp. 351–71.

A Schölch, 'The "Men on the Spot" and the English Occupation of Egypt in 1882', *Historical Journal*, 19, 3 (1996), pp. 773–85.

B Schwarz, 'Divided Attention: Britain's Perception of a German Threat to Her Eastern Position in 1918', *Journal of Contemporary History*, 28, 1 (1993), pp. 103–22.

A Seal, 'Imperialism and Nationalism in India', *Modern Asian Studies*, 7, 3 (1973), pp. 321–47.

A A Sikainga, 'Review Article: Empire on the Nile: The Anglo-Egyptian Sudan, 1898–1934', *International Journal of Middle Eastern Studies*, 21, 2 (1989), pp. 277–78.

R S Simon, 'The Hashemite "Conspiracy": Hashemite Unity Attempts, 1921–1958', *International Journal of Middle Eastern Studies*, 5, 3 (1974), pp. 314–27.

C D Smith, 'The "Crisis of Orientation": The Shift of Egyptian Intellectuals to Islamic Subjects in the 1930s', *International Journal of Middle Eastern Studies*, 4, 4 (1973), pp. 382–410.

C D Smith, 'Review Article: Islam, Nationalism and Radicalism in Egypt and the Sudan', *International Journal of Middle Eastern Studies*, 18, 4 (1986), pp. 519–23.

M Smith, 'The Royal Air Force, Air Power and British Foreign Policy, 1932–1937', *Journal of Contemporary History*, 12, 1 (1977), pp. 155–74.

Z Steiner and M Dockrill, 'The Foreign Office Reforms, 1919–1921', *Historical Journal*, 17, 1 (1974), pp. 131–56.

E Stokes, 'Traditional Resistance Movements and Afro-Asian Nationalism', *Past and Present*, 48 (1970), pp. 100–18.

Major-General Sir Frederick H Sykes, 'Imperial Air Routes', *The Geographical Journal*, 55, 4 (1920), pp. 241–70.

M Thomas, 'Bedouin Tribes and the Imperial Intelligence Services in Syria, Iraq, and Trans-Jordan in the 1920s', *Journal of Contemporary History*, 38, 4 (2003), pp. 539–61.

M Thomas and R Toye, 'Arguing about Intervention: A Comparison of British and French Rhetoric surrounding the 1882 and 1956 Invasions of Egypt', *Historical Journal*, 58, 4 (2015), pp. 1081–1113.

M T Thornhill, 'Informal Empire, Independent Egypt and the Accession of King Farouk', *Journal of Imperial and Commonwealth History*, 38, 2 (2010), pp. 279–302.

A P Thornton, 'British Policy in Persia, 1858–1890', *English Historical Review*, 69, 273 (1954), pp. 554–79.

H H Tollefson, 'The 1894 British Takeover of the Egyptian Ministry of Interior', *Middle Eastern Studies*, 26, 4 (1990), pp. 547–60.

C Townshend, 'Going to the Wall: The Failure of British Rule in Palestine, 1928–31', *Journal of Imperial and Commonwealth History*, 30, 2 (2002), pp. 25–52.

C W E Tripodi, 'The Foreign Office and Anglo-Italian Involvement in the Red Sea and Arabia, 1925–1928', *Canadian Journal of History*, 42, 2 (2007), pp. 209–34.

T Tvedt, 'Hydrology and Empire: The Nile, Water Imperialism and the Partition of Africa', *Journal of Imperial and Commonwealth History*, 39, 2 (2011), pp. 173–94.

F Venn, 'A Futile Paper Chase: Anglo-American Relations and Middle East Oil, 1918–34', *Diplomacy and Statecraft*, 1, 2 (1990), pp. 165–84.

J Voll, 'Review Article: Imperialism and Nationalism in the Sudan', *International Journal of Middle Eastern Studies*, 6, 4 (1975), p. 508.

J Voll, 'The Sudanese Mahdi: Frontier Fundamentalist', *International Journal of Middle Eastern Studies*, 10, 2 (1979), pp. 145–66.

J O Voll, 'The British, the "Ulama," and Popular Islam in the Early Anglo-Egyptian Sudan,' *International Journal of Middle Eastern Studies*, 2, 3 (1971), pp. 212–18.

D Walker, 'Modernists, Particularism and the Crystallisation of Pan-Arabism in Egypt in the 1920s', *Islamic Culture*, 60, 2 (1986), pp. 57–96.

G Warburg, 'The Sudan, Egypt and Britain, 1889–1916', *Middle Eastern Studies*, 2, 2 (1970), pp. 163–78.

G Warburg, 'Review Article: Sir Eldon Gorst: The Overshadowed ProConsul', *International Journal of Middle Eastern Studies*, 14, 3 (1982), pp. 405–08.

G R Warburg, 'The Wingate Literature Revisited: The Sudan as Seen by Members of the Sudan Political Service during the Condominium 1899–1956', *Middle Eastern Studies*, 41, 3 (2005), pp. 373–89.

R Warman, 'The Erosion of Foreign Office Influence in the Making of Foreign Policy, 1916–18', *Historical Journal*, 15, 1 (1972), pp. 133–59.

H Weinroth, 'British Radicals and the Agadir Crisis', *European Studies Review*, 3, 1 (1973), pp. 39–61.

R Youngs, 'European Approaches to Security in the Mediterranean', *Middle East Journal*, 57, 3 (2003), pp. 414–31.

M E Yapp, 'Review: Curzon and British Imperialism in the Middle East, 1916–19', *Middle Eastern Studies*, 36, 1 (2000), pp. 184–87.

M E Yapp, 'Elie Kedourie and the History of the Middle East', *Middle Eastern Studies*, 41, 5 (2005), pp. 665–87.

Z N Zeine, 'Review Article: Foundations of British Policy in the Arab World: The Cairo Conference of 1921', *International Journal of Middle Eastern Studies*, 4, 1 (1973), pp. 121–22.

Theses

M S Hussain, *British Policy and the Nationalist Movement in Egypt, 1914–24*. (DPhil, Exeter, December 1996).
S Morewood, *The British Defence of Egypt, 1935–September 1939*. (unpublished PhD thesis, University of Bristol, 1985).
R C Mowat, *Lord Cromer and His Successors in Egypt. A Study of the Development from Anti-Colonial Radicalism to Liberal-Imperialism*. (MS DPhil, 1970).

Unpublished Material

S Shoul, 'British Riot Control in Egypt and the Punjab 1919', Conference Paper, Institute of Historical Research, December 2004.
J Whidden, 'A New Idea: British "Civilisation" – Para-Colonial Discourses on Syria, Iraq and Egypt'. British World Conference, Bristol, July 2007.

Online Resources

The British Cartoon Archive, University of Kent. http://www.cartoons.ac.uk
The Oxford Dictionary of National Biography, online edition. Ed. Lawrence Goldman. May 2006. http://www.oxforddnb.com

Index

Abd-el-Latif, Ali 80, 104–5, 107
Admiralty 24–6, 47, 57, 75. *See also* Royal Navy
Afghanistan 4, 15, 29
Africa, Scramble for 3, 7, 11–13, 21, 88, 179
Air Ministry 28, 57, 83. *See also* Royal Air Force
Allenby, General Sir Edmund 2, 4–5, 23, 37–41, 44–6, 48, 51–4, 60–9, 72–3, 76–83, 95, 97, 100, 102–9, 113–15, 117, 119–29, 131, 133, 148, 177, 179–80, 182
    Allenby declaration 69
    reaction to Stack assassination 120–9
    recommendations re Sudan 82–3
    relationship with Austen Chamberlain 120–9
    resignation 126–7, 180
al-Nahas Pasha, Mustafa 138–9, 142–3, 146–7, 151–2, 154, 158, 160–9, 174–6, 184
Amery, Leo 75, 133
Amos, Sir Sheldon 68, 119
Anglo-Egyptian treaty negotiations 33, 53–5, 62, 84, 135–6, 142–8, 150–66, 177, 180, 184–5
    al-Nahas Pasha, Mustafa 163–6
    Chamberlain, Austen 139–43
    Conservative government 133–48
    Foreign Office 155–63
    Henderson, Arthur 151–4, 163–6
    Labour government 121, 145, 149–77, 180–1
    MacDonald, Ramsay 83–5, 182
    Mahmoud, Mohammed Pasha 151–4
    Milner, Lord Alfred 53–5, 180
    reserved points 73, 78–9, 98, 103, 180
    Residency, Cairo 157–63
    Sarwat Pasha 139–47
    Zaghlul, Saad Pasha 53–5, 64–6, 78–9, 83–5, 109–10, 121

Arabi, Colonel Ahmed 2, 8–9, 11
Archer, Sir Geoffrey 23, 183
Army Crisis 134–5, 184
Asquith, Herbert 119, 124, 127

Baldwin, Stanley 73, 120, 129, 133, 149–50, 177
Balfour, Arthur 34–5, 37, 40–1, 43–4, 95
Barakat, Fatallah 139–40
Baring, Sir Evelyn, Lord Cromer 2, 23, 48–9, 52, 60, 88, 93
Bolshevism 2–3, 24, 38, 47, 52, 73, 145–6, 183–4
Bonar Law, Andrew 44, 60
Britain
    Cabinet 6, 56, 60–2, 66–9
    imperial defence strategy 23–30
    position in Middle East 15–16
British Army 24, 26–8. *See also* Chiefs of Staff
    in Egypt 50, 73–6, 82–4, 136, 140, 155, 157, 180
Bulfin, General 37–8

Cabinet
    British 6, 56, 60–2, 66–9
    Egyptian 8, 35
Campbell, Cecil 150, 158
Chamberlain, Austen 5, 67, 114–15, 133–7, 144–7, 149–50, 182, 184
    reaction to Stack assassination 120–30
    relationship with General Sir Edmund Allenby 120–9
    role in Anglo-Egyptian treaty negotiations 139–43
Cheetham, Sir Milne 36–8, 46, 89, 95
Chiefs of Staff 6, 71, 75, 78, 82–3, 141, 156–7, 180–1, 184. *See also* British Army
Churchill, Winston 56, 65, 67, 70, 126, 142, 149–50, 172–3

Clark Kerr, Archibald 119, 121–2, 125, 127
Clayton, Colonel Gilbert 31, 46–7, 68, 89
colonialism 11, 21–3, 118
Colonial Office 22–3, 27, 56, 70, 74, 88
Committee of Imperial Defence (CID) 27–8, 73–7, 83, 137, 155–7
communications, imperial 1, 3, 5–6, 22, 57, 69, 71, 74, 82–3, 137, 144, 155, 180
Conservative government
    Anglo-Egyptian treaty negotiations 133–48
    foreign policy approach 6, 71
Cromer, Lord. *See* Baring, Sir Evelyn
Curzon, Lord George 31–2, 35–8, 40–1, 43, 45–6, 48–9, 52, 54, 56–7, 60, 62–3, 65–8, 70, 76, 83, 95, 180

Dalton, Hugh 150, 154, 158, 164, 174
Derby, Lord. *See* Stanley, Edward

Ebeid, Makram 154, 164, 166
Egypt
    Army 101–2, 140
    British Army 50, 73–6, 82–4, 136, 140, 155, 157, 180
    British involvement 1, 3, 7, 20, 50, 71, 128
    British occupation 9–14, 179
    British Protectorate 2, 32, 40, 44–5, 50–1, 67, 69
    electoral law 168, 170–1, 173–4
    Expeditionary Force 42, 179
    foreign debt 7–8, 14, 33, 54, 83
    importance in British imperial defence 7, 23–30, 31, 179
    independence 2, 4, 5, 14, 17, 26–7, 53, 67–9, 71, 101, 180
    March 1919 uprising 4, 15, 29, 37–8, 41–3
    market for goods 7, 13–14
    Parliament 71–4, 78
    political violence 117–19, 182–3
    protection of minorities 43, 55, 69, 84, 136, 146
    relationship with Sudan 87, 94, 96
    secret societies 117–19
Empire
    British 1, 3–4, 179, 182
    Ottoman 1, 15, 31

Fahmi, Abd al-Aziz 33, 64
fellahin 9, 20, 37, 38, 42, 55, 92, 137
First World War 1, 3–4, 6, 12, 16, 29, 31, 42, 69, 177, 179–82
Foreign Office 2–4, 6, 23, 32–42, 53, 56–7, 63, 65, 67, 70, 73–6, 78, 88, 103, 105
    policy on Egypt 3, 32, 44–6, 119, 136–9
    policy on Sudan 82–3, 93, 95, 109–13, 115
    relationship with Cairo Residency 4, 120–9, 134, 148–51, 157–63, 172, 179–80, 182, 184
    role in Anglo-Egyptian treaty negotiations 155–63
France 9–10, 13, 31–2, 81, 88, 155
Fuad, King Ahmed 43, 78, 80, 107, 135–7, 145, 151–2, 158, 160, 164, 166–70, 175

Gandhi, Mohandas 4, 79
Ghali, Butros Pasha 88, 118
Ghali, Wassif 164, 166
Gladstone, William 9, 10, 13
Graham, Ronald 36, 39–40, 43, 93, 179

Hardinge, Charles 32–4, 36, 39–40, 58, 68
Henderson, Arthur 145, 148–52, 154, 156, 159, 161, 167, 169–73, 175–7, 182–4
    role in Anglo-Egyptian treaty negotiations 151–4, 163–6
Henderson, Nevile 124–7, 129, 134, 138–40, 182
High Commissioner
    relationship with Foreign Office 6, 71, 117
    role of 91, 180–1
Hoare, Rex 153–4, 160, 163, 166
Huddleston, Colonel Hubert 23, 107
Hurst, Sir Cecil 48, 140, 144

India 1, 10, 13–16, 26–9, 33, 39, 41, 47, 56–8, 60, 69–70, 79, 118, 141, 146, 164
Iraq 1, 15–16, 26–30, 144
Ireland 4, 9, 16, 27, 56, 58–9, 62, 69, 146
Italy 9, 47, 128, 148, 155, 177, 185

260   *Index*

Japan 3, 16, 24–6, 57, 180

Keown-Boyd, Alexander W. 77, 89, 91, 95–6
Khedive, authority of 8, 84
Kitchener, Lord Herbert 2, 23, 87, 90

Labour government
   foreign policy approach 6, 71, 73
   role in Anglo-Egyptian treaty negotiations 121, 145, 149–77, 180–1
League of Nations 3, 49, 74, 82, 110–12, 124, 136, 140
League of the White Flag 5, 80–1, 87, 105
Lindsay, Ronald 63, 150, 154, 158, 161
Lloyd George, David 40, 43, 44, 52, 56, 60, 62, 65–9, 173, 180
Lloyd, Lady Blanche 133, 147, 151
Lloyd, Lord George 2–3, 128, 133–6, 139–51, 172, 184
Loraine, Sir Percy 151–4, 157–74, 176–7, 184–5

MacDonald, Ramsay 5, 21, 71–3, 77–8, 81–2, 103, 107–9, 114–15, 121, 124, 152, 154–5, 159–61, 167, 171, 173, 176–7, 180
   role in Anglo-Egyptian treaty negotiations 83–5, 182
Maffey, Sir John Loader 23, 156, 165
Maher, Ahmed 163–4
Mahmoud, Mohammed Pasha 37, 64, 157–9, 162–3, 173–5, 184
   role in Anglo-Egyptian treaty negotiations 151–4
mass media, development of 19, 22
Maxwell, General Sir John 48, 50
McMahon, Sir Henry 2, 90–1
Mesopotamia 4, 15, 53, 59, 99
Middle East 1, 3–4, 7, 13–17, 19–20, 24, 26, 28–9, 31–2, 41, 55–6, 58, 74–6, 145–6, 173, 179
Milner, Lord Alfred 4, 11, 40, 45–6, 48–62, 65, 83, 95–6, 152, 179–80
   role in Anglo-Egyptian treaty negotiations 53–5, 180
Milner Mission 4, 31, 46–62, 92, 180
   aims of 48, 50
   background to 43–9

   composition of 48–9
   extension to Sudan 95–8
   failure of 52
   Wafd boycott of 46, 49–51
Montagu, Edwin 56, 58, 70
Murray, Jack 23, 62–3, 79, 82–4, 100, 103–4, 124–5, 138–40, 142, 144, 158–63, 170–2, 174

nationalism 11, 16–17, 19, 21–2, 30
   Egyptian 2, 4, 17–20, 23, 31–2, 34–6, 39–43, 47, 59, 71, 92, 98, 179, 181, 184
   Sudanese 5, 87, 94
Nationalist Watani Party 47, 77, 118
Nile Control Board 82, 102
Nile Valley 3, 4, 30, 97, 105–6, 108, 115, 184
non-intervention, principle of 5, 71, 171, 173, 180

Palestine 16, 24, 26–7, 30, 37, 39, 53, 74, 81, 84, 145, 177
Paris Peace Conference 4, 15, 33–5, 40, 43–4, 47, 93, 95, 168, 179
Parmoor, Lord 104, 108
Patterson, Sir Reginald 77, 119

Residency, Cairo 4–6, 36–9, 43–4, 63, 67, 71, 81, 105
   relationship with Foreign Office 45–6, 120–9, 134, 148–51, 157–63, 172, 179–80, 182, 184
   role in Anglo-Egyptian treaty negotiations 157–63
Royal Air Force 4, 24, 26–30, 57–8, 75. *See also* Air Ministry
Royal Navy 24–8, 74. *See also* Admiralty
Rushdy Pasha 33–6
Russia, Tsarist 2, 9, 15

Sarwat Pasha, Abd al Khaliq 50, 67, 133, 135–9, 142, 147, 184
   role in Anglo-Egyptian treaty negotiations 139–47
Selby, Walford 83, 125, 135–6, 140, 150, 172
self-determination 4–5, 15, 33–4, 41, 44, 179

Sidky Pasha, Ismail 37, 167–8, 170–1, 173–6
Singapore 24, 26, 30, 141
Snowden, Philip 76, 176
Society of Brotherly Solidarity 118–19
Spender, John Alfred 48–9, 54, 61–2, 65
Stack, Sir Lee 23, 80–3, 89, 91–105, 107–9, 112–13, 115, 181–2
   assassination 3, 5, 113, 115, 117, 119–20, 133, 140, 163, 182
   trial of assailants 129–30
Stanley, Edward, Lord Derby 46, 73, 75–6
Sterry, Wasey 89, 108–9, 121–2
Sudan 4–6, 54, 57, 66, 69, 74, 77, 79–85, 140, 155, 165, 181
   Anglo-Egyptian Condominium Agreement 5, 21, 23, 82, 87–8, 92, 100, 109–10, 115, 124
   Anglo-Egyptian settlement 5, 21, 50, 87–8, 98–101, 165–6
   army 91, 97–8, 101–2, 107
   British Army 155–6
   British policy 82–3, 128–9
   de-Egyptianization 80, 94, 96, 106, 114–15, 181
   demonstrations 106–8, 181, 183
   education 97, 183
   Egyptian Army 101–2, 109, 112–14, 120, 128–9, 155–6, 181
   Egyptian policy 79–80
   Egyptian propaganda 80, 87, 93, 98, 102–4, 107, 112, 181, 183
   First World War 88–92
   government 94, 98–9
   importance 5, 181–2
   independence 71–3, 88
   irrigation 5, 81, 87, 94, 96, 99–100, 114, 120–4, 127, 129–30, 156, 182
   mutiny 5, 87, 90, 113–15, 182
   political landscape 103–5
   relationship with Egypt 87, 94, 96
Sudanese Defence Force 80, 106–7, 113–14, 140, 181–3
Suez Canal 7, 10, 14, 20, 33, 54, 57, 60, 66, 72, 76, 164
   defence 9, 26, 29, 74–5, 84–5, 141, 155, 179
   strategic importance 1, 3, 24–5, 31, 74

supra-Egyptianism 17–18
Symes, Colonel George Stewart 36, 41, 89, 91

technological change 1, 18, 22
Trenchard, Sir Hugh 29, 57
Turkey 28, 31–2, 34, 38–9, 41, 47, 53
Tyrell, Sir William 77, 124, 125, 136, 139, 144

United States 2, 16, 25, 44, 57

Wafd Party 3–4, 42–4, 46–7, 78, 114, 120, 137–8, 142, 146–8, 153–5, 180, 184–5
   coalition 158–9, 173–4, 176
   election results 71, 163, 176
   power struggle with King Fuad 166–70
War Office 56, 73–7, 83, 155
Willis, C A. 23, 81, 90, 104, 106, 114
Wilson, Sir Henry 3, 57
Wilson, Woodrow 4, 33, 44, 179
   Fourteen Points 44
Wingate, Sir Reginald 2, 4, 23, 32–6, 38–41, 44, 49, 88–90, 92–7, 115, 126, 179, 181–2

Yakan Pasha, Adli 33–6, 54, 62–7, 74, 139–40, 153–4, 162, 175

Zaghlul, Saad Pasha 3–5, 23, 33, 35–7, 43–4, 46, 49, 51–2, 61, 63–7, 71–3, 80, 82–3, 101, 103, 105, 107, 119–20, 130, 151, 153, 168, 179, 182, 184
   death 137–8, 147
   demand for Egyptian independence 77
   deportation 37, 67
   reaction to Stack assassination 122–3, 128–9
   release 40
   resignation 79, 128–9
   role in Anglo-Egyptian treaty negotiations 53–5, 64–6, 78–9, 83–5, 109–10, 121
   Sudan 109–12
Ziwar Pasha, Ahmed 5, 128, 175

www.ingramcontent.com/pod-product-compliance
Lightning Source LLC
Chambersburg PA
CBHW070026010526
44117CB00011B/1720